Privacy and Data Protection Law in France

Privacy and Data Protection Law in France

Olivia Tambou

This book was originally published as a monograph in the International Encyclopaedia of Laws/Privacy and Technology Law.

Founding Editor: Roger Blanpain
General Editor: Frank Hendrickx
Volume Editors: Jos Dumortier, Pieter Gryffroy, Ruben Roex & Yung Shin Van Der Sype

Wolters Kluwer

Published by:
Kluwer Law International B.V.
PO Box 316
2400 AH Alphen aan den Rijn
The Netherlands
E-mail: lrs-sales@wolterskluwer.com
Website: www.wolterskluwer.com/en/solutions/kluwerlawinternational

Sold and distributed by:
Wolters Kluwer Legal & Regulatory U.S.
920 Links Avenue
Landisville, PA 17538
United States of America
E-mail: customer.service@wolterskluwer.com

ISBN 978-94-035-1269-3

e-Book: ISBN 978-94-035-1279-2
web-PDF: ISBN 978-94-035-1289-1

The Author

Dr Olivia Tambou studied Law at the University Lyon III (France), She has a LLM from the Christian Albrecht University of Kiel in Germany (1990) and a Phd in European Law from the University of Strasbourg (1997). From 1997 to 1999 she was awarded a Marie Curie scholarship to carry out research on cross-border cooperation at the Institut Universitari d'Estudis Europeus at the Universitat Autonoma of Barcelona (Spain). From 1999 to 2007 she was Associate Professor and director of the International Relations at the Law School of the University of Angers, (France). Since 2007, Olivia Tambou is a Associate professor at the Université Paris-Dauphine, PSL Research University, specialized in European digital Law in particular Data protection and regulation of Artificial intelligence. She is also the founder-editor of blogdroiteuropeen created in 2016. From 2018-2023 she was external Scientific Fellow at the Max Planck Institut Luxembourg for Procedural Law. Olivia Tambou is the author of more than 50 publications in French, English and Spanish mainly on data protection law including her *Manuel de droit européen des données*, Ed. Bruylant collection Droit administratif européen matériel, Bruylant (2020) and chapters in the *General Data Protection Regulation, Commentary article by-article*, edited by Indra Spiecker gen. Döhmann, Vagelis Papakonstantinou, Gerrit Hornung, Paul De Hert, Nomos, (2023). Olivia Tambou is reviewer for several review in Data protection and provides legal guidance in European research project on Data protection and artificial intelligence. She is also offen asked to deliver keynotes and participate to international conferences on these both topics.

The Author

Table of Contents

List of Abbreviations*

AAI	Autorité Administrative indépendante, Independent Administrative Authority
AID	AI Department
AMF	Autorité des Marché Financier, French Financial Market Authority
ANS	Agence du Numérique en Santé, Digital Health Agency
API	Autorité Publique Indépendante, Independent Public Authoriy
ARCOM	Autorité de Régulation de la Communication Audiovisuelle et Numérique, Audiovisual and Digital Communication Regulatory Authority
BCR	Binding Corporate Rule
CADA	Commission d'accès aux documents administratifs, Commission for Access to Administrative Documents
CGCT	Code Général des Collectivités Locales, General Code of Local Authorities
CISPE	Cloud Infrastructure Service Providers Europe
CNAOP	Conseil National pour l'Accès aux Origines Personnelles, National Council for Access to Personal Origins
CNCTR	Commission Nationale de Contrôle des Techniques de Renseignements, National Oversight Commission for Intelligence-Gathering Techniques
CNIL	Commission National Informatique et Libertés, French Data Protection Authority
CP	Code Penal, Criminal Code
CPCE	Code des Postes et des Communications Electroniques, Post and Electronic Communications Code
CPP	Code de Procedure Pénale, Code of Criminal Procedure
CRPA	Code des Relations entre le Public et l'Administration, Code of Relations Between the Public and the Administration

List of Abbreviations

CRPD	Convention on the Rights of Persons with Disabilities
CSE	Comité Social Et Économique, Social and Economic Committee
CSI	Code de la Sécurité Intérieure, Internal Security Code
DGA	Data Governance Act
DGCCRF	Direction Générale de la Concurrence, de la Consommation et de la Répression des Fraudes, Directorate-General for Competition, Consumer Affairs and Fraud Control
DGDDI	Direction Générale des Douanes et Droits Indirects
DGSE	Direction Générale de la Sécurité Extérieure, Directorate-General for External Security
DGSI	Direction Générale de la Sécurité Intérieure, Directorate-General for Internal Security
DPA	Data Protection Authority
DPIA	Data Protection Impact Assessment
DPO	Data Protection Officer
DRM	Direction du Renseignement Militaire, Directorate of Military Intelligence
DSA	Digital Services Act
ECHR	European Convention of Human Rights
ECtHR	European Court of Human Rights
EDPB	European Data Protection Board
EEA	European Economic Area
FACTA	Foreign Account Tax Compliance Act
FAED	Fichier Automatisé des Empreintes Digitales
FCC	Fichier Central des Cheques
FICOBA	Fichier des Comptes Bancaires
FICP	Fichier des Incidents de remboursement des Crédits aux Particuliers
FNAEG	Fichier National des Empreintes Génétiques
FNCI	Fichier National des Cheques Irréguliers
FPR	Fichier des Personnes Recherchées
GIC	Groupement Interministérielle de Controle, Interministerial Control Group
H3C	Haut Conseil du Commissariat aux Comptes, French High Council of Statutory Auditors
ICCPR	International Covenant on Civil and Political Rights
ISP	Internet Service Provider
JAP	Juge d'application des Peines

JLD	Juge des Libertés et de la Détention
LCEN	Loi pour la Confiance dans l'Economie Numérique, Law for a Trusty Digital Economy
LIL	Loi Informatique et Libertés, French Data Protection Act
NIR	Numéro d'Inscription au Répertoire, French National Identification Number
NOYB	None of Your Business
PCAOB	Public Company Accounting Oversight Board
SNAF	Société Nouvelle de l'Annuaire Français
SREN	Loi pour Réguler et Sécuriser l'Espace Numérique, Law Aimed at Securing and Regulating the Digital Space
TAJ	Traitement d'Antécédents Judiciaires
TES	Titres Électroniques Sécurisés, Secured Electronic Documents
TGI	Tribunaux de Grande Instance
TJ	Tribunal Judiciaire

* Priority is given to the common French abbreviations, which may explain the lack of correspondence with the English translation proposed by the author.

List of Abbreviations

General Introduction

§1. General Background of the Country

1. Understanding privacy and data protection in France requires having some basic knowledge of the French legal system and French constitutional history.

I. Basics on French Legal System

2. **France belongs to the Romano-Germanic tradition**. This has two main consequences. First, the legislative sources (Constitution, parliamentary statutes (*lois*)), government regulations, (*règlement, décrets, arrêtés*) are the primary sources of law in France, besides case law. France has a codification tradition, starting with the famous Code Civil (1804) enacted under Napoleon, which has served as a model for many countries. Second, the judiciary is historically considered secondary to the legislative and executive branches according to an interpretation of Montesquieu's Theory of the separation of powers.

3. These two preliminary remarks illustrate that the main features of the French legal system find their origins around the Revolution of 1789. First, the Declaration of Human and Civic Rights[1] was approved on 26 August 1789 and is a part of the current constitutional rules.[2] The before mentioned Code Civil, adopted in 1804, is still in force today, even though it has undergone numerous reforms, including one regarding privacy. French public/private law divide was formalised in the law of the 16–24 August 1790,[3] which remains in force today. Consequently, there are two separate branches of the judiciary: the ordinary one, also called the judiciary body and the administrative one, as detailed later. The French public/private law divide implies both the application of specific rules for the main activities of the Administration (exercise of public power, public services) and a specific judge for their control. The rationale of this divide is that the Administration acts for general interest and has exorbitant powers.

1. English version available at https://www.conseil-constitutionnel.fr/en/declaration-of-human-and-civic-rights-of-26-august-1789.
2. *See* CC Decision No. 71-44 DC 16 Jul. 1971 Law completing the provisions of Arts 5 and 7 of the Law of 1 Jul. 1901 on association agreements, available in English at https://www.conseil-constitutionnel.fr/en/decision/1971/7144DC.htm.
3. Loi des 16-24 août 1790 sur l'organisation judiciaire, available in French at https://www.legifrance.gouv.fr/loda/id/JORFTEXT000000704777.

4. Since 1875, France has been a Republic and is currently governed by the Constitution of the Fifth Republic, passed on 4 October 1958.[4] The Fifth Republic was elaborated by a Comity chaired by General De Gaulle. Originally, the Constitution intended to restore the authority of the executive, which had been undermined by previous regimes. The Fifth Republic regime is based on a strong executive, dominated by a directly elected President of the Republic, who chairs his government with the support of its parliamentary majority. Most laws are proposed by the government and passed by parliament. The parliament is composed of two chambers: the directly elected *Assemblée Nationale* and the indirectly elected *Sénat*, which represents local and regional authorities. It is an unequal bicameralism in which the government can ask the *Assemblée nationale* to pass a law alone in case of disagreement with the *Sénat*. The predominance of the executive is also marked by the possibility for the government to legislate by ordinance.[5] This technique of legislative delegation is widely used to transpose European obligations and/or to codify texts.[6]

5. **France is a Decentralised unitary state**. The first decentralisation laws date from the 1980s. Since then, France's territorial organisation has been based on three basic levels: *Régions, Département, Communes*, and the special status for the Overseas.[7] The various decentralisation laws that have followed have aimed to rationalise the French territorial organisation by reducing the number of local authorities either through mergers or federations. The laws and the regulations regarding the local authorities are codified in the Code Général des Collectivités Locales (CGCT). At this stage, it should be underlined that French local authorities play an important role in data area, digital services, and digital space development. Since the 2004 law on confidence in the digital economy (LCEN),[8] local authorities have been able to set up public-initiative networks where the offerings of the major

4. Constitution of 4 Oct. 1958, available at https://www.conseil-constitutionnel.fr/en/constitution-of-4-october-1958.
5. Article 38 of the Constitution provides:

> In order to implement its programme, the Government may ask Parliament for authorization, for a limited period, to take measures by Ordinance that are normally the preserve of statute law. Ordinances shall be issued in the Council of Ministers, after consultation with the Conseil d'État. They shall come into force upon publication, but shall lapse in the event of failure to table before Parliament the Bill to ratify them by the date set by the Enabling Act. They may only be ratified in explicit terms.
> At the end of the period referred to in the first paragraph hereinabove Ordinances may be amended solely by an Act of Parliament in those areas governed by statute law.

6. Ordonnance n° 2018-1125 du 12 décembre 2018 prise en application de l'article 32 de la loi n° 2018-493 du 20 juin 2018 relative à la protection des données personnelles et portant modification de la loi n° 78-17 du 6 janvier 1978 relative à l'informatique, aux fichiers et aux libertés et diverses dispositions concernant la protection des données à caractère personnel, which adapts the French Data protection Law to the GDPR, and the Police Justice directive.
7. *See* Art. 72 of the Constitution which mentioned the 'Special-Status communities and the Overseas Territorial communities.'
8. Loi n° 2004-575 du 21 juin 2004 pour la confiance dans l'économie numérique.

private operators are not satisfactory.[9] Local authorities then delegate the operation of these networks to operators. This contributes to regional development and digital access for all.

II. Justice Organisation and Conseil Constitutionnel

6. The administrative courts are headed by the French *Conseil d'Etat*, which was created in 1799. Beyond the *Conseil d'Etat*, the French administrative jurisdictional system comprises forty-two administrative tribunals and nine administrative courts of appeal. The *Conseil d'Etat* serves as first and last instance judge for cases for actions for annulment of administrative acts such as governmental decrees or ministerial decisions, individual cases involving certain high-ranking civil servants and decisions made by certain public agencies, such as the French Data Protection Authority (DPA). The *Conseil d'Etat* serves as a *juge de cassation* for all judgments issued by an administrative Court of Appeal and for some judgments of administrative tribunals in minor cases which cannot be appealed. It is worth to underline that for historical reasons, the French *Conseil d'Etat* is both an administrative court and an advisor to the Government. As such, the *Conseil d'Etat* examines each draft law and some government regulations to verify their legal validity and their appropriateness in terms of administrative action. At this stage, one should keep in mind that the French *Conseil d'Etat* plays an extremely important role in France, particularly both in the elaboration and implementation of privacy and data protection law.

7. The French *Cour de cassation* is the Supreme Court for cases between private individuals. It consists of three civils chambers, a commercial chamber, a social chamber, and a criminal chamber. The *Cour de cassation* does not rule on the dispute but assesses whether the rules of law and procedure have been correctly applied by the lower courts. The main Court of First Instance for civil matters in France is the *Tribunal judiciaire* (judicial tribunal).[10] The *Tribunal du commerce* (commercial court) and *Tribunal des prud'homme* (employment tribunals) are also judges of first instances in their respective matters, while the *Tribunal correctionnel* (Tribunal with crimes) and the *Tribunal de Police* (Tribunal of Police) for minor offences are the first instance judges in criminal matters. The *Cour d'Appel* deals both with civil and criminal matters, except for the most serious offences which are from the competences of the *Cour d'Assises* (Assisses Courts). Only the *Cour d'Assises* are made up of jury systems.

8. As a consequent, privacy and Data protection cases can be brought before both administrative and judiciary judges according to the status of the parties, as we will see later. Finally, the *Tribunal des Conflits* (Tribunal of Conflicts) arbitrates conflicts between the administrative and the judicial jurisdictional system. The court also aims to prevent the denial of justice in the case when neither the judiciary

9. Article L. 1425-1 CGCT.

10. The Tribunaux judiciaires replace the former Tribunals of Great instance (Tribunaux de Grande Instance, TGI) and the Tribunals of small instance (Tribunaux d'Instance, TI) since 2020.

courts nor the administrative courts consider themselves competent to settle a dispute.[11]

9. The Constitution of the Fifth Republic established the *Conseil constitutionnel.* It ensures the control of the conformity of the law with the constitution.[12] It is the guardian of the rights and freedoms, including privacy and data protection. The *Conseil constitutionnel* is not a Supreme Court by contrast to the *Conseil d'Etat* and the *Cour de cassation.* The *Conseil constitutionnel* exercises its control *a priori* and *a posteriori.* The *Conseil constitutionnel* can be seized just before the promulgation of a law by the President of the Republic, the Prime Minister, the President of the Assemblée Nationale or the President of the *Sénat* or sixty members of the *Assemblée Nationale* or sixty senators.[13] Since March 2000, the *Conseil constitutionnel* can be seized of an application for a priority preliminary ruling on the issue of constitutionality y the two Supreme Courts, the *Conseil d'Etat* and the *Cour de cassation.*[14] This *ex post* review aims to check whether a legislative provision which is already in force violates the rights and freedoms guaranteed under the Constitution.[15]

III. French Administrative Authorities from Interest for Privacy and Data Protection

10. Several independent administrative authorities (Autorité Administrative indépendante (AAIs)) play an important role in the fields of privacy, data protection, digital services, and new technologies. Since 2017, the status of such administrative authorities has been clarified by the Law.[16] This law makes a distinction between the authorities with a legal person called independent public authorities (Autorité Publique Indépendante (APIs)) and the other which are called AAIs. The list of those agencies has been reduced. Currently, there are seven APIs and twenty-four AAIs. Two AAIs deserve attention, besides the French DPA, the Commission National Informatique et Libertés (CNIL).[17]

11. First, the ARCEP is France's Electronic Communications, Postal and Print Media Distribution Regulatory Authority. Created in 1997, the ARCEP[18] was originally designed to accompany the opening competition in telecoms to the benefit of

11. The *Tribunal des Conflits* is a court composed equally of members of the *Conseil d'État* and the *Cour de cassation.*
12. The *Conseil constitutionnel* also ensures that the election of the President of the Republic and referendums are conducted in accordance with the law. It also decides on the division of powers between the State and certain overseas collectivities.
13. Article 61 of the Constitution.
14. Article 61-1 of the Constitution.
15. An overview of the main QPC in English in available at https://www.conseil-constitutionnel.fr/en/selection-of-qpc-decisions.
16. Loi n° 2017-55 du 20 janvier 2017 portant statut général des autorités administratives indépendantes et des autorités publiques indépendantes.
17. *See infra* para. 412.
18. It was originally called the Telecoms Regulatory Authority or ART.

users. Today, the ARCEP defines itself as 'the is the architect and guardian of communication networks in France'.[19] Its duties in the electronic communications sector are mostly to define the regulation that applies to all or some operators,[20] to allocate frequency and numbering resources through individual decisions,[21] and to define the national numbering plan.[22] It also oversees the financing and supply of the universal service.[23] As with all AAIs, in its area of expertise, the ARCEP issues opinions to the government, Parliament, and other regulatory authorities and prescribes soft laws such as guidelines or recommendations to clarify the duties or guide the stakeholder's behaviour. Finally, the protection of net neutrality, the digital transformation of territories and, more recently, the environmental impact of digital technology are at the core of the ARCEP's activities.

12. Second, the Audiovisual and Digital Communication Regulatory Authority (Autorité de Régulation de la Communication Audiovisuelle et Numérique (ARCOM))[24] is the guardian of the freedom of communication and expression in audiovisual and digital spaces. The ARCOM is responsible for regulating online platforms (social media, search engines, video sharing platforms, etc.), including overseeing the means they use to combat information manipulation and hateful, infringing, and harmful content.

§2. Telecommunications Infrastructure

13. Thanks to its extensive coastline and central location, France has several gateways for submarine internet cables. The city of Marseille is one of the largest French marine cable hubs. France's Atlantic seaboard has cables connecting it to the United States, the United Kingdom and Ireland.

As far as terrestrial internet access is concerned, the French government has launched a very high-speed broadband plan with the aim of rolling out optical fibre access throughout the country by the end of 2025, while in 2022, it was 79%.

14. The ARCEP's data gives an overview of the state of the roll-out of terrestrial optical fibre and the internet mobile network. There are still many disparities between regions. On the one hand, there are major disparities between very densely populated areas. Paris, for example, has 97% coverage, compared with just 81% for Marseille. On the other hand, very densely populated areas often have better coverage than less densely populated areas. In these areas the choice between operators may be more limited.

19. *See* the ARCEP Manifesto.
20. Articles L. 37-1 et seq. of the French Postal and Electronic Communications Code (CPCE).
21. CPCE Arts L. 42-1 et seq. and Art. L. 44.
22. CPCE Art. L. 44.
23. CPCE Arts L. 35 et seq.
24. The ARCOM is the result of the merger between the French broadcasting regulator (CSA) established in 1989 and the authority overseeing the dissemination of works and the protection of property rights online (Hadopi).

15. 5G has been rolled out in France since the end of 2020 by the four main operators: Orange, SFR, Bouygues Telecom and Free. The French National Frequencies Agency (ANFR) authorised almost 41,700 5G sites and 64,700 4G by 1 August 2023. But according to operator declarations, 77% of authorised sites are technically operational.

§3. THE INFORMATION AND COMMUNICATIONS TECHNOLOGY MARKET

16. The consumer electronic communications market in France is divided into four major fixed and mobile operators: Orange, SFR, Bouygues, Telecom, and Free. The strong competition between these operators has resulted in some of the lowest prices in Europe and high levels of investment.

Table 1 Main Indicators of the Four Largest Telecoms Operators in France

2021 Indicator	*Orange France*	*SFR (Altice France)*	*Bouygues Telecom*	*Free (Iliad France)*
Turnover in France[a]	EUR 18.1 billion	EUR 10.7 billion	EUR 7.3 billion	EUR 5.2 billion
Turnover growth rate (versus 2020)	–2.0%	+1.4%	+12.7%[b]	+3.8%
No. of fixed service subscribers (% of total)	12.3m *(40%)*	6.7m *(22%)*	4.4m *(15%)*	6.9m *(23%)*
No. of fixed FttH service subscribers[c] (% of total)	5.9m *(37%)*	4.0m[d] *(25%)*	2.3m *(14%)*	3.8m *(24%)*
No. of mobile service subscribers[e] (% of total)	20.0m *(29%)*	19.6m *(29%)*	14.8m *(22%)*	13.6m *(20%)*

a. Turnover includes market revenue between operators (*e.g.* interconnections, wholesale).

b. Excluding the acquisition of several virtual operators, the organic turnover growth rate of Bouygues Telecom is 5%.

c. FttH: Fibre to the Home. The concept differs from FttB (Fibre to the Building), where the last few metres of the cable can be made of copper (VDSL) or coaxial cable (DOCSIS).

d. The SFR figure for its fibre optic subscribers is greater than its FttH subscriber figure since it includes FttB and 4G Box customers.

e. The number of mobile service subscribers is the number of mobile plans taken out under a contract in France (excluding MVNOs, M2M and prepaid offerings).

Source: Annual operator results, DG Trésor calculations.

Note: The figures do not necessarily reflect those published by ARCEP in its analyses as the scopes used may differ slightly.

By contrast, on the business market, competition is not as strong. Orange, the historical provider, holds significant market shares in the retail, wholesale and wholesale markets (over 50% at the end of 2021).[25]

17. The France ICT market was valued at USD 114.24 billion in 2022 and will grow at a compounded annual growth rate (CAGR) of 11.35% to reach a value of USD 195.53 billion by 2027. The cumulative revenue generation opportunities for ICT providers in France is estimated at USD 895.96 billion between 2022 to 2027.[26]

§4. E-GOVERNMENT

I. Main Components of the Development of France's e-Government

18. According to the OECD, e-government refers to 'The use of information and communication technologies, and particularly the Internet, as a tool to achieve better government.'[27] Giving an overview of the main e-government developments in France requires presenting the evolution of the digital transformation of the French administration and the French Open Data policy, as well as recalling France's commitments to open government.

19. **The main steps of the digital transformation of the French Administration**. The administrative digital transformation dates back to the early 2000s. As in many other states, the first step was to put online practical resources to improve information for citizens, including information on administrative procedures. This led to the creation in 1999 of the *Légifrance website* which enabled the dissemination of French law.[28] In addition, in 2000, *service public.fr* was created as the government's digital portal. Since 2005, the second step in the development of the e-government in France has involved the gradual digitisation of relations between the administration and its users. This has been made possible by the adoption of various texts. An ordinance in 2005, modified in 2014,[29] established the to f users to communicate with their administration by email,[30] regulate the creation of administrative e-procedures[31] and offer to the users an online storage personalised space.[32] This has resulted in the widespread introduction of online administrative procedures and processes supported by various Action plans. After the latter one,

25. *See* for more details, Arthur Dozias, *La concurrence dans le marché français des communications électroniques*, TResor-Eco, January 2023.
26. *See* Global Data Report Store, published in July 2023.
27. OECD, *e-Government Studies: The e-Government Imperative*, 2003, http://pavroz.ru/files/egovimperetive.pdf, p. 23.
28. Since 2002, Legifrance has been qualified as public service for the dissemination of law via the internet. *See* décret n° 2002-1064 du 7 août 2002 relatif au service public de la diffusion du droit par l'internet.
29. Ordinance No. 2005-1516 8 Dec. 2005 which is partially codified in the CRPA.
30. Article L. 112-8 CRPA.
31. Article L. 112-9 CRPA.
32. Article 7 Ordinance No. 2005-1516 of 8 Dec. 2005.

the 'Public Action 2022', around 250 most used administrative procedures are dematerialised, such as the declaration of income, the payment of taxes and fines, the request for identity papers, the request for housing assistance, etc. The full list of online e-procedures, administrative forms and standard administrative letter templates are available on the *service public.fr* website.[33] Furthermore, an observatory[34] has been set up to assess the quality of the main administrative procedures every six months. The tool considers the opinions of users.

20. **French Open Data policy**. Although France had envisaged access to administrative documents as early as 1978,[35] it was under the influence of European directives on public sector information (2003, 2013)[36] that a genuine Open Data policy was introduced in France. The landmark law in this area is the so-called Digital Republic Act of 2016.[37] This law established the principle of free and open access to public sector data and general interest data.[38] This obligation applies to all French administrations and local authorities with more than 3,500 inhabitants, more than fifty employees, and their companies delegated for public service. Sectoral legislation specifying Open Data regimes in the fields of energy,[39] transport[40] and public procurement.[41] The Digital Republic Act also extended Open Data to source codes.[42]

21. Article L.321-4 Code of Relations Between the Public and the Administration (CRPA) enshrines the provision of reference data with a view to facilitating its

33. https://www.service-public.fr/particuliers/vosdroits/demarches-et-outils. There is also a business oriented website https://entreprendre.service-public.fr/.
34. *See* https://observatoire.numerique.gouv.fr/observatoire.
35. Loi n° 78-753 17 Jul. 1978 portant diverses mesures d'amélioration des relations entre l'administration et le public et diverses dispositions d'ordre administratif, social et fiscal, which is now codified in the Book III, Ch. 1 of the CRPA.
36. Directive 2003/98/EC of the European Parliament and of the Council of 17 Nov. 2003 on the re-use of public sector information, and Directive 2013/37/EU of the European Parliament and of the Council of 26 Jun. 2013 amending Directive 2003/98/EC on the re-use of public sector information Text with EEA relevance.
37. Loi n° 2016-1321 7 Oct. 2016 pour une République numérique. The Open Data principle is codified in the Book III of the CRPA.
38. The concept of general interest data covers by Arts 17 to 24 includes the data collected by concessionaires as part of their public service delegations and justice data. The Open Data of the French administrative court's decision is fully implemented since June 2022, https://opendata.justice-administrative.fr/ whereas there is only one search engine relative to the decision of the *Conseil d'Etat* and the Cour administratives d'Appel called Ariane Web https://www.conseil-etat.fr/decisions-de-justice/jurisprudence/rechercher-une-decision-arianeweb. The Open Data of the judiciary bodies is still underway, for the Tribunaux de commerce (forthcoming in December 2024) and the tribunaux judiciaires, (forthcoming in September 2025). *See* Arrêté 28 Apr. 2021 pris en application de l'article 9 du décret n° 2020-797 du 29 juin 2020 relatif à la mise à la disposition du public des décisions des juridictions judiciaires et administratives.
39. Articles L. 111-73-1 et seq. energy code.
40. Article L. 1115-1 Transport Code.
41. *See* Arts R. 2196-1, R. 2196-4 and D. 2396-2-1 public procurement code and the Arrêté du 22 décembre 2022 relatif aux données essentielles des marchés publics.
42. Article L. 300-2 CRPA.

reuse as a genuine public service mission falling within the remit of the State.[43] These reference data have been defined with three criteria. First, they are common references used to name or identify products, services, territories, or people. Second, this reference data is frequently reused by public or private bodies other than the administration that holds it. Lastly, their reuse requires them to be made available at a high level of quality. To date, nine datasets covering a wide range of subjects have been identified as reference data:

- National Address Database (BAN).
- Sirene database of companies and their establishments (SIRENE, SIRET).
- Official Geographical Code (COG).
- Computerised cadastral map.
- Registre Parcellaire Graphique (RPG): outlines of parcels and cropping islands and their majority crop groups.
- State administrative organisation reference system.
- Large-scale reference system (RGE).
- National Directory of Associations (RNA).
- Operational Directory of Professions and Jobs (ROME).

22. Administrative documents, public information and data must be published in an open format that can be easily reused and exploited in an automated format. Open Data comprises data from the public sector made accessible for reuse for non-commercial or commercial purposes.[44] Licensing remains optional unless the reuse is subject to a fee.[45]

23. Implementing these open Data obligations can prove complex, as they are subject to respect for the right to privacy[46] and the right to protection of personal data.[47] Technically, this may mean that data must be 'anonymised'. It may also involve obscuring certain information.[48] Furthermore, Open Data can be limited to data covered by secrecy[49] or property rights.

24. **The French Open government policy.** In 2014, France joined the Open Government Partnership. This international initiative brings together seventy-eight states and seventy-six local authorities, which produce action plans every two years to promote transparency, participation, and collaboration with civil society. France

43. The Etalab department of the Interministerial Digital Affairs Directorate (DINUM) is responsible for the implementation and governance of this public service. The platform *data.gouv.fr* is the open, community-based platform that aims to centralise and structure Open Data in France.
44. Article L. 321-1 CRPA.
45. Article D. 324-5-1 CRPA list the categories of data that can be submitted to fee. These data are mainly from the, Météo-France, French National Institute for Geographic and Forestry Information, French Naval Hydrographic and Oceanographic Service.
46. *See* Art. L. 311-6 CRPA which recalls the categories of administrative document which can only be communicate to the concerned person.
47. *See* CNIL, CADA, guide pratique de la publication en ligne et de la réutilisaiton des données publiques, Open Data, avalaible at https://www.cnil.fr/sites/cnil/files/atoms/files/guide-open-data.pdf.
48. Article L. 311-7 CRPA.
49. *See* Art. L. 311-5 CRPA which lists of administrative documents which cannot be communicated.

has already adopted three action plans. The last one is the 2021–2023 action plan, which is structured around a package of commitments from twelve ministers and has been extended to other lead public institutions such as the Conseil d'Etat, the government audit office, AAIs such as the CNIL, the ARCOM, the ARCEP, the High Authority for Transparency in Public Life, the Commission for Access to Administrative Documents (Commission d'accès aux documents administratifs (CADA)).

II. Mixed Progress

25. Digitalisation has obvious benefits for many users (greater availability of services, shorter processing times for certain administrative procedures, etc.) 71% of adults in 2022 said they had carried out an online procedure in France. However, the digitalisation raises three main concerns in France. First, the quality of the digital services offered is often called into question. The excepted simplification of the daily life of French citizens and users of digital administrative services is not always there. The physical fragility of certain digital administrative processes is often criticised. Internet users complain that the online procedure did not work, that they had difficulty joining files or reforming their submission, that the proposed form to be completed was inappropriate, and that the online procedure was not sufficiently adapted to the mobile format, not to mention all the cases where the lack of appropriate information makes it difficult to use the proposed service and that the lack of personal contact increase the delay of the user requests.[50]

26. Second, the administrative digital transformation can also be the source of territorial, economic and cultural inequalities. Technical difficulties in accessing certain services can have an impact on the most disadvantaged users. This has been pointed out in certain emblematic cases, such as the 'MaPrimeRénov', the flagship home renovation digital platform whose malfunctioning has had consequences for the payment of grants to low-income households.[51] More globally, access to public services is an essential condition for access to many fundamental rights, such as the right to health, housing, education, justice, and emergency. In 2022, the Defender of Rights listed some populations which are structurally penalised by the development of digital administration, such as persons with disabilities, prisoners, foreigners, the elderly, and young people who can be lost when carrying out administrative procedures online.[52] One of the main recurrent recommendations is 'not to trap the

50. *See* the user assessments from the digital observatory implemented by the government at https://observatoire.numerique.gouv.fr/observatoire#.
51. The French ombudsman, le défenseur des droits, received more than thousand claims regarding the defects of the digital platform concerned. *See* Décision du Défenseur des droits n° 2022-199 adopted in October 2022 and her hearing on the 13 Apr. 2023 available in French at https://www.senat.fr/compte-rendu-commissions/20230410/cere.html#toc6.
52. Defender of the Rights, *Report Dematerialisation of Public Services: Three Years Later, Where Are We?*, 2022, available in English at https://www.defenseurdesdroits.fr/sites/default/files/2023-07/ddd_rapport_dematerialisation_EN_2022_202205.pdf.

user in an exclusively digital relationship'.[53] The *Conseil d'Etat* has accepted that the administration may impose the use of an online administrative procedure provided that it guarantees the persons concerned the effective exercise of their rights. The *Conseil d'Etat* concluded that '*In view of the characteristics of the public concerned, the diversity and complexity of applicants' situations and the consequences that the registration of their application has on a foreigner's situation, in particular on their right to remain in France and, in certain cases, to work there, it is the responsibility of the regulatory authority, where it requires the use of a teleservice to obtain certain residence permits, to take the necessary steps to ensure that people who do not have access to digital tools or who have difficulty either in using them or in completing administrative procedures receive support.* It is also responsible, for the same reasons, for guaranteeing the possibility of resorting to an alternative solution in the event that certain applicants find it impossible to use the teleservice for reasons relating to the design of this tool or its mode of operation, despite this support.'[54]

27. Despite the legal obligation of accessibility for persons with disabilities,[55] only 6 of the 248 most common online procedures were 100% accessible in July 2023.[56] Seventy-eight standard procedures are not accessible to disabled people, including applications for student grants, registration on the national register of organ donation refusals and applications for European health insurance cards. For this reason, a 2023 ordinance provides that the administration's bad pupils will first receive a formal notice from the ARCOM before being penalised financially if they still fail to comply with the accessibility obligation, i.e., a fine of EUR 50,000 from 1 January 2024.[57]

28. Although digital coverage of the regions and household equipment is progressing, disparities remain at the national level. First, more than 7.5 million people in France do not have quality access to the Internet connection, especially in the countryside and ultramarine territories. Second, the Defender of Rights estimates that there are 13 million people in this situation of digital exclusion.[58]

29. Third, the lack of participation of the civil society in France illustrates the limit of the implementation of an open government. This is mentioned in the France

53. *See* above-mentioned report of the Defender of the Rights pp. 59–60. *See* the recent proposal to for the reopening of physical reception areas in public services, Bill 158.
54. CE, 3 Jun. 2022, n° 452798, Conseil national des barreaux et assoc. La Cimade et a. point 11.
55. Access for persons with disabilities to websites is a right recognised by the United Nations CRPD, which was ratified by France in 2010, by the Directive of the European Parliament and of the Council of 26 Oct. 2016 on the accessibility of websites and mobile applications of public sector bodies Arts 47 and 48 of Act No. 2005-102 of 11 February.
56. An administrative procedure is considered to be 100% accessible if it complies with all the criteria of its 'General accessibility improvement reference framework' (RGAA).
57. Ordonnance No. 2023-859 adopted on 6 Sep. 2023.
58. *See* above-mentioned report 2022.

Action Plan Review 2021–2023. The report underlines the 'lack of meaningful dialogue with civil society during the co-creation process, and most of the 59 commitments have unclear potential for results or lack sufficient detail to be assessed'.[59]

30. On an international scale, the EGDI (E-Government Development Index) created by the UN are aimed at comparing the level of e-government in the world. EGDI is a composite index between 0 and 1 used to determine the performance of e-governments. It is calculated by the average of three indices, quantifying respectively: the use of NTICs for public services, the degree of telecommunication connectivity in the country (internet access), and the human capacity of citizens (human capital). Currently, France is ranked 19th, whereas it was 4th in 2014.[60] This shows that compared to other countries, the deployment of e-government in France is becoming slower.

31. However, France is considered by the European Commission as the most mature country in the EU-twenty-seven regarding Open Data for the third time in 2023. Since 2015, this ranking has been highlighting the progress made by European countries in opening their data according to the following criteria: public policy, national portal, impact and quality. France has just achieved an overall score of 98.3% for Open Data maturity and comes top on three of the four aforementioned criteria: 100% for impact, 100% for public policy and 97% for quality.[61]

59. https://www.opengovpartnership.org/documents/france-action-plan-review-2021-2023/.
60. https://publicadministration.un.org/egovkb/en-us/Data/Country-Information/id/61-France.
61. *See* France Open Data Maturity report 2023, https://data.europa.eu/sites/default/files/country-factsheet_france_2023.pdf.

Part I. Privacy Protection in France

§1. The Affirmation of the Constitutional Value of the Right to Privacy

32. No article of the Constitution of the Fifth Republic[62] explicitly enshrines the principle of privacy. Nevertheless, in 1999,[63] the *Conseil constitutionnel* explicitly recognised the constitutional value of the right to privacy. The *Conseil constitutionnel* declared that freedom, proclaimed as a 'natural and imprescriptible human right' by Article 2 of the Declaration of Human and Civic Rights of 1789, 'implies respect for privacy'.[64]

33. The constitutionalisation of the right to privacy mentioned before was important because the *Conseil constitutionnel* cannot consider the consistency of a statute with the European Convention of Human Rights (ECHR).[65] Then, the derived constitutional value of the right to privacy allows the *Conseil constitutionnel* to review the constitutionality of the French legislation toward privacy rights.

62. Former French Constitutions contains some elements of the right to Privacy. Article 17, Chapter V on Judiciary Power provides that 'Slanders and insults against any person relating to the actions of their private life shall be punished on their prosecution.' Article 9, Chapter IV on Police of the Constitution of 1791 enshrines the inviolability of home.
63. In a former decision, the *Conseil constitutionnel* only linked the right to privacy to individual freedom, *see* Decision No. 94-352 DC, 18 Jan. 1995, *Loi d'orientation et de programmation relative à la sécurité*, §3.
64. *See* Conseil constitutionnel, Décision No. 99-416 DC, 23 Jul. 1999, Act Creating Universal Health Coverage (*Loi portant création d'une couverture maladie universelle)* §45. The *Conseil constitutionnel* confirmed in several decisions the constitutional nature of the right to privacy. *See* for instance, Decision No. 2004-492 DC, 2 Mar. 2004, *Act adapting the Administration of Justice to the changing face of crime* §75. English version available at https://www.conseil-constitutionnel.fr/en/decision/2004/2004492DC.htm, or more recently Decision No. 2021-828 DC of 9 Nov. 2021, *Law on various public health surveillance provisions*, §24, English version available at https://www.conseil-constitutionnel.fr/en/decision/2021/2021828DC.htm.
65. Conseil constitutionnel, Decision No. 74-54 DC, 15 Jan. 1975, Voluntary Interruption of Pregnancy Act, §7, English version available at https://www.conseil-constitutionnel.fr/en/decision/1975/7454DC.htm. Only the judicial and administrative judges can exercise such a so-called conventionality control.

34. The formal introduction of the right to privacy in the French constitution was discussed several times.[66] It has been so far rejected[67] mainly for two reasons.[68] First, such an enshrinement would not have an added value. It would be symbolically codifying the above-mentioned case law of the *Conseil constitutionnel.* Moreover, this would unnecessarily duplicate international provisions applicable in France which already explicitly enshrine the right to privacy: Article 12 of the Universal Declaration of Human Rights of 1948, Article 8 of the ECHR, and Article 7 of the EU Charter of Fundamentals Rights. Second, the law was considered more appropriate in facilitating the necessary adaptability and specifying privacy.

§2. Article 9 Civil Code: French Legal 'Matrix'[69] of the Right to Privacy

35. Historically, violations of privacy were sanctioned in France on civil liability basis under Article 1382 civil code[70] and/or criminal defamation. The inference in the private life of others constitutes a fault, entitling to reparation of the damage or to the cessation of the violation.[71] The emergence of the right to privacy is also linked to the need to limit press freedom by introducing press offences.[72] In other words, privacy in France was considered a civil and penal-protected interest.

66. Recently *see* la proposition de loi constitutionnelle n° 5241, 12 mai 2022, visant à transposer dans notre Constitution les dispositions de la Charte des Droits naturels et des Libertés fondamentales, Art. 10, available at https://www.assemblee-nationale.fr/dyn/15/textes/l15b5241_proposition-loi#.
67. Interestingly, the recent attempts to annex a digital charter to the French Constitution do not mention the Right to privacy *see* for instance the digital Charter proposed by the Working Group on the Rights et Freedoms in the Digital Age of Assemblée Nationale and the Senat in June 2018. The Charter introduced as the amendment No. 2343 of the constitutional proposal Pour une démocratie plus representative et efficace, was rejected by the Assemblée Nationale on the 11 Jul. 2018, available at https://www.assemblee-nationale.fr/dyn/15/amendements/0911/AN/2343.
68. *See* Redécouvrir le Préambule de la Constitution, rapport du Comité présidé par Simone Veil, rendu au Président de la République en décembre 2008, pp. 69 ff.
69. Expression originally borrowed from J. Ch. Saint-Pau, *L'article 9, matrice des droits de la personnalité: D,* 1999, p. 541.
70. Article 1382 Civil Code in its 1804 version provided that 'Every act whatever of man that causes damage to another, obliges him by whose fault it occurred to repair it.', David Gruning, et al., *traduction du code civil français en anglaise*, version bilingue 2015, available at https://halshs.archives-ouvertes.fr/halshs-01385107/document.
71. J. Ch. Saint-Pau considers that the first French decision on Privacy dates back to 1858, when the Civil Court of the Seine admitted that the sister of a great actress was entitled to prohibit to reproduce the portrait of the star on her deathbed. (T. civ. Seine, 16 juin 1858: DP 1858, jurispr. p. 62) *See* J. Ch. Saint-Pau, *Juriscl. Civil Code,* Fasc. 10 Jouissance des droits civils- Droit au respect de la vie privée. Définition conceptuelle du droit subjectif, §4.
72. *See* for instance, the Art. 11 of the Act of the 11 Mai 1868 which provided that 'any publication in a periodical relating to a fact of private life constitutes a contravention punishable by a fine of 500 francs'. For more details on the French sources of Privacy Right *see* J.L. Halpérin, *Protection de la vie privée et privacy: deux traditions juridiques différentes?,* Les Nouveaux Cahiers du Conseil constitutionnel, n° 48, juin 2015, pp. 59–68, available at https://www.conseil-constitutionnel.fr/nouveaux-cahiers-du-conseil-constitutionnel/protection-de-la-vie-privee-et-privacy-deux-traditions-juridiques-differentes.

36. It was only in 1970[73] that a new Article 9 was introduced in the civil code, which provides, in its paragraph 1, that: 'Everyone has the right to respect for his private life'. The second § declares that 'Without prejudice to the right to recover indemnification for injury suffered, judges may prescribe any measures, such as sequestration, seizure and others, suited to the prevention or the ending of an infringement of the intimate character of private life; in case of emergency those measures may be provided for by summary proceedings.' Thus, Article 9 civil code creates an autonomous right to privacy distinct from Article 1382 of the civil code.[74]

37. Article 9 French civil code is considered the French legal 'matrix' of personality rights. Unlike international texts, Article 9 of the Civil code does not specify the components of this right. This lack of definition will allow the object of protection to be progressively extended. Initially understood as a right to intimacy against the public or private inference, a right to secrecy, and a right to respect of home,[75] Article 9 civil code has been extensively interpreted under the influence of the European Court of Human Rights (ECtHR). Article 9 civil code today covers rights to identity and several domains,[76] as detailed hereinafter. At this stage, it is worth keeping in mind the importance of the ECtHR both on the concept of privacy and on the methodology for resolving the conflicts between right to privacy and other legitimate interests.[77] This occurs through the well-known technique of balance of interests and by an evaluation of the necessity and the proportionality of the inference in the right of privacy.

§3. National Application of European and International Conventions Regarding Privacy

I. Applicability in France of the Main European and International Conventions Including a Right to Privacy

38. France ratified the main International and European treaties, including protection of privacy, in particular the ECHR[78] and the International Covenant on Civil

73. Act No. 70-643 of 17 Jul. 1970. This Act contained a civil and a penal aspect. Beside the affirmation of a subjective and autonomous right to Privacy, introduced at the Art. 9 Civil Code, the Act reinforced the protection of the right to privacy with provisions in the penal code sanctioning audiovisual spying on private life and its exploitation. (Arts 368 ff. Penal Code).
74. This has been clarified by *the Cour de cassation* which declared: 'the mere finding of an infringement of privacy gives rise to a right to compensation', on the unique legal ground of Art. 9 Civil Code, *Cass. 1re civ., 5 Nov. 1996, n° 94-14.798.*
75. The right to respect of home in France was recognised very early on in the revolutionary era in Art. 76 of the Constitution of 22 Frimaire An VIII.
76. *See* S. Canas, *L'influence de la fondamentalisation du droit au respect de la vie privée sur la mise en œuvre de l'article 9 du code civil,* Nouveaux cahiers du Conseil Constitutionnel, n° 48, June 2015, pp. 47–58.
77. *See* J. Ch. Saint-Pau, *Juriscl. Civil Code,* Fasc. 10, mentioned above, §§23–24.
78. *See* Art. 8 EHCR.

and Political Rights[79] (ICCPR). This first observation calls for three types of complementary remarks. Those ratifications were late, and the applicability of those conventions was limited. For twenty years, French judges have been quoting more and more international provisions on privacy by giving priority to Article 8 ECHR.

39. First, France was the last founding state of the Council of Europe to ratify the ECHR on 3 May 1974, and it only ratified the ICCPR on 4 November 1980. The reasons mostly given for this delay were paradoxical. One the one hand, those ratifications were considered symbolic because most of their provisions were reflected in French domestic law. On the other hand, the integration of these conventions into French law raised legal difficulties.[80]

40. Second, at the beginning, the ratification of both conventions was incomplete.[81] It was only in 1981 that France accepted the right of individual application to the ECtHR and the individual complaints procedures in the ICCPR in 1984. This explains that it was mostly after the eighties that these conventions and, in particular, their provisions on privacy were more and more invoked by parties before the French judges and appeared in the decisions.

41. Third, French judges recognised the direct effect of the provisions on privacy of these Conventions based on Article 55 of the French Constitution. In most cases, Article 17 of the ICCPR is cited in addition to Article 8 of the ECHR. For instance, the criminal Chamber of the *Cour de cassation* ruled in 1994 that tax searches were in accordance with Articles 8 of the ECHR and 17 of the ICCPR.[82] To our knowledge, there are no French decisions on a violation of the only Article 17 ICCPR. The priority given to the ECHR implies that the French judges interpret Article 17 ICCPR in a consistent manner with Article 8 ECHR. Furthermore, the French judges do not feel bound by the reports[83] or communications[84] issued by the ICCPR's Human Rights Committee. It is true that such activities of the Committee

79. Article 17 ICCPR provides:

1. No one shall be subjected to arbitrary or unlawful interference with his privacy, family, home or correspondence, nor to unlawful attacks on his honour and reputation.
2. Everyone has the right to the protection of the law against such interference or attacks.

80. *See* for more details: Bonino Pauline, *La France contre les droits de l'Homme? La difficile ratification par la France de la Convention européenne des droits de l'Homme (1950–1974)*, Relations internationales, 2018/2, n° 174, pp. 91–108, https://www.cairn.info/revue-relations-internationales-2018-2-page-91.htm; Imbert Pierre-Henri, *La France et les traités relatifs aux droits de l'Homme.* In *Annuaire français de droit international*, volume 26, 1980, pp. 31–43, https://www.persee.fr/doc/afdi_0066-3085_1980_num_26_1_2379.
81. France also made declarations and reserves on both Conventions, which do not directly affect the right of privacy. For more details, *see* Dhommeaux Jean, *Les engagements souscrits par la France, Les Petites Affiches*, 25 May 2000, n° 104, p. 3 for the ICCPR and the above-mentioned articles on the ECHR note 80.
82. Cass. Crim., 12 Dec. 1994, 94-83.949, https://www.legifrance.gouv.fr/juri/id/JURITEXT000007559821/; for an example before the *Conseil d'Etat see* CE, 10 Mar. 1995, Demirpence, No. 141083.
83. *See* Jean Flauss, *Le pacte international relatif aux droits civils et politiques devant le juge administratif texte actualisé au 31 decembre 1999*, Les petites Affiches, 2020, p. 31.

are much more directed to the French Government. In addition, the Committee sometimes opts for an extensive interpretation of Article 17 ICCPR. The Committee, dealing with petitions submitted by Polynesians residing in Tahiti, had concluded that the construction of a hotel on ancestral burial grounds, which represent an important place in their history, culture and life, constituted 'an arbitrary interference with the author's right to family and privacy, in violation of Articles 17, paragraph 1, and 23, paragraph 1'.[85] Some member of the Committee declared in an opinion this extensive interpretation of the term family to all members of one's ethnic or cultural group aimed at circumventing the reservation formulated by France with regard to Article 27 (protection of minorities).[86]

42. Besides the ECHR and the ICCPR, France also ratified two less famous conventions of the UN with privacy provisions. The Convention on the Rights of the Child has been in application in France since 6 September 1990. Its Article 16 recalls that:

1. No child shall be subjected to arbitrary or unlawful interference with his or her privacy, family, home or correspondence, nor to unlawful attacks on his or her honour and reputation.
2. The child has the right to the protection of the law against such interference or attacks.

This provision is directly applicable in France but is usually mentioned in the complement of Article 8 ECHR or even Article 17 ICCPR.[87]

43. The Convention on the Rights of Persons with Disabilities (CRPD) has been in vigour in France since 20 March 2010. Its Article 22 on respect for privacy declares that:

1. No person with disabilities, regardless of place of residence or living arrangements, shall be subjected to arbitrary or unlawful interference with his or her privacy, family, home or correspondence or other types of communication or to unlawful attacks on his or her honour and reputation. Persons with disabilities have the right to the protection of the law against such interference or attacks.
2. States Parties shall protect the privacy of personal, health and rehabilitation information of persons with disabilities on an equal basis with others.

---

84. *See* Cohen Jonnathan, *La France, la convention européenne des droits de l'homme et le pacte international relatif aux droits civils et politiques*, Les petites affiches, 2020 p. 39.
85. *See Francis Hopu and Tepoaitu Bessert v. France*, Communication No. 549/1993, U.N. Doc. CCPR/C/60/D/549/1993/Rev.1. (1997), point 10.3, available at http://hrlibrary.umn.edu/undocs/549-1993.html.
86. *See* points 4 and 5 of the opinion anexed to the former mentioned communication.
87. *See* for instance CE, 10 Mar. 1995, *Demirpence*, requête No. 141083, mentioned above or CE, 19 Jul. 2010, M. F. et Mme C., Décision No. 317182, 323441 relatif à la décision *'Base élèves 1er degré'*. *See also* CE, 31 Oct. 2008, No. 293785 in which Art. 8 has been invoked against a French decree on detention in combination with the Art. 3 of the Convention on the Rights of the Child.

This Article 22 has been invoked before the French judges in some cases,[88] most of the time in combination with other provisions, and sometimes in a very extensive way. For instance, French administrative judges refer to Article 22 CRPD in cases of conflicts between family and physicians regarding the continuation of artificial feeding and hydration of a relative.[89] Such cases are much more related to the respect of human dignity in the sense of Article 2 of the ECHR. The main issues raised by application of the CRPD in France are focused on non-discriminations. More globally, France lacks an inclusive policy based on a human right of disability instead of a pure 'medical model, paternalistic approaches to disability'.[90]

To sum up, national jurisprudence on privacy is mostly substantially in relation to Article 8 ECHR, even though France ratified other international Conventions with privacy provisions.

II. National Application of Article 8 ECHR

44. The application of Article 8 ECHR led to important legislative changes in France as general measures to execute judgments.[91] Today, Article 8 is widely invoked before the French judges, who mention on a regular basis the case law of the ECHR. The right to privacy was even the topic of the first advisory opinion under Protocol No. 16 to the Convention, which was requested by the *Cour de cassation* to the ECtHR. This illustrates that the right to privacy is an important element of the dialogue between French judges and the ECtHR.[92]

---

88. *See* for instance Conseil d'État, 7e chambre, 2 Oct. 2017 – n° 408364, regarding the inscription of the term 'invalidty' on a military pension certificate delivered by the Ministry of the Finances. This mention was necessary to calculate the pension and did not attempt to the Health secrecy or the private life because such certificate was only delivered to the beneficiary, who could have another one without the mention for communication to third parties. In the point 4 the *Conseil d'Etat* denied direct effect to Art. 22, §2 of the CRPD after it declared the non-violation of Art. 8 ECHR and the non-applicability of Art. 8 of the CFR. 'M. B ... ne peut non plus utilement invoquer les stipulations du paragraphe 2 de l'article 22 de la convention relative aux droits des personnes handicapées ... qui requièrent l'intervention d'actes complémentaires pour produire des effets à l'égard des particuliers'.
89. *See* for instance Conseil d'État, Juge des référés, 24 Avril 2019 – n° 428117, in the famous Lambert Case.
90. *See* Concluding observations on the initial report of France, Committee on the Rights of Persons with Disabilities, CRPD/C/FRA/CO/1, 4 Oct. 2021, avalaible at https://docstore.ohchr.org/SelfServices/FilesHandler.ashx?enc=6QkG1d%2fPPRiCAqhKb7yhsppzG2aGV9V7jwwTt3BTgywsT00cPcBs4teRNpzwZ%2f8e90S8SG9WCEivodoQxam9M%2byTPRnagoi6mSW97seE%2fnlqsZLuMpsLxXaWJmPl04w3.
91. For instance, France amended the legislation on telephone tapping about interceptions ordered by the judicial authorities after the case of *Kruslin and Huvig* on 24 Apr. 1990 in which, the ECHR considered that the lack of clarity of the French law on telephone tapping violated Art. 8. This was the first case of violation by France of Art. 8. The Case of B from 25 Mar. 1992 led a reform of national practice concerning the possibility for the civil status of transgender persons to match their new gender identity. This was the second violation of Art. 8 by France.
92. Advisory opinion, concerning the recognition in domestic law of a legal parent-child relationship between a child born through a gestational surrogacy arrangement abroad and the intended mother request No. P16-2018-001.

45. The object of the protection is to say that private and family life has not been explicitly defined in a theoretical manner but is reflected mostly by the case law of the ECtHR. Most of the time, when the judges consider that the right to privacy is applicable in the case, their main task is to asset whether the inference in the private and family life is disproportionate. This would be illustrated hereinafter in the most relevant areas of application of Article 8 ECHR for France.

A. *Facts and Figures on the French Violations of Article 8 ECHR*

46. According to the search engine Hudoc, in January 2023, France has been condemned in fifty-seven decisions for violations of Article 8 ECHR.[93] According to the statistics of the ECtHR,[94] France is the eighth most condemned state by the Court for violation of Article 8 after Russia, Italy, Turkey, Poland, Romania, Ukraine, Bulgaria, and the UK, tied with Croatia. Globally, Article 8 is the third most violated article of the ECHR by France after Article 6 and Article 5 ECHR.[95]

47. At the national level, Article 8 ECHR is frequently invoked before the judicial judges and the administrative judges based on their respective competences. The database of the *Conseil d'Etat* refers only to fourteen judgments of violation of this article; while it has been invoked in 75 cases, there are 7,558 cases dealing with inference in privacy.

48. In July 2022, the right to privacy was invoked in 532 case laws before the *Conseil constitutionnel*: 303 times in post-review and 229 times in ex ante review. Although the parties and parliamentarians often invoke privacy, it appears only 362 times in the summaries of the decisions of the *Conseil constitutionnel*.

49. While the number of decisions that have led to the existence of a violation of the right to privacy in France seems to be relatively small, this article has been used in very emblematic cases which illustrate social and political issues of the French society. One should mention, among others, the still lively debates on civil status of transsexuals, rights of the parents and the children in the context of gestational surrogacy and the claim for new forms of parenthood. The French structural prison overcrowding also led to a finding of violation of privacy rights of the

93. https://hudoc.echr.coe.int/fre%23%7b%22languageisocode%22:%5b%22FRE%22%5d,%22respondent%22:%5b%22FRA%22%5d,%22article%22:%5b%228%22%5d,%22documentcollectionid2%22:%5b%22JUDGMENTS%22%5d,%22violation%22:%5b%228%22%5d%7d#{%22languageisocode%22:[%22FRE%22],%22respondent%22:[%22FRA%22],%22documentcollectionid2%22:[%22GRANDCHAMBER%22,%22CHAMBER%22,%22DECISIONS%22],%22violation%22:[%228%22]}.
94. *See* the statistics of the ECtHR on violation Article by State 1959–2022 https://www.echr.coe.int/documents/d/echr/stats_violation_1959_2022_eng.
95. *See* The ECtHR and France, p. 5 available at https://www.echr.coe.int/documents/d/echr/CP_France_ENG.

prisoners and recommendation for more effectivity of this right.[96] The successive waves of terrorist attacks in France have led to new surveillance measures with intrusive technologies, which raised privacy and data protection concerns. Lately, the multiple restrictions and controls aiming at fighting against the COVID-19 pandemic have given rise to new violations of Article 8.

B. *Noteworthy French Application of Article 8 ECHR*

1. Liberalisation of the Sexual Civil Status

50. **Progressive liberalisation of the change of sexual civil status.** In France, the change of the mention in the civil status for transgender people has long been the subject of controversy in both doctrine and jurisprudence. Initially refused by the *Cour de cassation,*[97] the modification has been admitted since 1992[98] after the condemnation of France in the *B v. France* Case.[99] However, the *Cour de cassation* only recognised that '*when, following medical and surgical treatment undergone for therapeutic purposes, a person suffering from transsexualism syndrome no longer possesses all the characteristics of his or her original sex and has taken on a physical appearance that brings him or her closer to the other sex, to which his or her social behaviour corresponds, the principle of respect for privacy justifies that his or her civil status should henceforth indicate the sex he or she appears to be; ... the principle of the unavailability of personal status does not prevent such a change'*.[100] The change of the transsexual's gender in civil status was subject to four conditions:

- the proof of the reality of the 'transsexual syndrome' established by judicial expertise;
- the existence of 'medical and surgical treatment' undergone for therapeutic purposes;
- a physical appearance close to the other sex.; This excluded sexual changes by hormone therapy;
- social behaviour corresponding to the 'psychological sexe'.

51. In 2012, the *Cour de cassation* maintained its controversial jurisprudence by ruling that to obtain a change of gender in civil status, 'the person must establish,

96. *See* for instance the opinion of the Commission Nationale Consultative des Droits de l'Homme, l'effectivité des droits fondamentaux en prison, mars 2022 available at https://www.cncdh.fr/publications/avis-sur-leffectivite-des-droits-fondamentaux-en-detention-2022-5.
97. *See* Cass. 1st civ., 16 Dec. 1975: JurisData n° 1975-000374; JCP G 1976, II, 18503, J. Penneau; D. 1976, p. 397, R. Lindon; Bull. civ. I, n° 374 et 376, and Cass. 1re civ., 21 May 1990, n° 88-12.829 but accepted by others judges TGI Toulouse, 25 May 1978: JurisData n° 1981-763674; JCP G 1981, II, 19529, J. Penneau. – TGI Paris, 24 Nov. 1981: JurisData n° 1981-000552; JCP G 1982, II, 19792.
98. Cass. ass. plén., 11 Dec. 1992, n° 91-12.37.
99. 25 Mar. 1992, *Botella v. France,* n° 13343/87.
100. Cass., ass. plén., 11 Dec.. 1992, n 91-11.900.

in the light of what is commonly accepted by the scientific community, the reality of the transsexual syndrome from which he or she suffers, as well as the irreversible nature of the transformation of his or her appearance'.[101] Those conditions led in 2017 to a second condemnation of France by the ECtHR. In its A.P., Garçon and Nicot Case,[102] the Court ruled that France had infringed the right to respect for private life by making recognition of sexual identity conditional on undergoing an operation involving a high probability of sterility.

52. Since 2016, the procedure of gender change in civil status has been demedicalised by the law on the modernisation of Justice of the twenty-first Century. A new Article 61-5 was introduced in the Civil code. It clarifies that:

> '*Any person of full age or emancipated minor who demonstrates by a sufficient number of facts that the mention of his or her sex in the civil status records does not correspond to the sex in which he or she presents himself or herself and in which he or she is known, may obtain a change in the record.*
>
> *The main facts, which may be proven by any means, may be*
>
> *1 That she presents herself publicly as belonging to the sex claimed;*
> *2 That she is known as the claimed sex by her family, friends or professional circle;*
> *3 That she has obtained a change of her first name to correspond to the claimed sex.*'

This article relaxes the conditions of proof for a change of sex in civil status[103] by removing the prior requirement for surgery, by evading any consideration of the irreversibility of the change of sex and by promoting a non-exhaustive list of ways to prove the new sex status. The main condition is the social recognition of the change of sex. Immediately applicable, this law allowed the change of sex for a person who has presented herself as a female for the past five years to all her family, friends, and professional contacts and beyond (fidelity card, train tickets, order on the Internet) and is accepted as a woman in her environment.[104]

---

101. Cass. 1st civ., 7 Jun. 2012: JCP G 2012, 753, Ph. Reigné; Dr. famille 2012, comm. 131, Ph. Reigné; D. 2012, p. 1648, F. Vialla; RDSS 2012, p. 880.
102. 6 Apr. 2017, A.P, *Garçon et Nicot v. France*, Nos 79885/12, 52471/13 and 52596/13.
103. It also explicitly authorises the change of sex in the civil status for emancipate person which is a novelty. For a recent extension to a request of change of sex to a female to male minor, after an analysis *in concreto see* Cour d'Appel de Chambery, 25 Jan. 2022, n° 25-01-2022. The Court of Appeal said that 'The prohibition for unemancipated minors of acting to modify their civil status as derived from the provisions of Article 61-5 of the Civil code does not make it possible to guarantee in the present case [the < minor's >] right to respect for his private life within the meaning of Article 8 of the European Convention on Human Rights. They must therefore be regarded as disproportionately infringing his rights by obliging him to reveal his personal background, in particular because of the mention of his female gender, which will be entered on his diplomas certifying the end of his schooling'. *See* L. Carayon et L. Marguet, *Changement de la mention du sexe à l'état civil pour un mineur trans*, Dalloz actualité, 28 mars 2022.
104. *See* CA de Montpellier, 3rd Chamber, 15 Mar. 2017, n° 16/02691.

53. **Consequences of the judicial change of sexual status.** Article 61-6 Civil code maintains the need for a judicial request for the change of sex status. Article 61-7 Civil code declares that: '*A mention of the decision to change the sex and, where applicable, the forenames is made in the margin of the birth certificate of the person concerned, at the request of the public prosecutor, within fifteen days of the date on which this decision has become final.*'

54. As far as the change of first name is concerned, such change can also be requested by the civil registrar[105] prior to the change of sex since the above-mentioned 2016 law of modernisation of justice.[106] In 2017, a circular proposed a list of legitimate interests, which include 'reasons relating to the applicant's trans-sexuality'. It clarified that there is a legitimate interest in '*the change of first name in order to match the civil status to a physical appearance including independently of the introduction of procedure of change of sexe*'.[107] However, it is up to the civil registrar to consider *in concreto* that the request is based on a legitimate interest. In case of conflict with the civil registrar, the refusal to change the first name should be brought before the judge.

55. The change of sex includes only a mention in the birth certificate of the concerned person but no mention in the marriage certificate or birth certificate of the children of the person, which would be an infringement of its right to privacy. Article 61-7 civil code clarifies that the change of first name can only be added to their civil status with their consent.

56. Since 2013, marriage between persons of the same sex has been accepted in France.[108] Therefore, there is no legal issue with the application of the *Goodwin v. RU case* of the ECtHR in France. As far as the children of the person concerned by a change of sex are concerned, the situation is more complex. Article 61-8 civil code only clarified that the change of sex has no consequences on parentage established before the change of sex. Then, the change of sex raised some issues regarding the effectiveness of new form of parenthood, which will be seen hereinafter.

57. **Refusal of the gender neutral.** In France, the birth certificate mentions the sex of the children, which should be female or male gender.[109] This raised ethics[110] and legal concerns for intersexual children. According to statistics, there are around

105. *See* Art. 60 civ. Code.
106. Before 2016, the change of 'psychological sex' was one of legitimate interests accepted by the judges, see after the change of sexe *see* Cass. 1st civ., 21 mai 1990, 4e esp., Suzanne J.: JCP G 1990, II, 21588, rapp. J. Massip, concl. F. Flipo, CA Paris, 24 Feb. 1978: JCP G 1979, II, 19202, note J. Penneau and sometimes in case of refusal of a change of sexual status.
107. Circulaire du 17 février 2017 de présentation de l'article 56, I de la loi n° 2016-1547 du 18 novembre 2016 de modernisation de la justice du XXIe siècle, available at https://www.legifrance.gouv.fr/download/pdf/circ?id=42004.
108. *See* Loi n° 2013-404 du 17 mai 2013 ouvrant le mariage aux couples de personnes de même sexe, and Art. 143 Civil Code.
109. Article 57 Civil Code does not explicitly provide such binary approach. It is much more a common understanding founded in the case law, mentioned hereinafter.

two hundred children per year who cannot be assigned a sex birth year in France.[111] In 2021, the bioéthic law introduced the possibility for the civil registrar to postpone the mention of sex in the birth certificate but only for a maximum of three months and with the authorisation of the public prosecutor.[112]

58. More globally, it has been admitted that French law doesn't recognise gender neutrality. In 2017, the Cour de cassation declared that 'if sexual identity falls within the sphere protected by Article 8 of the Convention for the Protection of Human Rights and Fundamental Freedoms, the duality of statements relating to sex in civil status records pursues a legitimate aim in that it is necessary for the social and legal organisation of which it constitutes a founding element; that the recognition by the judge of a "neutral sex" would have far-reaching repercussions on the rules of French law constructed on the basis of the binary nature of the sexes, and would imply numerous coordinating legislative amendments. That the Court of Appeal, which found that Mr Y ... had, in the eyes of third parties, the appearance and social behaviour of a person of the male sex, in accordance with the indication in his birth certificate, was able to deduce, without being required to follow him in the detail of his argument, that the infringement of his right to respect for his private life was not disproportionate in relation to the legitimate aim pursued'.[113] In this case, the ECtHR considered that it has not to assess whether the refusal of this neutral gender is a legitimate inference in the private life of the applicant.[114] The ECtHR approaches the case from the perspective of a positive obligation. It underlined that there is no European consensus on the recognition of non-binary gender status. The ECtHR concluded that France enjoyed a wide margin of appreciation in implementing its positive obligation to secure the applicant's effective respect for his private life and that there was no violation of Article 8 ECHR.

2. Effectivity of New Forms of Parenthood

59. **Difficulties of parenthood after a change of sexual status.** Case law illustrates two types of difficulties left open by the law, including the above-mentioned 2021 bioethics law, which only refers to the possibility of double female parenthood in case of gestational surrogacy.

In 2005, the *Cour de cassation* judged the annulation of the paternity of a transsexual born with a female sex for the child of his partner, a woman who made after

---

110. *See* Avis n° 2022.0015/AC/SBP-UDCAP du 10 Mar. 2022 du collège de la Haute Autorité de santé portant sur le projet d'arrêté fixant les règles de bonnes pratiques de prise en charge des enfants présentant des variations du développement génital en application de l'article L.2131-6 du code de la santé publique.
111. *See* Avis 132 du Comité consultatif national éthique pour les sciences de la vie et de la santé, sur les questions éthiques soulevées par la situation des personnes ayant des variations du développement sexuel, 2019 p. 12.
112. *See* Art. 57, §2 Civil Code.
113. *See Cour de cassation,* 1re civ., 4 May 2017, n° 16-17.
114. *See Y v. France,* 31 Jan. 2023, Request No. 76888/17, legal summary in English. https://hudoc.echr.coe.int/fre#{%22itemid%22:[%22001-222780%22]}.

the birth of her child a surgery change of sex and obtained a change of sexual civil status. The child had maternal filiation towards the woman who gave birth and paternal filiation towards the transsexual. The sexual otherness required in matters of filiation under common law was thus respected. The legal issue occurred at the separation of the couple. The biological mother denounced the paternity. The *Cour de cassation* accepted the annulation of the paternity of the transsexual was '*not contrary to Articles 8, 12 and 14 of the European Convention on Human Rights'*. It is true that following the Article 3. One of the Conventions of 26 January 1990 on the Rights of the Child, the Court of Appeal, took into account the best interests of the child within the meaning by organising visiting rights.

60. In 2020, the *Cour de cassation* imposed on a transgender woman to be recognised as the father and not the 'biological parent'.[115] According to the *Cour de cassation* '*a transgender person, male to female, who, after the modification of the mention of his sex in the civil status records, procreates with his wife by means of his male gametes, is not deprived of the right to have a biological parent-child relationship recognised with the child, but can only do so by having recourse to the methods of establishing parent-child relationship reserved for the father*'.[116] The *Cour de cassation* considered that it is not possible by law to create a new category of civil status record of 'biological parent'. The Court of Appeal did not follow the reasoning of the *Cour de cassation* after underlining that 'the parties agree on the exclusion of paternal filiation'.[117] The Court of Appeal stated that '*the best interests of the child and the right to respect for private life, as enshrined in the New York Convention and the European Convention for the Protection of Human Rights and Fundamental Freedoms respectively, make it imperative to allow a child born to a couple one of whose members is transgender to have his or her filiation doubly established with regard to both parents, provided that this does not contravene the fundamental principles of national law*'.[118] In the absence of 'any conflict or contradiction between the filiations of the two biological parents', it admitted the judicial establishment of maternal filiation between the child and his transgender mother.

61. **Difficulties of parenthood in case of gestational surrogacy.** Gestational surrogacy has been prohibited in France by law since the first bioethics law in 1994.[119] This law codified the jurisprudence of the *Cour de cassation* which considered that this practice was contrary to the principle of the unavailability of the human body and the status of persons. In addition, the *Cour de cassation* declared that '*the adoption being only the final phase of a process intended to allow a couple to receive in their home the child, conceived in execution of a contract tending to*

115. *Cour de cassation*, 1st civil chamber, 16 Sep. 2020 – n° 18-50.080.
116. *See* point 18 of the above-mentionned case.
117. *See* CA Toulouse, 9 Feb. 2022, n° 20/03128.
118. CA Toulouse, 9 Feb 2022, n° 20/03128.
119. Loi de bioéthique n° 94-653 du 4 Aug. 1994.

abandon it at birth by its mother, [...] this process constituted a misuse of the institution'.[120] Then, since 1994, Article 16-7 civil code provides that 'All agreements relating to procreation or gestation for the benefit of another are null.' and void on public-policy grounds. Several legal difficulties have arisen when couples circumvent this prohibition by carrying out gestational surrogacy abroad. In the beginning, in such circumstances, the couple was obliged to conceal the operation to grant an adoption.[121] The couple was unable to obtain in France the legal recognition of parent-child relationships that had been legally established abroad.[122]

62. **Issues regarding the transcription of the birth certificate of the child born through gestational surrogacy abroad.** After the condemnation of France by the ECtHR in the *Mennesson* case, the *Cour de cassation* reversed its jurisprudence. First, the *Cour de cassation* admitted the full transcription of regular birth certificates of a child born through a gestational surrogacy arrangement abroad when the certificate mentioned the biological parents (father and surrogate mother).[123] The *Cour de cassation* only authorised a partial transcription with the biological father when the birth certificate mentioned the 'legal mother' instead of the surrogate mother.[124] In 2019, after the advisory opinion of the ECtHR, the *Cour de cassation* liberalised its jurisprudence. It admitted the possibility of recognition in domestic law of a legal parent-child relationship between a child born abroad through a gestational surrogacy arrangement and the intended parents designated in a regular birth certificate established abroad as the 'legal parent'. According to the *Cour de cassation*: '6. *It can ... be deduced from Article 8 of the Convention for the Protection of Human Rights and Fundamental Freedoms that, with regard to the best interests of the child, the fact that the birth of a child abroad originated from a surrogate motherhood agreement, which is prohibited by Articles 16-7 and 16-9 of the Civil Code, cannot, on its own, without disproportionately infringing the right to respect for the child's private life, prevent the transcription of the birth certificate drawn up by the authorities of the foreign State, as far as the child's biological father is concerned, nor the recognition of the parent-child relationship with regard to the mother of intention mentioned in the foreign certificate, which must take place at the latest when this link between the child and the mother of intention has been materialised.*'[125] In this case, the *Cour de cassation* argued that the adoption, which needs the introduction of the new procedure, '*would, in view of the time that has*

120. Cass. plen., 31 May 1991, n° 90-20.105.
121. *See* for instance: Cass. 1st civ., 29 Jun. 1994, n° 92-13.563 in which the adoption was refused because of a gestational surrogacy. In France, the adoption between person of same sex has been accepted since 2013.
122. *See* for instance, Cass. 1st, 6 Apr. 2011, n° 10-19.053.
123. *See* Cass. plen., 3 July 2015 n° 15-50.002; Cass. Plen. 5 October 2018, n° 12-30-.38.
124. *See* Cass. 1st civ., 5 Jul. 2017, n° 15-28-597 in case of a heterosexual couple and 1st civ., 20 Mar. 2019, n° 18-11-815 in case of a homosexual couple. In the first case, the *Cour de cassation* recalled that the transcription in the French registar is not submitted to a judicial expertise.
125. *See* Cass. plen., 4 Oct. 2019, n° 10-19.053 (for a heterosexual couple) confirmed by Cass. 1st civ., 18 Dec, 2019, n° 18-14.751, (for a homosexual couple with two women), Cass. 1st civ., 18 Dec, 2019, n° 18-11.815 (for a homosexual couple with two men) *See also* – Cass. 1st civ., 18 Nov. 2020, n° 19-50.043, Cass. 1st civ., 13 Jan. 2021, n° 19-17.929 et 19-50.046.

elapsed since the link between the children and the mother of intention became a reality, have manifestly excessive consequences with regard to the right to respect for private life'.[126]

63. In 2021, the French legislator intended to limit the transcription of the civil certificate established abroad to the only biological parent. The 2021 bioethics Law introduced Article 47 civil code for such purpose. This article clarified that the foreign civil status record is not authentic 'if it is irregular, falsified or if the facts declared in it do not correspond to reality', the precision according to which 'this reality must be assessed with regard to French law'. According to Article 47 civil code, the second parent, the intended parent, must proceed to the adoption of the child of his/her spouse or his or her partner in a civil solidarity pact or cohabitant, if the legal conditions are met.[127] In its recent case law, the ECtHR seems to acknowledge the efforts in France to elaborate concrete solutions in the best interest of the child to establish or not establish parentage with the social parent.[128]

64. **Issues regarding the adoption by the intended parent.** Article 345-1 civil code provides that 'the plenary adoption of the spouse's child is allowed: 1° Where the child has a lawfully established parentage only with regard to that spouse;'. This article authorised the adoption of the child by the intended parent in case of gestational surrogacy abroad. The consent of the biological mother is not required when the birth certificate contains only the name of the father.[129] In 2021, the *Cour de cassation* even accepted the adoption of a child conceived by medically assisted procreation abroad by its intended mother separated from its legal mother.[130] In this case, the Court based its rationale on the existence of a common parental project for the couple and the behaviour of the intended mother included after the separation. It considers both the interest of the child and the interest of the intended mother despite the opposition to the adoption of the legal mother. This approach could be applied by analogy to the child born through a gestational surrogacy abroad in case of a request for adoption after a separation of the couple.

65. **Issues regarding nationality in the context of gestational surrogacy**. There are also a few cases before the *Conseil d'Etat* on the recognition of the French nationality of the child born through a gestational surrogacy arrangement abroad. In 2014, the *Conseil d'Etat* refused the annulation of a circular of the Minister of Justice, which enabled such recognition of nationality when the legal conditions were

126. *See* Cass. plen., 4 Oct, 2019, n° 10-19.053, point 17. It is true that this dispute has been going on for over fifteen years.

127. These two last possibilities were introduced by the Loi n° 2022-219 du 21 Feb. 2022 visant à réformer l'adoption. There is still a debate in France on the necessity to modernise the adoption Jean-Jacques Lemouland Filiation – 1972–2022. Et maintenant? Droit de la famille n° 6, June 2022 dossier 11.

128. *See* 24 Mar. 2022, Nos 29775/18 et 29693/19, C.E. *et a. v. France*, 7 Apr. 2022, No. 13344/20, *A. L. v. France*.

129. Cass. 1st civ., 4 Nov. 2020, No. 19-15.739, P+B+I.

130. Cass. 1st civ., 3 Nov. 2021, n° 20-16.745, Boisson, Julien, Gouëzel, Antoine L'adoption de l'enfant issu d'une PMA à l'étranger par sa mère d'intention séparée de sa mère légale ou l'anticipation de la réforme de l'adoption 1.2.2022 – Revue Juridique Personnes et Famille (RJPF) – n° 36-39.

met, to say when one of the parents at least is French. The French administrative Supreme Court declared that '*the mere fact that the birth of a child abroad originates from a contract that is void under French public policy cannot, without disproportionately infringing what the child's right to respect for his or her private life implies in terms of nationality, guaranteed by Article 8 of the European Convention for the Protection of Human Rights and Fundamental Freedoms, lead to the deprivation of the child of the French nationality to which he or she is entitled, by virtue of Article 18 of the Civil codeand under the control of the judicial authority, when his or her filiation with a French national is established*'.[131] In 2019, the Conseil led to the same solution in the situation of naturalisation. '5. While the Minister responsible for naturalisation could, in the exercise of his broad discretionary powers in this area, refuse to grant Mr E ... s application for naturalisation by taking into consideration the fact that he had had recourse to surrogate motherhood, which is prohibited in France by the above-mentioned provisions of the Civil Code, such a circumstance could not, on the other hand, be taken into consideration, even though it is not argued that the civil status records of the two children, established according to the law applicable to the facts in the State of Colorado, would be vitiated by fraud or would not be in conformity with that law, lead to depriving these children of the effect which in principle attaches, by virtue of Article 22-1 of the Civil Code, to the decision to naturalise Mr. E ... E ..., without disproportionate interference with what is implied, in terms of nationality, by the right to respect for their private lives, guaranteed by Article 8 of the European Convention for the Protection of Human Rights and Fundamental Freedoms.'[132]

More globally, this case shows that the administrative Supreme Court accepts that nationality as a social identity enters into the scope of Article 8 ECHR which matches with the case law of the ECtHR.[133]

66. **Specific case law related to gametes export.** The French Public Health Code subjects the export of gametes to compliance with strict conditions, which does not, in principle, allow export for a use contrary to French law. This is at the core of case-law on the export for a post-mortem insemination.[134] The *Conseil d'Etat* has consistently refused to allow gametes to be exported to circumvent the ban on *post-mortem* insemination in France. This is the solution chosen in cases where the woman is of French nationality and has no link with the country of export.[135]

131. CE, 12 Dec, 2014, n° 365779, ECLI:FR:CESSR:2014:365779.20141212, point 11.
132. CE, 31 Jul, 2019, n° 411984.
133. *See* 21 Jun. 2016, n 76136/12, *Ramadan v. Malte*, §85; 25 Jun. 2020, n 52273/16 and a., *Ghoumid et a. v. France* which declared that the deprivation of French nationality based on a conviction for a terrorism offence committed over ten years earlier doesn't violate Art. 8 ECHR.
134. *See* Arts 2141-11 et seq. code of public Health which limit the export 'to pursuit of a parental project through medically assisted procreation or the restoration of the applicant's fertility or hormonal function' and provides that in case of the death of the person and in the absence of his written consent for a future insemination, the storage shall be terminated which unable the export.
135. CE 17 May 2023, n 473666

67. Recently, the ECtHR recalled that there was no European consensus on whether or not posthumous conception should be authorised. A wide margin of appreciation is thus granted to States, which must strike a fair balance between existing competing interests. The Court declared that the case law of the *Conseil d'Etat* complied with Article 8 ECHR.[136] The ban on gamete exports[137] is not absolute under French law. It may be authorised in exceptional circumstances, as in the *Gomez* case. The initial plan of the couple was to carry out an artificial insemination in France, which could not take place because of the husband's worsening health. Before his death, he had agreed that his wife could benefit from artificial insemination with his gametes posthumously in Spain, which was her country of origin. This concrete evaluation shows the absence of any fraudulent intent on the part of the widow. Then, the judge is obliged to review the proportionality of French legislation about the infringement of the right to respect for private life as guaranteed by Article 8 ECHR, even in urgent proceedings. Due to the specific situation of the deceased husband and his widow, the *Conseil d'Etat* decided that such prohibition was '*a manifestly excessive interference with his right to respect for private and family life protected by the provisions of Article 8 of the European Convention for the Protection of Human Rights and Fundamental Freedoms. In so doing, it seriously and manifestly unlawfully infringes a fundamental freedom*'.[138] In another case, the *Conseil d'Etat* delivered such a balance between the prohibition of gametes export and other legitimate interests regarding the right to privacy. The *Conseil d'Etat* considered that the export prohibition of gametes for a woman of 61 old age did not constitute 'an excessive interference with the exercise of his right to respect for his private and family life protected by Article 8 of the European Convention for the Protection of Human Rights and Fundamental Freedoms'.[139] The prohibition was based on the consensus in the scientific community. The maximum age for gamete retrieval was set at 59 years to avoid the risk of birth defects and genetic diseases.

3. Other Specific Issues on Private and Family Rights

68. **Privacy and Right to know your origins.** French judges[140] and the ECtHR[141] considered that the effectiveness of the right to know one's origins and to have one's filiation established is guaranteed by Article 8 ECHR. However, this right is not absolute and can conflict with other rights. Judges and the French legislator are engaged in a delicate exercise of balancing the interests involved in three situations: the right to give birth anonymously, the right to the gamete donor anonymity, and the post-mortem genetics analysis.

136. 14 September, *Baret and Caballero v. France*, No. 22296/20 et 37138/20
137. In an *obiter dictum*, the ECtHR call into question the maintaining of the prohibition of posthumous embryo transfer since French law extend the right to medically assisted reproduction to single women and femal couples since 2021. Cf. para. 90.
138. CE, 31 May 2016, n° 396848, ECLI:FR:CEASS:2016:396848.20160531, point 11.
139. CE, 17 April 2019, n° 420468, ECLI:FR:CECHR:2019:420468.20190417, point 11.
140. Cass., 5 Oct. 2016, n° 15-25.507.
141. 13 Feb, 2003, *Odièvre v. France*, n° 42326/98, §44.

69. **Right to discover one's origins and the right to give birth anonymously.** The possibility for any woman, married or not, to give birth anonymously to the child she is carrying was generalised in France on 28 June 1793. Currently, Article 326 Civil code provides that 'At the time of delivery the mother may request that the secrecy as to her admittance and identity be preserved.' The impact of this secrecy has been progressively mitigated in a way that reconciles the mother's right to secrecy and the child's right to know his/her history.

70. First, in 2002,[142] the Law organised the reversibility of the secrecy of birth through two mechanisms. At the time of the birth, the mother who desires to give birth anonymously is invited to seal an envelope with her history and if she accepts her identity. The mother is the only one to know the exact content of the sealed envelope. The name, date and place of birth of the child are written on an envelope which is stored by the Conseil National pour l'Accès aux Origines Personnelles (CNAOP).[143] It is only at the request of the child for access to personal origins that the CNAOP will contact the anonymous mother to find out if she agrees to lift the secrecy of her identity. At any time, the mother can decide to reveal her identity which will be communicated to the child only when he asks for access to personal origins, again through the CNAOP. When the mother refuses the lifting of the secrecy of her identity, the CNAOP can only reject the child's request for access to his or her origins,[144] even after the mother's death.[145] In 2003, the ECtHR judged that the balance interest introduced by the 2002 Law was considered to conform to Article 8 by the ECHR in its *Odièvre v. France* case.[146] In 2024, the ECtHR confirmed the mother's almost absolute right to keep her identity secret. The CNAOP's refusal to disclose her mother's identity to an applicant constitutes interference in her right to privacy.[147] This interference is nevertheless justified in order to protect the privacy of the biological mother and/or her family. The Court did not take into account the argument that the French legislation was in the minority. Most States, if they allow secret births, give the majority of children the opportunity to have access to the identity of their birth parents. However, the Court seems to question whether a mother can oppose the transmission of her identity after her death. Moreover, it encouraged the applicant to refer the matter to the CNAOP again at that point, and if it refused to submit the decision to the domestic courts. The Court

142. Loi n° 2002-93 du 22 Jan. 2002 relative à l'accès aux origines des personnes adoptées et pupilles de l'Etat, *see* Art. 326 Civil Code.
143. Recently the decree n° 2022-360 du 14 Mar. 2022 relatif aux conditions de traitement des données à caractère personnel permettant l'accès aux origines personnelles creates the ORPER personal data processing. The decree clarifies the modalities for processing requests for access to origins to be respected by the CNAOP.
144. *See* CE, 16 Oct. 2019, n° 420230.
145. CAA Paris, 18 Oct. 2018, n° 17PA01844.
146. 13 Feb. 2003, *Odièvre v. France*, n° 42326/98.
147. 30 Jan. 2024, *Cherrier v. France*, No. 18843/20. In this case, the applicant learned of her adoption when her second adoptive parent died. She was 56. The CNAOP had been able to obtain information mentioning the surnames, first names, dates and places of birth of the mother and biological father, as well as the circumstances of the abandonment. Due to the refusal of her biological mother, the applicant had been only able to obtain non-identifying information about her birth.

clearly considers that when the mother dies, the balance of interests is likely to be assessed differently[148] and tilted in favour of the right to recognition of her origins.

71. Second, at the origin, Article 325 Civil code provides that the child of an anonymous mother was deprived of the right to sue for maternity, while this was not the case for the paternity suit. This difference was abolished in 2009 to prevent a violation of discrimination according to Article 14 the ECHR.

72. **Right to discover one's origins in case of medically assisted procreation.** Since the first bioethics law, France has opted for a system of voluntary, free, and anonymous gamete donation.[149] This approach deprived the child of any possibility of access to knowledge of his or her genetic origins. In this context, the French judges have always rejected the possibility of lifting anonymity, arguing that this rule aims '*at respecting family life within the legal family of the child conceived from gametes resulting from this donation, it being specified, however, that, as far as the recipient is concerned, this rule of anonymity cannot, in any event, constitute an infringement of privacy within the meaning of Article 8 of the European Convention on Human Rights and Fundamental Freedoms*'.[150]

73. The 2021 bioethics law tries to find a compromise between the different interests involved by introducing two novelties. First, at the time of the gamete donation, the donor must consent to give information on his identity and listed non-personal data,[151] which will be kept secret until the majority of the child. While the French Biomedicine Agency is the data controller of this processing, a new commission is entitled to grant requests to this agency for access to the identity of third-party donors.[152] Second, the child has the possibility to access the identity and non-identifying data of the third-party donor at the age of majority.[153] The access to the donor information is submitted at a prior request of the adult child to the above-mentioned commission. The former consent of the donor enables that the death of donor will have no impact on the right to access to discover one's origins. There is no obligation to the parent to reveal to the child the secret of its conception. Article L.2141-10 Public Health Code mentions that 'The members of the couple or the

148. 30 Jan. 2024, *Cherrier v. France*, No. 18843/20, §73.
149. *See* Art. 16-8 Civil Code which provides 'No information enabling the identification of both the person who donates an element or a product of his body and the person who receives it may be divulged … In case of therapeutic necessity, only the physicians of the donor and recipient may have access to the information enabling the identification of these two persons.'
150. *See* CE, avis, 13 Jun. 2013, n° 362981 and also CE, 12 Nov. 2015 – n° 372121; CE, 28 Dec. 2017, n° 396571.
151. *See* Art. R.2143-5 Health Code. From 31 Mar. 2025, only gamete donations for which the donor has agreed to disclose his identity will be possible. *See* Décret n° 2023-785 16 Aug. 2023 fixant la date mentionnée au C du VII de l'article 5 de la loi du 2 août 2021 relative à la bioéthique d'utilisation exclusive des gamètes et embryons pour lesquels les donneurs ont consenti à la transmission de leurs données non identifiantes et à la communication de leur identité.
152. The commission d'accès aux données non identifiantes et à l'identité du tiers, *See* Art. L.2143-6 of the Health Public code.
153. *See* Art. L.2143-2 Public Health Code.

unmarried woman are encouraged to anticipate and create the conditions that will allow them to inform the child, before he or she reaches the age of majority, that he or she is the product of a donation.'

74. **Right to discover one's origins and post-mortem genetics analysis.** The *Cour de cassation* recognised that a person could have 'a vital interest in obtaining the information he needs to discover the truth about his ancestry, even if it means exhuming and carrying out a genetic analysis of the body'[154] of his deceased presumed biological father. Nevertheless, the *Cour de cassation* judged that the Court of Appeal violated the Article 8 ECHR by not considering the right of the heirs of the presumed biological father. The Court should have declared ex officio inadmissible in the action seeking recognition of a genetic ancestry by means of an expert report in the absence of a summons to the heirs of the person whose exhumation is requested. This solution differs from the ECtHR case *Pascaud v. France.*[155] In this case, the ECtHR considered that the invalidation of the genetic expertise based on the lack of consent of the biological deceased father constituted an 'unjustified infringement of the right to privacy' of the applicant. This solution seems to consider the very special circumstances of the case, in particular, the absence of heirs of the biological father and the lack of alternatives for a legal establishment of the parentage. It is still not clear whether Article 8 should always prevail over French rule, which provides that 'Unless there is express agreement by the person manifested while alive, no identification of that person may be carried out after his death.'[156]

75. The ECtHR has continuously declared that 'the private life of a deceased person from whom a DNA sample was to be taken could not be adversely affected by a request to that effect made after his death'.[157] However, the formulation of Article 16-11 civil code has been maintained so far by the legislator, in particular, after the *Conseil constitutionnel* declared its constitutionality. In 2011, the French *Conseil constitutionnel* considered 'that deceased individuals are presumed not to have consented to identification through DNA testing, the legislator intended to prevent exhumations in order to ensure respect for the dead; that it is not for the *Conseil constitutionnel* to substitute its appraisal for that of the legislator with regard to the consideration given in such matters to the respect due to the human body; that accordingly, the complaints relating to the lack of knowledge of privacy and the right to conduct a normal family life must be rejected'.[158]

76. **Right to biological filiation.** There are situations where the right to privacy cannot be usefully invoked to have a biological filiation recognised. First, Article

154. Cass. 1st civ., 13 Nov. 2014, n° 13-21.018.
155. *Pascaud v. France*, 16 Jun. 2011, n° 19535/08.
156. Article 16-11 Civil Code.
157. *Jäggi v. Switzerland*, No. 58757/00, §42.
158. CC Decision No. 2011-173 QPC of 30 Sep. 2011 *Mr Louis C. and others* [Conditions for the performance of genetic testing on deceased persons for the purposes of filiation actions], §6, available in English at https://www.conseil-constitutionnel.fr/en/decision/2011/2011173QPC.htm.

320 Civil code provides that 'As long as it has not been contested in court, a lawfully established parentage is a bar to establishing another parentage which would contradict it.' Thus, the *Cour de cassation* considered that the right to privacy does not permit the cumulation of adoptive and biological filiation '*if the impossibility for a person to have his or her paternal filiation link recognised constitutes an interference with the exercise of the right to respect for his or her private and family life guaranteed by Article 8 of the Convention for the Protection of Human Rights and Fundamental Freedoms, the obstacle imposed on [the applicant] is provided for in Article 320 of the Civil code and pursues a legitimate aim insofar as it is intended to guarantee the stability of the filiation link and to protect children from conflicts of filiation;*'.[159] Recently, the *Cour de cassation* reaffirmed this position by delivering a control of the proportionality of the judgment of a Court of Appeal, which had declared admissible the paternity action of an adopted person. The *Cour de cassation* considered that the Court of Appeal had failed 'to strike a fair balance between the competing interests involved' and that, therefore, its judgment 'violated Article 8 of the European Convention on Human Rights'.[160] In both cases, the *Cour de cassation* considered that the right to know one's origins has been respected and that the link with the child was insufficient to fall within the scope of family life because the child did not really have a relationship with his biological father in comparison to his legal father. Therefore, these French case laws conform to the ECtHR case law.[161]

77. Second, Article 8 ECHR has been invoked in cases where the biological father wants to intervene in an adoption procedure of his child when the mother gives birth anonymously.[162] In principle, such an intervention is inadmissible for lack of interest in acting when there is no legal or social link to the child.[163] It is also an illustration of the rule when a child is placed in care; it is an obstacle to recognition by the biological father according to Article 351 Civil code. The main difficulty is that the father does not always have the means to recognise his child, particularly when he is unaware of the child's existence and/or in the case of births under X. To find a better balance between the interests involved, the legislator has offered the father, who is in need, the possibility of asking the Public Prosecutor's Office for help in finding his child.[164] More recently, a biological father was allowed to challenge the placement order if he wished to take charge of his child.[165]

159. Cass. 1st civ., 5 Oct. 2016, n° 15-25.507.
160. Cass. 1st civ., 14 Oct. 2020, n° 19-15.783.
161. *See* 29 Jun. 1999, *Nylund v. Finland*,n° 27110/95.
162. For an overview of the debate on this delicate issue *see*, Hugues Fulchiron, *Quelle place pour le père d'un enfant né sous X? Autour d'un dialogue muet entre Conseil constitutionnel et CEDH*, Dalloz Sirey, 2020, p. 695.
163. 1st civ., 8 Jul. 2009, n° 08-20.153 in this case, the inadmissibility concerned the intervention in the adoption procedure of the grand fathers of the child of a woman who gave birth anonymously. *A contrario,* when the paternal recognition of the child takes place before the adoption, the latter is no longer valid. *See Cour de cassation* 1st civ., 7 Apr. 2006, n° 05-11285.
164. Article 62.1 Civil Code introduced in 2002.
165. Article L.224-8 CASF introduced in 2013. This right is extensively open included to all member of the family of the child.

78. In 2019, the *Conseil constitutionnel* was seized of a priority question of constitutionality to verify whether the impossibility for the biological father to ask for the restitution of the child after his placement with a view to adoption infringed the right to lead a normal family life and the requirement to protect the best interests of the child. The *Conseil constitutionnel* took into consideration the above-mentioned possibilities legally granted to the biological father to avoid the adoption of his child. Then, it considered that it was not for it '*to substitute its assessment for that of the legislature on the reconciliation that should be made, in the best interests of the child handed over to the child welfare service, between the right of the birth parents to lead a normal family life and the objective of fostering the adoption of this child, provided that this reconciliation is not manifestly unbalanced.*' It concluded by declaring that '*the claims that the right to lead a normal family life and the constitutional requirement to protect the best interests of the child have been disregarded*'.[166]

79. In 2021, the *Cour de cassation* considered that Article 8 ECHR can be invoked in favour of a biological father who didn't have the possibility to assert his rights during the administrative phase of the procedure.[167] This intervention right of the biological father does not necessarily imply that his action will be considered well-founded. It would be up to the judge, in the light of the circumstances of the case, to balance the interests of the child, which takes precedence over those of the birth parents and of the applicants for adoption.

80. Finally, Article 310-2 Civil code[168] prohibits the establishment of a double parent-child relationship in the case of absolute incest.[169] This strict prohibition is based on the child's supposed interest and the public social order. In addition, the *Cour de cassation* prohibits, for the same reasons, the circumvention of this prohibition through adoption by the second parents.[170] Thus, when the child's paternal filiation has already been established, an action to establish his maternal filiation should be inadmissible. However, a recent case law illustrated that this rule must be set aside sometimes in 'the best interests of the child'.[171] A Court of Appeal judged that, in this case, the parents were siblings who had been in care and had not lived together as children. The father had carried out an antenatal recognition. Then, the

---

166. CC Decision No. 2019-826 QPC du 7 Feb. 2020, M. Justin A.
167. 27 Jan. 2021 Cass. n° 19-15.92; Damien Sadi, *L'espoir de paternité à l'épreuve de l'accouchement sous X,* Gazette du Palais, 30 March 2021, pp. 16–19.
168. For an overview on the legal and social status of the incest in France *See* L'inceste, un tabou civil, Aline Cheynet de Beaupré, Revue Juridique Personnes et Famille, n° 4, 1er avril 2021; on the penal aspects *see,* Charlotte Dubois, *l'inceste en droit pénal ou la consécration de la famille selon Vianney,* Y'a pas que les gènes qui font les familles, 'La Semaine Juridique Edition Générale n° 23, 7 Juin 2021, doctr. 622'.
169. This is the case when the parents are related by descent (ascendants and descendants for instance mother and son including step-mother and adopted son or father and daughter including step-father and adopted daughter) or collaterally (brothers and sisters including half-brother and half-sister). However, this does not apply to children born from the union of an uncle and his niece.
170. Cass. 1st civ., 6 Jan. 2004, n° 01-01.600 8.
171. CA, Caen, 3rd civ., 8 Jun. 2017 – n° 16/01314.

child's maternal filiation was established at a second stage. Afterwards, the prosecutor obtained its annulation according to Article 310 Civil code. Faced with this conflict of filiation, the Court of Appeal decided that '*the link of maternal filiation must nevertheless be maintained' because, since his birth, the child has lived with the mother and has no relationship with the father. The Court of Appeal refers explicitly to Articles 8 and 14 ECHR. It considered that having no means to reform the father filiation, the maternal filiation has to be maintained 'In view of the particular interest of this child, and the damaging consequences for her, in the construction of her identity, of the annulment of a filiation link on which her place in the family history has been built up to now.*'[172] More globally, there is a debate in France about the legitimacy and the conformity of the prohibition of double filiation in case of absolute incest with Article 8 ECHR. Some authors argued that France could be condemned on the rationale of the ECHR case law on prohibition of incestuous marriage.[173] Other authors underlined that Article 310 Civil code prohibition has huge consequences, including patrimonial ones and incoherences for the incestuous child, who is not responsible for the circumstances of his birth.[174]

4. Privacy in the Context of the Prisons

81. Prison overcrowding is a chronic and well-known problem in French prisons. After two decisions of the ECtHR which condemned France for inhuman or degrading treatment in detention,[175] the respect of fundamental rights in prisons still raises important concerns.[176] The prison population has continued to grow with occupancy rates in some establishments being over 200%.[177] France has been obliged to invest in a prison plan and to introduce a new interim procedure[178] allowing prisoners to challenge their living conditions in French prisons before the liberty and custody judge (Juge des libertés et de la detention, JLD) or the sentence enforcement judge (juge d'application des peines, JAP) of the competent judicial court (Tribunal judiciaire, TJ).[179] With 75,677 people imprisoned in December

---

172. CA, Caen, 3rd civ., 8 Jun. 2017 – n° 16/01314.
173. C. Gris, *Les droits de l'enfant à l'épreuve des droits parentaux: l'exemple du rattachement familial de l'enfant*, Thèse de doctorat en Droit, Université de Bordeaux 4, 2013, p. 530 quoted by Sofia Sellami, *La double filiation d'une enfant issue d'un inceste absolu*, village justice, 14 Dec. 2018, available at https://www.village-justice.com/articles/double-filiation-une-enfant-issue-inceste-absolu,26918.html.
174. *See* article above-mentioned of Aline Cheynet de Beaupré.
175. *J.M.B. and others v. France*, 30 Jan. 2020, No. 9671/15; 6 Jul. 2023 *B.M. and Others v. France*, No. 84187/17 and five others; *Leroy and others* 18 April 2024 No32439/19.
176. *See* for instance, the recent opinion of the National Consultative Commission on Human Rights (CNCDH) adopted en 22 Mar. 2022 or the report the Assemblée Nationale No. 4906 adopted on the 12 Jan. 2022 on identifier les dysfonctionnements et manquements de la politique pénitentaire française. The Opinion of the Controller General of Places of Deprivation of Liberty adopted on 25 Jul. 2023 relatif à la surpopulation et à la régulation carcérales, JORF 14 Sep. 2023, n° 213, texte 89.
177. *See* statistics of in the above-mentioned opinion of the CNDH, p. 7.
178. Article 803-8 Criminal Procedure Code.
179. *See* for instance ord. JAP, TJ de Créteil, 25 Feb. 2022; ord. JLD, TJ Toulouse, 17 Dec. 2022.

2023[180] and prisons still obsolete, France is struggling to ensure the effectiveness of prisoners' fundamental rights, including those guaranteed by Article 8 of the ECHR, besides issues with human dignity rights of the prisoners and inhuman or degrading treatment.[181] While the rights of the prisoners are mostly at stake, case law illustrates that Article 8 ECHR application in France was also usefully invoked by the employees of the prisons.

82. **Right to privacy of the prisoners in prison overcrowding context.**[182] The chronic overcrowding of prisons in France has revived the debate on the need to maintain a right to individual cell housing.[183] Since 1875, this right has been enshrined in French law but cannot be respected in practice. Therefore, its application is continuously postponed by moratoria, the last one expiring on 31 December 2027.[184] Recently, members of parliament proposed to focus 'on ensuring dignified conditions of detention rather than on the individualisation of cells, which is not always relevant'.[185] In the meantime, some cases show that the indecent conditions of detention necessarily lead to violations of the right to privacy of prisoners. In 2020, the *Conseil d'Etat* declared that '*Where a cell is occupied by more than one person, the absence of a partition between the sanitary facilities ... to provide sufficient privacy is likely to infringe the privacy of prisoners to an extent exceeding the restrictions inherent in detention.*'[186] On this basis, the judge ordered the administration to ensure the separation of the sanitary area from the rest of the cells.

83. The electronic bracelet is often seen to combat overcrowding in prisons. Introduced in France in 1997, it was generalised in 2019. Since then, the electronic bracelet has been used both as an alternative to pre-trial detention and a fitting out of a sentence.[187] The new sentence of 'house arrest with electronic monitoring' is presented as one of the major innovations of the 2019 Law on Reform of Justice. It is up to the judges to consider the balance between the legitimate interest at stake for the implementation of the bracelet and the right to privacy of the holder. The electronic bracelet is considered both an inference on the private life of the holder and a way to preserve his private and family life. Article 131-4-1 Criminal Code (Code Penal (CP)) provides that '*The convicted person shall be allowed to be absent*

180. *See* statistics of the French Justice Minister available at https://www.justice.gouv.fr/documentation/etudes-et-statistiques/statistiques-mensuelles-population-detenue-ecrouee.
181. *See* recently, TA French Guyana, 28 Dec. 2023, n° 2201112.
182. For a recent analysis of the causes of prison overcrowding, *see* the report of the French Court of Auditors, une surpopulation carcerale persistante, une politique d'exécution des peines en question, October 2023, https://www.ccomptes.fr/sites/default/files/2023-10/20231005-surpopulation-carcerale-persistante.pdf.
183. The CNDH is in favour of this maintain while the aboved mentioned report of the Assemblée Nationale proposed *See* report No. 4906 adopted on the 12 Jan. 2022, p. 259, proposal 23.
184. *See* Art. 190 Loi n° 2022-1726 du 30 Dec. 2022 de finances pour 2023.
185. *See* above-mentioned report the Assemblée Nationale n° 4906 adopted on the 12 Jan. 2022, proposal 23, p. 44.
186. CE, 19 Oct. 2020, n° 439372, ECLI:FR:CECHR:2020:439372.20201019.
187. The electronic bracelet is also used as device for monitoring perpetrators of domestic violence to prevent them from approaching their victims. *See* Décret n° 2021-1820 du 24 décembre 2021 relatif aux mesures de surveillance applicables lors de leur libération aux auteurs d'infractions commises au sein du couple.

from home for periods determined by the court or the enforcement judge only for the time necessary to carry out a professional activity, to attend an education, a training course, a course of study or medical treatment, to seek employment, to participate in family life or to carry out any integration or reintegration project.' In 2017, the *Conseil d'Etat* rejected the annulation of the decree implementing the electronic bracelet on the basis of Article 8 ECHR. The administrative Supreme Court considered that the electronic bracelet '*implements a measure which, in the context of the execution or adjustment of a sentence, makes it possible, by virtue of its technical characteristics, to reconcile the objective of preventing recidivism and the right to respect for the convicted person's private and family life, under more satisfactory conditions than incarceration authorises; that, consequently, the plea that the aforementioned stipulations have been disregarded cannot be accepted;*'.[188]

84. **Right to respect for family life of prisoners.** Title IV of the new penitentiary code[189] contains various provisions concerning the maintenance of the prisoner's relations with the outside world. It illustrates that maintaining family ties is one of the tasks of the prison administration. This right to respect for family life of prisoners is mainly exercised through visits and communications (written correspondence and calls). In 2016, the *Conseil constitutionnel* declared unconstitutional the impossibility of judicial appeal against a decision which refused access to the telephone and the visit of a person who is not a member of his family to a person placed in pre-trial detention. The *Conseil constitutionnel* considered that these two impossibilities deprived '*the constitutional protection of the right to respect for private life and the right to lead a normal family life of legal guarantees*'.[190] It applied the same solution to the impossibility of a person placed in pre-trial detention to dispose of a judicial appeal to the decision which denies him the right to write correspondence.[191]

85. While French law contains various provisions that in theory allow for the respect of prisoners' family life, the lack of resources often makes it difficult to exercise these rights. For instance, a prisoner may be granted an escorted leave to attend the funeral of a member of his family.[192] Although authorised by the judges, many of these outings are not carried out due to a lack of staff. This could affect the family rights, particularly of pre-trial detention prisoners.

188. CE, 12 Dec. 2007, n° 293993.
Section française de l'Observatoire international des prisons.
189. The French penitentiary code came into force on 1 May 2022. It aims at ending to the scattered nature of prison law and has made it more accessible and readable.
190. CC, Decision No. 2016-543 QPC 24 May 2016, §14.
191. CC, Decision No. 2018-715 QPC du 22 Jun. 2018.
192. *See* Art. D.143.5 and Art. D.147 Code of criminal procedure on escorted exit permit.

86. The ordinary visitation areas are small, crowded and under the continuous and direct supervision of prison staff,[193] which is legitimate for security reasons.[194] Familial visiting rooms[195] from 12 to 15 metres square allow all prisoners to meet with their relatives for a maximum of six hours during the day without such continuous surveillance. According to the Minister of Justice, only 124 such familial visiting rooms were functioning in 33 prisons in 2019. Family living units[196] are furnished two- or three-room flats, separate from the detention facility, where the prisoners can receive relatives in privacy. These facilities are reserved as a priority for convicts who are not eligible for a temporary leave or a modified sentence. For accused persons, this right is subjected to an agreement of the competent judicial authority. In practice, 170 family living units were in operation in 52 prisons in 2019.[197] Finally, French law contains specific rules for detained pregnant women and mothers. When a mother gives birth while in detention, she may, if she wishes, keep her child with her in her cell until the child is 18 months old.[198]

87. Despite this progress, the maintenance of family ties depends to a large extent on the proximity of the prison to the place where the prisoners have family or social ties. This could be difficult when the prisoner is relocated to another facility because of the undignified conditions of detention in the prison near his family. It is also more complicated for women because of the limited number of facilities available to them. That is why, recently, the CNDH proposed to cover the travel costs of the most vulnerable relatives in the event of imprisonment away from home.[199]

88. The exercise of the right to family approximation (rapprochement familial) for the prisoners raised several practical, legal and political difficulties. In 2019, the *Conseil constitutionnel* had to consider the incapacity of the administrative judge to control the legality of the decision of the civil judge to reject the family approximation of the prisoner whose investigation has been completed and who is awaiting trial. It declared that such incapacity violated the right to an effective remedy.[200] By contrast, in 2021, the *Conseil constitutionnel* declared that '*by determining the place of incarceration of a person placed in pre-trial detention, in the course of an investigation, without imposing the taking into account of the place of residence of his family, the legislator did not deprive of legal guarantees the right to lead a normal*

193. Videosurveillance in the collective areas of the visiting rooms (waiting room, entrance and exit, corridors) is even compulsory in prisons opened after the entry into force of the 2009 Penitentiary Law. *See* Art. R.341-14 of penitentiary code.
194. In the past France was condemned for exceeding this limit by instituting a systematic recording of conversations in the visiting room for other purposes which were not clearly included in the Law. *See* EHCR, 20 Dec. 2005, *Wisse v. France*, n° 71611/01 §§29–34.
195. *See* Art. R.341-15 penitentiary code.
196. *See* Art. R.341-16 penitentiary code, and circulaire de la DAP du 26 mars 2009 relative aux unités de vie familiale which recalls that they were initiated through an experimentation in 2003.
197. *See* French Ministery of Justice Website, http://www.justice.gouv.fr/prison-et-reinsertion-10036/la-vie-en-detention-10039/le-maintien-des-liens-familiaux-12006.html.
198. Article D.216-22 Penitentianary Code.
199. *See* above-mentioned CNDH opinion March 2022, p. 21.
200. Cons. Const., 8 févr. 2019, n° 2018-763 QPC.

family life enjoyed by the persons concerned within the limits inherent in pre-trial detention'.[201] The complaints were dismissed because the *Conseil constitutionnel* considered that the choice of where to incarcerate an accused person should be guided primarily by a concern for the efficiency of the procedure and not by the preservation of the right to family life. The judge underlined that the right to family of the pre-trial person could be exercised through the above-mentioned rights to visit, including familial visiting rooms and family living units.

89. The family approximation of the prisoners detained for terrorism is a matter of much debate. Usually, this family approximation is rejected because the prisoner has a particularly high profile, which requires him to be placed in institutions with high-security measures. This is the core of the political issue on the detention of Corsican prisoners in mainland France. The recent murder of Yvan Colonna in prison of the Parisian Region led to the transfer to the island of two other Corsican prisoners after seven years of request.

90. By contrast, in 2017, the Administrative Court of Appeal of Paris[202] declared that Article 8 ECHR 'do not grant prisoners the right to choose their place of detention and the separation and estrangement of the detainee from his or her family are inevitable consequences of such detention'. However, detaining a person in a prison so far away from his family that any visit is in fact very difficult or impossible may, in specific circumstances, constitute an interference with the family life of the detainee, since the possibility for family members to visit the detainee is an essential factor for the maintenance of family life.[203] Nevertheless, the judge considered after a concrete evaluation of the situation that Article 8 ECHR was not violated by the posting of the prisoner in Paris, since it 'does not make it impossible, particularly in the context of a family life unit, the visit his mother, his partner and their daughter, born in January 2014 in Spain, more than three years after her father's incarceration, as well as his first daughter, born in Annecy in August 2009, whose mother is also being held in the Paris region'.[204]

91. **Privacy and the rights of the prison employees**. In 2012, the *Conseil d'Etat* partially annulled a decree which prohibited natural persons and agents of legal persons involved in the public prison service from maintaining relations with persons who have a link with prisoners beyond their mission. The administrative Supreme Court based its judgment on Article 8 ECHR. It is considered that prohibiting relations with prisoners, their relatives, or friends meets security requirements and does not constitute an excessive interference with the exercise of the right to respect for the private and family life of these employees. By contrast, extending

201. Cons. Const., 21 Jan. 2021, Décision n° 2020-874/875/876/877 QPC du 21 janvier 2021, §13.
202. *See* CAA Paris, 1rst, 28 Sep. 2017, n° 16PA03671 concerning an ETA terrorist.
203. *See* §7 of the above-mentioned judgment.
204. *See* §8 of the above-mentioned judgment.

this prohibition to the former prisoners, their family, and friends '*introduces a general prohibition, of an absolute nature and without any time limit, which imposes excessive hardship with regard to the provisions of Article 8 of the Convention*'.[205]

5. Privacy and Respect for Home

92. **Constitutional value of the inviolability of home**. The inviolability of home which is a component of the right to respect for the home was introduced into French law well before its affirmation in Article 8 ECHR. The inviolability of home acquired a constitutional value during the revolutionary period.[206] Even though the principle of the inviolability of the home was no longer explicitly enshrined in a French Constitution since 1875, French judges ensured the effectiveness of this right, first on basis of the CP,[207] second on basis of Article 9 Civil Code and Article 8 ECHR. In 1983, the *Conseil constitutionnel* confirmed the constitutional value of the principle of inviolability of the home based on Article 66 of the Constitution in relation to a legislative provision specifying the procedures for tax searches.[208]

93. **Broad scope of the notion of 'home'**. Currently, both the French courts and the ECtHR adopt a broad conception of the notion of home[209] based on similar criteria. This leads to general agreement on the scope of protection.

94. **Home goes beyond the domicile.** Like the ECtHR, the French courts have a broad conception of the notion of home. While Article 102 Civil code provides a definition of domicile limited to the place where the person has its principal establishment, the French judges have progressively opted for a more concrete and voluntary definition of home which differs from the legal domicile. In 1957, the Criminal Chamber of the *Cour de cassation* affirmed for the first time that the notion of home '*does not only mean the place where a person has his or her principal place, but also the place where, whether or not he or she lives there, he or she has*

205. CE, 11 juil. 2012, n° 347148, ECLI:FR:CESSR:2012:347148.20120711.
206. *See* Art. 359 of the Constitution of the 5 Fructidor an VIII (22 Aug. 1793) which enshrined the inviolability of the citizen's home against arbitrary entry by agents of the public forces; Art. 76 Constitution of 22 frimaire an VIII (13 Dec. 1799) which extended this right to any person living in the French territory. For an historical overview of the judicial protection of the inviolability of home, *see* Isabelle Gravelais, La protection juridictionnelle de l'inviolabilité du domicile, PhD 2013, Université de Bourgogne, available at https://hal-univ-bourgogne.archives-ouvertes.fr/tel-01563871.
207. To start with Art. 184 Criminal Code adopted in 1810 and currently Arts 226-4 and 432-8 Criminal Code.
208. CC, 29 Dec. 1983, n° 83-164 DC, Cons. 28-30.
209. The French judges also are in line with the limits of the broad concept of home. Recently, the *Cour de Cassation* denied the classification as a home of a bin bag deposited in a communal waste bin, which the police had searched while it was on the street. Thus, the *Cour de Cassation* validated the seizure of the content of the bin on the street by the police. The *Cour de Cassation* considers that the seizure does not constitute an invasion of privacy within the meaning of Art. 8 of the European Convention on Human Rights, requiring judicial authorisation prior to exploitation of its content. *See* Crim., 6 Apr. 2022, F-B, n° 21-84.092.

the right to call himself or herself at home, regardless of the legal title of his or her occupation and the use to which the premises are put'.[210]

95. **Illustrations.** Therefore, a hotel room,[211] a hospital room,[212] a yacht,[213] a caravan,[214] and a camping tent under which holidaymakers live[215] are home and protected as such. Judges also extend the protection of the home to its outbuildings, such as gardens,[216] garages,[217] terraces,[218] etc. This concept covers an individual's business premises.[219] Even an operating block of a hospital is considered the home of the hospital.[220] This illustrates that French judges admit that the right to respect home also applies to legal persons and individuals. However, a 5-metre boat without any fittings serving only as a means of transport has not been considered a home.[221] The judges considered in a debatable manner that 'a cell in a prison cannot be a home because it has not been chosen'.[222]

96. **French Illustrations of possible interference with the right to respect for one's home.** France has been condemned eight times before the ECtHR for violation of respect for home.[223] Seven cases are related to home searches and seizures,[224] and one case is on eviction measures of French travellers.[225] National case laws are mostly on such topics. Article 8 ECHR is invoked also in some cases where the free choice of the home is at stake.

97. **Control of the eviction and demolition measures.** After the *Winterstein* case, the French judges have made a change in jurisprudence. Since then, the French

---

210. Cass. Crim., 20 Jun. 1957, Bull Crim., 1957, n° 518, pp. 941–944.
211. Cass. Crim., 31 Jan. 1914, D.P. 1918.1. 76 and more recently Cass. Crim., 30 May 1980, Bull Crim., 1980-1, n° 165, pp. 41–413.
212. CAA Paris, 17 Mar. 1986, Gaz Pal. 1986, pp. 429–431.
213. Cass. Crim., 20 Nov. 2004, 84-91.829.
214. Cass. Crim., 30 Oct. 2006, Bull Crim., n° 261, pp. 964–966.
215. Cass. Crim., 18 Oct. 1972, Gaz Pal. 1973, 1st sem., pp.100–101.
216. Cass. Crim., 13 Mar. 1974, Bull Crim., 1974, n° 110, pp. 280–281.
217. Cass. Crim., 29 Mar. 1994, 93-84.995.
218. Cass. Crim., 8 Feb. 1994, 92-83.151.
219. Cass. Crim., 7 Feb. 1994, 93-80.520.
220. Cass. Crim., 27 Nov. 1996, n° 95-85.118.
221. Cass. Crim., 20 novembre 1984, 84-91.829.
222. Cass. Crim., 18 octobre 1989, 89-80.462.
223. *See* https://hudoc.echr.coe.int/eng#{%22languageisocode%22:[%22ENG%22],%22respondent%22:[%22FRA%22],%22kpthesaurus%22:[%22426%22],%22documentcollectionid2%22:[%22JUDGMENTS%22],%22violation%22:[%228%22]}.
224. 16 May 2019, *Halabi v. France* – 66554/14; 2 Apr. 2015, *Vinci Construction and GTM Génie Civil et Services v. France* – 60567/10 and 63629/10; 21 Oct. 2010, *Xavier Da Silveira v. France* 43757/05; 24 Jul. 2008, *André and Other v. France* – 18603/03; 16 Apr. 2002, *Société Colas Est and Others v. France* – 37971/97; 25 Feb. 1993, *Funke v. France* – 10828/84; 25 Feb. 1993, *Crémieux v. France* – 11471/85.
225. 17 Oct. 2013, *Winterstein and Others v. France* – 27013/07. In the case ECtHR, *Hirtu and others v. France*, n° 24720/13, it has been considered that the encampment where the Rom's applicants had been living unlawfully for six months was not 'a home' in absence of a sufficient and continuous link with the place in question.

judges have exercised a review of the proportionality of the interference[226] in the context of the eviction proceedings in accordance with the requirements of Article 8. The *Cour de cassation* no longer limits itself to verifying that the Courts of Appeal have indeed characterised the existence of an unlawful disturbance. It does not hesitate to censure the decision of the Court of Appeal which orders the removal of structures and caravans installed on a plot of land in violation of the local town planning scheme, without investigating, as requested, whether the measures ordered were proportionate with regard to the right to respect for the private and family life and the home of the owners of the land and these facilities, as guaranteed by Article 8 ECHR.[227] The judges exercise proportionality control not only on the enforcement measure but also on the time limit within which this measure must be taken. For instance, a delay of a five-day deadline for evacuating illegal settlements was deemed manifestly insufficient, especially as it involved vulnerable people. Such a timeframe did not allow for the rehousing needs of those concerned to be considered.[228]

98. The judges apply the same methodology for controlling demolition measures of an illegally constructed property. For instance, the Cour de cassation cancelled a judgment of a Court of Appeal which based the demolition of a building erected in disregard of town planning rules only on environmental protection considerations without proportionality review about the right to respect for the complainant's home.[229]

99. However, in several cases, the eviction or the demolition are ordered because of an infringement of property rights. Therefore, the control of proportionality seems to be very formal in comparison to the ECtHR case law. In such cases, the Cour de cassation usually declared that '*Since eviction is the only measure likely to enable the owner to recover the full extent of his right to the unlawfully occupied property, the resulting interference with the occupier's right to respect for his home, protected by Article 8 of ECHR, cannot be disproportionate in view of the seriousness of the infringement of the right of ownership.*'[230] In other terms, the judges consider that the right to property overrides the right to respect for the home of the occupant without right or title and that summary eviction can be ordered. This solution is based on Articles 544[231] and 546[232] Civil code as well as Article 17 of the

226. *See* for a first application of this change of jurisprudence at the level of the *Cour de Cassation* 3rd civ., 22 Oct. 2015, n° 14-21.515 et 14-11.776. In this case the *Cour de Cassation* considered that the eviction was justified on grounds of public order; *See also* judgments of Court of Appeal; Cour d'appel de Pau, 7 Aug. 2014, 14/2768; Cour d'appel de Montpellier, 26 Jun. 2014, n° 13/08074; Cour d'appel de Paris, 22 Jan. 2015, n° 13/19308; Cour d'appel de Paris, 2 Jul. 2015, n° 13/12287.
227. Cass. 3rd civ., 17 Dec. 2015, n° 14-22.095.
228. *See* Cour d'appel de Paris, 29 Jan. 2015, n° 13/12287.
229. *See* for instance Cass. 3rd civ., 16 Jan. 2020, n° 19-10.375.
230. Cass. 3rd civ., 17 May 2018, n° 16-15.792; Cass. 3rd civ., 4 Jul. 2019, n° 18-17.119; Cass. 3rd civ., 28 Nov. 2019, n° 17-22810.
231. Article 544 Civil Code provides that 'Ownership is the right to enjoy and dispose of things in the most absolute manner, provided they are not used in a way prohibited by statutes or regulations.'
232. Article 545 Civil Code provides that 'No one may be compelled to yield his ownership, unless for public purposes and for a fair and previous indemnity.'

Declaration of Human and Civics Rights[233] which give an absolute character to the right of ownership in France and Article 1 of the additional protocol No. 1 of the ECHR.

100. The *Cour de cassation* also considered that an overriding legitimate public order interest may circumvent the need for a deeper proportionality review. For instance, the *Cour de cassation* considered that 'Having found that there was a compelling social need to preserve the safety of persons exposed to a natural risk of flooding and to avoid any new construction or reconstruction within the flood-prone areas subject to the strongest hazards, the Court of Appeal … has, on these grounds alone, legally justified its decision to order the demolition.'[234] In such an extreme situation, the Cour de cassation refused to consider the applicant's family and financial situation as a single parent with three minor children, the tolerance of the municipality for seven years since the reconstruction and the absence of third-party rights at stake.

101. **Home visits, searches and seizures.** French law contains several provisions allowing public officials to conduct home visits for legitimate purposes. The ECtHR considered in its *Funke and Cremieux case v. France* that States encountered serious difficulties in the prevention of capital outflows and tax evasion and might '*consider it necessary to have recourse to measures such as house searches and seizures to obtain evidence of exchange-control offences and … prosecute those responsible. Nevertheless, the relevant legislation and practice had to afford adequate and effective safeguards against abuse*'.[235] ECtHR and national cases law show the extent to which French law has had to strengthen its guarantees on several occasions.

102. In *Funke and Cremieux,* the breach of Article 8 ECHR was due to the very wide powers of the customs authorities which had exclusive competence to assess the expediency, number, length, and scale of inspections and, above all, the absence of any requirement of a judicial warrant. France had already anticipated that such a version of Article 64 Customs code contained disproportionate interference in the right to respect for home by amending this provision. Thus, since 1986, home visits must be authorised by a judge, except in case of a flagrante offence. In 2013, the *Conseil constitutionnel*[236] invalidated the specific regime of customs home visits of ships at sea, which also did not provide sufficient safeguards. Likewise, the ECtHR, the *Conseil constitutionel* criticised the Custom code provisions because it allowed '*the inspection by customs officials of any vessel located at sea, in a port or in a harbor or along rivers and canals under all circumstances; that such visits are also*

233. Article 17 of this Declaration provides 'Since the right to Property is inviolable and sacred, no one may be deprived thereof, unless public necessity, legally ascertained, obviously requires it, and just and prior indemnity has been paid.'
234. *See* for instance 16 Jan. 2020, Cass. n° 19-13.645.
235. 25 February *Funke v. France*, n° 10828/84, §56.
236. *See* CC Decision No. 2013-357 QPC of 29 Nov. 2013 Société Wesgate Charters Ltd [Inspection of vessels by customs officials], English version available at https://www.conseil-.fr/en/decision/2013/2013357QPC.htm.

permitted during night hours;' … and that '*appropriate forms of appeal have not been provided such as to enable a control of the implementation of these measures, within the conditions and according to the procedures provided for by law*'.[237] Nevertheless, the *Conseil constitutionnel* did not declare invalid the lack of prior judicial warrant because it took into account the mobility of the vessels and the difficulties in controlling vessels on high seas.

103. The French regime of home visits, search and seizure for tax purposes has also undergone several changes to better meet the requirements of Article 8 ECHR. Until 1985, French law did not really contain specific provisions to allow the tax authorities to search and seize documents to control the taxation of companies.[238] In 1983, the first text that introduced such a regime was censured by the *Conseil constitutionnel.*[239] On the one hand, it did not sufficiently specify the offences for which such a search could be undertaken. On the other hand, the intervention of the judge was not explicitly detailed enough. The text did not really include an obligation for the judge, who has the power to authorise such searches, to verify in a concrete way the validity of the tax administration's request. The subsequent intervention of the judge to control the implementation of the authorised operations was not provided for. Finally, it was not specified that searches on premises not exclusively used for residential purposes should be subject to judicial authorisation. The infringement of the right to respect for home was, therefore, one of the reasons for the invalidation[240] of this first provision. As various new guarantees were introduced by the legislator, the *Conseil constitutionnel* declared the second version constitutional.[241] Since 1985, Article L.16.B of the tax procedure book described in detail the course of the visit and seizure procedure in tax matters. Home visits, searches and seizures can only be authorised if there is a presumption of tax fraud listed exhaustively. Tax administration must be authorised by a judge to conduct such tax inspections and seizures.[242] ECtHR has on several occasions examined the conventionality of Article L.16.B tax procedure book both regarding Article 6 ECHR[243] and Article 8 ECHR.[244] First, the ECtHR considered that this provision placed the entire search and seizure procedure under the supervision of the judge and that the 'interference with the applicant's right to respect for his private and his home was proportionate to the legitimate aims' of obtaining evidence confirming

237. *See* §11 of the Decision No. 213-357.
238. Tax procedure book only provided visit of professional (Art. L.26) or not professional premises (Arts L.38 to L. 41) of persons subject, by reason of their profession, to the legislation on indirect taxes.
239. CC, 29 Dec. 1983, n° 83-164 DC, points 28–30.
240. The violation of the right to an effective remedy was also at stake.
241. CC, 29 Dec. 1984, n° 84-184.
242. According to the last version of L.16 B tax book, the judicial authorisation has to be made by order of the liberty and custody judge (juge des libertés et dela detention) of the judicial court (tribunal judiciaire) in whose jurisdiction the premises to be visited are located.
243. 21 Feb. 2008, *Ravon v. France*, n° 18497/03.
244. 8 Jan. 2002, *Kelassy v. France*, n° 51578/99.

fraud by the applicant.[245] Second, the ECtHR found that despite the existence of certain safeguards in the law, some court orders authorising home visits were still drafted in very broad terms and gave overly extensive powers to tax officials.[246]

104. In practice, the tax administration sends the judges a pre-filled draft order authorising a home visit, which the judges often simply validate. Whereas this practice raised some concerns regarding its conformity to Article 8 ECHR and the *Conseil constitutionnel*'s case law,[247] the *Cour de cassation* validates such a very formal and pragmatical approach.[248] The authorisation order is deemed to have been issued by the judge once he has signed it. The *Cour de cassation* takes into account that judges have to statue in a breve delay on a lot of documents given by the tax administration. At this stage, it is, above all, required that the tax administration provide the judges with convincing evidence of presumed fraud. The *Cour de cassation* even considered that the judge is not obliged to mention that the authorisations of the agents who carried out the visit and seizure were presented to him by the tax authorities.[249] The applicant rightly considered that this reference made it possible to ensure the reality of the judge's control over the application for authorisation.

105. This very pragmatic approach is balanced by the fact that if authorisations are acquired based on unlawful documents, they can be cancelled later.[250] However, the complainant must have an effective remedy against the order authorising these visits and seizures. This was not the case before the *Ravon v. France* ECtHR case. In this case, the ECtHR declared that the impossibility of challenging validity of orders authorising search and seizure operations in the applicant's home by the tax authorities violated Article 6, §1 ECHR. Since 2008,[251] the taxpayer has had a double appeal: an appeal against the order of the judge having authorised, at the request of the tax administration, the implementation of the home visit and an appeal against the report established at the end of the home visit operation.[252] Such access to a tribunal allows the people concerned to have a concrete review of the legality of the extend of the documents seized in relation to the legitimate objective of seeking evidence of tax fraud. This enables the protection of third persons which could have their documents seized because they are in business with the person under suspicion of fraud. The judge may order the return of seized documents that are not related to the presumption of fraud.[253] This review also allows to assess, if

245. 8 Jan. 2002, *Kelassy v. France,* n° 51578/99.
246. 24 Jul. 2008, *André v. France*, n°18603/03, *see* §45.
247. *See* CC, 29 Dec. 1983, n° 83-164 DC, cons. 28–30 above-mentioned.
248. *Cour de cassation* Com., 14 Dec. 2010, n° 10-13.601, and more recently, *Cour de cassation* Com., 14 Nov. 2018, n° 17-16.071 et 17-16.072.
249. Cass. Com., 4 Mar. 2020, n° 18-20244.
250. *See* for instance, Com., 31 Jan. 2012, n° 11-13.097; CE, 20 Oct. 2016, n° 390639. *See also* Conseil constitutionnel,14 Dec. 2013, n° 2013-679 DC, in which the *Conseil constitutionnel* invalided a bill's provision which authorised the tax and custom administration to use any information including illegal ones to base its request for home visit and search.
251. Act No. 2008-776 adopted the 4 Aug. 2008, for the modernisation of the Economy (Loi sur la modernisation de l'économie).
252. This appeal must be made before the First president of the concerned Court of Appeal.
253. *See* for instance Com., 13 Oct. 2021, n° 17-13/008.

needed, whether the concrete home visits respect professional secrecy. The ECtHR has condemned France on three occasions for violating Article 8 ECHR in cases concerning home visits and seizure of documents in lawyers' offices. The ECtHR considered that the seizures carried out on the applicant companies' premises had, in the circumstances of the case, been disproportionate to the aim pursued. In two cases, the seizure contained unnecessary information covered by the lawyer-client privilege.[254] In the last case,[255] the ECtHR considered that the French judges had wrongly deprived the applicant of the guarantees granted to lawyer's home visits simply because he was a Franco-Brazilian lawyer who was no longer attached to a French bar. Indeed, visits to a lawyer's home can only be made with the President of the Bar or his representative and in the presence of the judge or his representative.

106. Beyond tax and customs matters, French law contains similar provisions in several codes which detail how home visits, search and seizure can be carried out by the financial markets authority (Autorité des marches financiers),[256] the Competition Authority (Autorité de la concurrence),[257] Competition, Consumer Affairs and Fraud Control Officers,[258] the Energy Regulation Commission officers,[259] Environmental inspectors,[260] investigators from the anti-doping agency[261] … One of the main differences between these provisions is their scope. Some provisions are limited to visits to professional premises, while others cover visits to all places, including private ones and/or living places and can lead to seizure of documents.

107. The last condemnation of France by the ECtHR in terms of violation of the home concerns the field of town planning. After the *Halabi v. France* case, Act No. 2018-1021 of 23 November 2018 brought domestic law into line with conventional requirements, as home visits can only be carried out in the presence and with the agreement of the occupant (C. urb., Article L.461-2) or, failing that, by order of the judge (C. urb., Article L.461-3).

108. The *Conseil d'Etat* has on several occasions considered that inspections carried out based on other texts were in conformity with Article 8 ECHR. For instance, the supreme administrative judge declared that the possibility for public

254. *See* 2 Apr. 2015, *Vinci Construction and GTM Génie Civil et Services v. France* – 60567/10 and 63629/10; 24 Jul. 2008, *André and Other v. France* – 18603/03.
255. 21 Oct. 2010, *Xavier Da Silveira v. France* 43757/05.
256. Article L.621-10 and L.621-12 Monetary and Financial Code. *See* Conseil d'Etat, 21 Nov. 2016, n° 386249 in which the *Conseil d'Etat* declared Art. L.621-10 conform to Art. 8 ECHR. *See also* CE, 9e et 10e sous-sect., 20 janv. 2016, n° 374950, Caisse d'épargne et de prévoyance du Languedoc-Roussillon.
257. Article L.450-4 Commerce Code.
258. Article L.512-51 Consummer Code.
259. Article L.135-4 Energy Code.
260. Article L.172-5 Environmental Code.
261. Article L.232-18-17 Sport Code.

health inspectors to conduct inspections of pharmacists without the latter being able to object was in line with Article 8 ECHR.[262]

109. By contrast, the *Conseil d'Etat* declared that Article 8 ECHR and the 1978 Data Protection Act were violated because the data protection agent did not inform the plaintiff of its right to object to the visit within this case, which needs to be authorised by the judge.[263] Since then, the home visits and seizure powers of the French DPA have been clarified.[264] Safeguards measures have been reinforced in case of home visits and seizures. The DPA agent cannot access health data that is covered by medical confidentiality. Therefore, the communication of individual medical data may then only take place under the authority and in the presence of a doctor.[265] Professional secrecy can justify a refusal to allow access to computer programs or to communicate documents to the agents when the data relate to correspondence between a lawyer and his client or are covered by the secrecy of journalistic processing.

110. **Freedoms related to home.** Several French judgments based on Article 8 ECHR recalled that individuals enjoy certain freedoms related to their homes. First, the *Cour de cassation* judged that a clause in a residential lease which deprived the tenant of the possibility of accommodating his relatives violated Article 8 ECHR.[266] This judgment put an end to the practice of social landlords who considered that such a clause ensured that their housing was allocated based on the actual resources of the occupants.[267] Second, the *Cour de cassation* has repeatedly held that '*the free choice of personal and family residence is one of the attributes*'[268] of the right to respect for the home guaranteed by Article 8 ECHR. Therefore, the *Cour de cassation* declared null and void residence clauses which obliged the employee to reside in the vicinity of his place of work. It extended this to the mobility clauses,[269] which obliged the employee to transfer his home and follow his company when moving to another region. The Court also annulled the dismissal of employees based on these clauses for lack of legal basis.

111. This free choice of personal and family residence is not absolute. The *Cour de cassation* underlined that 'a restriction on this freedom of residence by the

262. CE, 21 Nov. 2016, n° 386249. In the health context, *see also* 26 Jan. 2007, n° 281516 in which the *Conseil d'Etat* dismissed the violation of Art. 8 by a doctor mandated by the labour inspectorate for a counter visit at the home of an employee on sick leave. In this case, after the opposition to the home visit, the doctor proposed to make the visit in the premise of the building or at his office.
263. CE, 6 Nov. 2009, n° 304300.
264. *See* Art.19 French Data protection Act, LIL.
265. *See* Art. 19 III. LIL. *See infra* para. 559.
266. *See* Cass. 3rd civ., 6 Mar. 1996, Mel Yedei, 93-11.113; Mrs Mel Yedei took in the father of her two children and her sister. *See also*, Cass. 3rd civ., 22 Mar. 2006, *Zaline c/ Élisée*.
267. *See* former judgments of Courts of Appeal which validated such clauses CA Paris urgences 4 December 1986, *OPHVP c/ Dormante*, in case of accommodation of a cohabitant; CA Paris 6e ch. A, 5 Dec. 1989, *OPAC c/ Fairfort*, in case of the accommodation by the tenant of his child and grandchildren.
268. Cass. soc., 28 Feb. 2012, n° 10-18308.
269. Cass. soc., 12 Jan. 1999, Spileers n° 96-40755.

employer is only valid if it is essential for the protection of the legitimate interests of the company and proportionate, taking into account the job held and the work required, to the aim sought'. This is not the case for a job as a sales representative or housekeeper. Recently, a Court of Appeal accepted the legality of a dismissal based on an employee's refusal to reside near his company and moved 442 km away. Curiously, the Court considered that 'no disproportionate interference with the free choice of personal and family residence under the right to respect for the home, protected by Article 8 of the European Convention for the Protection of Human Rights and Fundamental Freedoms, appears to be characterised in view of the essential obligation to preserve the health and safety of the employee'.[270] It is expected to see whether the *Cour de cassation* will accept or agree to give precedence to the employer's obligation of security over the employee's free choice of domicile based on Article 8 ECHR.

112. Finally, French law had tried to respect the free choice of the Travellers to live in caravan by developing a housing offer adapted to their lifestyle. In 1990, the so-called Besson Law[271] obliged the French municipalities with more than 5,000 inhabitants to provide stopping places for travellers. In 2000, a specific law on the Reception and Housing of Travellers tried to give more effectivity to this obligation[272] This law created an obligation for the departments to plan the creation of reception areas, the implementation of which is entrusted to the municipalities with more than 5,000 inhabitants and, since 2015, intermunicipal authorities.[273] Each departmental scheme should provide for the geographical implementation of three kinds of hosting. Beyond the permanent access area, local collectivities must create rental family plots for the prolonged installation of mobile homes[274] and large-scale transit areas designed to accommodate travellers who move collectively to traditional or occasional gatherings. In 2017, a new law promoted the development of family rental plots by counting them as part of the 25% of social housing that every French municipality is supposed to provide.[275] In 2018, a new law clarified the competencies between the local actors involved in the creation and management of the areas and family rental plots. This law also reinforced the sanctions against illicit parking. Beyond the criminal penalties, a municipality that fulfils its obligations to host travellers is entitled to evacuate illegal camps. Since 2007, this eviction has been an administrative procedure and can be ordered by the Prefect.

270. Court of Appeal Versailles, 10 Mar. 2022, n° 20/02208.
271. Act No. 90-449 du 31 May 1990 for the implementation of the right to housing.
272. Act No. 2000-614 of 5 Jul. 2000 on the reception and housing of travellers. In return for new obligations imposed on local authorities to provide accommodation for travellers, this law reinforces the penalties for the illegal parking of travellers.
273. This new actor was introduced by the Act No. 2015-991 of 7 Aug. 2015 on the new territorial organisation of the Republic, known as the NOTRe law.
274. *See* Art. L.444-1 Urban Planning Code. This family rental plots should allow not only the installation of caravan but also of all kinds of demountable residence constituting the permanent home of its user (This could be yurte, for instance).
275. Act No. 2017-86 of 27 Jan. 2017 on equality and citizenship.

113. Despite these efforts, a recent report by the Human Rights Defender considers that the effective recognition of the itinerant lifestyle of travellers remains incomplete in France.[276] The fact that a caravan is considered a home but not a dwelling is still a source of difficulties for travellers. The implementation of reception possibilities is still insufficient. The areas created are often problematic in terms of health and environment. One could consider that the localisation of these areas near classified installations, such as landfills or even wastewater treatment plants, could constitute a violation of the *Lopez case* law on Article 8 ECHR.[277] The 2018 Act above-mentioned facilitates expedited eviction of illegal camps. This issue is the core of the recent condemnation of France in the *Hirtu Case*[278] for violation of the respect of the private and family life of the applicant. This case concerns the eviction of an illegal Rom camp based on the same rules as the above-mentioned for travellers.

6. Privacy and Secrecy of Correspondence

114. **Main French sources on secrecy of correspondence**. In France, the secrecy of correspondence is protected both by Article 8 ECHR and Articles 226-15 and 432-9 CP. The first article deals with violations of the secrecy of correspondence by private individuals, and the second with violations by persons holding public authority. The first criminalisation of violations of the secrecy of correspondence coincides with the French Revolution,[279] which enshrined this right to privacy. While the secrecy of correspondence is not explicitly written in the current French Constitution, the *Conseil constitutionnel* has established its constitutional value since 2004.[280]

115. **Broad concept of correspondence.** As at the European level, the notion of 'correspondence' is widely interpreted. The aim is to protect correspondence of all kinds, regardless of how it is sent or delivered. This includes not only written letters but also phone conversations, SMS, emails, conversations exchanged using a video camera, etc. The medium and the form of the message are of little importance. The concept of correspondence is defined by the existence of an exchange between two types of people: the sender and a third person to whom the message is addressed. The protection, therefore, does not apply in the case of communication to the public targeting an unlimited number of unidentified persons.

---

276. Défenseur des droits, *Rapport: Gens du goyage – lever les entraves aux droits, Contribution à la stratégie nationale*, 2021, p. 11.
277. *López Ostra v. Spain*, 9 Dec. 1994, Series A No. 303-C.
278. *Hirtu and Others v. France,* No. 24720/13, 14 May 2020.
279. Loi 17–22 Aug. 1790 which obliged the requiring postal employees to take an oath to respect the secrecy of correspondence, and finally by a decree of 10 Jul. 1791 on the secrecy and inviolability of letters; *see also* Part II, Title I, s. II, Art. 23 Penal code of 25 Sep. 1791.
280. CC, 2 Mar. 2004, Decision No. 2004-492 DC Evolution de la criminalité, §4.

116. **Main features of the protection by Article 226-16 CP**. Article 226-16 CP states that it is irrelevant whether the correspondence reached its addressee. Violation of the secrecy of correspondence can take several forms, ranging from opening the message to deleting it or simply delaying its transmission. It also includes the simple act of becoming aware of the message by reading it, for example. According to Article 226-15 of the French Criminal Code, the protection of the confidentiality of correspondence is subject to the existence of an intentional element. The breach of protection must be committed in bad faith. The perpetrator must have been aware that the communication was not intended for him or her. No penalty may be imposed if the third person can prove that he accidentally opened an email or letter. Otherwise, the penalty may be up to one year's imprisonment and a fine of EUR 45,000. An aggravated penalty was introduced in 2020 in cases where the violation of correspondence is committed by the spouse of a victim of domestic violence.[281] Besides the controversial use of correspondences as proof in divorce cases,[282] the protection of the secrecy of correspondence is often invoked in relations between employers and their employees. In particular, the question arises as to the extent to which an employer can have access to his employees' emails without violating the secrecy of correspondence and breaching Article 8 ECHR. Personal emails received or sent by an employee at work are protected by Article 226-15, paragraph 2 CP.[283] The following paragraphs will focus on three specific domains of application of the secret of correspondence, which deserve attention in France.

117. **Protection of Correspondence in Prisons.** Since 2009, a law has been in force in France to protect the secrecy of correspondence of the prisoners.[284] This law forms the legal basis on which prison authorities must justify any interference with prisoners' correspondence under Article 8 ECHR. Article L.345-3 prison code states that: '*Mail sent or received by detainees may be inspected and detained by the prison administration when such correspondence appears to seriously compromise their rehabilitation or the maintenance of good order and security.*' In addition, Article L.345-4 Prisons Code lists three main categories of correspondences that cannot be inspected and detained by the prison administration. This includes correspondence between prisoners and their defence counsel[285] or with certain administrative or judicial authorities strictly defined by decree, as well as exchanges

281. Law No. 2020-936 of 30 Jul. 2020 aimed at protecting victims of domestic violence, which provided in such case a penalty of two years' imprisonment and a fine of EUR 60,000. This completes the prohibition already enshrined in Art. 259-1 Civil Code, under which a spouse may not introduce into the proceeding's letters exchanged between his or her spouse and a third party that he or she may have obtained by violence or fraud.

282. *See* for illustrations where the French judges accepted emails which, although on the spouse's personal computer, had 'no protection to minimise access'. 1st civ., 18 May 2005, n° 04-13.745; 1st civ., 26 Oct. 2011, n° 10-27.872.

283. More details on this protection *see infra* paras 526–527.

284. Law 2009-1436 du 24 Nov. 2009 pénitentiaire, in particular Arts 39 and 40, which have been codified in Art. L.341-1 to L.341-4 of the prison code created in 2022.

285. *See* Circulaire du 27 mars 2012 relative aux relations des personnes détenues avec leur défenseur. The *Conseil constitutionnel* validated the legal framework of the confidentiality in its Décision No. 2021-945 QPC du 4 Nov. 2021, *M. Aristide L. (Communication entre la personne détenue et son avocat)*, para. 5 et 7.

with chaplains approved by the prison. Although these legislative provisions broadly comply with the conditions laid down by the ECHR, their implementation by the prison administration raises criticisms from the Defender of Rights. According to the Defender of Rights, French prisons systematically open correspondence between prisoners and their outside doctors, even when the doctor's or hospital's stamp is displayed on the envelope. This administrative practice seems to be contrary to respect for medical confidentiality. Furthermore, its systematic nature runs counter to the letter of the above-mentioned Article L.343-3 of the Prisons Code. According to this provision, the opening of prisoners' mail should be limited to cases where it appears strictly necessary for their rehabilitation or the maintenance of good order and security. According to the Defender of Rights, the prison administration justifies this systematic opening of letters between prisoners and outside doctors because doctors are not on the list of protected correspondence provided by the above-mentioned decree. The Defender of Rights recently recommended that the government take action to put an end to this administrative practice by reminding prison administrations of the need to make the opening of letters subject to the strict purpose of the checks on correspondence established by law.[286]

118. In conclusion, it is also worth underlining that since 2016, there has been a specific regulation on prison intelligence, which has been codified in the title V bis of the Internal security Code (Code de la Sécurité Intérieure (CSI)). Article L.855-1 CSI details the purpose, the categories of agents and the surveillance techniques[287] that can be used by prison intelligence services. This article provides a legal base of inference in the correspondence of the detainees '*for purposes of preventing escapes and ensure security in prisons or health establishments intended to hold detainees*'. The use of technical devices to capture, fix, transmit and record private or confidential speech or images in a private place is limited to high-risk prisoners. The regime of such inference on the secrecy of the correspondence of the prisoners is aligned to the one intelligence interception.[288]

119. **Protection of Correspondence with Lawyers.**[289] While the protection of correspondence with the lawyers is an essential element for the functioning of justice in a democratic state, it does not constitute an autonomous fundamental right guaranteed as such by the Constitution.[290] The *Conseil constitutionnel* nevertheless

286. Décision of the Defender of Rights No. 2022-038, adopted on 9 Feb. 2023, p. 2. Curiously, the Defender of Rights is calling for a change to the circular of 9 Jun. 2011 on the application of Arts 4, 39 and 40 of the Prison Act 2009-1439 of 24 Nov. 2009, relating to telephone correspondence and correspondence with prisoners. However, the principle of finality is explicitly stated in this text, which once again shows that the difficulty lies much more in the practical implementation of the rules on the confidentiality of prisoners' correspondence.
287. *See* Art. L.851-1, L.851-4, L.851-5 and L.851-6, au I de l'article L. 852-1, Arts L.852-2 et L.853-1 CSI.
288. More detailed further paras 140–145 and National securities services processing and paras 609–612, and note 1277.
289. *See also* professional secrecry of the lawyer, para. 560.
290. *See* CC, Decision No. 2015-478 QPC, 24 Jul. 2015, Association French Data Network, in which the *Conseil constitutionnel* stated that no constitutional provision specifically enshrines a right a right to secrecy of exchanges and correspondence of lawyers not even Art. 2 of the DDH, points

considers that it has a duty to verify the constitutionality of potential breaches through its review of respect for the right to secrecy of correspondence, the right to privacy and the exercise of the rights of defence. Furthermore, the protection of correspondence of the lawyers is enshrined in Article 66-5 of the 1971 law on legal professions.[291] The scope of protection for lawyers' correspondence has been the subject of debate in France. The criminal chamber of the *Cour de cassation*[292] has been reluctant to recognise the confidentiality of correspondence relating to legal advice, which was not the case of the commercial chamber[293] or the *Conseil d'Etat*.[294] Since 2022, a preliminary article introduced into the Code of Criminal Procedure (Code de Procedure Pénale (CPP))[295] explicitly provides that the confidentiality of a lawyer's correspondence applies to all matters, whether in the field of defence or legal advice.[296]

120. The protection of the correspondence applies to both the correspondence sent by the lawyer to his client or intended for the client. The criminal chamber of the *Cour de cassation* extends the protection to the correspondence to internal emails from a company containing the analyses and advice of a lawyer in the context of a competition investigation on the premises of a company.[297] In the case of phone interception, it has even been ruled that the prohibition on transcribing correspondence between a lawyer and his client extends to correspondence exchanged on this subject between the lawyer and the client's relatives.[298] It is also worth underlining that the ECtHR recalls to the French judges that the concept of correspondence has to be interpreted widely and included a piece of paper folded in two by a lawyer that he handed ostentatiously to one of his two customers during the audience.[299]

121. The confidentiality of a lawyer's correspondence must sometimes be balanced with respect for the rights of the defence. For example, the *Cour de cassation*

31–37. The *Conseil d'Etat* has classified independence and respect for 'lawyer-client confidentiality' as 'principles' that must be observed by the regulatory authority. the 'secrecy of relations between lawyers and their clients': CE, Ass., 9 Apr. 1999, Mme Toubol-Fisher and Bismuth, No. 196177. By contrast, French lawyers consider that the professional secrecy of the laywer is 'general, absolute and unlimited' *See* Art. 2 of the règlement intérieur de la profession d'avocat (RIN) drawn up by the French National Bar (Conseil national des barreaux).

291. Law No. 71-1130 du 31 Dec. 1971 portant réforme de certaines professions judiciaires et juridiques.
292. *See* for instance Cass. Crim., 30 Jun. 1999, n° 97-86.318.
293. *See* for instance Cass. Com., 5 May 1998, n° 96-30116; Com., 9 Mar. 1999, n° 97-30.029, et 26 Nov. 2013, n° 12-27.162.
294. CE, Section, 10 Apr. 2008, n° 296 845; CE, 12 Dec. 2008, n° 414088.
295. Law No. 71-1130 du 31 Dec. 1971 has been modified in 2021.
296. For more details *see* the Circulaire présentant les dispositions de la loi n° 2021-1729 du 22 décembre 2021 pour la confiance dans l'institution judiciaire renforçant la protection des droits de la défense.
297. Cass. Crim., 26 Jan. 2022, 17-87.359.
298. *See* Crim. 13 Dec. 2022, FS-B, n° 21-87.435.
299. While the Criminal Court of the *Cour de cassation* considered that this note was not cover by the secrecy of the correspondence, Crim., 16 Oct. 2012, n° 11-88.136, the ECHR condemned France for the violation of Art. 8 in its case *Laurent v. France* 28798/1.

has held that confidentiality may be waived when the lawyer is defending himself against his client's claims that would call into question the steps he has taken to carry out his task.[300] Furthermore, correspondence exchanged between lawyers and their colleagues is covered by professional secrecy, except for correspondence marked 'official'.

122. More globally, the strengthening of the confidentiality of lawyers' correspondence is essentially reflected in the guarantees relating to the conditions under which lawyers' correspondence may be intercepted in his/her office or at home. Those guarantees are listed by Article L.56-1 CPP.[301] Interception of a lawyer's correspondence with his client is subject to authorisation by the liberty and custody judge (JLD). This judicial decision must state the reasons and indicate the nature of the offence being investigated, the reasons justifying the measure, its purpose, and its proportionality regarding the nature and seriousness of the facts. The seizure can only be made by a judge under the control of the President of the bar and only for the purposes mentioned by the judicial authorisation. Recently, the constitutionality of these provisions has been validated by the *Conseil constitutionnel.*[302] For its part, the *Cour de cassation* has also strengthened the procedural guarantees relating to the seizure of information from the mobile phone of a lawyer involved in criminal proceedings.[303]

123. **Surveillance of Correspondence for Law Enforcement.** Until 1991, French civil and criminal law contained no explicit provisions for the recording of the conversation which was an interference with the right to respect for correspondence in the sense of Article 8 ECHR. However, case law had accepted that telephone tapping was admissible as evidence, based on Articles 81 and 151 of the CPP, which allow the investigating judge to order 'all useful acts', provided that they are ordered by the judge, for a limited period, on the presumption of a specific offence, and that they are carried out without artifice or stratagem.[304] In its *Kruslin and*

300. Crim., 16 May 2000, n° 99-85.304.
301. A similar legal regime applies to taping on lawyers' office *see* Art. 100 CPP which provides that 'No interception may be made on a line depending on a lawyer's office or home, unless there are reasonable grounds for suspecting the lawyer of having committed or attempted to commit, as perpetrator or accomplice, the offence that is the subject of the proceedings or a related offence within the meaning of article 203 and provided that the measure is proportionate to the nature and seriousness of the facts. The decision is taken by reasoned order of the liberty and custody judge, referred for this purpose by reasoned order of the investigating judge, taken after consulting the public prosecutor.' *See also* Art. 100-7 CPP.
302. *See* CC, Decision No. 2022-1031 QPC du 19 Jan. 2023.
303. Cass. Crim, 5 Mar. 2024 n°23-80.229. In this ruling, the Court of Cassation reiterates the requirement to review the need to seize correspondence, which must be selective in order to be proportionate to the aim sought. It also refers for the first time to two rights that may be claimed by lawyers in criminal proceedings: notification of the right to remain silent and the assistance of a defendant.
304. Crim., 18 1958, P, n°163 – Crim., 16 mars 1961, *JCP* 1961. II. 12157, note J. Larguier – Crim., 9 Oct. 1980, n°80-93.140, P, n°255; *D.* 1981. 332, note J. Pradel; *JCP* 1981. II. 19578, note Di Marino; *JCP* 1981. I. 3029, obs. P. Chambon – Crim. 23 avr. 1981, n°80-93.475, P, n°117 – Crim., 23 juill. 1985, n°85-92.574, P, n°275; *D.* 1986. 61, note P. Chambon.

Huvig cases,[305] the ECtHR held that French law, written and unwritten, did not indicate with reasonable clarity the scope and manner of exercise of the relevant discretion conferred on the public authorities in violation of Article 8, §2 ECHR. Thus, it was under the influence of the ECtHR that France had to adopt the law of 10 July 1991 on the confidentiality of correspondence following its condemnation.[306] Currently, the surveillance of correspondence for law enforcement in France is covered by the concept of interception of correspondence sent by electronic communications (hereinafter 'interception'). This concept is not limited to the interception but also the recording and the transcription of such interception. There are mainly two kinds of such interceptions: administrative interception, ordered by judicial judges, and security interception, ordered with the authorisation of the Prime Minister. The latter is related to surveillance for State intelligence services.

124. Judicial interception in France is currently governed by Articles 100 to 100-7 of the CPP. These provisions contained three main guarantees which answer to the standard required by Article 8, §2 ECHR. First, such interception must be authorised by the investigating judge (juge d'instruction) in writing. Second, this written authorisation must include all the information needed to identify the connection to be intercepted, the offence for which the interception is required and the duration of the interception. In principle, this authorisation may not be taken for more than four months, renewable for up to one year, or even two years for mostly organised crimes listed exhaustively.[307] The *Cour de cassation* held that Article 8 of the ECHR was not infringed insofar as the successive or cumulative interception, pursuant to these texts, of different telephone lines used by the same person suspected of serious offences was a necessary measure to protect public order and prevent criminal offences.[308] Third, the interception may only be used for offences involving a serious disturbance of public order. Therefore, Article 100 CPP provides that it applies in criminal and misdemeanour cases if the penalty is three years' imprisonment or more. Judicial interception on offences punishable by a lesser term of imprisonment remains possible if requested by the victim of an offence committed via electronic communications.[309]

125. This system has been refined over the years to cover specific aspects. Four points merit attention. First, the preliminary article of the CPP recalls in line with Article 8 ECHR that *'During criminal proceedings, measures affecting a person's private life may only be taken, by decision of or under the effective supervision of the judicial authority, if they are, in the light of the circumstances of the case, necessary to establish the truth and proportionate to the seriousness of the offence'*.[310]

305. *Kruslin v. France*, http://hudoc.echr.coe.int/eng?i=001-57626; *Huvig v. France*, http://hudoc.echr.coe.int/eng?i=001-57627.
306. Loi n° 91-646 du 10 juillet 1991 relative au secret des correspondances émises par la voie des communications électroniques.
307. *See* Art. 706-73 and 706-73-1 CPP.
308. Crim., 8 juill. 2015, n°15-81.731, P, n°174.
309. For instance, this makes possible to wiretap the line of a person who is the victim of repeated malicious telephone calls, punishable by one year's imprisonment under Art. 222-16 of the CP.
310. This provision was introduced in 2019.

126. Second, France's condemnation by the ECtHR in the *Lambert* case[311] in 1998 has shown the weaknesses of French law regarding procedural rules on interception. The French criminal chamber of the *Cour de cassation* considered that only the person who has personally been the victim can claim that the rules of procedure have been breached, thereby violating privacy. Thus, the person under investigation is not entitled to rely on the irregularity of a search and recordings of conversations made at the home of a third party.[312] The ECtHR questioned this narrow conception of the applicants' interest in bringing proceedings before the French criminal courts. According to the ECtHR, an accused person must be able to challenge the legality of a wiretap originating from another procedure and concerning a third party if it is attached to the procedure.[313] This forced the criminal chamber of the *Cour de cassation* to change its jurisprudence.[314]

127. Third, interceptions may be authorised by the liberty and custody judge (JLD) as part of a *flagrante delicto* investigation or a preliminary investigation into listed offences against organised crime[315] at the request of the Public Prosecutor. In such cases, the measure shall be ordered for a maximum of fifteen days. It may be renewed once under the same conditions of form and duration.

128. Fourth, French law provides several guarantees for the judicial interception of deputies, senators, judges, lawyers, and journalists. Such interception is submitted to an additional condition. The investigation judge needs to prior inform the President of the chamber in case of an interception of a member of the parliament, the first president, or the public prosecutor of the court where the concerned judge resides, the President of the Bar in case of the interception of a lawyer.[316]

129. To sum up, even after the introduction of solid legal guarantees regarding the condition for the implementation of judicial interception, national case law paradoxically illustrates that when public officials commit the offence of violating the confidentiality of correspondence, they are rarely punished.[317] Furthermore, the Surveillance by State Intelligence Services which includes interception for fighting against organised crime and terrorism is the core of important disputes between the French judges and the European Courts.

---

311. *Lambert v. France*, 24 Aug. 1998.
312. Crim., 7 Dec. 2005, n° 05-85.876.
313. *Matheron v. France* 57752/00, 29 Mar. 2005.
314. Cass. Crim., 6 Sep. 2006, Bull Crim., n° 208. Filniez, *L'arrêt Mathéron de la Cour européenne des droits de l'homme et ses suites*, RSC 2007, p. 333.
315. *See* Art. 706-73 of the CPP.
316. *See* Art. 100-7 CPP.
317. *See* P. Collet, *Les interceptions téléphoniques judiciaires et les conversations avec un avocat*, Dalloz, 2023, p. 1410. The author considers that this lack of repression is linked to the strictness of the conditions of Art. 6-1 of the CPP, which requires that 'when a crime or offence allegedly committed in the course of criminal proceedings or proceedings before a court involves the violation of a rule of procedure, the public prosecution may only be brought if the unlawful nature of the prosecution, of the decision taken or of the act performed in the course of the prosecution has been established by a final decision of the criminal court hearing the case or pursuant to the remedies provided by law or regulation'.

7. Surveillance by State Intelligence Services

130. **Main aspects of the French law on intelligence**. In 2015, France adopted its first law on intelligence[318] which has been introduced in its CSI. Article L.801-1 CSI recalls explicitly that the legal framework applicable to the intelligence activities needs to be aligned with the right to privacy, in particular, the secrecy of the correspondence, data protection, and respect for home. Furthermore, Article L.801-1 CSI lists the fundamental principles governing the use of intelligence techniques inspired by Article 8, §2 ECHR. Such a use is subject to the following requirements:

(1) the technique must be authorised by an authority with the legal competent to do so;
(2) it must be the result of a procedure that complies with the law;
(3) it must correspond to the missions entrusted to the intelligence services by law;
(4) it must be justified by the threats, risks and issues relating to the fundamental fundamental interests of the Nation;
(5) it must not infringe on a person's right to privacy except in a way that is proportionate to the reasons given.

131. The French fundamental interests of the Nation are listed exhaustively in Article L.811-3 of the CSI. It covers the seven following purposes:

(1) the national independence, territorial integrity and national defence;
(2) the Major foreign policy interests, the fulfilment of France's European and international commitments and the prevention of any form of foreign interference;
(3) France's major economic, industrial, and scientific interests;
(4) the prevention of terrorism;
(5) the prevention of attacks on the republican form of institutions; the prevention of collective violence likely to cause serious damage to public peace; actions aimed at maintaining or reconstituting groups disbanded for such collective violence reasons;
(6) prevention of organised crime and delinquency;
(7) the prevention of the proliferation of weapons of mass destruction.

Despite some imprecisions, the *Conseil constitutionnel* has validated this list of seven purposes.[319] It considered that the criteria were in line with the objective pursued by these administrative policy measures.[320] The *Conseil constitutionnel* argued that most of the purposes referred to criminal offences are defined in the CSI, the defence code or the penal code. This is particularly the case of the prevention of

318. Loi n° 2015-912 du 24 Jul. 2015 relative au renseignement.
319. In addition, the Art. L.855-1 CSI enables the prison intelligence service to pursue specific objectives, namely preventing escapes and ensuring security in prisons.
320. CC, DC n° 2015-713, 23 Jul. 20215.

terrorism, which is the purpose based on which the greatest number of people are monitored by the French intelligence services since 2015.[321] In practice, the Commission Nationale de contrôle des techniques de renseignements (CNCTR) ensures that these purposes are not interpreted too broadly by the intelligence services.[322] The CNCTR is the AAI whose opinion must be received by the Prime Minister to authorise the use of intelligence techniques. In its annual reports,[323] the CNCTR reiterates its vigilance regarding the request based on the purpose of 'the prevention of collective violence likely to cause serious damage to public peace'. Indeed, the use of this purpose does not allow technical surveillance of individuals targeted because of their political or trade union activities or their involvement in social mobilizations. Here, it goes beyond privacy and includes issues of freedom of expression, opinion, association and demonstration.

132. To comply with the requirements of Article 8, §2 ECHR, the CSI lists not only the purposes that may be pursued by the intelligence services but also the various authorised intelligence techniques by specifying the conditions for implementing each of them. The more privacy-intrusive the technology, the more restrictive its conditions of application.

133. The CSI provides a legal basis for four categories of security interceptions, which enable the intelligence services to access communications content and connection data. First, Article L.852-1, I CSI enables security interception of the electronic communications operators. The groupement interministérielle de controle (GIC), an intermediary department reporting to the Prime Minister, has been created. The GIC centralises the requests of the intelligence services and transfers to them the data from the electronic communications operators. The number of interceptions that can be carried out simultaneously is limited to 3,800.

134. Second, Article L.852-1, II CSI authorises the interception by an IMSI catcher, which is also called proximity interception and is used for mobile communications. As it is a very intrusive technique, its implementation has been limited in two different ways. On the one hand, such interceptions can only be granted for a maximum period of forty-eight hours renewable compared with up to four months for ordinary security interceptions. On the other hand, such interception can only be used for three purposes:

- prevention of terrorism;
- national independence, territorial integrity and national defence; and
- prevention of attacks on the republican form of institutions.

---

321. *See* CNCTR, *Annual Report*, 2022, pp. 13–14. Prevention of terrorism is the purpose used for 30% of the monitored persons in France, while 25% for Prevention of organised crime and delinquency in 2022.
322. *See* Art. L.833-5 CSI that explicitly charges the CNCTR of the control of the alignment of the request of surveillance with all the requirements of Art. L.801-1 which includes a control of the purposes.
323. *See* for instance CNCTR, *Annual Report*, 2022, pp. 75–88.

Security interception of communication with IMSI catchers by intelligence services seems exceptional. Apparently, the CNCTR has not received any requests to implement this highly intrusive interception technique since 2018.[324]

135. Third, Article L.852-2 CSI provides a legal basis for the interception of communications exchanged within a private network using the airwaves exclusively and not involving an electronic communications operator. This concerns radio communications and communications between connected objects.

136. Fourth, intelligence services have the power to intercept correspondence sent or received by satellite themselves, using a special interception device, without having to seek the assistance of the communications operators concerned. In 2021,[325] the legislator authorised this experiment until 31 July 2025 and under strict conditions. Interception of satellite communications:

- are authorised only on a subsidiary basis, i.e. only when technical or confidentiality reasons prevent the use of these operators;
- are subject to a quota system, under which the maximum number of authorisations simultaneously in force may not exceed a quota set by the Prime Minister after consulting the CNCTR;
- are limited to the purposes of national defence, counter-intelligence, the fight against terrorism or the prevention of organised crime and delinquency;
- cannot be carried out for a period that exceeds thirty days;
- can only be carried out by the so-called first circle of specialised intelligence.[326]

137. Beyond the security interception, the CSI provides for other intelligence techniques such as speech recording, image recording in a private place and computer data collection.[327] The use of those techniques may require entry into a private area, such as a home or a car to set up, use or remove a tag. This is why such intelligence techniques are limited to situations where other less intrusive techniques are not available.[328]

138. Finally, intelligence services are enabled to obtain access to connection data from internet operators either in deferred time[329] or in real time.[330] The legal regime of connection data, which has been the subject of numerous disputes in

324. *See* CNCTR, *Annual Report*, 2022, p. 18. By contrast, the report mentions 641 uses of IMSI Cather to access to connection data in 2022. These uses are based on Art. L. 851-6 CSI. This figure seems particularly high given that the simultaneous collection of connection data by IMSI Catcher is capped at 100.
325. *See* Loi n°2021-998, 30 Jul 2021 relative à la prévention des actes de terrorisme et au renseignement.
326. *See* further the definition of the first circle intelligence services, para. 140, and note 1277.
327. Article L.853-1 CSI.
328. *See* Art. L.853-3 CSI.
329. Article L.851-1 CSI.
330. Article L.851-2 CSI, with a quota of 720 simultaneous authorizations.

France to bring it into line with European standards, will be analysed in the following paragraphs, as it arises in part from the transposition of the e-Privacy Directive.

139. In addition, intelligence techniques' regime can vary depending on whether the aim is to monitor national territory or international communications. The French provisions relating to intelligence techniques applicable to international communications proposed originally in 2015 were not sufficiently detailed by the legislator as required by Article 8, §2 ECHR. Thus, it was invalidated by the *Conseil constitutionnel.*[331] The current regime has been validated by the *Conseil constitutionnel.*[332] The constitutional judge considered that the new law does not constitute a manifestly disproportionate infringement of the right to respect for private life and the secrecy of correspondence. '*the legislator has precisely defined the conditions for implementing measures to monitor international electronic communications, those for using, storing and destroying the information collected, and those for the control exercised by the national commission for the monitoring of intelligence techniques*'.[333] The purposes for which international electronic communications may be monitored are identical to those that govern the use of these techniques for the sole purpose of monitoring French territory. However, the procedure differs because such intelligence techniques of international electronic communications need two successive authorizations. The first one is for the interception itself, and the second one is for the exploitation by a specific intelligence service of the data received from the interception. In both cases, the authorisation needs to be done by the Prime Minister. The exploitation of international communication requires in addition the prior opinion of the CNCTR.[334]

140. At this stage, it is worth to recap that since 2015, France has put in place a sophisticated legal regime to govern intelligence surveillance techniques. This system is based on three main characteristics. First, the definition in law within the meaning of Article 8, §2 ECHR of three essential elements that are closely linked. On the one hand, the possible purposes are exhaustively listed. On the other hand, the techniques likely to be used to implement each of these purposes are detailed. Finally, the competent authorities to deploy each of these intelligence techniques for each of these purposes are defined. This so-called French intelligence community is divided into two categories. Only six specialised intelligence services are considered the 'first circle'.[335] This includes the well-known Directorate-General for Internal Security (DGSI) and the Directorate-General for External Security (DGSE). Such services are entitled to use most of the techniques provided for by law.[336] The

331. CC, DC 2015-713, 23 Jul. 2015, point 78 the legal argument is based in the lack of respect of the public liberties including the right to privacy.
332. *See* CC, DC 2015-722, 26 Nov. 2015.
333. *See* CC, DC 2015-722, 26 Nov. 2015, point 15.
334. *See* Art. L. 854-2 CSI.
335. *See* Art. R 811-1 CSI.
336. *See* Art. R 811-2 CSI. Only the Directorate of Military Intelligence (DRM) and the national department responsible for processing intelligence and combating clandestine financial circuits (TRACFIN) have more limited competences.

so-called intelligence services of the second circle[337] are made up of around twenty services for which intelligence is only part of their mission or which are part of an administration whose mission goes beyond intelligence. This includes the Directorate-General of the National Police, the Directorate-General of the National Gendarmerie, the Prefecture of Police and the Prison Administration. As a result, they can only use some of the intelligence techniques provided by law for a limited number of purposes. In addition, the second circle includes four services with an exclusive intelligence mission.[338]

141. Second, the uses of intelligence techniques are submitted to a specific procedure of prior authorisation by the Prime Minister with the opinion of the CNCTR, while the use of these same techniques in criminal proceedings is subject to judicial authorisation.[339]

142. Third, the CNCTR also exercises *a posteriori* control over the way the intelligence services have complied with the authorisation given for the implementation of surveillance techniques. While the existence of this *a posteriori control* is a particularly positive feature of this system, the CNCTR's reports attest that such controls are far from systematic. To improve this control, the CNCTR claims for a more centralised access to data collected, as well as mechanisms for tracing the use of data.[340]

143. In conclusion, the French system of intelligence techniques attempts to provide numerous guarantees to meet the standard of Article 8, §2 ECHR. However, it does raise several concerns. One of these is the risk of the participation of the intelligence services in criminal procedure.[341] Intelligence is an administrative police activity and, as such, should not be used to establish offences. However, the administrative authorities are obliged to notify the judicial authorities when they become aware of a crime or offence.[342] In practice, it is once again to the CNCTR to be the guardian of the border between administrative intelligence surveillance and judicial procedure. The main current difficulties remain the regime of connection data as we shall *see supra* III C.

---

337. *See* Decree No. 2015-1639 of 11 Dec. 2015.
338. Namely, the Central Territorial Intelligence Service (le service central du renseignement territorial, SCRT) within the General Directorate of the National Police, the Intelligence Directorate of the Police Prefecture (la direction du renseignement de la prefecture de police DRPP), the Sub-Directorate for Operational Anticipation (la sous-direction de l'anticipation opérationnelle, SDAO) within the General Directorate of the National, the Gendarmerie and the National Prison Intelligence Service within the Prison Administration Directorate,(le service national du renseignement pénitentiaire, SNRP).
339. *See* before paras 123–127, Surveillance of Correspondence for Law Enforcement for the interceptions, and Art. 230-232 CPP for the geolocalisation techniques, Art. 706-96-20 for the uses of IMIS catcher, Art. 706-96 CPP for the sonotisation and fixation of images of certain places or vehicles.
340. *See* CNCTR, Annual Report, 2022, pp. 51–55.
341. *See* A. Guillard, *Sonorisation et fixation d'images au croisement de la procédure pénale et du renseignement*, AJ Pénal, 2023, p. 484.
342. This has been underlined by the *Conseil constitutionnel see* CC 2005-532 DC, 19 Jan. 2005, point 6.

III. Privacy in Electronic Communications (National Transposition of the e-Privacy Directive)

144. **French sources of the transposition of the e-Privacy Directive**. The e-Privacy directive (ePD) was transposed in France in 2004 by three laws. The first one amended the French Data Protection Law, also called loi informatique et libertés (LIL).[343] Currently, the main provisions related to the transposition of the ePD are introduced in Title II, which is dedicated to the national adaptation of the GDPR under Chapter IV, called Rights and Obligations for Processing in the Electronic Communication Sector. The second law is a law on electronic communications and audiovisual services,[344] which has been mainly introduced in the Post and Electronic Communications Code (Code des Postes et des Communications Electroniques (CPCE)). The third law is the law for a trusty digital economy, loi pour la confiance dans l'economie numérique, hereinafter 'LCEN'.[345]

145. **Security breach notification**. Article 83 LIL related to the security breach notification does not call for any comment. It aligns with the security breach notification of Article 4-1 ePD and that provided by Article 33 GDPR.[346] Article 83 LIL provides that such personal data and security breach are to be notified to the CNIL immediately and to the person involved when his/her privacy is at stake. The notification to the person is not necessary when 'appropriate protection measures have been implemented by the provider in order to render the data unintelligible to any person who is not authorized to access it, and that those measures were applied to the personal data affected by the personal data breach'.

146. Privacy in electronic communications in France raises three main issues regarding cookies and similar techniques: the processing of different kinds of data such as traffic, location, and connection data as a national restriction of the confidentiality of communications, and finally, the Unsolicited Direct Marketing Communications legal framework.

A. *Cookies and Similar Techniques*

147. As mentioned in recital 24 of the ePD, 'Terminal equipment of users of electronic communications networks and any information stored on such equipment are of the private sphere of the users requiring protection under the European Convention for the Protection of Human Rights and Fundamental Freedoms.' This

343. Loi n° 2004/801 du 6/8/2004 relative à la protection des personnes physiques à l'égard des traitements de données à caractère personnel et modifiant la loi n° 78 -17 du 6/1/1978 relative àl'informatique, aux fichiers et aux libertés.

344. Loi n° 2004-669 du 9 juillet 2004 relative aux communications électroniques et aux services de communication audiovisuelle.

345. Loi n° 2004-575 du 21 juin 2004 pour la confiance dans l'économie numérique. The LCEN also transposed the directive 2000/31 EC on certain legal aspects of information society services, in particular electronic commerce, in the Internal Market ('Directive on electronic commerce').

346. *See* further para. 373.

means Article 8 ECHR. The concept of terminal equipment refers to the Directive 2008/63/EC,[347] which gives a large definition of it. This includes tablets, smartphones, fixed or mobile computers, video game consoles, connected television consoles, connected TVs, a connected car, a voice assistant, etc. Article 5, §3 ePD imposes to the Member States 'to ensure that the use of electronic communications networks to store information or to gain access to information stored in the terminal equipment of a subscriber or user is only allowed on condition that the subscriber or user concerned is provided with clear and comprehensive information in accordance with Directive 95/46/EC, inter alia about the purposes of the processing, and is offered the right to refuse such processing by the data controller'. Article 82 LIL transposes in France Article 5, §3 eDP. In 2020, the CNIL adopted guidelines on the application of Article 82 LIL which refers to cookies and other tracking devices (guidelines cookies).[348] At the same time, the CNIL also adopted some recommendations[349] to help stakeholders comply.

1. Scope

148. **Cookies and beyond.** According to the CNIL, cookies and tracking devices mean 'any operation of reading and/or writing of information (hereinafter referred to as "tracers") in the subscriber's or user's electronic communications terminal equipment'.[350] The cookies are small files stored by a server on a user's terminal (computer, telephone, etc.) and associated with a web domain. A distinction is made between 'internal' cookies, which are deposited by the site visited by the Internet user, more specifically on the site's domain, and so-called third-party cookies, which are deposited on domains other than that of the main site, generally managed by third parties who have been consulted by the site visited and not by the Internet user himself.[351]

149. The CNIL considers that Article 82 LIL applies not only to cookies but also to a range of similar techniques such as local shared objects, sometimes called Flash

347. *See* Art. 1 Directive 2008/63/EC of 20 Jun. 2008 on competition in the markets in telecommunications which provides that means an 'equipment directly or indirectly connected to the interface of a public telecommunications network to send, process or receive information; in either case (direct or indirect), the connection may be made by wire, optical fibre or electromagnetically; a connection is indirect if equipment is placed between the terminal and the interface of the network'.
348. CNIL, Délibération n° 2020-091 du 17 septembre 2020 portant adoption de lignes directrices relatives à l'application de l'article 82 de la loi du 6 janvier 1978 modifiée aux opérations de lecture et écriture dans le terminal d'un utilisateur (notamment aux 'cookies et autres traceurs') et abrogeant la délibération n° 2019-093 du 4 juillet 2019.
349. CNIL, Délibération n° 2020-092 du 17 septembre 2020 portant adoption d'une recommandation proposant des modalités pratiques de mise en conformité en cas de recours aux 'cookies et autres traceurs'.
350. *See* Guidelines cookies n°2.
351. *See* CNIL website https://www.cnil.fr/fr/definition/cookie#:~:text=La%20d%C3%A9finition&text=Les%20cookies%20ont%20de%20multiples,fins%20statistiques%20ou%20publicitaires%2C%20etc.

cookies, local storage implemented as part of the HTML 5 standard, identifiers generated by terminal fingerprinting, identifiers generated by operating (whether advertising or not: IDFA, IDFV, Android ID, etc.), hardware identifiers (MAC address, serial number or any other device identifier), etc.[352] Thus, Article 5, §3 should still be applied to a range of tracking devices after the announced end of the third cookies by digital platforms. The future of the legal framework on cookies and other tracking devices is still dependent on the adoption of the e-Privacy regulation.[353]

150. **Personal data and not personal data.** Article 82 LIL, as Article 5, §3 ePD, covers any information, whether personal data or not. However, the French DPA, the CNIL, is responsible for monitoring compliance with the legality of cookies and other tracking devices.

2. Right to Prior Information

151. Article 82 recalls that 'any subscriber or user of an electronic communication service will be informed in a clear and comprehensive manner by the controller or his representative, except if previously notified, … ' this information should cover the purpose of any access to information stored in its terminal or any record data on its device. In addition, Article 83 LIL almost copies and pastes the two possible exceptions to the right to prior information from Article 5.3 ePD. First, no prior information is needed when access to data stored in the terminal or the recording of data from the terminal is exclusively intended to enable or facilitate communication by electronic means. Second, such prior information is not required when this access or recording is strictly necessary for the provision of an online communication service at the user's express request. Beyond the right to prior information, Article 82 LIL transposes in France the obligation to prior consent to the access of data stored or any record of data in the terminal of an individual. This raises several issues regarding cookies and consent.

3. Consent Issues

152. **Evolution of the prior consent requirement for the cookies and other tracking devices**. The wording of Article 82 LIL has not been changed since the GDPR. It provides that '*such access or recording may only be carried out provided that the subscriber or user has expressed after receiving said information, his*

---

352. *See* Guidelines cookies n° 13. This seems in line with the recent EPDB Guidelines 2/2023 on Technical Scope of Art. 5(3) of e-Privacy Directive, which also considered new tracking techniques such as URL and pixel tracking.
353. Proposal for a regulation concerning the respect for private life and the protection of personal data in electronic communications and repealing Directive 2002/58/EC (Regulation on Privacy and Electronic Communications), adopted by the European Commission on 10 Jan. 2017, COM(2017) 10 final.

consent, which may result from appropriate parameter settings on their connection device or any other system under their control'.[354] Before the GDPR, the CNIL admitted that continued browsing implies consent to cookies being deposited on a terminal.[355]

153. However, like the European Data Protection Board (EDPB),[356] the CNIL has changed its position on the conditions for valid consent in the case of cookies and other tracking devices. The CNIL clarifies that '*the possibilities for configuring browsers and operating systems cannot, on their own, enable users to express valid consent*'.[357] The CNIL clearly applies the GPDR requirements on the consent to the cookies and other tracking devices. Therefore, the consent must be freely given, specific, informed, and unambiguous, as mentioned in Article 4(11) GDPR.[358]

154. **The partial validation of cookie walls.** The CNIL initially mentioned in its guidelines cookies the EDPB's position, which considered that the practice of blocking access to a website or mobile application for those who do not consent to be tracked (cookie walls) did not comply with the GDPR. The argument was that the practice of cookie walls did not respect the free nature of the consent of the persons concerned. The CNIL endorsed this argument, pointing out that '*The consent can only be valid if the person concerned is able to exercise his or her choice validly and does not suffer any major inconvenience in the event of the absence or withdrawal of consen*t.'[359] The *Conseil d'Etat* challenged this general and absolute ban on cookie walls.[360] In other words, the supreme administrative judge imposed on the CNIL a case-by-case analysis of cookie walls to assess whether consent is freely given. The reformulated guidelines cookies cautiously only acknowledge the need for such a systematic analysis. By contrast, the CNIL's website gives a few clues as to the factors that the CNIL want to consider in its examination of cookie walls. The CNIL will assess 'the existence of real and satisfactory alternative(s) offered in the event of refusal of cookies'.[361] The CNIL is asking publishers to impose a cookie wall to demonstrate that Internet users will be able to go to another publisher to

354. Article 83(2) LIL.
355. *See* CNIL 5 décembre déliberation 2013-378 portant adoption d'une recommendation relative aux cookies.
356. *See* EPDB, Guidelines 05/2020 on consent under Regulation 2016/679, point 7.
357. *See* point 4 of the Deliberation n° 2020-092. The approach has been validated by the Conseil d'Etat, *see* CE, 6 Jun. 2018, Société Editions Croque Futur, n° 412589, points 7–8.
358. More details on the requirements for the consent under the GDPR *see* Jos Dumortier, Pieter Gryffroy, Ruber Roex & Yung Shin Van der Sype, *Europe, Privacy and Data protection Law*, §§537 et seq.
359. CNIL, Délibération n° 2019-093 du 4 juillet 2019 portant adoption de lignes directrices relatives à l'application de l'article 82 de la loi du 6 janvier 1978 modifiée aux opérations de lecture ou écriture dans le terminal d'un utilisateur (notamment aux cookies et autres traceurs) (rectificatif), Art. 2.
360. CE, 19 Jun. 2020, n° 434684B, point 10.
361. *See* https://www.cnil.fr/fr/cookie-walls-la-cnil-publie-des-premiers-criteres-devaluation, 16 May 2022.

access an equivalent service without having to consent to cookies. The CNIL website also addresses the question of the legality of pay walls. This is a form of cookie walls in which the publisher makes access to its content conditional either on acceptance of tracers that help remunerate its service or on payment of a sum of money. While the CNIL accepts that this is not prohibited in principle, it stresses that the fee charged to Internet users must remain reasonable. The CNIL reserves the right to assess this reasonableness on a case-by-case basis while informing publishers that they will have to be able to explain why the amount is not excessive. In the interests of transparency, the CNIL is encouraging publishers to make public the details of how they have calculated the amount charged. In practice, while there are many pay walls, players are usually not transparent about calculating the prices they charge Internet users. Finally, the CNIL website implicitly refers to a log wall, which is a technique whereby the editor requires the user to register with the site to access it. The CNIL recalls that such registration obligation needs to be justified in relation to the purpose, and the collection of data is limited to the necessity of those purposes. Since their partial validation, the legal regime for cookie walls has become particularly sophisticated. However, this practice has not yet been the subject of litigation in France.

155. **Consent-exempted cookies and tracking devices.** These exemptions are provided for in the letter of Article 5, §3 eDP. Article 82 2°) LIL recalls that no consent is required '*when the access to data stored on the terminal device of the user or the recording of information on the terminal device of the user is:*

1. Either exclusively intended to enable or facilitate communication by electronic means.
2. Or, is strictly necessary for the provision of an online communication service at the user's express request'.

The guidelines cookies entailed a non-exhaustive list of tracking devices, which the CNIL considers consent exempted. The CNIL mentions as examples:

– the tracers preserving the choice expressed by the users on the deposit of cookies;
– logs used for authentication to a service, including those designed to ensure the security of the authentication mechanism, for example by limiting robotic or unexpected access attempts;
– tracers designed to keep a record of the contents of a shopping basket on a merchant site or to invoice the user for the product(s) and/or service(s) purchased;
– logs used to personalise the user interface (for example, to choose the language or the presentation of a service), where such personalisation is an intrinsic and expected element of the service;
– tracers used to balance the load of equipment providing a communication service;

– tracers enabling paying sites to limit free access to a sample of the content free access to a sample of content requested by users (predefined quantity and/or over a limited period);
– certain audience measurement tracking devices.[362]

156. Acknowledging that most websites use audience measurement tracers, the CNIL considers that only those that are strictly necessary for the operation and administration of the sites are consent exempted.[363] This does not apply, however, to tracers that enable the overall tracking of a person's browsing by using different applications or browsing different websites.

157. The *Conseil d'Etat* pointed out that consent-exempted cookies are subject to strict interpretation. It ruled out such an exemption for the use of connection cookies to determine whether the Internet user who makes a purchase on a site has connected to this site via a link appearing on an affiliated operator. The *Conseil d'Etat* rightly pointed out that these cookies were used primarily for billing purposes between operators but were not necessary to enable an Internet user to connect to an e-commerce website, nor were they necessary for the provision of the service requested by the Internet user.[364]

158. The CNIL has also recently pointed out that to determine whether a cookie falls within the scope of the consent exemption, all its purposes must be examined. Thus, a ReCaptach mechanism whose purpose is to secure the authentication mechanism for the user's benefit and to analyse user behaviour, needs prior information and consent from the Internet user.[365]

4. Illustrations of the Control of the CNIL Regarding Cookies

159. After its 2020 guidelines, the CNIL has established a transitional period to allow website publishers to comply with the new rules before launching enforcement actions as of April 2021. The CNIL is particularly active in monitoring changes in the practices of players in the field of cookies and other tracking devices.

362. *See* point 49.
363. *See* point 50 where the CNIL mentioned for example tracers whose purpose is limited to measuring the audience for the site or application in order to meet various needs (performance measurement, detection of browsing problems, optimisation of technical performance, etc.), detecting navigation problems, optimising technical performance or ergonomics or ergonomics, estimating the power of the servers required, analysing the content content consulted, etc. For a list given that could be in the scope of the consent exemption *see* https://www.cnil.fr/fr/cookies-et-autres-traceurs/regles/cookies-solutions-pour-les-outils-de-mesure-daudience, September 2023.
364. *See* CE, n° 4526688, April 2022, Syndicat national du marketing à la performance (SNMP), point 13.
365. *See* CNIL, SAN 2023-003 du 16 mars 2023 concernant la société CITYSCOOT, point 86. *See also* CNIL, SAN-2022-025 du 29 décembre 2022 concernant la société Apple Distribution International, point 98 on the DSID.

It argues that it had a 'substantial impact'[366] on the evolution of these practices. It is true that the CNIL adopted numerous significant sanctions not only on major digital players such as Google,[367] Facebook,[368] Amazon,[369] Microsoft,[370] and Apple[371] but also on major French players such as Criteo ad'tech[372] or doctissimo website[373] and even less important French companies.[374] Most of the cases revealed infringements to Article 82 LIL for lacking information, depositing of cookies without prior consent, failure of the refusal mechanism, or impossibility to refuse cookies as easily as to accept them.

160. Finally, it is worth underlining that there is no GDPR 'one-stop shop' mechanism[375] for the application of Article 82 LIL. Thus, the CNIL is materially competent in verifying and sanctioning operations related to cookies deposited by all companies on the terminals of Internet users located in France.[376]

B. *Unsolicited Direct Marketing Communications*

161. Article L.34-5 French CPCE transposes Article 13 ePD and lays down a prohibition in principle on direct marketing communication.

---

366. *See* the review of its action plan on cookies (2020 to 2022), https://www.cnil.fr/en/evolution-practices-web-regarding-cookies-cnil-evaluates-impact-its-action-plan-0#:~:text=A%20cookie%20refusal%20rate%20on%20the%20rise&text=The%20rate%20of%20people%20declaring,tend%20to%20configure%20cookies%20less, 21 Jun. 2023.
367. CNIL, SAN 2021-023, 31 Dec. 2021 concernant les sociétés X et Y, The CNIL issued a fine of EUR 150 million against Google (EUR 90 million for Google LLC and EUR 60 million for Google Ireland Limited) for not proposing a bottom enabling the Internet user to easily refuse the deposit of these cookies.
368. CNIL, SAN 2021-024, 31 Dec. 2021 concernant Facebook Ireland Limited, a EUR 60 million fine.
369. CNIL, SAN 2020-013, 7 Dec. 2020 concernant la société X, EUR 35 million fine.
370. CNIL, SAN 2022-023, 19 Dec. 2022 concernant la société Microsoft Ireland Operations Limited infringement of Art. 82 for by depositing cookies subject to consent on the user's terminal prior to any action on his or her part and lack of possibility to refuse cookies as easily as to accept them. The CNIL imposed a penalty of EUR 60 million.
371. CNIL, SAN 2022-025, 29 Dec. 2022 concernant la société Apple Distribution International, EUR 8 millions fine.
372. CNIL, SAN 2023-009, 15 Jun. 2023 concernant la société Criteo: a EUR 40 million fine in particular for failing to verify that the persons from whom it processed data had given their consent.
373. CNIL, SAN 2023-006, 11 May 2023 concernant la société Doctissimo, *see* points 105–114 Infringement of Art. 82 of the LIL for depositing cookies subject to consent on the user's terminal prior to any action on his or her part and by rendering ineffective the refusal to deposit and read cookies for advertising purposes.
374. CNIL, SAN 2023-008, 8 Jun. 2023 concernant la société Kg Com, EUR 30,000 fine for a French society which operates several websites to offer clairvoyance consultations to its customers without respecting the prior information and consent of its visitors.
375. Articles 55 and 56 GDPR.
376. CE, 28 Jan. 2022, Societés Google LLC et Google Ireland Limited, n° 449209, point 12.

1. Scope of the Ban of Unsolicited Direct Marketing Communication of Article L.34-5 CPCE

162. **Large concept of direct marketing communication**. This covers the sending of any message intended to promote, directly or indirectly, goods, services or the image of a person selling goods or providing services. This is also extended to calls and messages designed to encourage the user or subscriber to call a premium-rate number or send a premium-rate text message, which also falls within the scope of direct prospecting.

163. **Limitation to certain modes of communication**. The ban is limited to direct marketing communications by means of automated electronic communications systems, faxes or emails, SMS, and MMS that use the contact details of a natural person, subscriber, or user without their prior consent. By contrast, this provision is not applicable to direct marketing communication by post or by phone without the use of an automatic calling machine. It such cases, which usually need a prior collect of personal data (names, addresses, phone numbers), the GDPR and the LIL should apply. This means that these direct marketing communications are possible when the data subject has been informed at the time of the collect of the use of his or her data for direct marketing purposes and was able to object to this use according to Article 21, §2 GDPR.[377]

164. **Exclusion of the application to the legal person.** France clearly opts for the limitation of the ban on individuals and excludes an application to the legal person, for instance, direct marketing communications to a generic business email (info[@]nameofthecompanie.fr).

2. The Relative Need of a Prior Consent

165. **Alignment of the required prior consent with Article 4 GDPR**. Article L.34-5 CPCE lays down an opt-in approach. This means that Direct Marketing Communications is prohibited unless the individual has given prior consent. Article L.34-5 CPCE recalls that such a consent must be freely given, informed and specific. Since the GDPR, the CNIL considered that the consent as mentioned in Article 4 GPDR should be unambiguous. This requires a positive and specific action on the part of the person concerned (for example, a dedicated tick box that is not preticked). Acceptance of the general terms and conditions of use is not sufficient. In practice, this implies that the individual should be able to withdraw his or her consent at any time. The CNIL considers that a controller does not comply with Article L.34-5 CPCE when it only indicates to the person concerned in its form at the time of collecting their data that the information provided, including their email address, may be used by the company to 'present its offers to them at a later date'.[378] The

377. *See infra*, para. 361.
378. CNIL, SAN 2022-011, 23 Jun. 2022 concernant la société Totalenergies Electricité Et Gaz France, point 17.

form should enable the data subject to object to further uses of its data for direct marketing purposes. In addition, any further communication must contain a link to unsubscribe. The CNIL also recalls that the informed consent requires that a data controller, which has not directly collected the data from the data subject, must check that its processor has informed the data subjects of the name of the partners who may send him or her direct marketing messages.[379] The CNIL considers that when a large number of partners are involved, this can be done through an exhaustive and updated list that may be made available to individuals at the time their consent is obtained via a hypertext link to the said list and to the confidentiality policies of the service providers and suppliers.[380] These requirements apply to all kinds of sales of prospect files. It avoids any legal possibility to transfer consent from partners to partners without prior information. It imposes the renewal of the consent of the data subject in case of new partners involved.

166. **The two basic exemptions of prior consent**. The first one covers the situation where the individual is already a client to whom the trader wishes to send an offer of goods or services similar to those initially purchased by the customer. This exemption requires a prior sale or provision of service. Only the same company and not a third party can use it.[381] The second exemption only applies to direct marketing communication, such as charity or communication of a political nature.

3. French Attempts to Reinforce the Regulation of Unsolicited Direct Marketing Communications

167. In addition to Article L.34-5 CPCE, several French laws have attempted to tighten the rules on abusive canvassing, whereas the results of their effectivity are mixed. This is why, recently, the French NGO, *UFC-Que Choisir?,* created new tools for facilitating the consumer to object to the transfer of his or her personal data to major French telecom companies and internet providers.[382] This website aims to help consumers regain control over their data by using the potential of the GDPR.

168. **Bloctel free of charge oppositions list**. Since 2014, the so-called Hamon Law[383] has allowed consumers to register free of charge on an opposition list against telephone canvassing.[384] This opposition list called Bloctel has been in application since 2016. Professionals are prohibited from calling people who are registered on Bloctel. Professionals are obliged to subscribe to Bloctel to remove all Bloctel subscribers from their prospect files. Article L.223-3 consumer code bans the sales or the renting of prospects who are Bloctel subscribers. Bloctel subscribers who

379. CNIL, SAN 2023-015, 12 Oct. 2023 concernant la société Groupe Canal+, point 30.
380. CNIL, SAN 2022-021, 24 Nov. 2022, concernant la société Électricité De France, point 22.
381. In such cases, the legal basic of the processing could be the legitimate interest of the data controller.
382. *See* https://www.respectemesdatas.fr/.
383. Loi n° 2014-344 du 17 Mar. 2014 relative à la consommation.
384. This has been codified in Art. L.223-1 French consumer code.

received unsolicited calls can report that on the Bloctel website. In the event of prohibited canvassing, professionals may be subject to administrative fines of up to EUR 75,000 for natural persons and EUR 275,000 for legal entities. The French administrative authority in charge of consumer protection, the Directorate-General for Competition, Consumer Affairs and Fraud Control (Direction Générale de la Concurrence, de la Consommation et de la Répression des Fraudes (DGCCRF)), controls these rules and can make public its fines.[385]

169. **Time restrictions for unsolicited phone calls for direct marketing purposes.** Since March 2023, telephone canvassing of consumers is only permitted from Monday to Friday and from 10 am to 1 pm and from 2 pm to 8 pm excepted if the consumer has given a prior and explicit consent to be reached outside of these slots. In addition, a professional may not approach the same consumer more than four times in the same month.[386]

170. **Websites for reporting unwanted communications**. The website 33700[387] enables the consumer to report unwanted SMS, including vocal spam and ping calls.[388] By contrast, the website signals spam enables to report spam related to email. More globally, the website Pharos[389] allows reporting any illegal content, including phishing[390] attempts, by sending unsolicited communications.

171. **The enlargement of the ban on unsolicited direct marketing communication**. First, since 2020,[391] Article L.223-1 consumer code includes the ban on commercial canvassing of consumers by professionals by telephone, with the aim of selling equipment or carrying out work on dwellings with a view to making energy savings or producing renewable energy. The only exception is a solicitation made in the context of the performance of an ongoing contract. Second, in 2022,[392] a law added a ban on canvassing for the personal training account (CPF). The CPF gives every working person access to a sum of money in euros for training, which was intended to democratise training. The massive success of the CPF has paved the way for abusive commercial practices aiming at forcing the purchase of training courses against the will of the worker. One of the most current practices was to make workers believe that their training rights were about to expire when this was not the case. Therefore, French law bans such canvassing, whether by telephone, by message, by email or via social networks. Failure to comply can result in a fine of

385. *See* the last published fines here https://www.bloctel.gouv.fr/sanctions.
386. Article D.223-9 Consumer Code.
387. https://www.33700.fr/.
388. Ping call is a scam that consists of receiving a call that only rings once, encouraging the consumer to call back a number that is in fact heavily overcharged in a foreign country.
389. https://www.internet-signalement.gouv.fr/PharosS1/.
390. Phishing is a fraud by which an email user is duped into revealing personal or confidential information which the scammer can use illicitly.
391. Loi n° 2020-901 du 24 Jul. 2020 visant à encadrer le démarchage téléphonique et à lutter contre les appels frauduleux.
392. Loi n° 2022-1587 du 19 Dec. 2022 visant à lutter contre la fraude au compte personnel de formation et à interdire le démarchage de ses titulaires, which introduces this ban at Art. L.6323-8-1 of the French Labour Code.

up to EUR 375,000 for a legal entity. Only canvassing relating to a training course in progress between the CPF holder and the training organisation is authorised. The DGCCRF is responsible for enforcing this ban. Third, the French Telecom administrative authority, the ARCEP, prohibited commercial canvassing platforms from making mass calls or sending text messages to individuals using numbers beginning with 06 or 07.[393]

C. French Approach on Retention of Connection Data for Enforcement Law and National Security Purposes

172. **Definition of the connection data.** Connection data, also named metadata, are not data on the content of exchanges. This includes three categories:

- **identity data** related to the identification of the user of an electronic communication system, such as the name linked to a phone number or an IP address which identifies a computer. These data are considered less privacy sensitive;
- **traffic data** which according to Article 2 ePD '*means any data processed for the purpose of the conveyance of a communication on an electronic communications network or for the billing*'. These data correspond to the list of telephone contacts, text messages, and emails received and sent, recorded in the detailed invoices of a person's communications. Based on this data, precise information about a person's private life can be revealed;
- **location data** '*means any data processed in an electronic communications network, indicating the geographic position of the terminal equipment of a user of a publicly available electronic communications service*;'.[394] This data can be used to determine a user's location more or less precisely by identifying the base station to which his smartphone or other connected object is attached.

173. A recent parliamentary report states that in France, connection data plays a major role in 85% of criminal investigations and lists in detail the several uses of these data.[395] These facts illustrate the importance of the issue of access by public authorities to connection data.

174. **The exception provided by Article 15 ePD**. Currently, data retention and access on data connection are covered by Article 15 ePD which must be read in relation to Article 5 ePD which enshrines the principle of confidentiality of communications. Article 5 ePD lays down that Member States '*shall prohibit listening, tapping, storage or other kinds of interception or surveillance of communications and the related traffic data by persons other than users, without the consent of the*

393. Décision No. 2022-1583 de l'Autorité de régulation des communications électroniques, des postes et de la distribution de la presse en date du 1er septembre 2022 modifiant la décision établissant le plan national de numérotation et ses règles de gestion.
394. Article 2 ePD.
395. Rapport du Sénat n°110 de la Commission des lois sur les modalités d'investigations recourant aux données de connexion dans le cadre des enquêtes pénales, November 2023, p. 33.

users concerned, except when legally authorised to do so in accordance with Article 15(1)'. Article 15(1) ePD provides in a similar way to Article 8, §2 ECHR that such exceptions need to be necessary, appropriate, and proportionate measures within a democratic society to safeguard a limited number of legitimate objectives of general interest: '*the prevention, investigation, detection and prosecution of criminal offences or of unauthorised use of the electronic communication system* ...'.

175. **CJEU's Jurisprudential movement on connection data**. Since the wave of terrorist attacks in London (2004) and Madrid (2006), the EU Member States are seeking a pragmatic legal framework that will enable them to use the various types of data held by digital operators to fight terrorism. Therefore, in 2006, they adopted the Directive 2006/24 EC, known as the data retention directive, which amended the ePD. The main issue was to determine to what extent Member States can adopt legislation to oblige internet service providers (ISPs) and telephone operators to retain data relating to their customers in a general and undifferentiated manner and allow public authorities access to retained data, where necessary, to fight against terrorism or organised crime. In this context, a competitive dialogue has been established between national courts and the CJEU. This leads to a particularly sophisticated body of case law establishing a framework for data retention and access to the retained data by public authorities. The famous *Digital Rights* ruling marks the starting point of this jurisprudential moment. In this case, the CJEU invalidated the retention Directive 2006/24 EC for entailing a wide-ranging and particularly serious interference with privacy and data protection fundamental rights.[396] The CJEU subsequently confirmed its approach by reiterating the ban on general and indiscriminate retention of all traffic and location data and access of public authorities to the retained data, except for fighting serious crime.[397]

176. **The rationale of French position on data retention and data access**. Referred to by the French *Conseil d'Etat* in the *La Quadrature du Net case*, the CJEU was asked to clarify whether this ban could be lifted for national security reasons. The French approach was to encourage the CJEU not to consider this issue from the angle of interference with the fundamental right to privacy and data protection, which requires compliance with a principle of proportionality to be justified. France wanted this issue to be resolved as a conflict between two fundamental rights guaranteed by the CFR. This would have meant seeking a horizontal reconciliation between the right to privacy and personal data protection on the one hand and the right to security guaranteed by Article 6 of CFR on the other hand. Furthermore, France invoked the EU's lack of competence in matters of national security according to Article 4 TEU to justify the non-application of the ePD. Although the CJEU in the *La Quadrature du Net* has relaxed its previous case law by defining a more flexible regime for data retention measures for reasons of national security, it has not followed the French approach. It, therefore, leaves Member States with little

396. *See* Europe, Privacy and Data Protection Law, paras 153 et seq.
397. CJEU, Joined Cases C-203/15 and C-698/15, Judgment of 21 Dec. 2016, Tele2 Sverige AB, ECLI: EU:C:2016:970.

room for manoeuvre when it comes to implementing a system that provides them with the means to prevent and combat the various forms of crime, including terrorism.

177. **CJEU's position in *La Quadrature du Net* case**. The CJEU has proposed an assessment grid for ranking the possibilities of interference with the fundamental rights to privacy and data protection, taking into account both the purposes for which they are processed and the types of data concerned. Only data that does not provide precise information on entire areas of the private lives of the people concerned is subject to a lighter regime. Therefore, the CJEU accepted national legislative measures that allow general and indiscriminate retention only for data relating to the civil identity of users of electronic communications systems and for the purposes of safeguarding national security, combating crime and safeguarding public security. Above this first level, the CJEU accepted general and indiscriminate retention of IP addresses assigned to the source of an Internet connection, only for the purposes of safeguarding national security, combating serious crime and preventing serious threats to public security, and for a period that is limited in time to what is strictly necessary. The more intrusive the data, the less acceptable is its general and indiscriminate retention. Therefore, the CJEU accepted only the limited possibility of general and indiscriminate retention of traffic and location data for the purposes of safeguarding national security. Three guarantees are required to implement this form of retention. First, the Member State concerned should demonstrate that it is confronted with a serious threat to national security that is shown to be genuine and present or foreseeable. Second, the decision imposing such an instruction needs to be subject to effective review, either by a court or by an independent administrative body whose decision is binding. This review should aim to verify that a serious threat exists and that the conditions and safeguards are observed. Third, the instruction should be given only for a period that is limited in time to what is strictly necessary but which may be extended if that threat persists. More generally, the CJEU confirmed the possibility of targeted retention of traffic and location data. This applies to purposes of safeguarding national security, combating serious crime and preventing serious threats to public security. Such targeting can take three forms. Targeting can be linked to people, which need to be chosen based on objective and non-discriminatory factors. Targeting can also be geographic. Finally, targeting is also temporal. The retention is limited in time to what is strictly necessary but may be extended.

178. **The impact of the CJEU's position on French law.**[398] After the *La Quadrature du Net* case, the *Conseil d'Etat,* the *Cour de cassation* and the *Conseil constitutionnel* tried to implement the interpretation of the CJEU in French law. First, the *Cour de cassation* strictly applied the CJEU ruling. It considered that Article L.34-1 of the CPCE did not comply with EU law because it allowed for the general retention of so-called connection data. Second, the *Cour de cassation* also

398. On this issue *see* n° spécial RFDA September 2023 Les données de connexion, droits fondamentaux et lutte contre la criminalité, pp. 603–640.

declared that several articles of the CPP did not conform to the EU law, which provided access to retained data by the French public authorities by the authorisation of the public prosecutor. The *Cour de cassation* argued that only the investigating judge is an independent authority who can authorise access to retained data.[399]

179. By contrast, the *Conseil d'Etat* was more reluctant to accept the position of the CJEU. While it refused to rule *ultra vires* against the CJEU as requested by the French government,[400] the *Conseil d'Etat* has clearly established itself as the guardian of the fundamental interests of the French Nation.[401]

180. First, the *Conseil d'Etat* implicitly validated the existence of a serious and persistent threat to national security in France,[402] justifying in practice general and indiscriminate retention of traffic and location data for the purposes of safeguarding national security. Second, the *Conseil d'Etat* accepted that the expedited retention mechanism allows police and judicial authorities access to data initially collected for national security purposes.[403] However, the CJEU had clearly stated that the expedited retention of traffic and location data was acceptable for national security reasons but that access to this data should not be open to use for other purposes.[404] These two adjustments enabled the *Conseil d'Etat* not to call into question the ongoing criminal proceedings while asking the legislator to introduce into French law the guarantees requested by the CJEU. On the one hand, the possibility of general and undifferentiated retention of traffic and location data had to be limited to purpose of safeguarding national security.

181. Second, French legislator had to introduce a periodic review of the existence of a serious, actual, present, or foreseeable threat to national security. Finally, the lawmaker was required to implement retention measures subject to prior control by an AAI with the power to give its assent or by a court, except in duly justified cases of urgency. Following these rulings, two French laws were passed to bring French law into line. In 2021, the first one amended Article L.34-1 of the French Data Protection Code (CPCE), grading retention obligations according to data category and purpose.[405] In 2022, the second one introduced Article L.60-1-2 CPP, which restricts access to traffic and location data to investigations into the most serious criminal offences. Despite this progress, France's compliance with the CJEU's requirements remains fragile. It should be noted that the analysis grid proposed by

399. Cass., 12 Jul. 2022, n° 21-83.710, 21-83.820, 21-84.096, 20-86.652.
400. *See* CE, 21 Apr. 2021, n° 393099, point 8.
401. CE, 21 Apr. 2021, n° 393099, points 9, 10 and the English Press release Connection data: the Council of State conciliates the implementation of European Union law and the effectiveness of the fight against terrorism and crime, https://www.conseil-etat.fr/en/news/connection-data-the-council-of-state-conciliates-the-implementation-of-european-union-law-and-the-effectiveness-of-the-fight-against-terrorism-and.
402. CE, 21 Apr. 2021, n° 393099, point 44.
403. CE, 21 Apr. 2021, n° 393099, point 55.
404. CJEU, Joined Cases C-511/18, C-512/18 and C-520/18, Judgment of 6 Oct. 2020, La Quadrature du Net and Others, ECLI:EU:C:2020:791, point 164.
405. Loi n° 2021-998 du 30 Jul. 2021 relative à la prévention d'actes de terrorisme et au renseignement.

the CJEU for connection data is not fully respected in France. In practice, connection data continues to be stored in a generalised and undifferentiated manner. Similarly, the framework for public authorities' access to this data leaves much to be desired. Three points are particularly controversial. First, allowing police and judicial authorities access to data initially collected for national security purposes through the expedited retention mechanism calls into question the granularity of conservation regimes proposed by the CJEU. The CJEU recently reiterated the need to make a clear distinction between processing operations authorised for national security purposes and those relating to crime, including serious crime. Thus, the legality of the former cannot automatically be extended to the legality of the latter.[406] Second, one of the main difficulties is that the concepts of 'serious crime' and 'prevention of serious threats to public security' are imprecise. The question arises as to whether these concepts should be considered autonomous concepts of EU law, allowing the CJEU to interpret them uniformly on a case-by-case basis. If not, the room for manoeuvre left to the Member States could lead to contradictory interpretations, making it possible to circumvent the grid proposed by the CJEU.[407] It could also be an issue for the development of European judicial cooperation in case of the use of collected data in a Member State, which could be considered illegal in another Member State based on a different interpretation of those concepts.[408]

182. Third, the independence of the body authorising access to connection data is another sensitive issue. The French approach is to opt for a judge rather than an independent authority. There is, however, a debate on the nature of the judge likely to meet the criteria of independence referred to by the CJEU in its *H. K., Prokuratuur* judgment.[409] While the *Conseil constitutionnel* has raised no objection to the public prosecutor[410] taking on this role, the *Cour de cassation*[411] has ruled that only the investigating judge could be considered independent. However, to avoid invalidating many ongoing proceedings, the *Cour de cassation* considered that the absence of an independent review would lead to the invalidity of the proceedings only if the applicant could establish the existence of prejudice. In practice, this restrictive condition made it possible to cover the authorisations given by the French Public Prosecutors. To regularise this fragile situation, a recent parliamentary report[412] proposes that in the future, the power to authorise access to connection data by public authorities should instead be given to judges responsible for rights and freedoms (JLD). More generally, many French players, both institutional[413] and

406. CJEU C-140/20, Judgment of 22 Apr. 2022, Commissioner of An Garda Síochána, ECLI: EU:C:2022:258, points 63–64.
407. On this issue *see* Brunessen Bertrand, *La Cour de justice et les données de connexion: vers un European Data Network*, RFDA 2023, p. 615.
408. *See* the onjoing case before the CJEU, Case C-670/22.
409. CJEU C-746/18, 2 Mar. 2021, H. K., Prokuratuur, ECLI:EU:C:2021:152, points 53–54.
410. CC, Decision 2022-993 QPC, 20 May 2022.
411. Cass., 12 Jul. 2022, n° 21-83.710, 21-83.820, 21-84.096, 20-86.652.
412. Rapport du Sénat n° 110 de la Commission des lois sur les modalités d'investigations recourant aux données de connexion dans le cadre des enquêtes pénales, November 2023, p.17.
413. *See* above-mentioned senatorial report, p. 16.

scholars,[414] are questioning the relevance of the sophisticated analysis grid proposed by the CJEU and are calling for more practical solutions to secure criminal investigations while protecting the rights and freedoms of individuals.

414. *See,* recently, RFDA September 2023 Les données de connexion, droits fondamentaux et lutte contre la criminalité, pp. 603–640.

Part II. French Personal Data Protection Law

§1. Background

183. **Historical French Approach to Data Protection.** France is one of the pioneer European states in data protection law. The first French Data Protection Law was adopted in January 1978. It is called LIL.[415] This originally short law laid the foundations of French personal Data Protection Law. The unchanged Article 1 of the LIL provides that:

> Information technology must serve the needs of every citizen. It must evolve in the context of international cooperation. It must not violate human identity, human rights, privacy, or individual or civil liberties.

184. **The progressive evolution of the LIL under EU Law**. From its inception, the LIL applied to both the public and private sectors and gave rise to a national administrative and independent authority, the CNIL, to ensure that it was applied. The deep changes to the LIL were made to meet or anticipate European obligations. In 2004, the law, which transposed Directive 95/46 EC into French law,[416] rewrote practically the original LIL, of which only the title and Article 1 were retained. In 2016, the Digital Republic Law[417] modified the LIL in anticipation of the GDPR by introducing into French law new rights regarding the protection of minors and the use of the data of deceased persons, as well as improved the powers of the CNIL. Finally, the French adaptation to the GDPR and the transposition of the directive 2016/680[418] EU have led to a profound rewriting and codification of the LIL.

---

415. Loi n° 78-17 du 6 Jan. 1978 relative à l'informatique, aux fichiers et aux libertés, https://www.legifrance.gouv.fr/download/securePrint?token=JSG0YTMFEk0LvN@C!G2K.

416. Loi n° 2004-801 du 6 août 2004 relative à la protection des personnes physiques à l'égard des traitements de données à caractère personnel et modifiant la loi n° 78-17 du 6 janvier 1978 relative à l'informatique, aux fichiers et aux libertés.

417. Loi n° 2016-1321 du 7 Oct. 2016 pour une République numérique, JORF n° 0235 du 8 octobre 2016 Texte, n° 1.

418. Directive EU 2016/680 on the protection of natural persons with regard to the processing of personal data by competent authorities for the purposes of the prevention, investigation, detection or prosecution of criminal offences or the execution of criminal penalties, and on the free movement of such data, and repealing Council Framework Decision 2008/977/JHA, OJ L 119/89.

185. **Reform of the LIL with the 2016 EU personal data package.** France is part of the group of Member States which decided to adopt one law for both the adaptation of the GDPR and the transposition of the 2016/680 Directive. Therefore, the new LIL consists of five titles, including one part dedicated to the implementation of GDPR and one to the transposition of the Police Directive. More precisely, Title 1 contains common provisions divided into six chapters. Chapter 1 is dedicated to the principles and the definitions, with a lot of referrals to the GDPR. Chapter 2 is devoted to the CNIL, including the strengthening of its missions and powers due to the European Data Law package. Chapter 3 looks at the modalities of data processing of the national identification number.[419] Chapter 4 addresses the few remaining prior formalities. Chapter 5 deals with the remedies in data protection, and Chapter 6 with the penalties.[420] Title II of the LIL details the legal framework applicable to the GDPR processing with some uses of the margin of manoeuvre, also called opening clauses. In general, France has made moderate use of these open clauses, mostly for the benefit of public authorities or to grant some additional rights to data subjects. Title II is divided into five chapters. Chapter 1 includes general provisions regarding its scope, the lawfulness of the processing, conditions for the consent of the minor, processing of personal data relating to criminal convictions and offences and automated individual decision-making. Chapter 2 is dedicated to the rights of the data subject. Chapter 3 details the obligations of the data controller and the processor. It includes some provisions for specific processing situations. It looks at health processing and processing for archiving purposes in the public interest, scientific, historical research purposes, or statistical purposes, or processing for journalistic purposes and the purposes of academic, artistic, or literary expression. Chapter 4 provides rules on electronic communication, which are the transposition of the Directive (EC) 2002/58 (e-Privacy Directive). Chapter 5 contains provisions on the processing of personal data of deceased persons. Title 3 of the LIL focuses on the transposition of the Directive (EU) 2016/680 (Police Justice Directive),[421] whereas Title 4 rules the processing relating to the defence and national security. Finally, Title V included some provisions relating to the French overseas.

186. **LIL decree's application**. Furthermore, in 2019, a new application decree of the LIL was adopted.[422] The decree details the composition and the functioning of the CNIL for the accomplishment of its different missions, some elements of the rights of the data subjects, the obligations of the data controllers and processors, and specific processing situations.

419. Also called in French NIR national d'identification des personnes physiques, NIR.
420. Some GDPR violations can be punished by five years' imprisonment and by a fine of EUR 30,000 according to Art. 226-16 to 24 of the French penal code. These penalties existed before in French law and were not used in praxis.
421. Directive (EU) 2016/680 of the European Parliament and of the Council of 27 Apr. 2016 on the protection of natural persons with regard to the processing of personal data by competent authorities for the purposes of the prevention, investigation, detection or prosecution of criminal offences or the execution of criminal penalties, on the free movement of such data, and repealing Council Framework Decision 2008/977/JHA, OJ L 119, 4.5.2016, pp. 89–131.
422. Décret n° 2019-536, 29 May 2019 pris pour l'application de la loi n° 78-17 du 6 janvier 1978 relative à l'informatique, aux fichiers et aux libertés.

187. While the LIL underwent a few changes between 2018 and 2023, its structure was affected in 2024 by the law aimed at securing and regulating the digital space, abbreviated in French as SREN (Loi pour Réguler et Sécuriser l'Espace Numérique, law aimed at securing and regulating the digital space). The SREN is a flagship text which adapts French law to the new texts of the digital single market, mainly the Digital Services Act (DSA),[423] and the Data Governance Act (DGA)[424] while anticipating the adaptation to the Data Act.[425] The adoption of the SREN led to the addition of two new titles to the LIL. The title IV bis relates to the data altruism and the title IV ter relates to the provisions applicable to online platform providers under the DSA. These two titles extend the tasks and strengthen the powers of the CNIL.[426]

188. **Data protection rules beyond the LIL.** Around thirty-five French codes contain articles with specific provisions on personal data protection, such as the CPCE, the Energy Code, the Defense Code (CD), the CP, and the CRPA. The CSI covers the processing of personal data in connection with video protection systems and those implemented in the context of intelligence. In 2024, the above mentioned SREN introduced into French law a system for monitoring the processing of personal data carried out by the courts in the exercise of their judicial functions (Articles 45 and 47 SREN). These provisions have been incorporated into the Code of Administrative Justice, the Code of Judicial Organisation and the Code of Financial Courts. The *Conseil d'Etat* is now the competent supervisory authority for compliance with personal protection law by administrative courts and the Tribunal des conflits in the exercice of their judicial functions,[427] while the *Cour de cassation* performs this role for the judiciary[428] and the Cour des comptes for financial courts.[429]

§2. Scope of the National Law

I. A Broad Material Scope

189. The LIL has a broad material scope. According to its Article 2, it applies not only to all processing by both private persons and public authorities, processing

423. Regulation (EU) 2022/2065 of the European Parliament and of the Council of 19 Oct. 2022 on a Single Market For Digital Services and amending Directive 2000/31/EC (Digital Services Act), *OJ L 277, 27.10.2022, pp. 1–102.*
424. Regulation (EU) 2022/868 of the European Parliament and of the Council of 30 May 2022 on European data governance and amending Regulation (EU) 2018/1724 (Data Governance Act), *OJ L 152, 3.6.2022, pp. 1–44.*
425. Regulation (EU) 2023/2854 of the European Parliament and of the Council of 13 Dec. 2023 on harmonised rules on fair access to and use of data and amending Regulation (EU) 2017/2394 and Directive (EU) 2020/1828 (Data Act), *OJ L, 2023/2854, 22.12.2023.*
426. *See* for more details paras 426, 428 and 432.
427. *See* Art. L.115-1 Code of Administration justice
428. *See* Art. L.453-1 to Art. L.453-2. Code of the judiciary Organisation,
429. *See* Art. L. 111-18 Code of Financial Courts.

in the scope of EU law[430] but also in the sole scope of national law. As such, the LIL[431] applies to the processing of personal data of deceased persons[432] and processing of data in the interests of state safety and defence.[433] This illustrates the French political will to maintain a single data protection law. In a way, LIL is part of France's legal heritage. The consequence of this choice has been a creeping harmonisation between the regime for purely national processing operations and those covered by the European data protection package

190. Recently, the CNIL stated that processing relating to national sovereignty, such as the organisation and holding of presidential and legislative elections or referendums, did not fall within the competence of the EU.[434] Formally, that processing could not be considered processing in the interests of state safety and defence. Consequently, only the first title of the LIL should apply to them. The issue was that the first title of the LIL only contained principles and did not include any rights for the data subject. Therefore, the government decided to extend the scope of the GDPR to this category of national processing. This anticipated a solution adopted by the CJEU.[435]

191. Article 2 LIL defines its material scope by mentioning that it applies to automated and non-automated processing of personal data except for strictly personal or domestic activities. This exception, which dates to Directive 95/46 EC, has been maintained by the GDPR. Due to the European harmonisation, the LIL contains no definition of personal data or processing and merely states that the definitions applicable in principle are those in Article 4 GDPR.

II. A French Territory-Oriented Geographical Scope

192. The LIL applies to 'the processing of personal data which takes place in the context of the activities of a single establishment of a controller or processor in French territory, whether or not the processing takes place in France'.[436]

193. France added a provision regarding the law applicable in cross-border cases in the exercise of the national margin of manoeuvre. This provision aims to resolve potential horizontal conflicts between national laws regarding the implementation of opening clauses. In such hypothesis and according to Article 3, §2, the LIL applies

430. This means GDPR and Police Justice Directive.
431. *See* Arts 84–86 LIL.
432. Recital 27 GDPR records that the GDPR does not apply to the personal data of deceased persons but let it to Member States.
433. *See* Title IV of the LIL. The LIL uses the outdated term 'State Safety' and not 'State Security' *see* para. 600.
434. CNIL, Délibération 2021-007, 14 janvier 2021 portant avis sur un projet de décret en *Conseil d'Etat* instituant une télé-procédure pour l'établissement des procurations de vote.
435. CJEU, C-306/21, -Case-- *omisia za zashtita na lichnite danni, Tsentralna izbiratelna komisia* 20 Oct. 2022, ECLI:EU:C:2022:813.
436. *See* Art. 3 LIL.

to the data subjects, who are residents of France. Therefore, the data subject rights of France's residents are secured. The LIL provides an exception for processing carried out for journalistic purposes or academic, artistic, or literary expression. In this situation, the establishment of the controller or processor is the criterion for the application of the LIL. This provision could produce a conflict with Member States, which will use an alternative criterion.

194. Furthermore, in application of Article 3 GDPR, the LIL applies to processing of personal data of data subjects who are in France by a controller or processor established outside of the EU when it offers services to data subjects or when it monitors their behaviour in France. Consequently, the CNIL declared its competence for examination of processing of Discord Inc. based on three grounds. First, Discord Inc. processes personal data of people living in France. Second, all the pages of this application are available in French. Third, Discord Inc. through its website and application is directly related to the offering of services to the French data subject such as '*the creation of an account, the provision of the Discord messaging platform and social network or the purchases*'.[437] The CNIL recalled that the controller established outside of the EU does not benefit from the one-stop-shop mechanism of Article 56, which enables each national DPA to control the conformity of their processing of people who are in their territory.[438]

195. The CNIL also had the opportunity to declare its competence in controlling the processing of personal data of people based in France by Clearview AI, which was established in the USA. Therefore, the CNIL considered that the facial recognition software developed by Clearview AI is based on the extraction of publicly available images from the Internet, including personal data of people living in France. The CNIL detailed that Clearview processing aims at creating a behavioural profile of each person whose personal data is collected with the purpose of identifying and gathering information about the person. The CNIL declared that '*the automated processing of data allowing the creation of this behavioural profile and its availability to persons making queries in the company's search engine must be qualified as Internet monitoring*'.[439] It concluded that this matches the concept of monitoring of behaviour which takes place in the EU described in Article 3.2.b GDPR.[440]

196. By contrast, the CNIL has declined its competence and the application of the LIL based on Article 3 GDPR in a recent *Luscha* case.[441] The CNIL considered that the foreign company processes personal data of people living in the EU but that

437. *See* CNIL, SAN 2022-020, 10 Nov. 2022 concernant la société Discord Inc., point 20. The CNIL also checked that Discord.Inc has a representative in Europe according to the Art. 27 GDPR.
438. *Ibid.*, point 25.
439. CNIL, SAN 2022-019, 17 Oct. 2022 concernant la société Clearview AI, point 37.
440. Similarly, the CNIL claimed its competence on the processing of personal data by Monsanto for monitoring the behaviour of French person potentially useful for the renewal of the authorisation of glyphosate in Europe within the elaboration of a data base by a public relation agency qualified as processor established in France. *See* CNIL, SAN-2021-012, 26 Jul. 2021, points 49 to 55.
441. CNIL, SAN 2022-024, 20 Dec. 2022 concernant la société Lusha Systems Inc.

those processes could not be qualified for monitoring their behaviour. The CNIL declared that '*the constitution of the database by the company is based solely on the reconciliation of professional contact data (telephone, e-mail address) with the identity of people whose profiles are visited on LinkedIn in order to verify their veracity*'.[442] To get around this difficulty, an amendment was introduced in 2024 by the SREN, amending the LIL. It is now stipulated that the LIL applies to 'the processing of personal data relating to individuals present on French territory by a controller or processor who is not established in the European Union, where such processing relates to the monitoring of the behaviour of such individuals within the European Union, in particular by collecting their personal data with a view to reconciling it with data relating to their online activity'.[443] However, the final formula chosen remains ambiguous and its added value in relation to Article 3 of the GDPR has yet to be demonstrated.

197. Finally, the LIL applies not only in Metropolitan France but also in the French overseas, sometimes with some specificities mentioned in its Articles 125–128.

§3. CONCEPTS

198. While there are certain particularities in French data protection law, the French authorities respect the European harmonisation of concepts. This paragraph will, therefore, give some illustrations of the implementation of the GDPR concepts in France.

I. Personal Data

199. **A concept imported from EU Law**. Originally, the LIL did not know the concept of personal data but referred to the concept of nominative information, *informations nominatives*. Article 4 of the 1978 LIL declared that nominative information '*is information which allows, in any form, directly or indirectly, the identification of the natural persons to whom it applies, whether the processing is carried out by a natural person or a legal person*'. This notion was less extensive than that of personal data.[444] The concept of personal data was introduced in France in 2004 with the transposition of the 1995 Directive. Currently, the LIL no longer contains a definition of personal data and simply refers to Article 4 of the GDPR.[445]

200. **Examples of French Case law on personal data concept**. In various case laws, French judges had the opportunity, including before the GDPR, to clarify the

442. *See* point 47.
443. *See* new article 3 I last paragraph LIL.
444. Anne Debet, Jean Massot & Nathalie Metallinos, *Informatiques et Libertés*, Lextenso, 2015, pp. 239 et seq.
445. *See* Art. 2 LIL.

concept of personal data. As an illustration, in 2016, the *Cour de cassation* qualified an IP address as personal data.[446] The *Conseil d'Etat* considered that addresses Mac of mobile phones are personal data.[447] More recently, the *Conseil d'Etat* qualified data collected by drones with cameras as personal data even though the disputed use of the camera did not allow the identification of the persons filmed and no images were recorded. Those drones were used by the police only for the purpose of controlling the respect of the lockdown. Nevertheless, the *Conseil d'Etat* declared that the drones were 'likely to collect identifying data and do not include any technical device to prevent the information collected from leading to the identification of the persons to whom it relates for purposes other than those currently in use'.[448] Therefore, the *Conseil d'Etat* illustrate that the mere potential for identification is sufficient to qualify data as personal data.

201. **CNIL's statements on personal data concept**. Deliberations of the CNIL included clarification on the delimitation of concept of personal data. In its *Criteo* case, the CNIL pointed out that pseudonymised data retain their status as personal data. Criteo collects the browsing data of Internet users thanks to the Criteo tracker (cookie) which is placed on their terminals when they visit certain Criteo partner websites. Through this tracker, the company analyses browsing habits to determine which advertiser and for which product it would be most relevant to display an advertisement to a particular user. Then, it participates in real-time bidding and displays personalised advertising if it wins the bid. The CNIL emphasised although the company does not directly have the identity of the individuals to whom the terminals on which cookies are stored are linked, it can re-identify them by 'reasonable means'.[449]

202. In its *Société nouvelle de l'annuaire français (SNAF)* case, the CNIL clarified the distinction between personal data and data of legal person. A directory company claimed that the data it processed was company data. The CNIL has reiterated its consistent position in this area. *'The records relating to the companies listed in the directory accessible from the company's website include, in particular, the surnames, first names and addresses of individuals when they have the status of self-employed entrepreneur or when they practise a liberal profession without being a member of a practising body. Consequently, the data on the forms relates to an identified natural person and is therefore "personal data" within the meaning of the GDPR.'*[450]

---

446. *See* Cass., 1st civ., 12016, n° 12-22-595.
447. CE, 8 fév. 2017, n° 393714, point 5.
448. CE, 18 May 2020, n° 440442 point 16.
449. CNIL, SAN 2023-009, 15 Jun. 2023 Criteo, point 41. The CNIL underlined that 'in certain cases, in addition to data relating to browsing events, the company collects other data which facilitates re-identification, such as the electronic addresses of people who have browsed from an authenticated (or "logged") environment, in hashed form, corresponding identifiers generated by other players, the IP address in hashed form or the user agent of the terminal used.', point 40.
450. CNIL, SAN 2021-014, 15 Sep. 2021 concernant la Société nouvelle de l'annuaire français (SNAF), 25. *See* before the GDPR, CNIL n° 85-45, 15 Oct. 1985, and the CE, 30 Dec. 2015, n° 376845, point 8.

203. **Personal data of deceased persons.** France has opted for a broad definition of the concept of personal data by including the data of deceased persons. Thus, Chapter V of the Title II of the LIL is devoted to the processing of personal data of deceased persons. This chapter was introduced by the Digital Republic Act of 2016. This chapter specifies the conditions under which a data subject may define directives on the retention, erasure, and disclosure of his or her personal data after death.[451]

II. Filing System

204. Curiously, Article 2 LIL has maintained the definition of a filing system, which repeats word for word that of Article 4.6 GDPR. '*Filing system*' means any structured set of personal data which are accessible according to specific criteria, whether centralised, decentralised or dispersed on a functional or geographical basis;' This copy-past of the GDPR may be due to the title of the law, which includes the term filing systems. This concept is used in the context of manual processing, as French case law illustrates. Personal data contained in the personal file of an employee detained by his employer constitutes a filing system within the meaning of the provisions of Article 2 LIL.[452] On this basis, the *Conseil d'Etat* granted a right of access to his personal data contained in his personal file. In the same way, the *Cour de cassation* considered that notes containing personal assessments of a person's service in the administration, recorded by the secretary of a department head in a computerised directory, constituted a filing system within the meaning of the LIL.[453] Such processing of personal data needed a prior authorisation which was lacking in this case.

III. Processing of Personal Data

205. The concept of processing of personal data is not defined in the French LIL. Even before the GDPR, this concept was broadly interpreted in French case law and by the CNIL. It includes not only the collection and the recording of personal data, such as comments introduced in the customer database of bank[454] but also the disclosure of personal data through the online publication of a not totally anonymised case law database.[455]

451. *See* below para. 320.
452. CE, 20 Oct. 2010, n° 327916, Société Centrapel.
453. Crim., 8 Sep. 2015, n° 13-85.587.
454. CE, Ass., 3 Dec. 1999, n° 197060 Caisse crédit mutuel de Bain Tresboeuf.
455. CE, 23 Mar. 2015, Lexeek n° 35317.

206. Recently, the CNIL adopted guidelines regarding cookies and other tracking devices[456] which clarified the use of such tracking devices for collecting IP addresses, emails, and other technical identifiers in processing of personal data.

207. In the context of the COVID-19 pandemic, the *Conseil d'Etat* clarified under which conditions the processing of thermal cameras constituted processing of personal data within the meaning of the GDPR. '*Where a thermal imaging camera, installed at the disposal of a given public, has the sole function of providing instantaneous information to persons who wish to do so, without the intervention of a third party or a person handling the equipment, without any consequences as to access to a place, good or service, and without recording or communication of the data other than to the person concerned, so that the instantaneous information captured by the equipment is not accessible or usable by the person responsible for it, who does not collect any data with this equipment, this camera cannot be considered as giving rise to processing within the meaning and for the application of the GDPR. On the other hand, even though the thermal imaging cameras used do not record data, if they allow information to be captured by a person acting on behalf of the person who decided to use them, and if the latter, on the basis of this data, decides on an action, they must be considered as giving rise to data collection and use operations, and therefore to processing within the meaning of Article 4 of the GDPR.*'[457] As a result, the installation of a thermal camera by a city in its premises to indicate to people who so wish by a colour code that their temperature is higher than normal does not in itself constitute processing of personal data. By contrast, the use of a portable thermal camera by communal agents in schools to control and ask people with an abnormal temperature to leave the school immediately and in case children ask their parents to pick them up is qualified as a processing health data. The context of such temperature collection implies a prior knowledge of the identity of the data subjects which is a decisive criterion for the qualification of processing of personal data.

208. Similarly, the use of a surveillance device to collect data through the capture of images by drone, to transmit them, in some cases, to the command centre of the police for real-time viewing and to use them to verify compliance with containment rules during the COVID-19 pandemic was qualified as processing personal data.[458] Such a qualification is maintained if the images collected by the drone are blurred prior to transmission to the command centre of the police.[459] The judge considers that blurring is an intermediate step in a set of processing of personal data. In other words, blurring does not affect the nature of the collected data which remains personal data because natural persons are likely to be identified at least indirectly.

---

456. Délibération n° 2020-091, 17 Sep. 2020 portant adoption de lignes directrices relatives à l'application de l'article 82 de la loi du 6 janvier 1978 modifiée aux opérations de lecture et écriture dans le terminal d'un utilisateur (notamment aux 'cookies et autres traceurs') et abrogeant la délibération n° 2019-093 du 4 juillet 201.
457. CE, 26 Jun. 2020, n° 441065, point 15.
458. CE ord., 18 May 2020, n° 440442.
459. CE ord., 22 Dec. 2020, n° 446155, points 6–7.

IV. Controller Versus Processor or Recipient

209. The controller is the person which determines the purposes and means of processing, while the processor processes personal data on behalf of the controller. The recipient is a person to whom personal data is disclosed. A reading of the CNIL's deliberations gives some significant examples of cases where the distribution of these roles between the players was decisive in determining the extent of their obligations. Furthermore, these concepts are dynamic and need to be interpreted *in concreto* for each category of processing.[460]

210. **The controller can be a specific service of public authority**, as illustrated by the *OCEAN* case. The database OCEAN is a processing of personal data for the management of school examinations and competitions created by the Ministry of National Education based on the arrêté of 22 April 2013.[461] The Ministry is the controller of OCEAN because it determines its purposes and its means in this arrêté. By contrast, the rectorate services are described as the recipient of the processing to which the personal data of OCEAN are disclosed.[462] Nevertheless, a rectorate service who decides to send an Excel file extracted from OCEAN containing the baccalaureate holders of his department who obtained a very good mention to a parliamentarian has been qualified as a controller by the CNIL. In its deliberation, the CNIL underlined the autonomous decision of the rectorate service to transfer this file to the parliamentarian without controlling whether this third party was habilitated for such disclosure, which was not the case.[463] Furthermore, the CNIL noted that the rectorate service delivered more data than the parliamentarian was asking and decided alone without consulting the Data Protection Officer (DPO) of the Ministry of the means of extraction. The CNIL denounced the fact that this sending of large quantities of minors' data had also been done without any security measures, which constituted an aggravating fact for the controller.

211. **Delimitation between data controllers and processors**. In its *Monsanto* case,[464] the CNIL had to determine who was the controller of a file entitled 'French Monsanto stakeholders database – cultivating trust', which contained personal data of 201 people such as members of environment, farmers, health NGOs, journalists, civil servants, academics, and politicians. The file was created by a public relations agency to influence the renewal of the authorisation of the use of glyphosate in Europe. Monsanto claimed the public relations agency took the initiative on its own to create this file. Monsanto argued that it was only the beneficiary of a service and

---

460. *See also* CNIL, SAN 2021-020 du 28 Dec. 2021 Slimpay software company which sales solutions for managing subscriptions and recurring payments in the Single Euro Payments Area as a processor and became controller for the processing of internal research into an anti-fraud mechanism in a situation of data breach. Points 30–32.

461. Arrêté du 22 avril 2013 portant création d'un traitement automatisé de données à caractère personnel relatif à la gestion des examens et concours scolaires dénommé OCEAN, Jorf n° 0104 du 4 mai 2013.

462. *See* Art. 3 of the above-mentioned arrêté.

463. CNIL, SAN 2020-006, 3 Sep. 2020, point 2.

464. CNIL, SAN 2021-012, 26 Jul. 2021.

not the controller. By contrast, the CNIL qualified Monsanto as the controller because it considered that by contracting the public relations agency, Monsanto had a clear purpose of '*mapping the stakeholders in the debate on the renewal of the authorisation of the use of glyphosate in the European Union*'. The CNIL deduced from the analysis of several clauses of the contract between Monsanto and the public relations agency that the agency was '*explicitly required to list stakeholders in the campaign to renew the authorisation of glyphosate in Europe*'.[465] Furthermore, the investigation allowed the CNIL to find evidence of the implication of Monsanto in the follow-up of the tasks carried out by the public relations agency in relation to this conflicted file.[466] According to the CNIL, '*it was the fact that Monsanto, the principal, decided to accept the proposal made by … [the public relation agency], and to contractually ask it to carry out operations on its behalf as a service provider, that allowed the processing to exist*'.[467] The fact that Monsanto then claims that it did not use this file does not make it any less of a controller.

212. In another case, CNIL qualified a parent company as the controller for the data processing of all its subsidiaries. In this case, data processing is concerned with the creation of a user account on mobile applications or websites and the collection of geolocation data on rented vehicles.[468] The parent company was the one which determined the means and the purposes of all these processing.

213. **Illustrations of joint controllers**. Recent CNIL cases illustrate the implementation of the concept of joint controller, where the purposes and the means are determined jointly by several companies. For example, Tik Tok Irlande and Tik Tok UK are joint controllers for processing '*consisting of operations of access or registration of information in the terminal of users residing in France when using the TIKTOK social network, in particular on the "tiktok.com" site and the TIKTOK sub-domains*'.[469] The CNIL applies the concept of joint controller by mentioning the CJEU's case on the witnesses of Jehovah.[470] The interweaving of players in the field of targeted advertising also provides examples of joint controllers. In its *Criteo* case, the CNIL underlines that '*the company and its partners' sites from which the Criteo cookie is deposited on the Internet user's terminal are jointly responsible for depositing the Criteo cookie and for the collection of Internet user data using this cookie*.'[471]

465. *Ibid.*, point 38.
466. *Ibid.*, point 39.
467. *Ibid.*, point 43.
468. *See* CNIL, SAN 2022-015, 7 Jul. 2022, concernant la société Ubeeqo International, point 28. *See also* SAN 2022-009, 15 Apr. 2022 concernant la société Dedalus Biologie, point 30.
469. *See* CNIL, SAN 2022-027 du 29 décembre 2022 concernant les sociétés Tiktok Information Technologies Uk Limited et Tiktok Technology Limited, point 52.
470. *See* CJEU, 10 July 2018, Case C-25/17.
471. *See* CNIL, SAN 2023-009, 15 Jun. 2023, Criteo, point 55.

§4. MINORS

214. Children, as vulnerable persons, merit specific online protection[472] which includes protection of their personal data. Such protection aims at preventing misuse of their personal data and premature and intensive use of social networks that could have a negative impact on their development. In France, this protection takes several forms. On the one hand, it imposes obligations to control the age for access to certain services. On the other hand, it gives additional personal data rights to minors. CNIL has also taken initiatives to support players in improving data protection for minors. More recently, in connection with the French adaptation of the DSA, the CNIL has been granted new powers to ensure that providers of online platformsestablished in France comply with their obligation to prohibit the presentation of profiling-based advertising to minors.[473]

I. The Double Consent of Parents and Children under 15 Years of Age to Information Society Services

215. Article 8 GDPR imposes a minimum age of 16 for a child to be able to consent to a direct offer of information society services.[474] However, Article 8 GDPR leaves to the Member States the freedom to reduce this kind of digital maturity age as long as it does not exceed 13 years. In France, the threefold of 15 years old has been chosen for the valid consent of the minor according to Article 8 GDPR. The new LIL introduced a form of double consent. Article 45 LIL provides that when a minor is less than 15 years old, both the parent/guardian and the child should give consent. This approach is designed to respect both parental authority and the wishes of the children. In theory, a parent cannot force a child to register for an information society service without his or her agreement, just as a child cannot register or modify important elements of these services without parental agreement. The *Conseil constitutionnel* validated this double consent approach by considering that Article 8 GDPR distinguishes between the given consent (by a child that has capacity to consent) and the authorised consent by the holder of parental responsibility over a child that does not have capacity to consent. According to the *Conseil constitutionnel*, this means that consent can be given by the parents of a minor or that the parents can authorise a minor to consent.[475] The rationale of the double consent is based on this second interpretation. To sum up, in France, minors under the age

472. Therefore, the French government created in 2021 a dedicated website on digital parenting called https://jeprotegemonenfant.gouv.fr/.

473. *See* Art. 124-5 LIL introduced by the 2024 SREN Act.

474. This concept is defined by Art. 1(b) of the e-Privacy Directive as a 'services, normally provided for a remuneration, at a distance, by electronic means and at the individual request of a recipient of services'. It includes the social media services such as Tik Tok, Snapchat, Instagram, and other website of video games such as Fortnite, which are very popular among the minor.

475. *See* CC 2018-765 DC du 12 Jun. 2018, point 63.

of 15 must consent with their parent(s) to direct offers of company information services. Minors over the age of 15 may consent alone. The other conditions for the consent to be valid according to the GDPR must also be met.[476]

216. Parental authority is exercised by both parents.[477] The question, therefore, arises as to whether the agreement of just one parent is sufficient or whether both parents must expressly consent. The CNIL considers that according to French civil law, consent is a 'usual act'[478] of the parent authority. Therefore, the consent of one parent implies acceptance by the other parent with parental authority.[479]

II. The Legal Obligations of Online Verification of the Age

217. **From Article 8 GDPR and beyond.** The implementation of Article 8 of the GDPR, as well as several texts protecting children, requires verification online of their age. There are several legal obligations which impose the verification of the age for providing certain services or products, such as alcohol purchases,[480] online gambling, and certain banking services. In July 2020, a law reinforced the obligation of the verification of the age for sites broadcasting pornographic content[481] which in the event of violation may be subject to criminal penalties.[482] The ARCOM, the audiovisual and digital communications regulatory authority, has obtained the power to issue formal notices to sites that fail to comply with their age verification obligations.[483] Until now, however, ARCOM has been obliged to go to court to request that French ISPs block these sites.[484] A recent Act[485] reinforces the ARCOM powers. From now on, the ARCOM can issue formal notices to online

476. The consent needs to be freely given, specific, informed, and unambiguous *see* below paras 357 et seq.
477. *See* Art. 372 Civil Code.
478. The concept of usual act refers to Art. L.372-2 civil Code, which provides that 'With regard to third parties acting in good faith, each parent is deemed to act with the agreement of the other when he or she alone performs a usual act of parental authority in relation to the person of the child.'
479. *See* CNIL Recommandation 4: rechercher le consentement d'un parent pour les mineurs de moins de 15 ans, available at https://www.cnil.fr/fr/recommandation-4-rechercher-le-consentement-dun-parent-pour-les-mineurs-de-moins-de-15-ans.
480. This prohibition was introduced in French law by the so-called Loi Evin (Loi No. 91-32, 10 Jan. 1991 relative à la lutte contre le tabagisme et l'alcoolisme) and is also codified at Art. L3342-1 Health Code.
481. Loi 30 Jul. 2020 visant à protéger les victimes de violences conjugales.
482. *See* Art. 224-27 CP.
483. Cf. décret n° 2021-1306 'relatif aux modalités de mise en oeuvre des mesures visant à protéger les mineurs contre l'accès à des sites diffusant un contenu pornographique'.
484. In application of this power, the ARCOM asked recently the *Tribunal judiciaire* of Paris to block five porn websites Pornhub, xHamster, Xnxxx, Tukif and Xvideos. *See* the judgement of the Tribunal judiciaire of Paris 7 Jul. 2023 n° 22/55687. The tribunal judiciaire of Paris has decided to stay the proceedings pending a ruling by the *Conseil d'Etat* on the validity of the decree on which ARCOM is basing its request to block the sites. While the the *Conseil d'Etat* dismissed several general critiscims of the decree and the act, it decided to refer to the CJEU for a issue regarding the application of the single market clause. The Conseil d'Etat considered that the recent *Google Ireland* Case (No. C-376/22) calls into question the ability of France to ensure that a digital service based in another EU Member State complies with French criminal law. More details see it press

video-sharing providers who allow minors to access pornographic content. If the formal notice fails, ARCOM can not only impose fines, but also require Internet providers to block access to such pornographic content. This Act also provide that the ARCOM establishes and publishes a reference system determining the minimum technical requirements applicable to age verification systems. In March 2024, ARCOM submitted a proposal for a reference framework for consultation.[486] The future reference system will refer on the CNIL's previous work.

218. **CNIL's statements on the verification of the age**. In this context, the CNIL published several documents regarding the issue of the verification of age which implies processing of personal data. In 2021, the CNIL published eight recommendations to strengthen the protection of minors online after a large consultation of the stakeholders.[487] In July 2022, the CNIL published a statement on the control of the age of minors which aim to promote a balance between protection of minors and privacy.[488] Therefore, the CNIL recommends age verification and parental consent systems based on six pillars: '*minimisation, proportionality, robustness, simplicity, standardisation and third-party intervention*'.[489] In this document, the CNIL listed six current possible solutions and stressed that none of them is fully satisfactory. The verification by validation of the credit or debit card raises several security issues, such as fishing. The verification by facial analysis without identifying the person is very intrusive and seems not sufficiently reliable. It will need a minimisation of the risk of data breach. Offline age verification for adults or use of the State identity digital tools could not be implemented only for pornographic content because it will be too stigmatising. Inferential age verification systems could only apply to services which already process data on a large scale and with important GDPR guarantees. While the CNIL is trying to provide its expertise on the issue of age verification systems, it is up to ARCOM to establish the technical solutions that sites should implement to prevent minors from accessing pornographic sites. Therefore, the CNIL reaffirmed the urgent need to develop a more virtuous system

---

release in English available at https://www.conseil-etat.fr/en/news/online-access-to-pornographic-content-the-conseil-d-etat-refers-the-issue-of-protecting-minors-to-the-court-of-justice-of-the-european-union

485. Cf. Loi No. 2024-449, 21 May 2024 to secure and regulate the digital space also called in France Loi SREN (Loi visant à Sécuriser et à Réguler l'Espace Numérique) in particular article 2. This provision applies only to providers established in France or outside the EU, to prevent any risk of non-compliance with the Google Ireland case, mentioned in the note above. By way of derogation, suppliers established in the EU may be concerned within the limits of the conditions set out in Art. 3, §4 of the e-commerce directive for derogating from the so-called internal market clause.
486. Consultation publique sur le projet de référentiel déterminant les exigences techniques minimales applicables aux systèmes de vérification de l'âge mis en place pour l'accès à certains services de communication au public en ligne et aux plateformes de partage de vidéos qui mettent à disposition du public des contenus pornographiques, available at https://www.arcom.fr/sites/default/files/2024-04/Arcom-Consultation-publique-projet-referentiel-determinant-exigences-techniques-minimales-applicables-aux-systemes-verification-age-acces-contenus-pornographiques-en-ligne.pdf.
487. *See* https://www.cnil.fr/fr/les-droits-numeriques-des-mineurs.
488. *See* https://www.cnil.fr/fr/controle-de-lage-sur-les-sites-web-la-cnil-invite-developper-des-solutions-plus-efficaces-et.
489. *See* https://www.cnil.fr/fr/verification-de-lage-en-ligne-trouver-lequilibre-entre-protection-des-mineurs-et-respect-de-la-vie.

for the access of pornographic websites or applications.[490] The LINC proposed an open-source solution with a trusted third party. However, in March 2023, the government launched its own experiment to develop an age verification solution that respects the principle of double anonymity.[491] Thus, the ARCOM reference framework is eagerly awaited by stakeholders to help them achieve compliance.

III. The Parental Control Tools

219. Since 2022, there has been a legal obligation to install a free parental control system in connected objects.[492] The activation of such tools must be proposed when a device is first put into service. This obligation applies to computers, smartphones, tablets, video game consoles and connected objects such as televisions, watches and speakers. Guarantees have been added to ensure that these systems include data protection by design and by default approach. '*personal data of minors collected or generated when this device is activated must not be used for commercial purposes, such as direct marketing, profiling and behaviour-targeted advertising, even after they have reached the age of majority*'.[493]

220. In July 2023, two decrees clarified the functionalities and technical characteristics of parental control systems and the conditions of certification of these parental system tools. These parental control mechanisms must, therefore, include compulsory functions enabling parents to block sites that are legally off-limits to minors, such as pornographic sites. To comply with a data protection by design approach, it has been stipulated that the functionalities and technical characteristics of the parental control devices '*are implemented locally without involving the collection or processing of personal data of the minor user by servers*'. It is also provided that the parental control devices '*Do not result in the processing of personal data relating to the minor user, with the exception of identification data strictly necessary for the operation of the parental control system.*'[494]

221. While parental tools constitute an alternative to protect minors, here again, the technical solutions are not always very effective.

IV. The Minor Data Subject Rights

222. Article 51 II LIL foresees the right for a data subject to obtain for a controller the erasure of his or her personal data collected in relation to information society services when he or she was a minor. This right was introduced in French

490. https://www.cnil.fr/fr/controle-de-lage-pour-lacces-aux-sites-pornographiques.
491. *See* Damien Leloup et Florian Reynaud, *Blocage de sites porno: où en est l'expérimentation d'outils de vérification d'âge en 'double anonymat'?*, Le monde, 7 Jul. 2023.
492. Loi n° 2022-300, 2 Mar. 2022 visant à renforcer le contrôle parental sur les moyens d'accès à internet, which is integrated in the CPCE.
493. Article L.34-93 CPCE.
494. Article R.20-29-10-1 CPCE.

Law before the GDPR by Article 63 of the Digital Republic Law of 2016. It allows the data of a person who has reached the age of majority to be deleted if it was collected when he or she was a minor. In February 2024, a revision of the LIL introduced additional guarantees to ensure the effectiveness of a minor's right to erasure. Article 21 LIL now allows the President of the CNIL to bring an application for interim measures before the competent court in the event of non-execution or failure to respond to a request for erasure from a minor.

223. Furthermore, Article 70 LIL provides that for processing of minors in the health sector,[495] the holders of parental authorities are the recipients of the information and exercise the rights of the data subject. It is only by way of derogation and in the case of medical research in the public domain that information may be provided to only one of the holders of parental authority, if it is impossible to inform the other parent or if this cannot be done in the time required. However, if the minor is aged 15 or over, he or she may object to access to this data by his or her parents. In this case, the minor is informed and exercises his or her rights alone.

V. CNIL Standard for Processing in Children's Sector

224. In February 2022, the CNIL adopted a standard providing a better framework for processing in the children's sector,[496] except for the processing related to adoption. This standard is a tool for all private or public organisations '*involved in the reception, accommodation and/or support of minors and young adults under the age of 21 in social, medico-social, educational and/or legal terms*'.[497] It is also a guideline for complying with the obligation of the data protection assessment. Processing for the purpose of the social and medico-social support of persons is included in the French list of types of processing operations for which a data protection impact assessment (DPIA) is required[498] according to Article 35 GDPR.

---

495. *See infra* para. 323.
496. *See* https://www.cnil.fr/sites/default/files/atoms/files/referentiel_relatif_a_la_protection_de_lenfance.pdf.
497. *See ibid.*, point 1 with include a non-exhaustive list of the bodies concerned.
498. Délibération n° 2018-326 du 11 Oct. 2018 portant adoption de lignes directrices sur les analyses d'impact relatives à la protection des données (AIPD) prévues par le règlement général sur la protection des données (GDPR).

Part III. General Principles

225. Chapter II GDPR mentions a set of general principles which are at the core of the European personal data Law. Currently, these principles are mentioned in Articles 4 to 6 of the LIL. Article 4 copy-pastes Article 5.1 GDPR on the core principles relating to processing of personal data. Article 5 LIL recalled the legal grounds for processing similarly to Article 6 GDPR. Finally, like the GDPR, the LIL contains several provisions for special categories of data.

§1. French Illustrations on the General Principles of Article 5 GDPR

226. Article 4 LIL recalls the European general principles relating to personal data processing. Article 4.1 provides that '*personal data must be processed fairly, and lawfully*' and, for processing in the scope of GDPR, '*transparent with regard to the data subject.*' Both at the European and French levels, fairness, lawfulness and transparency have been formally grouped into a single paragraph, although they constitute three distinct principles.

I. Fairness Principle

227. The fairness principle is not defined in the GDPR nor in the LIL. It is mainly used by the CNIL in the context of the relation between the data subject and the controller to balance the risk of information asymmetry. Therefore, the fairness principle is mainly used in two situations. First, the fairness principle aims to prohibit the collection of personal data without prior information about the data subject. Second, the fairness principle prohibits further processing without the data subject's knowledge

228. **Fairness applied to collects without prior information**. Even before the entry into force of the GDPR, the CNIL referred to the need for fair collection by implementing cookies and other tackers. For instance, Facebook violated this principle when it implemented cookies for collecting personal data, including those on non-subscribers when visiting or liking a Facebook page.[499] Similarly, even before the GDPR, the fairness principle was invoked against the collection and indexation

499. CNIL, SAN 2017-006, 27 Apr. 2017.

of public profiles of users of social networks. The *Conseil d'Etat* declared that due to the lack of prior information on the extraction of their profiles, the collect of personal data was not fair and lawful.[500]

229. On a broader level, the fairness principle is also used to contextualise at what point the information on data processing should be usefully given. For instance, the *Cour de cassation* considered that the fair collection of data does not imply that the person is individually informed in a systematic way at the time of the collection of his or her data, as long as he or she has prior general information on the data that may be collected, the rights that he or she may oppose to this collection, as well as the possibility of accessing all of his or her collected data at any time.[501]

230. Furthermore, the CNIL often warns of the need to respect the fairness principle in its opinion on bills aiming at extending surveillance technologies. Recently, the CNIL recalled that fairness implies that the deployment of augmented camera devices during events such as the Olympic Games 2024 should be submitted with a minimum amount of information with regard to the data subject. The CNIL recommended that exclusion of the information should be extremely limited and carefully grounded.[502] By contrast, the bill provided for the possibility of excluding information to individuals in cases where such information would be in contradiction with the purposes pursued.[503] Finally, the law took into account the opinion of CNIL.[504]

231. **Fairness applied to non-informed further processing.** Fairness principle can be invoked in the context of sharing personal data with third parties, including when the information given by the controller is unclear or misleading. As an illustration, the CNIL considered that the fairness principle was violated by a controller which collected personal data for a credit card service and proposed to its customer to link this service to a loyalty programme without saying that by doing so a set a personal data will be transferred to a third party. From the given information, the data subject could not understand that the loyalty programme was managed by another company which was controller of further processing of this personal data.

500. CE, 12 Mar. 2014, n° 353193, pages jaunes.
501. Cass. soc., 13 Jun. 2018, FS-P+B, n° 16-25.301.
502. CNIL, Deliberation n° 2022-118, 8 Dec. 2022 portant avis sur un projet de loi portant sur les jeux Olympiques et Paralympiques de 2024.
503. *See* Art. 7 VI 4°) of the Bill.
504. Article 10(III) provides for the public to be informed in advance of the use of algorithmic processing on images collected by means of video protection systems. While it retains the same wording as the bill, additional guarantees are envisaged in the decision to authorise such processing. On the one hand, the Ministry of the Interior will provide general information to the public. On the other hand, Art. 10 VII 4°) specifies that this reasoned and published decision must include 'the arrangements for informing the public, in particular of their rights, or, where such information contradicts the objectives pursued, the reasons why the controller is exempted from providing it, accompanied by a reference to the general information organised by the Ministry of the Interior ...'.

The misleading information was not only about the reality of the loyalty programme but also about the extent of the personal data transferred to the loyalty programme. The web site provided that the link between the credit card service and the loyalty programme was submitted to agree to transfer limited personal data, such as first name, second name, email and nothing else, to the loyalty programme. In practice, the investigation of the CNIL revealed that much more personal data was transferred, such as the postal address, the phone number, the number of children, etc. Interestingly, the CNIL declared in this deliberation that the fairness principle is '*an autonomous principle provided for in Article 5(1)(a) of the GDPR, the breach of which by a controller is likely to result in a remedial measure being taken by the supervisory authority*'.[505] It clearly distinguished the violation of the fairness principle from the violation of information obligations of the controller according to Articles 12 and 13 GDPR.

II. Transparency Principle

232. **A GDPR's principle**. The transparency principle has a special status since it is only explicitly stated for processing covered by the GDPR at both the European and French levels. Therefore, the *Conseil d'Etat*'s case law on Directive Police Justice processing and processing in the Interests of State Safety and Defense only controls the application of the requirement of fairness and lawfulness to the exclusion of any reference to the requirement of transparency.[506]

233. **A principle rarely invoked on its own**. Even for processing covered by the GDPR, the CNIL and the French judges rarely rely on Article 4 LIL about the transparency principle. Most transparency cases are based on the specific obligations of the controller to provide accessible and intelligible information to the data subject according to Article 12 GDPR. This was at the core of the first sanction post-GDPR given by the CNIL to Google.[507] In particular, the CNIL criticised the lack of ergonomics of the Google website, which sometimes required up to five or six actions from the Internet user to find information when creating an email account. Furthermore, the CNIL refers to the transparency principle in combination with the exercise of the data subject rights, such as the right to access. The CNIL considered '*that the data subject's right of access constitutes a fundamental guarantee of the transparency of the data processing methods. It deduced that the data controller must in principle communicate "the specific source" of the data and that the limitation of the right of access to indications of the "nature of the sources, types of organisations, companies and sectors" can only be done when the data controller does not have this information, as it is impossible to identify the specific source of*

505. CNIL, SAN 2020-009, 18 Nov. 2020, point 32.
506. *See,* CE, 21 Dec. 2021, n° 442360, Assoc. La Quadrature du Net, point 4, – CE, 24 Dec. 2021, n° 447518, Ligue des droits de l'homme et a., point 21.
507. CNIL, SAN 2019-001, 21 janv. 2019.

the data subject's personal data'.[508] In its deliberations[509] relating to the obligation of transparency, the CNIL often refers to the EDPB guidelines on this topic.[510]

III. Lawfulness Principle

234. The lawfulness principle is not limited to the need to have a legal ground for the processing according to Article 6 GDPR.[511] It includes more broadly that the processing needs to conform to data protection law and more globally to all the rules in application in the State. The judge will consider that a processing operation is unlawful if the data collected goes beyond what the act authorising the processing allows.[512]

IV. Purpose Principle

235. The purpose principle is a 'cardinal principle of personal data protection', as recalled by the CNIL's opinion on the Stop Covid application.[513] Article 4.2 LIL provided that 'personal data must be obtained for specific, explicit and legitimate purposes, and not subsequently processed in a manner that is incompatible with those purposes'. As Article 5.1.b) GDPR, Article 4.2 LIL also mentions the possibility of further processing for legitimate interests, such as data processing for archiving purposes in the public interest, scientific and historical research purposes, and statistical purposes.[514]

236. **Control prior to authorisation of processing by public authorities.** The application of the purpose principle in France has given rise to various issues in the context of processing operations that have been authorised for implementation by public authorities. Most of the time, it is a question of verifying the purpose that the processing can pursue. As the CNIL recorded in its opinion on the *Stop Covid application*, the purpose principle means that '*data may only be used for a specific, predetermined purpose. Any other use of the data is in principle prohibited*'.[515] Therefore, the CNIL warned the government that the application has only a contact tracking purpose for the benefit of the data subject. French Stop Covid application aimed at informing the data subject that his phone has been in proximity in the past few days to that of a person who has tested positive for COVID-19, so that there is

508. CNIL, SAN 2022-022, 30 Nov. 2022, FREE, point 37.
509. *See*, SAN 2020-009, 18 Nov. 2020, points 46–47, point 54.
510. EDPB Guidelines on Transparency under Regulation 2016/679 (wp260rev.01).
511. *See* further paras 256 et seq.
512. *See* for example CNIL, SAN-2021-016, 24 Sep. 2021 concernant le ministère de l'intérieur, in which the CNIL notes that the Ministry of the Interior is processing data not covered by Decree No. 87-249 and deduces that this processing is unlawful. This case is relating to the French automated fingerprint database called FAED.
513. Délibération 2020-046 du 24 avril 2020 portant avis sur un projet d'application mobile dénommée 'StopCovid'.
514. *See* further para. 554.
515. *See* the above-mentioned SAN 2020-046 Stop Covid.

a risk that he may have been contaminated as well. By contrast, Stop Covid application could not be used for monitoring the lockdown or other heath requirements.

237. In 2021, the *Conseil d'Etat* examined decrees which extended the administration authorisation of databases of the Minister of Interior. The police database PASP aims at the prevention of information management and prevention of public security breaches. The database GIPASP has the same purpose but relates to the French military police called the Gendarmerie. The EASP database facilitates the administration investigations for the recruitment of certain professions, such as police officers, prison guards, judges, and security guards.[516] Whereas some liberties associations were concerned by the extent of categories of data processed and the variety of the purposes authorised, the *Conseil d'Etat* almost validated all the amendments made by the government by considering that the purposes were sufficiently detailed. In these cases, the *Conseil d'Etat* clarified that processing could have mixed purposes grounded on separate titles of the LIL.[517] It ruled that the purposes of the processing were well defined both for the public security purposes covered by the Police Justice Directive and for State safety purposes. For the latter, the *Conseil d'Etat* simply pointed out that the data concerning the State safety as well as the notion of attacking the security of the State are defined in the CSI. As far as the control of the legitimacy of the purposes is concerned, the *Conseil d'Etat* merely argued that the modification of the decree was justified because it had a different purpose than the existing processing. In other words, the *Conseil d'Etat*'s ruling on the legitimacy of the purpose of a processing operation is limited to verifying the necessity of the processing operation and not really to rule on the appropriateness of the new processing operation. In these PASP and GIPASD cases, the extension was necessary in order to collect data on people who are likely to attend to public security or State security without being wanted.

238. By contrast, the *Conseil d'Etat* declared that the Gendnotes application did not have specified, explicit and legitimate purposes. Gendnotes was an application of notes taken for the French military police, the Gendarmerie, in the context of interventions and investigations carried out by members of the gendarmerie, in particular for the purposes of prevention, detection, investigation and prosecution of criminal offences or the execution of criminal sanctions, including protection against threats to public safety. As a processing relating to the Police Justice Directive scope, it needs authorisation by decree in France.[518] The decree provided that the processing aimed at facilitating '*the collection and storage, "with a view to their subsequent use in other data processing", in particular by means of a pre-intelligence system, of information collected by members of the national gendarmerie during preventive actions, investigations or interventions and, secondly, to facilitate the transmission of reports to judicial authorities*'. The *Conseil d'Etat*

516. More details on the main public security files further para. 605.
517. *See* CE, 24 Dec. 2021, n° 447518, point 22. The *Conseil d'Etat* based its interpretation on Art. 91 LIL.
518. *See* further para. 583.

considered that the first purpose was too vague because it did not specify '*the nature and the object of the further processing, nor the categories of collected data*'.[519]

Beyond the principles of lawfulness, fairness, transparency, and purpose limitation, Article 4 LIL recalls other principles that are more focused on the data.

V. Minimisation Principle

239. **A formally new principle**. The principle of minimisation is enshrined in Article 4.3 LIL. This provision recalls that personal data must be '*Adequate, relevant and limited to what is necessary for the purposes for which they are processed*', which is a copy-past of Article 5.1.c) GDPR. Article 4 LIL adds another criterion for the processing under the Police Justice Directive and for the processing in the interests of State safety and defence. That processing must *'be not excessive.'* Whereas the formal concept of minimisation has been introduced by the European Data protection package, it echoes the well-known principle of proportionality.[520] Such proportionality principle has been applied in France spontaneously since the eighties.[521] It has been explicitly enshrined since 2004 in French LIL with the transposition of the 1995 Directive. The adequate, relevant, and not excessive criteria have sometimes been considered largely synonymous.[522] Those criteria are often not separately analysed by the doctrine, the CNIL and the judges. Often, the review focuses on the excessive nature of the data collection, both quantitatively and qualitatively.

240. **Illustrations**. The minimisation principle is frequently invoked in the context of surveillance tools such as video surveillance or geolocation. For instance, the CNIL rejected the constant surveillance of employees' posts except in special circumstances (handling of money or valuables or in case of theft or damage committed on the premises). Information on the student's state of health or family situation was deemed disproportionate in a processing operation for educational purposes.[523] The collection of geolocation data of rented cars[524] and scooters[525] was considered unjustified and excessive regarding the stated purposes, such as billing, processing, traffic violations, management of claims and theft.

241. The minimisation principle also implies a qualitative approach to the collection of data within the purposes. Therefore, the CNIL stated that it is a violation

519. CE, 13 Apr. 2021, n° 439360, point 8.

520. *See* Romain Perray, *Jusriclasseur Fasc. 274-23: Données à caractère personnel.* Principes fondamentaux relatifs aux traitements de données à caractère personnel. Minimisation.

521. *See* for instance, CNIL, SAN 81-89, 21 Jul. 1981, Art. 3; CE, Ass., 3 Dec. 1999, Nos 197060 and 197061, Caisse de crédit mutuel de Bain-Tresbœuf and others old decision of the CNIL and French judges mentioned by Romain Perray Fasc. 274-23.

522. *See* for instance Rapp. G. Braibant au Premier ministre, Données personnelles et société de l'information: Doc. fr., 1998., mentioned by Romain Perray who tries to bring subtle elements of distinctions.

523. CNIL, MED 2018-041, 8 Oct. 2018, point 1.

524. CNIL, SAN 2023-003, 16 Mar. 2023 geolocation data was collected every 500 metres.

525. CNIL, SAN 2022-015, 7 Jul. 2022, geolocation data was collected every thirty seconds.

of the minimisation principle when a company that conducts campaigns with prospects collects phone numbers even though it only uses emails for its activity.[526] The minimisation principle may also involve an assessment of the tools used to collect data about the chosen purposes. Therefore, the judge considered disproportionate the implementation of facial recognition devices at a high school entrance in absence of a demonstration that other less intrusive technical solutions could meet the same objective of security.[527]

242. The recent *RATP* case illustrates the relevant criterion of the principle of minimisation.[528] The Parisian public transportation establishment created a processing for the evaluation of its agents. It determined the categories of data to be collected for this processing which included the attendance at work. Several departments of the *RATP* included in the column of its register the number of days the agent was on strike. The CNIL considered that the criterion of the attendance of work was relevant. Nevertheless, including the number of days the agent was on strike during the evaluation period was too excessive regarding the purpose of the processing. In this situation, the knowledge of the reason for the absence was not relevant. Interestingly, the CNIL recalled in its case that it is up to the data controller to impose on its departments the respect of the minimisation principle through technical and organisational measures.[529]

243. **CNIL's referentiels and minimisation principle**. The CNIL specifies in numerous referential ('referentiels')[530] how to implement this principle of minimisation by listing by category of purposes the type of personal data that should be collected. For instance, in its referential for rental management,[531] the CNIL details the data that can be collected for housing search, the assessment of the solvency of the candidates to rent, during the rental, and at the end of the rental. CNIL limits the pertinent data for each purpose by adding comments on data that are not pertinent to collect. For instance, the CNIL considers only three categories of data for the housing search: identification such as first and second name, contact (email, phone number) and criteria for the search (location, rent, and surface). By contrast, data on the personal situation such as the professional or financial status of the data subject, are not pertinent at this stage.

VI. Accuracy Principle

244. **History of the accuracy principle in France.** The principle of accuracy is enshrined in Article 4.4 LIL which is a copy-paste of Article 5, §1, d) GDPR. This principle means that '*the personal data must be accurate and, where necessary, kept*

526. *See* CNIL, Deliberation SAN 2020-016, 7 décembre 2020, point 50.
527. TA Marseille, 9e ch., 27 févr. 2020, n° 1901249, la Quadrature du Net et a.
528. *See* Délibération SAN-2021-019 du 29 octobre 2021, *RATP*, points 29–32.
529. *See* Délibération SAN-2021-019 du 29 octobre 2021, *RATP*, points 39–40.
530. *See* further para. 423.
531. CNIL, Référentiel relative aux traitements des données à caractère personnel mis en oeuvre dans le cadre de la gestion locative, 6 May 2021, point 6.

up to date. Every reasonable step must be taken to ensure that personal data that are inaccurate, having regard to the purposes for which they are processed, are erased, or rectified without delay'. An 'obligation to supplement or correct *ex officio*'[532] has existed in French LIL since 1978. It is after the 1995 Directive that the principle of accuracy has taken on a broader pro-active approach, which has been confirmed with the 2016 European Data Law package.

245. **Obligation of result v. obligation of means**. In 2016, the CNIL stated that accuracy 'is unambiguously an obligation of result in that it requires the data controller to ensure the accuracy of the personal data it processes by taking all appropriate measures to rectify or erase inaccurate data … It is thus a matter of the data controller achieving a specific objective and not of deploying his best efforts to achieve it'.[533] In this case, because of a computer bug, an Internet access provider wrongly identified the address IP of a person concerned as the one who had committed counterfeiting offences. It is in this context that the CNIL has issued a warning to the Internet provider as data controller for violation of the principle of accuracy. Nevertheless, the French judges have recognised that in certain circumstances, the principle of accuracy may be relativised into an obligation of means. This was the case when the error was based on the technical failure to consider an accent in the name of the person[534] or in the spelling of the name of the person concerned due to 'the absence of risk of confusion or error about the person'.[535] These differences recalled that both for the CNIL and the judges, the principle of accuracy is appreciated within the purposes of the processing and the impact on the data subject. The principle of accuracy is interconnected with the right of rectification and the right of erasure mentioned in section 3 of the chapter on the rights of the data subject in the GDPR.[536]

246. **Main areas of application**. In praxis, the CNIL has often had occasion to sanction the respect of the principle of accuracy in the context of files such as the national file of credit repayment incidents to individuals (Fichier des incidents de remboursement des crédits aux particuliers (FICP)).[537] The CNIL is also very vigilant with respect to the principle of accuracy in case of data transfer[538] or public

532. Sénat Rapport No. 72, 10 Nov. 1977, p. 39. More details on this principle of accuracy *see* Romain Perray, Juriscl. Fasc. 274-24 Données à caractère personnel. Principes fondamentaux relatifs aux traitements des données à caractère personnel. Exactitude.
533. CNIL, SAN 2016-053, 1 Mar. 2016.
534. Cass. 1st civ., 4 May 2012, n° 10-27.208, Mr K. c/ Banque Postale.
535. CE, 3 October 2018, n° 405939, M. B.
536. *See* below paras 336 et seq.
537. J. Morel-Maroger, *Les dysfonctionnements récurrents du FICP: Gaz. Pal. 13 juin 2017*, n° 297, p. 83.
538. CNIL, SAN 2019-034, 21 Mar. 2019 authorising the implementation of an administrative arrangement to regulate transfers of personal data between the AMF and its counterparts outside the EEA.

authorities' files.[539] For example, the CNIL recalled *'the need of the implementation of different measures or parameters to anticipate the risk of false positives'* in the Stop Covid application.[540]

VII. Storage Limitation Principle

247. The principle of storage limitation means that 'the personal data must be kept in a form that permits identification of data subjects for no longer than is necessary for the purposes for which they are processed' accordingly to Article 4.5 LIL, which is a copy, cut of Article 5, §1, e) GDPR. Similarly, as this GDPR provision, the LIL provides limited exceptions 'for archiving purposes in the public interest, for scientific or historical research purposes, or statistical purposes'.[541] Besides these exceptions, each processing must have a storage limitation.

248. **CNIL's practical guide on storage limitation.**[542] In this 2020 guide, the CNIL details three phases of the data life cycle.[543] The latter one is an obligation of definitive storage for processing which exists mainly for the public sector and will be discussed further.[544] First, 'the active base' for current use in which the data 'is accessible, in the immediate work environment, by all those in charge of processing current cases'. The CNIL recalls that when the purpose of the processing is achieved, the data usually must be deleted or anonymised. Second, the 'intermediate storage' covers situations in which storage is necessary for an administrative interest or for a legal ground. For instance, the French commercial code provides that invoice data must be kept for ten years, even if the person concerned in no longer a customer.[545] Intermediate storage will also be necessary for the management of the litigation. When intermediate storage is necessary, it is submitted to four conditions. First, the data controller must sort the data in the intermediate storage to ensure that only the data necessary for the purpose of this kind of storage is retained. Second, the data controller must define the intermediate storage duration. When the intermediate storage duration is not defined by law, it is up to the data controller to define it regarding the purpose of this storage. Third, the data controller must operate a physical or logical separation between the active base and the intermediate archive. A physical separation implies that the data is stored in a new dedicated database. This type of archiving includes different functionalities, such as being able to visualise the type of data stored to respond to a data subject for the exercise of his rights. Logical separation implies that the data remains in the active database, but

539. CNIL, Deliberation 2018-322 du 4 Oct. 2018 opinion on a draft decree of the *Conseil d'Etat* concerning the validation of the long-stay visa as a residence permit; Deliberation n° 2020-001 du 9 Jan. 2020 opinion on a draft decree creating an automated processing of personal data called 'weapons information system'.
540. CNIL, SAN 2020-056, 25 May 2020, point 35.
541. *See* below para. 555.
542. https://www.cnil.fr/sites/default/files/atoms/files/guide_durees_de_conservation.pdf.
543. *See* the mentioned guide, p. 4.
544. *See* below paras 544 et seq.
545. *See* Art. L123-22 Commercial code.

access to it is restricted so that it is inaccessible to people who no longer have an interest in processing it. Fourth, the data controller must provide security measures aiming at protecting the destruction, loss, alteration, communication, or unauthorised access to the data.

249. Furthermore, the CNIL practical guide gives a list of categories of sources that can be used to determine storage limitations. As mentioned before, the storage duration can be provided by law. It can be either a minimum[546] or maximum duration[547] or a precis duration.[548]

250. **Limitation storage in other soft law documents of the CNIL**. The CNIL elaborates on several documents in which it detailed the storage duration for categories of processing. For instance, the CNIL recommends, in principle, a retention period of two months for the geolocation data by an employer of its employees.[549] For the processing of credit cards for sale or goods or for the provision of services at a distance, first, the CNIL recalls that the storage of the cryptogram after the transaction is prohibited. Second, the CNIL distinguishes the case of one-off purchases from subscriptions involving staggered payments. In the case of single payments, the card details can be kept to the time required to complete the transaction. Regarding subscriptions involving payment in instalments, the retention of bank details is justified until the last payment due date, if the subscription does not provide for tacit renewal or until the subscription is terminated in the event of tacit renewal.[550]

251. Since the GDPR, the CNIL adopted 'referentiels', including issues on data retention periods. For instance, the referential relating to the processing of personal data implemented for staff management purposes includes a table with practical illustrations of the retention periods that can be retained by the organisations concerned depending on the context.[551] Similarly, the CNIL listed different retention periods in its referentiel on data processing for the management of medical and

546. Data relating to employees' pay slips must be kept for at least five years in accordance with Art. L.3243-4 of the French Labor Code.
547. Article L.252-3 of the Internal Security Code limits the period of conservation of video protection images to one month.
548. Article L.123-22 Commercial code limits the period of retention of the accounting records and supporting documents to ten years.
549. *See* CNIL norme simplifiée NS-51geolocalisation des véhicules des employés. Since the GDPR, this document has no longer any legal value, but it still used in praxis. Longer period of detention can apply such as one year for the purpose of proving the performance of a service where it is not possible to provide such proof by any other means and for tour optimisation purposes. Five years of detention can apply in the context of working time monitoring, only for data relating to the hours worked.
550. CNIL, Deliberation n° 2018-303, 6 Sep. 2018 portant adoption d'une recommandation concernant le traitement des données relatives à la carte de paiement en matière de vente de biens ou de fourniture de services à distance et abrogeant la délibération n° 2017-222 du 20 juillet 2017.
551. *See* CNIL, référentiel relatif aux traitements de données à caractère personnel mis en œuvre aux fins de gestion de personnel adopted in 2019, point 7, and the mentioned table, p. 11.

paramedical practices.[552] In addition, the CNIL elaborated two referentiels focused on the retention periods in the context of health: the first for health research,[553] the second for health processing, excluding research.[554] Despite all this information, the lack of respect for the principle of storage limitation is often sanctioned by the CNIL

252. **CNIL Case's law on storage limitation.** Most of the cases illustrated the lack of a data retention policy following the above-mentioned rules. For instance, Discord did not mention the duration of the processing in its register, and some data on inactive users was kept for more than six years.[555] Some companies do have a policy for data retention but do not really follow it.[556] Some cases illustrated that the storage duration was not connected to the purposes. This was the case of a car rental company that kept geolocation data of rented vehicles for three years after they were returned to the rental companies. The CNIL considered that first, the purpose of the geolocation processing was not a general commercial relation which could allow a retention period of three years after the last contact but a specific rental contract. Second, other purposes of the processing were theft prevention and assistance in case of an accident. Both purposes were achieved by the restitution of the car. For all these reasons, the CNIL concluded that the company '*kept the geolocation data in question for longer than was necessary for the purposes for which they were processed and thus failed to comply with its obligations under Article 5.1.e of the GDPR*'.[557] In its *RATP* case, the CNIL recalled the storage limitation principle implies that the data controller must have '*a differentiated and adapted approach to the retention of data for the specific purposes for which they are process*'.[558] This was not the case with the application Dora, which was a data visualisation tool for human resources management of the bus department with the purpose of 'operational data mining'. On the one hand, the CNIL judged that such a purpose was too broad because the operational needs were not sufficiently defined. On the other hand, the CNIL considered that the six-year retention period for all the data processed was not appropriate for certain categories of data. The CNIL noted

552. *See* CNIL, référentiel relatif aux traitements de données personnelles pour les cabinets médicaux et paramédicaux, p. 7.
553. CNIL, référentiel des durées de conservation dans le domaine de la recherche en santé.
554. CNIL, référentiel des durées de conservation dans le domaine de la santé hors recherche.
555. *See* CNIL, SAN 2022-020, 10 Nov. 2022, Discord Inc.
556. *See* CNIL, SAN 2022-018, 8 Sep. 2022, GIE Infogreffe, for a retention period of thirty-six months announced by the general conditions of the data controller which was not effective for lack of an automatic erasure procedure. *See* CNIL, SAN 2021-019, 29 Oct. 2021, *RATP*. The CNIL's investigation revealed that the data used for the preparation of the classification commissions for the promotion of the agents were kept until more than three years after the holding of the concerned commissions, whereas the announced retention period was eighteen months. Point 57. *See* CNIL, SAN 2022-015, 7 Jul. 2022, Ubeeqo International in which the CNIL investigations revealed that some geolocation data were storage more than eight years in the rental system, while the announced retention duration was three years.
557. CNIL, SAN 2022-015, 7 Jul. 2022, Ubeeqo International, point 77.
558. CNIL, SAN 2021-019, 29 Oct. 2021, *RATP*, point 51.

that data concerning the number of strike days per employee were necessary for calculating pay and social contributions. Once the pay slip had been drawn up, the storage of this data for six years was excessive.

253. **Storage limitation of traffic and location data before French judges.**[559] The principle of limiting the duration of data retention has been the subject of significant cases in the context of preventive retention of traffic and location data for purposes of combating serious crime and safeguarding national security. The former wording of Article L.34-1 of CPCE is the starting point for these French cases. This provision imposed on telephony and Internet providers a general and indiscriminate retention of traffic and location data for crime-fighting purposes for one year. After a preliminary ruling,[560] the French *Conseil d'Etat*[561] declared that this did not conform to European Law. The *Conseil d'Etat* considered that general and indiscriminate retention is only authorised under strict conditions[562] for safeguarding national security purposes, as interpreted by the CJEU.[563] The *Cour de cassation* also came to the same conclusions in a series of judgments in July 2022.[564] For the processing for safeguarding national security purposes, the *Conseil d'Etat* argued that at the time of the case and since 1994, France has been facing a serious, real, and present threat to its national security. This justified that the retention duration of one year was strictly necessary.[565]

VIII. Integrity and Confidentiality Principles

254. The principle of integrity and confidentiality means that 'personal data must be processed in a manner that ensures appropriate security of the personal data, including protection against unauthorized or unlawful processing and against accidental loss, destruction or damage, or access by unauthorized persons, using appropriate technical or organisational measures', according to Article 4.6 LIL. Since 1978, the LIL has integrated a security obligation, which was much more at this time an obligation to protect the integrity of data, and it has been extended by European law to the confidentiality principle. Nethertheless, it has been only since the

559. More details on connection data *see* paras 172 et seq.
560. CJEU, 6 Oct. 2020, C-511/18, La Quadrature du Net e.a.
561. CE, 21 Apr. 2021, n° 393099, French Data Network, *see* point 48 for the reference of the CJEU case law, and the non-conformity of the French law, point 58.
562. The *Conseil d'Etat* underlined that such retention did not give rise to prior review by a court or by an AAI with binding powers as required by the CJEU case law. However, the *Conseil d'Etat* only annulled decrees on which the retentions were based, but non the retentions themselves, *see* point 97 and it enjoined the government to adapt this regulation within six months.
563. CE, 21 Apr. 2021, n° 393099, French Data Network, *see* point 48 for the reference of the CJEU case law, and its the non-conformity of the French law, point 58.
564. Crim., 12 Jul. 2022, FS-B+R, n° 21-83.710, points 24–26; Crim., 12 Jul. 2022, FS-B, n° 21-83.820; Crim., 12 Jul. 2022, FS-B, n° 21-84.096; Crim., 12 Jul. 2022, FS-B, n° 20-86.652. The *Cour de Cassation* published an explanatory note summarising the regime for the retention of connection and access data available at https://www.courdecassation.fr/getattacheddoc/62cd0e6ce91c8e9fcf07120d/4a99d09b7172bb5cb704fcf2d11cdca3.
565. *See* CE, 21 Apr. 2021, n° 393099, point 57.

last European data protection package that integrity and confidentiality have been enshrined as fundamental data principles.[566] Article 4.6 LIL is a copy-paste of Article 5, §1, f) GDPR with a small precision that the risk protected included the 'access by unauthorized persons', which was in the former LIL.

255. In 2020, the CNIL edited a guide relating to authorised third parties,[567] which listed the points that the data controller or processor must be verified when a third party requires access to data to prevent a violation of the confidentiality of the data. Recently, the *Conseil d'Etat* partially annulled a decree on the basis that it did not provide for any technical and organisational protection measures to restrict access to health data to external providers and auditors to avoid a breach of confidentiality.[568] More globally, the principles of integrity and confidentiality are closely linked to specific security obligations imposed on controllers and processors.[569]

§2. Legal Grounds

256. Article 5 LIL is a copy-paste of Article 6 GDPR and recalls the six general legal grounds for processing of personal data. The following paragraph will give some illustrations of the French application of the most used legal grounds. Before going further, it is worth remembering two points. The absence of a legal basis for the implementation of a processing operation naturally leads the CNIL to consider the processing operation unlawful.[570] The CNIL judges also that the controller must informed clearly on the legal ground it uses for each processing.[571]

I. Consent

257. Consent is certainly the most famous legal ground for personal data processing. Interestingly, consent was not a legal ground in the original 1978 LIL. It was only introduced in France by the transposition of the Directive 95/46. Since the GDPR, sanctioning the non-respect of the regime of the consent as a legal base for processing related to the cookies[572] is an important part of CNIL's activities.[573] In

566. For more details *see* Romain Perray, *Juriscl. 274-28 Données à caractère personnel*. Principes fondamentaux relatifs aux traitements de données à caractère personnel. Intégrité et confidentialité.
567. *See* https://www.cnil.fr/sites/default/files/atoms/files/guide_tiers_autorises.pdf, and the table of the main procedures of access for authorised third party in French law https://www.cnil.fr/sites/default/files/atoms/files/recueil-procedures-tiers-autorises.pdf.
568. CE 25 November 2020, n° 428451 point 14.
569. *See* further paras 372 et seq. and paras 380-381.
570. *See* recently the Clearview case CNIL, SAN 2022-019 du 17 Oct. 2022.
571. CNIL, SAN 2019-001, 21 Jan. 2019.
572. *See supra* paras 152 et seq.
573. *See* CNIL, SAN 2022-023, 19 Dec. 2022 concernant la société Microsoft Ireland Operations Limited, (60 million fine), SAN 2022-027, 29 Dec. 2022 concernant les sociétés Tiktok (5 million fine), SAN 2022-025, 29 Dec. 2022 concernant la société Apple Distribution International (8 million fine), SAN 2022-026, 29 Dec. 2022 concernant la société Voodoo, (3 million fine), SAN 2021-023, 31 Dec. 2021 concernant les sociétés Google LLC, (150 million fine); SAN 2021-024, 31 Dec.

these cases, involving most of the time big American digital platforms,[574] the CNIL recalls that consent must be given before the processing of personal data and that the consent needs to be freely given and specific. This means that bunded consent in which the user gives consent for all processing operations purposes is not valid. Furthermore, refusing consent should be as easy as giving it. Finally, the consent needs to be sufficiently informed. In its emblematic 2019 *Google* case, the CNIL notes the lack of clarity and comprehensibility with regard to the mention of the legal basis for the processing of personalised advertising. In particular, the CNIL criticised Google for not clearly specifying which processing operations were subject to consent and which were based on the legitimate interests of the data controller.[575] Otherwise, it is not simply a question of providing prior information to enable the person concerned to give valid consent. For each category of processing, the data subject must also be informed of the legal basis used.

258. Recently, the CNIL looked at commercial prospecting and in particular at how data brokers fulfil their legal obligations when collecting and reselling data. In this context, the CNIL issued an emblematic decision against a French company called Tagadamedia which mainly operates online competition websites and product testing websites, through which it collects data for propects. Based on its doctrine on cookies, the CNIL considered that the form put online by the company did not allow data to be collected on the basis of free, specific, informed and unambiguous consents. The first form only included an 'I validate' button, which in practice, obliged users wishing to take part in the competition to accept that their data would be used to send them offers from the company's partners. The second form integrated two buttons, but the user was not encouraged to click on the 'I decline' button because it was made less accessible by using dark pattern.[576]

259. Apart from the cases concerning cookies, the only noteworthy feature concerns the consent of minors. As mentioned before, the age at which a minor may consent to a direct offer of information society services in France is fifteen.[577] In other kinds of processing, French case law illustrates that the consent of both parents can be required where parental authority is exercised jointly.[578]

2021 concernant la société Facebook (60 million fine) and also cases with French companies such SAN 2021-013, 27 Jul. 2021 concernant la Societe Du Figaro (EUR 50,000 fine).

574. In such cases the CNIL is competent because there is no One-stop-shop mechanism in application of the directive 2002/58 and its competent is founded on Art. 82 LIL. *See* para. 420.

575. CNIL, SAN- 2019-001, 21 Jan. 2019.

576. CNIL SAN-2023-025, *Tagadamedia,* 29 December 2023, points 29, 38-50, in which the CNIL issued a fine of 75,000 euros against Tagadamedia, and decided to make its decision public. In April 2024, the CNIL closed the injunction. *See* CNIL SAN-2024-007, 25 April 2024.

577. *See* Art. 45 LIL, *see supra* para. 215.

578. *See* CA Versailles, 25 juin 2016, n° 13/08349; CA Paris, 9 février 2017, n° 15/13956, Cass. 1er civ., 27 février 2007, n° 06-14.273. These cases concern the publication of photographs of children in newpaper o social network where one of the parents had objected.

II. Performance of a Contract

260. The legal ground, bases on the need for the performance of a contract, does not call for any comment in France. As an illustration, the CNIL has had occasion to point out that this contractual requirement must be interpreted strictly in relation to the purposes of the contract. Accordingly, the CNIL found that Facebook's '*combination of user data for the purpose of targeting advertising did not correspond either to the main purpose of the contract or to the reasonable expectations of users with regard to the performance of the agreement entered into when registering for the service*'.[579]

III. Legal Obligation

261. The legal obligation ground often echoes the existence of national rules and/or specific processing duties for the controller or processor. National legal obligations of processing are numerous and diverse. For instance, online gaming and betting operators must check the identity of each new player, their age and address, and identify the payment account.[580] There are also numerous legal obligations to process personal data in the field of human resources. Management of professional elections, organisation of meetings of staff representative bodies, and nominative social declarations are based on legal obligations to process personal data.[581] French monetary and financial code contents several whistleblowing mechanisms with legal obligations of processing.[582]

262. Article 89 I LIL also requires certain types of processing to be based on a legislative or regulatory provision. This is a form of legal obligation which can be likened to the need for authorisation for certain types of processing generally covered by the Police Justice Directive. This is the case for processing carried out on behalf of the State by public authorities for public interest. For instance, the database SIRENE contains the personal data of passengers on the ships inspected, specifically information on their marital status, address, occupation, function onboard the ship, information on the ownership or hire of the ship and their geolocation collected by several French customs departments. The CNIL recently noted that such a database has been implemented without the needed authorisation. Therefore, the CNIL asked the Ministry of the Economy, which is responsible for processing this file, to rectify the situation.[583]

579. *See* CNIL SAN-2017-006 du, 27 Avril 2017, prononçant une sanction pécuniaire à l'encontre des sociétés X et Y.
580. *See* Art. 17 Loi n° 2010-476, 12 mai 2010, relative à l'ouverture de la concurrence et à la régulation du secteur des jeux d'argent et de hasard en ligne.
581. *See* Référentiel de la CNIL relatif aux traitements des données à caractère personnel mis en œuvre aux fins de gestion de personnel adopted in November 2019, p. 5.
582. *See* Art. L561-5, or Art. L225-102-4I.
583. Décision n° MED-2023-018 du 3 avril 2023 mettant en demeure le ministère de l'économie, des finances et de la souveraineté industrielle et numérique.

IV. Performance of a Task Carried Out in the Public Interest in the Exercise of Official Authority Vested in the Controller

263. The legal ground of the necessity for the performance of a task carried out in the public interest or in the exercise of official authority vested in the controller is broadly used in the public sector. It can be the managing requests for information on teleservices linked to the public service mission of the authority in question. It also applies to management of the claims relating to the concerned administration services.

V. Legitimate Interests

264. **The legitimate interests pursued by the controller or by a third party** can be used as legal grounds for processing according to Article 5.5 LIL which echoes Article 6.1.f GDPR. The *Conseil d'Etat* recalls that this ground implies assessing whether the legitimate interests of the controller prevail over those of the data subject. Therefore, the legitimate interests pursued by the controller must be weighed against the interests or fundamental rights and freedoms of the data subjects, having regard to the nature of the data processed, the purposes and methods of the processing and any expectations the data subjects may reasonably have regarding the lack of further processing of the data collected.

265. **Illustrations of balance of interest**. In a case, an internet website argued that keeping the bankcard numbers of customers could be based on a legitimate interest of facilitating the next payments by eliminating the need for the customer to enter this information each time they make a purchase as part of a 'one-click' purchase function. The *Conseil d'Etat* declared that '*this interest cannot take precedence over the customers' interest in protecting this data, given the sensitivity of this banking information and the harm that could result for them from its capture and misuse, and when many customers who use e-commerce sites in order to make one-off purchases cannot reasonably expect the companies concerned to keep such data without their consent*'.[584] Furthermore, the *Conseil d'Etat* validated the CNIL's recommendation related to the processing of payment card data relating to the distance sale of goods or provision of services. In this document, the CNIL considered that explicit consent of the data subject should be required to store the bank card numbers of customers of e-commerce sites to facilitate subsequent purchases.[585]

266. The balance of the legitimate interests of the controller and those of the data subject can be analysed in connection with its data subject rights, such as the

584. CE, 20 décembre 2020, n° 429571, point 9.

585. *See,* Deliberation n° 2018-303, 6 Sep. 2018 portant adoption d'une recommandation concernant le traitement des données relatives à la carte de paiement en matière de vente de biens ou de fourniture de services à distance et abrogeant la délibération n° 2017-222 du 20 juillet 2017.

right of information. This can be illustrated by the *Monsanto* case. In its deliberation, the CNIL incidentally considered that the processing of personal data for lobbying purposes could be carried out based on the legitimate interest pursued by the controller.[586] In this case, the people on file could reasonably expect Montsanto to be interested in their public stance on glyphosate and even to deal with their professional details. However, they should have been informed of the processing of their personal data under Article 14 GDPR.

267. In other cases, the balance of the legitimate interest involved the fundamental rights of the data subject, which prevailed over the economic interest of the data controller. For instance, in its 2017 *Facebook* case, the CNIL considered that '*combining user data for the purpose of displaying personalised content and advertising can arise from an economic interest and enables companies to offer a free and relevant service to users can be qualified as legitimate. However, the potentially unlimited combination of all user data, which is collected not only on the [...] site but also on third-party sites or applications, in particular via the [...] cookie, is of such a scale as to disregard users' interests and infringe their right to privacy*'.[587] More specifically, the fact that users have no means of controlling the combination of their personal data and putting an end to massive monitoring of their behaviour constitutes a violation of their right to privacy.

§3. Special Categories of Data

268. The LIL contains two distinct sets of provisions on special categories of data. First, some provisions recall the prohibition of the processing of so-called sensitive data and list national exceptions for such processings. Second, the LIL contains a provision relating to the processing of personal data relating to criminal convictions and offences.

I. Processing of Personal Data Relating to Criminal Convictions and Offences

269. The LIL and the GDPR include a regime for the processing of personal data relating to criminal convictions and offences without defining this concept. According to the CNIL and French judges, this concept covers the processing of data qualified as a conviction by a competent authority,[588] as well as the processing of data

586. CNIL, SAN 2021-012, 26 Jul. 2021, point 74. The CNIL described lobbying processing 'which consist of the collection of information to identify influential persons with whom a company wishes to represent its interests may, subject to certain conditions'. *See* SANc2021-012, 26 Jul. 2021, point 74.

587. CNIL SAN 2017-006, 27 Apr. 2017, point 6.

588. *See* for instance Crim., 13 Jan. 2009, n° 08-84. 088 P. The CNIL in its website give the example of Mr X's sentence of two years' imprisonment for tax fraud. It is case *B v. Latvijas Republikcas Saeima,* the CJEU emphasised that the application of Art. 10 GDPR required an autonomous and

collected for the purpose of establishing the existence or preventing the commission of offences.[589] This excludes the processing of data relating to non-criminal offences (such as a simple breach of internal rules). This excludes the processing of data relating to criminally punishable conduct that is not collected for the purpose of establishing the existence or preventing the commission of offences. This is a case of the data collected for the sole purpose of ensuring the safety of sporting events by enabling the organisers of these events to prevent certain people from accessing their sports venues on the grounds of dangerous behaviour in breach of contractual obligations.[590]

270. Article 46 LIL lists five national exceptions allowing the processing of personal data relating to criminal convictions, offences, or related security measures. The rationale behind this provision is that personal data relating to criminal convictions and offences may only be processed by a limited number of categories of players. Unauthorised access or storage might have grave consequences for data subjects, such as being discriminated against or stigmatised. The aim is to ensure that individuals' rights and freedoms are not disproportionately affected. For example, the CNIL recently condemned a company for violating Article 10 of the GDPR by storing extracts from criminal records in the personal files of employees whose contracts were in progress. However, under French law, in principle, employers can only consult employees' criminal records. As an exception, for certain jobs subject to clearance, this consultation is not carried out directly by the employer but must be done by the police or gendarmerie.[591]

271. Processing of personal data relating to criminal convictions and offences might be necessary to achieve general interest objectives. Therefore, Article 46 LIL echoes Article 10 GDPR, which gives two different legal grounds for the processing of such data. Personal data relating to criminal convictions and offences may be processed under the control of a public authority, or such processing can be authorised by EU or national law.

272. The list in Article 46 LIL meets these requirements. Article 46 LIL broadens the categories of players likely to be able to process this type of data while trying to provide safeguards. As before, the LIL authorises the processing of such data by the courts, public authorities, and entities managing a public service acting within the scope of their powers, court officers strictly for the purposes of carrying out their duties legally entrusted to them by law, and legal persons acting for the

---

uniform interpretation of the concept of criminal offence throughout the EU. *See* CJEU, *B v. Latvijas Republikcas Saeima*, judgment of 22 Jun. 2021, Case C-439/19, ECLI:EU:C:2021:504, point 85.

589. *See* for instance CE, 11 May 2015, *Renault Trucks* n° 375669P. This case concerned the processing of data to identify the consultation by employees of child pornography content with a view to possible reporting to the competent authorities. The *Conseil d'Etat* ruled that such processing by a private company did not comply with French law in force prior to the GDPR because it had not been authorised by the CNIL.

590. *See*, CE, 6 Apr. 2018, association nationale des supporteurs et autres, n° 406664 B.

591. *See* CNIL SAN-2023-013, 18 Sep. 2023, *Logistics*, points 61–63.

rights they manage or on behalf of victims of a violation of the rights provided for the purpose of defending these rights according to the CPI. The unique novelty is that the entities managing a public service acting within the scope of their powers are specified in Article 76 LIL application decree.[592] In addition, Article 46 LIL legalises the processing of personal data relating to criminal convictions and offences for two categories of players. Article 46-3 LIL authorises the processing of such data by 'natural or legal persons, for the purpose of enabling them to prepare for and, if applicable, bring and pursue a lawsuit as a victim, accused party, or on behalf of the victim or accused party and to enforce the decision issued, for a period strictly proportionate to these purposes'. Article 46-3 LIL includes an additional guarantee. It limits the communication of this data to third parties. This can only take place if these third parties also process this data to the extent strictly necessary for the same purposes. This paragraph clarifies the prior regime.[593] While the law specifies the conditions for the processing of personal data relating to criminal convictions and offences for what can be named as litigation files, the creation of such files is no longer subject to prior authorisation by the CNIL. Second, Article 46-5 LIL provides an exception for the processing of personal data relating to criminal convictions, offences or related security measures, allowing such processing for persons re-using public information. The rationale is to promote the Legal tech sector. By way of guarantee, it is specified that '*the purpose or effect of these processing operations is not to allow the re-identification of data subjects*'.[594]

273. Finally, it should be underlined that Article 46 LIL provides a separate legal regime for the processing of sensitive data (Article 9 GDPR, Article 6 LIL) and processing of personal data relating to criminal convictions and offences. This means that the exceptions to the prohibition of the processing of sensitive data should not applied. In particular, the explicit consent of the data subject should not give the data controller a legal ground for processing. However, recent case law shows that there are ways of processing personal data relating to criminal convictions and offences that can be justified over and above Article 10 GDPR. Access to such data could be justified by the right to freedom of information under Article 86 GDPR. This involves that the person requesting access must establish a 'specific interest in obtaining those data'.[595] In France, the *Conseil d'Etat* has, on several occasions,

592. This covers nine entities, including associations helping victims under agreement with the Ministry of Justice, associations helping victims approved by the Ministry of Justice, associations providing assistance with the reintegration of persons placed under house arrest, certain social and medico-social establishments and services, certain health establishments, public and private educational institutions, or approved vocational training establishments, etc.
593. The Constitutional Council has twice intervened to limit the possibilities for private individuals to process this data. It has reiterated that this possibility must be strictly limited by law. *See* CC, Decision No. 2004-499 DC, 19 Jul. 2004, and CC, Decision No. 2018-765 DC, 12 Jun. 2018. In addition, under the previous system, the CC considered that the possibility of creating a file to combat theft, non-payment and other offences to which legal entities could fall victim was subject to authorisation from the CNIL.
594. *See* Art. 46.5 LIL.
595. CJEU, 7 Mar. 2024, C-740/22, *Shine Finland Oy*, point 58, ECLI:EU:C:2024:216.

weighed up the prohibition on processing data relating to convictions or criminal proceedings against the right to information in the context of de-listing right.[596]

II. Processing of Sensitive Personal Data

274. Article 6.1 LIL reiterates the principle of prohibiting the processing of so-called sensitive data of Article 9.1 GDPR. It is supplemented by Article 44 LIL, which sets out a list of six exceptions to this prohibition. Some of these exceptions overlap with the specific processing situations for scientific research and statistical purposes, which will be addressed in Part IX. Finally, Articles 31 and 32 set up the legal framework applicable to the processing of sensitive data by or on behalf of the State. Five categories of sensitive data in the French context deserve attention.

A. *Personal Data Revealing Racial or Ethnic Origin*

275. Processing of personal data revealing racial or ethnic origin is strictly prohibited in France. Therefore, Article 6.I LIL includes a small but significant difference in wording in comparison to Article 9 GDPR. The prohibition is related to processing 'revealing "alleged" racial origin' because, more globally, France prohibits racial classifications. This principle is anchored in a French-style universalist approach that goes beyond the principle of non-discrimination by asserting a principle of non-racial distinction between human beings.[597] In 2007, the *Conseil constitutionnel* declared that the creation of a national nomenclature of ethno-racial categories would be contrary to the Constitution.[598] '*Although the processing of data necessary for carrying out studies regarding the diversity of origin of peoples, discrimination and integration may be done in an objective manner, such processing cannot, without infringing the principle laid down in Article 1 of the Constitution, be based on ethnicity or race.*' In its comment[599] on its decision, the *Conseil constitutionnel* gave two useful clarifications. It illustrated that collecting name, geographical origin or nationality prior to French nationality could be an objective manner to evaluating diversity.[600] It also validated the collection of subjective data, such as data based on 'feelings of belonging'. The investigation 'Trajectories and origins' is one of famous investigations based on both objective and subjective

596. CE, 20 Apr. 2023, n° 463487, n° 429154. More details on de-listing right *See* paras 343 et seq.
597. Article 1 of the current French Constitution: 'France shall be an indivisible, secular, democratic and social Republic. It shall ensure the equality of all citizens before the law, without distinction of origin, race or religion. It shall respect all beliefs.'
598. CC, 2007-557 DC, 15 Nov. 2007, point 29.
599. Commentaire de la décision n° 2007-557 DC du 15 novembre 2007, Cahiers du Conseil constitutionnel, n° 24, p.6.
600. *See* CE, 11 Mar. 2013 Association SOS racisme n° 348613, which also validated this possibility. This possibility has been exploited by the INSEE (French public statistic entity), in population census, employment survey, family budget survey, housing survey.

approaches.[601] These public statistical studies need a prior authorisation of the CNIL, in which it evaluates the respect of the principles enshrined in *Conseil constitutionnel* aforementioned 2007 decision.[602]

276. Apart from the processing of objective data such as nationality, country of birth, speaking languages, etc., employers may not process data '"revealing alleged" racial origin', even with the explicit consent of the person concerned. Article L.1221-6 French labour code provides that during a recruitment procedure, an employer must only collect information for the purpose of assessing the applicant's ability to do the job offered or his/her professional aptitudes. This article explicitly recalls 'This information must have a direct and necessary link with the job offered or with the assessment of professional skills.'

277. More globally, the strict nature of the prohibition on processing data that may reveal racial or ethnic origin must be assessed in the light of its necessity regarding the purpose of the processing. For example, the CNIL ruled that the creation of a file of postal addresses of people of foreign origin, selected on their first and last names, was not compliant with the LIL, since it was not relevant to the service insurance offered.[603] Finally, racial or ethnical data processing can be criminally condemned under the principle of non-discrimination.[604]

B. Data Concerning Health

278. Data concerning health are at the core of a complex articulation of European and French rules.[605] Data concerning health raises several legal and political issues in France,[606] as in most other countries. Among them, the scope of the data concerning health is still debated[607] even after the harmonised definition given by

601. Trajectoires et origines, Enquête sur la diversité des populations en France, sous la direction de Cris Beauchemin, Christelle Hamel et Patrick Simon, Collection: Grandes Enquêtes 2016.
602. *See* Deliberation 2011-255, 21 Sep. 2011 autorisant l'accès des chercheurs et des services statistiques ministériels aux données à caractère personnel collectées dans le cadre de la réalisation de l'enquête statistique dénommée 'Trajectoires et Origines'; Deliberation 2015-309, 10 Sep. 2015 autorisant l'Institut National d'Etudes Démographiques (INED) à mettre en œuvre des traitements automatisés de données à caractère personnel ayant pour finalités la réalisation et l'analyse des résultats d'enquête statistique portant sur les mutations sociodémographiques dans le département d'Outre-mer de Mayotte dénommée 'Migration, Famille, Vieillissement' (MFV Mayotte).
603. Delibération 2008-028, 31 Jan. 2008 sanctionnant la société X.
604. Article 225-4 CP.
605. LIL, Public Health Code in particular. It is worth to underline that in 1978, the LIL did not contain provision on health. It is with the adoption of the EC Directive 95/45 and its transposition in French law in 2004 that this concept was integrated in the LIL.
606. *See* Conseil d'Etat, Droits et débats, Santé et protection des données, La documentation française, 2019; M. Lanna, *La protection des données à caractère personnel à l'épreuve de l'automesure connectée*, thèse, Paris 2, 2019; Biometric data and genetic data can sometimes be considered data concerning health but will be adressed further on.
607. More details *see* Lorraine Maisnier-Boché, *Juriscl. Fasc. 945: Donnees De Sante a Caractere, Personnel. – Regime General; See also* Gaël Burroni, *L'influence de la finalité sur la qualification juridique des données de santé, Revue internationale de droit économique,* 2022/3, pp. 63–76.

Article 4.15 GDPR. Furthermore, the French government introduced a specific regime for health data in the LIL when adapting it to the GDPR.

1. The Scope of the Concept of Health Data

279. Before the GDPR, the *Conseil d'Etat* agreed on a strict definition of health data. According to the French administrative judge, health data need to give '*information on the nature, duration or seriousness of the pupil's condition*'.[608] Therefore, the registration of a child in a non-specialised primary school in an inclusive education class according to a code identifying the type of disability was health-related data.[609] By contrast, the judge considered that use of a code for a healthcare facility that makes it possible to know that a pupil has been ill without knowing what the illness was does not constitute health data.[610] After the GDPR, the French judges continue to interpret the notion of health data strictly. For example, the *Conseil d'Etat* ruled that data relating to vaccination appointments made during the COVID-19 pandemic did not constitute data relating to health.[611] In the same way, the *Conseil d'Etat* judges that information that '*indirectly reveals that the persons recruited in this capacity suffer from a handicap, it does not directly give any information on the nature or seriousness of this handicap', does not constitute data relating to health.*[612] Similarly, the *Cour de cassation* considers that information relating to a work stoppage, which does not indicate the reason for the absence, does not constitute data relating to health.[613]

280. **CNIL's approach**. The CNIL proposed a three-categories classification:[614]

- **Health data per nature**, such as medical history, illnesses, care received, test results, treatments, disabilities, etc.
- **Health data in combination with other** data which enables to draw a conclusion about a person's state of health or health risk. Combining a weight measurement with other data (number of steps, calorie intake measurement, etc.), combining blood pressure with effort measurement, etc.
- **Health data based on its intended use**, i.e., its medical application.

This classification intends to tackle the grey zone where it is only indirectly through further processing that precise information on the state of a person's health can be found. This classification has enabled the CNIL to consider that developers

608. CE, 19 Jul. 2010, n° 334014.
609. CE, 19 Jul. 2010, n° 317182.
610. CE, 19 Jul. 2010, n° 334014. Similarly, the CE judged that the 'mention of the permanent incapacity rate or disability rate … is not data "relating to health"'. *See* CE, 28 Mar. 2014 n° 361042, point 15.
611. CE, 12 Mar. 2021, n° 450163.
612. CE, 10 Jun. 2021, n° 431875.
613. Cass. soc., 13 Jun. 2018, n° 16–25/30.
614. https://www.cnil.fr/fr/recherche?search=donn%C3%A9es%20de%20sant%C3%A9.

of mobile health or wellness applications are exempt from the regulation on personal data when this data is exclusively recorded and stored locally on a smartphone or tablet, without any external connection and for exclusively personal purposes.[615] By contrast, health concerning data will be processed when the apps are based on data sharing, such as the follow-up by professional monitoring and medical surveillance, and involve an external connection, such as saving the data in the cloud.

2. French Exceptions to the Prohibition of Health Data Processing

281. The processing of health data is prohibited in principle, like all other special categories of data, but it is possible under a series of strictly defined exceptions. In this context, the French Health Data framework is fragmented into three main categories. The data concerning health processing which are based on Article 9, §2 GDPR, the processing in the health sector[616] and the processing for medical research, study or evaluation purposes (hereinafter 'research Health data').[617] France has used its room for manoeuvre in the last two categories to promote useful and/or legitimate sharing while ensuring that this particularly sensitive data is protected.

282. **Explicit consent**. Data concerning health processing based on Article 9, §2 GDPR includes all processing of health data based on the explicit consent of the data subject.[618] On numerous occasions, the CNIL has noted the absence of explicit prior consent for the processing of health data. Recently, the CNIL fined Doctissimo because its website provided online tests without special warning or consent mechanisms to ensure that the users were aware of the processing of their health data and gave their consent.[619] Similarly, the CNIL fined KG COM, an online clairvoyance company, because it collected and stored information about the health of its customers without obtaining its customers' prior explicit consent to process their sensitive data.[620]

283. It should be emphasised that consent encounters two types of reservations in the healthcare field. First, the consent is not seen as a pertinent legal ground for a healthcare relationship, and in the context of relations between employees, it may

615. Nevertheless, the provider must secure the storage of the data by following, in particular, the good practice guidelines on health apps and smart devices, adopted in October 2016 by the French Haute autorité de santé, https://www.has-sante.fr/upload/docs/application/pdf/2017-03/dir1/good_practice_guidelines_on_health_apps_and_smart_devices_mobile_health_or_mhealth.pdf.

616. Articles 65–71 LIL.

617. Articles 72–77 LIL.

618. Article 65 details all the processings which are not in the scope of the French Health Data regime. It includes the processing necessary to protect the vital interest (Art. 9.2.c GDPR), the processing carried out by foundation, association etc. (Art. 9.2.d GDPR), processing made public by the data subject, (Art. 9.2.e), processing necessary for the establishment, exercise or defence of legal claims (Art. 9.2.f) and some processing made by medical authorities or agencies.

619. CNIL, SAN 2023-006, 11 May 2023 concernant la société DOCTISSIMO.

620. CNIL SAN 2023-008, 8 Jun. 2023 concernant la société KG COM.

be difficult to consider that it is free given. In such a situation, the legal ground is often legal obligations. Second, French law prohibits the processing of certain health data that cannot be lifted by consent. For instance, it is forbidden to sell personal health data.[621] In addition, a patient cannot, in principle, release a professional who is bound by the obligation of medical confidentiality.[622] This means that the patient's consent cannot be used as a legal ground for processing health data covered by medical confidentiality.[623] French law also prohibits insurance companies, mutual insurance companies and provident societies from taking into account the results of an examination of the genetic characteristics of a person applying for disability or death cover, even with that person's consent.[624]

284. **French additional criteria**. The LIL completes the Article 9, §2 GDPR framework on health data by using two essential criteria: the purpose of the processing and the professional secrecy.[625] Therefore, Article 44 1°) LIL authorised processing for '*operations for the purposes of preventive medicine, medical diagnosis, the administration of care or treatment, or health services management carried out by a health professional, or by another person upon whom the obligation of professional secrecy is incumbent by reason of his duties, and any violation of which is punishable under Article 226-13 of the Penal Code*'. Furthermore, Article 44-3 LIL) is focused on the possibility of '*processing of data concerning health which is in the public interes*t' and when the processing meets the requirements set out by a specific section of the LIL dedicated to processing in the health sector. This additional condition of public interest applies to research health data processing and processing in the health sector. As the CNIL pointed out, '*the pursuit of the public interest is not restricted to public bodies alone'.*[626] *Nevertheless, there is a kind of presumption of public interest in studies, research and evaluations that are requested by public authorities.*[627]

285. **Prior formalities**. The CNIL plays an essential role in assessing this public interest thought a system of prior formalities. The LIL provides only a few exceptions in which the health data are not submitted to prior formalities, which mainly echoes the provisions of the GDPR.[628] Apart from these exceptions, prior formalities can take two forms. Research health data processing and processing in

---

621. *See* Art. L.1111-8 VII Public Health Code provides that VII – 'Any act of transferring directly or indirectly identifying health data for consideration, even with the consent of the person concerned, is prohibited, subject to the penalties ... .' and subjected to penalties of five years' imprisonment and a fine of EUR 300,000. *See also* the Art. L.41113-7 Health Public Code.
622. *See* Art. L.871 Public Health Code on medical confidentiality.
623. *See* Lorraine Maisnier-Boché, Fasc. 945, point 48.
624. *See* CSP, Art. L.1141-1. – CSS, Art. L.932-39. – C. assur., Art. L.133-1. – C. mut., Art. L.110-4.
625. *See also* Art. L.1100-4 Public Health code on medical confidentiality.
626. *See* Délibération n° 2018-289 du 12 juillet 2018 autorisant la société IQVIA Opérations France à mettre en œuvre un traitement automatisé de données à caractère personnel ayant pour finalité la constitution d'un entrepôt de données à caractère personnel à des fins de recherche, d'étude ou d'évaluation dans le domaine de la santé, dénommé base de données LRX (n° 2120812).
627. *See* INDS, Principes d'appréciation de l'intérêt public, 11 févr. 2019, p. 5.
628. *See* Art. 67 LIL which provides an exception for 'the processing of personal data concerning health carried out by the organisations or departments entrusted with a public service task contained on a

the health sector may be based on either an authorisation[629] or a declaration of compliance with a referential adopted by the CNIL that needs to be transmitted to the CNIL.[630] For instance, the CNIL adopted in 2019 a referential on personal data processing implemented for the purposes of health vigilance management[631] and a referential on health data warehouses.[632] Each of these referentials sets out a legal framework (nature of the data processed, data recipients, information, etc.) and technical frameworks for health data processing.

286. **The health research data regime**. The health research data regime is subject to two main particularities. On the one hand, the referentials are called 'methodology of references'.[633] On the other hand, the CNIL is supported by an expert committee[634] for the assessment of the purpose and the methodology of the research, the need for personal health data, the ethical relevance and the scientific quality and eventually, the public interest of the projected research.[635] The CNIL may disregard this opinion, but it may also use it to justify its refusal of authorisation.[636]

---

list established by decree of the ministers responsible for health and social security, passed following an opinion of the CNIL, whose sole purpose is to respond, in the event of an emergency, to a health alert and to manage the consequences'. Furthermore, studies internal to a care team have been exempted from prior formalities by Art. 65.2 LIL.

629. Article 33 LIL detailed common categories of information needed for asking the authorisation.
630. *See* Art. 66, for the general health data processing and Art. 73 LIL for health data processing for research purposes.
631. Deliberation n° 2019-057, 9 May 2019 portant adoption d'un référentiel relatif aux traitements de données à caractère personnel mis en œuvre à des fins de gestion des vigilances sanitaires.
632. *See* Deliberation n° 2021-118, 7 Oct. 2021 portant adoption d'un référentiel relatif aux traitements de données à caractère personnel mis en œuvre à des fins de création d'entrepôts de données dans le domaine de la santé, https://www.cnil.fr/sites/cnil/files/atoms/files/referentiel_entrepot.pdf.
633. In 2018, the CNIL adopted six methodologies of references *see* https://www.cnil.fr/fr/traitements-declaration-conformite?field_norme_numerotation_type_value%5B0%5D=6; In 2022, the CNIL adopted two new methodologies allowing pharmaceutical laboratories to process the personal data required to give patients access to certain medicines without marketing authorisation. https://www.cnil.fr/fr/traitements-declaration-conformite?field_norme_numerotation_type_value%5B0%5D=6.
634. Comité d'Expertise pour les Recherches, les Études et les Évaluations dans le domaine de la Santé (CESREES). The is made up of around twenty members (appointed by decree) and a network of external experts in research in the fields of health, epidemiology, genetics, biostatistics, human and social sciences, ethics, law and algorithmic processing and personal data processing in the health field. Its secretary is assumed by the French Health Data Hub.
635. In 2018 the CNIL adopted six methodologies of reference, some of them have been since updated. MR-001 applicable to research involving the human subjects and research requiring an examination of genetic characteristics; MR-002 applicable to non-interventional studies of the performance of in vitro diagnostic medical devices; MR-003 applicable to research involving the in which the person concerned does not object to after having been informed; MR-004 applicable to research not involving human beings; MR-005 and MR-006, which govern access to hospital data; *See* https://www.cnil.fr/fr/les-referentiels-et-methodologies-de-reference-sante.
636. *See* CNIL Decision 2022-103, 20 Oct. 2022, in which the CNIL refused to authorise a health research processing asked by the Newspaper Le Point for the purpose the elaboration of an annual ranking of hospitals and clinics. The CNIL based its refusal on the negative opinion of the CESREES which criticised the methodology used and consequently its lack of public interest. More details on https://www.cnil.fr/fr/palmares-des-hopitaux-cnil-precise-les-raisons-de-son-refus-dautoriser-le-point-base-donnees-hopitaux.

287. The above-mentioned documentation should not be confused with others 'referentials', which are not binding. Indeed, some referentials simply intend to help data controllers comply with the GDPR for processing which are not submitted in principle to prior formalities. This is the case of the referential for medical and paramedical practice to manage their day-to-day health processing based on legal obligation and legitimate interest.[637]

288. Despite this dense legal framework, the CNIL recently felt that it would be necessary to clarify and secure the legal framework for exchanges of health data between the health insurance scheme and supplementary insurance companies (mutuelles). These exchanges aim to facilitate the reimbursement of healthcare costs to patients. Nevertheless, it raised issues regarding their legal ground and the respect of medical confidentiality.[638] The *Conseil d'Etat* recalled that '*the sharing, between professionals who are not part of the same healthcare team, of information necessary for the care of a person requires his or her prior consent, obtained by any means, including electronically*'.[639]

289. On data protection law point of view, Health Data processing framework in France illustrated a form a privacy by design in which the CNIL plays an important role. It is first in this area that the CNIL has chosen to personalise its support for players by opening up sandbox possibilities.[640]

290. Furthermore, the legal framework of health data in France includes a series of specific obligations, such as carrying out a DPIA.[641] It also entails specificity regarding the rights of the data subject.[642]

3. Health Data Processing and French Digital Health Strategy

291. **Overview of the French Digital Health Strategy** Understanding the French health personal data regime requires replacing it in the broader context of France's digital health strategy. This strategy is based on three main components which date back to the 2016 Law on the modernisation of the French healthcare system.[643] The French ambition is to structure the different health data bases with the purpose of elaborating a national health data system (SNDS). Centralising these

---

637. Référentiel pour la gestion des traitements courants des cabinets médicaux et paramédicaux. In addition the CNIL published also a two referentials on the data storage limitation: one in the Health sector expect research and another which covers the health research. *See* https://www.cnil.fr/fr/la-cnil-publie-trois-referentiels-pour-le-secteur-de-la-sante.
638. *See* the legal analysis of the CNIL published on its website https://www.cnil.fr/fr/assurance-maladie-complementaire-la-cnil-appelle-clarifier-et-securiser-le-cadre-juridique-pour.
639. CE, 15 novembre 2022, n° 441387, point 5.
640. *See* CNIL, rapport annuel 2021, pp.86–88.
641. *See* below para. 389.
642. *See* below para. 323.
643. Loi n° 2016-41 du 26 January 2016 de modernisation de notre système de santé.

data should make it possible to create the largest medico-administrative database[644] in the world and gradually extend to certain medical data.[645] The purpose is to provide data for analysing and improving the health of the population. Therefore, the second component of France's digital health strategy is to organise the conditions to enable access to and reuse of these data by all public and private players with a public interest. Such an opening up has necessitated the creation of a health data platform, also called the French Health Data Hub.[646] Eventually, this national platform should become part of the future European Health Data Space.[647] The third component of France's digital health strategy is to ensure the exchange and sharing of health data in a trustworthy environment for e-health and patient monitoring. In 2018, digital health became one of the five priorities of the 'Ma Santé 2022' plan. The aim was to set up by 2022 an individual, customisable digital health space personalised for each user, giving access to their data and offering a range of services to them throughout their life. Therefore, a digital health agency (Agence du Numérique en Santé, ANS) was created in 2020. In 2019, a new programme called the *Segur du numérique* was launched to enable the seamless, secure sharing of healthcare data between professionals and patients.

292. **Security issues**. Security conditions relating to the storage of common health data are frequently called into question. Many French hospitals have made them prime targets for cyber-attacks.[648] The CNIL imposed several fines for heath data breaches in laboratories,[649] medical practices,[650] or excessive retention of health data by insurance companies.[651] In 2021, a judge even asked ISPs to block access to a site hosting the health data of nearly 500,000 people's health data people made available by a hacker.[652]

---

644. Originally, the Caisse Nationale de l'Assurance Maladie (Cnam) was the controller of the data base which aggregated the public health insurance data, the hospital data, medical causes of death collected by the Inserm, the data relating to disability a sample data from complementary health insurance organisations. These health data are in principle pseudonymised. The *Conseil d'Etat* declared the SNDS conform to the GDPR.
645. First application was with some data related to the COVID-19. *See* Arrêté du 21 Apr. 2020 complétant l'arrêté du 23 mars 2020 prescrivant les mesures d'organisation et de fonctionnement du système de santé nécessaires pour faire face à l'épidémie de covid-19 dans le cadre de l'état d'urgence sanitaire.
646. The Health data Hub was created by the Loi n° 2019-774 relative à l'organisation et à la transformation du système de santé. The French Health Data hub involves fifty-six stakeholders, mostly from the public sector (CNAM, CNRS, Haute Autorité de santé, France Assos Santé, etc.). It is rules by Arts L.1460-1 et seq. of the Public Health Code.
647. *See* the European Commission proposal of regulation on the European Health Data Space, COM(2022) 197 final.
648. The outdated IT systems of many French hospitals have made them prime targets for cyber-attacks, which forced the French government to improve the support to these bodies including with a new Heath Digital Agency. For example, the data breach from Assistance Publique-Hôpitaux de Paris (AP-HP) concerning 1.4 million people tested against COVID-19 in mid-2020. *See* Le Monde, 8 Oct. 2021.
649. CNIL, SAN 2022-009, 15 Apr. 2022, concernant la société Dedalus Biologie or the formal notice n° MED-2021-093, 4 Oct. 2021 prise à l'encontre de la société Francetest.
650. CNIL, SAN 2020-014 and SAN 2020-015, 7 Déc. 2020.
651. CNIL, SAN 2021-010, 20 Jul. 2021.
652. TJ Paris, 4 Mar. 2021, n° 21/51823.

293. **E-health**. Beyond the LIL, several provisions linked to the development of e-health in France have been introduced in the Health Public Code. Article L.1110-4 Health Public Code fixes the legal framework for exchange and sharing of health data. It is based on health data security and interoperability standards. In 2022, the ANS has been given broader powers to develop interoperability and security standards and to monitor compliance with these standards by publishers and healthcare professionals.[653] Financial support has been allocated to manufacturers so that they can propose software which guarantees the exchange and sharing of healthcare data. At the same time, IT solutions that comply with these technical standards are included in a list that practitioners, hospitals, etc., should use to update their software.

4. French Compulsory Heath Data Host Certification[654]

294. According to Article L.1111-8 of the French Public Health Code, all public or private organisations that host, operate or back up healthcare information systems on behalf of a healthcare institution or third party must be certified.[655] The scope of this obligation is doubly limited by the wording of this article. The obligation of certification is not extended to all data concerning health, and the hosting and intra-group hosting are excluded.[656] The certification procedure is based on an assessment of compliance with the certification standard elaborated by the ANS, which was reformed in December 2023.[657] Applicants must apply for a certificate from a body which has been accredited by the French Accreditation Committee (Cofrac).[658]

295. **Health Data hosting and digital sovereignty**. During the COVID-19 pandemic, the hosting of the Health Data Hub by Microsoft, an American company, has been the subject of much criticism as it runs counter to the political affirmation of the government's desire to assert its digital sovereignty. Several associations have asked the *Conseil d'Etat* to suspend this health data hosting contract. From a legal point of view, the associations argued that French health data had been transferred to the United States in breach of the GDPR. The *Conseil d'Etat* initially ruled that there was no evidence of such no conformed to the GDPR transfers.[659] According

653. *See* Arts L.1470-5 et seq. Public Health Code.
654. In practice, there are two kinds of certification: the Physical infrastructure hosting certification and a certification as a 'hosting provider'.
655. *See* TJ Paris, 6 Nov. 2020, n° 20/54799 where the judge considered that the non-certification of a website that put patients and doctors in touch with each other constitutes a manifestly unlawful breach of public order that must be brought to an immediate end. In 2023, there were 284 certified health data hosts. *See* https://esante.gouv.fr/offres-services/hds/liste-des-herbergeurs-certifies.
656. Maisnier-Boché, Lorraine Certification hébergeurs: un projet de référentiel, entre clarifications et interrogations, Expertises janvier 2023, n° 486, p. 16.
657. *See* the decree of 26 Apr. 2024, approving the new HDS certification framework, was published in the Official Journal on 16 May 2024 and will come into effect on 17 Nov. 2024.
658. In 2023, nine bodies are accredited by the COFRAC, *See* https://esante.gouv.fr/offres-services/hds/liste-des-organismes-de-certification.
659. *See* CE Ord., 19 Jun. 2020, n° 440916.

to the *Conseil d'Etat*, personal data was hosted in the Netherlands, and Microsoft contractually engaged itself that no data will be transferred outside the European Union. After the CJEU's *Schrems II*[660] ruling, the *Conseil d'Etat* temporarily validated the situation. While acknowledging the existence of a risk of access to personal data, the *Conseil d'Etat* encourage the government to find a solution that will eliminate such a risk.[661] Despite the French government promises to migrate the Health Data Hub to a purely European hosting solution, the Health Data Hub continues to be hosted by Microsoft.

296. However, one of the main novelties of the 2023 reform of the above-mentioned health data host certification is the introduction of four requirements relating to data sovereignty. Thus:

- Health data must be physically hosted exclusively in a country within the European Economic Area (EEA) (Requirement 28).
- Where the service offered by the Host or one of its processors involves remote access from a non-EEA country which is such access must be based on an adequacy decision or, failing that, on appropriate guarantees (Requirements 29 and 30). The hosting provider must inform its customers of this in the contract and specify the associated risks, as well as the technical and legal measures implemented to limit them.
- (Require hosting providers to publish, on their websites, a map of any transfers of the data they host to countries outside the EEA (Requirement 31).

C. *Biometric Data*

297. **French GDPR's exceptions of the use of biometric data.**[662] The LIL contains two major national exceptions to the prohibition of biometrics data. Article 44.4 LIL provides a possibility of such processing '*carried out by employers or administrations, which involve biometric data strictly required to verify access to the workplace and to the devices and applications used in the tasks entrusted to employees, officers, trainees or providers*'. Therefore, the biometrics processing needs to conform to a model regulation ('règlement type') adopted by the CNIL. In 2018, the CNIL adopted such model regulation for biometric access control in the workplace.[663] The model regulation authorises only '*the biometric authentication based on the morphological characteristics of the data subjects. The choice of biometric type(s) (iris, fingerprint, hand vein, etc.) must be justified and documented by the employer, including the reason for using one biometric characteristic rather*

660. CJEU, 16 Jul. 2020, Data Protection Commissioner c/ Facebook Ireland Ltd, Maximillian Schrems, C-311-/18.
661. *See* CE Ord., 13 Oct. 2020, n°444937.
662. For the use of a sensitive data in the context of the Directive 2016/680 *see infra* para. 578.
663. CNIL Deliberation n° 2019-001, 10 Jan. 2019 portant règlement type relatif à la mise en œuvre de dispositifs ayant pour finalité le contrôle d'accès par authentification biométrique aux locaux, aux appareils et aux applications informatiques sur les lieux de travail. *See* more para. 534 on this binding standard regulation on the CNIL.

than another'.[664] The possibility of using biometric processing within the framework of this model regulation is limited to two purposes: control access either to premises requiring a restriction or professional IT equipment and applications strictly specified by the employer. To comply with this model regulation, the CNIL reminds employers that they must justify the need for biometric access control in terms of the sensitivity of the premises or of the devices concerned, take appropriate security measures, and document their choices.

298. The LIL contains a second derogation for 'the processing of personal data carried out on behalf of the State, in the exercise of its public powers, in connection with genetic or biometric data necessary for the authentication or verification of individuals' identities.'[665] Such processing needs to be authorised by decree of the 'after a reasoned and published opinion of the CNIL. It was on this legal basis that the secure electronic documents file (also called TES (titres électroniques sécurisés)), created in 2016, was modified to enable the rollout since 2021 of the French electronic identity cards (CNIe).[666] Such CNIe is a bank card format with a highly secured microchip which integrated biometric data such as fingerprint and a digital photo. In its opinion on the CNIe, the CNIL reiterates its opposition to the creation of a centralised database of fingerprints for both electronic passports and national identity cards. It encourages the government to develop solutions that are more respectful of privacy such as 'the possibility of retaining a photograph of fingerprints in the form of a template'.[667]

299. More globally, it should be noticed that processing of biometrics data of vulnerable data subjects (patients, employees, children, etc.) for the purpose of recognising the data subject is submitted to an obligation of a priori DPIA.[668]

300. **Use of biometric data and consent**. The processing of biometric data may be based on the explicit consent of the data subjects according to Article 9, §2, a) GDPR.[669] In recent years, the use of biometric data processing in conjunction with facial recognition technologies has been debated.[670] The use of this highly intrusive technology by public authorities has raised several concerns. In 2020, the *Conseil*

664. Biometric authentication requiring a biological sample (saliva, blood, etc.) is prohibited.
665. *See* Art. 32 LIL.
666. *See* decree n° 2021-279, 13 Mar. 2021 portant diverses dispositions relatives à la carte nationale d'identité et au traitement de données à caractère personnel dénommé 'titres électroniques sécurisés' (TES) This Decree specifies the procedures for implementing European Regulation 2019/1157 of 20 Jun. 2019, aimed to strengthen the security of identity cards and residence documents within Member States.
667. Deliberation n° 2021-022, 11 Feb. 2021 portant avis sur un projet de décret modifiant le décret n° 55-1397 du 22 octobre 1955 instituant la carte nationale d'identité et le décret n° 2016-1460 du 28 octobre 2016 autorisant la création d'un traitement de données à caractère personnel relatif aux passeports et aux cartes nationales d'identité (demande d'avis n° 20015262).
668. *See* below para. 389.
669. The CNIL recalled that Biometric authentication mechanisms on smartphones when the template is stored on the device, under the sole control of the individual, may be based on the exception of processing for domestic purposes of Art. 2.2.c. GDPR. https://www.cnil.fr/fr/biometrie-dans-les-smartphones-des-particuliers-application-du-cadre-de-protection-des-donnees.
670. *See* CNIL Reconnaissance faciale- Pour un débat à la hauteur des enjeux, 15 novembre 2019.

d'Etat validated the use of a secure government digital identity solution which contained a biometric authentication system to access certain public teleservices via a smartphone.[671] The main legal issue was to assess whether this type of biometric processing could be based on the free consent of the data subjects. The *Conseil d'Etat* considered that data subject has the choice of accessing the teleservices in other ways without facial recognition. The judge also ruled that '*the use of biometric data processing authorised by the contested decree must be regarded as required by the purpose of that processing*'.[672] It invoked that at the date, there was '*no other means of authenticating the identity of the user in an entirely dematerialized manner with the same level of guarantee as the facial recognition system*'.[673] However, due to political opposition to the system, the government decided not to implement it. A new *France Identité numérique*[674] created in 2022 dispenses with facial recognition altogether. It is the CNIe which generates a digital identity via France Identité numérique.[675] Similarly, the project of biometric 'Carte vitale',[676] a personal smartcard with all information needed to be reimbursed for medical care, but with the integration of a digital image of the holder's fingerprints, was finally abandoned. The use of biometrics data to combat social security fraud has been deemed excessive both in terms of the privacy issues at stake and the costs involved.

301. Clearview AI's sanctions. In 2021, the CNIL was sanctioned with a EUR 20 million fine for processing biometric data from images collected from people located in France, including facial recognition by the American company Clearview AI. The CNIL considered that the company had no legal basis for this particularly intrusive and massive processing carried out without the prior consent of individuals.[677]

302. **Towards the use of facial recognition in public space by French public authorities**? The use of facial recognition techniques by public authorities in public spaces has also been hotly debated in France. Such was the case of the much-publicised experiment of facial recognition by the city of Nice during the Carnival

671. *See* Décret n° 2019-452 du 13 mai 2019 autorisant la création d'un moyen d'identification électronique dénommé 'Authentification en ligne certifiée sur mobile' also called Alicem.
672. *See* Conseil d'État, 4 novembre 2020, n° 432656.
673. *Ibid.*
674. Décret n° 2022-676 du 26 avril 2022 autorisant la création d'un moyen d'identification électronique dénommé 'Service de garantie de l'identité numérique' (SGIN) et abrogeant le décret n° 2019-452 du 13 mai 2019 autorisant la création d'un moyen d'identification électronique dénommé 'Authentification en ligne certifiée sur mobile'. This decree abrogated the above-mentionned Alicem decree.
675. More details of the position of the CNIL on the use of biometric data for digital identification. *See,* CNIL Dossier thématique L'identité numérique, mars 2023. https://www.cnil.fr/fr/la-cnil-publie-son-premier-dossier-thematique-dedie-lidentite-numerique.
676. *See* proposition de loi du Sénat tendant à instituer une carte vitale biométrique, n° 183, 3 décembre 2020.
677. *See* Délibération de la formation restreinte n° SAN-2022-019 du 17 octobre 2022 concernant la société Clearview AI.

in 2019.[678] In this case, the processing was based on the explicit consent of data subjects to this experiment and to give their biometrics data for this purpose.[679] By contrast, the experiment on the use of facial recognition for accessing public high schools was invalidated. The judge ruled that the prior consent of the minor and their legal representatives was not freely given because 'the target audience is in a position of authority vis-à-vis those in charge of the public educational establishments concerned'.[680] The consent was given by the signature of a simple form, so it wasn't really informed consent. In addition, the judge censured the adequation of the use of such intrusive techniques for purposes of fluidification and securing of controls at high school entrances.

303. Recently, the need to secure the use of facial recognition in public spaces by public authorities in France has been debated.[681] On the one hand, this translates into the reaffirmation of the explicit prohibition on the use of facial recognition and biometric processing as a guarantee for the acceptance of surveillance tools that are in themselves sufficiently intrusive. For example, the *Conseil constitutionnel* has reiterated that the explicit prohibition on using facial recognition technologies on images captured by drones does not constitute authorisation to use facial recognition on images captured using other technologies.[682] While algorithmic video surveillance was authorised for the first time on an experimental basis to ensure security at the Paris 2024 Olympic Games, the law explicitly prohibits the '*use of any biometric identification system, process any biometric data or implement any facial recognition technique*'.[683] One the other hand, currently, a bill anticipating the European regulation on AI attempts to draw red lines and allow certain uses,[684] which fall mostly in the scope of the Police Justice Directive or strictly national data processing.

678. *See* C. Rotily, *L. Archambault, Données biométriques issues d'expérimentations de reconnaissance faciale sur le territoire français: un défi à l'aune du droit 2.0?,* Dalloz IP/IT 2020, p. 54.
679. According to the city, 5,000 persons participated in these two days of experimentation whose purpose was to evaluate to social acceptability of the use of facial recognition in public space and the need of the improvement of the legal framework for the development of such uses. *See* Rapport de la Ville de Nice sur l'expérimentation reconnaissance faciale. https://s3.documentcloud.org/documents/6350838/Bilan-Reconnaissance-Faciale.pdf.
680. TA Marseille, 27 Feb. 2020, n° 1901249.
681. *See* Rapport d'information Sénat n° 627, Commission des lois, M.P. Daubesse, et A. de Belenet, Jérôme Durain, *La reconnaissance biométrique dans l'espace public: 30 propositions pour écarter le risque d'une société de surveillance*, mai 2022.
682. CC 2021-834 DC, 20 Jan. 2022, point 30.
683. *See* Loi n° 2023-380, 19 May 2023 relative aux jeux Olympiques et Paralympiques de 2024 et portant diverses autres dispositions, Art. 10, point 4.
684. *See* proposition de loi n° 1342 sur la reconnaissance biométrique dans l'espace public, 12 juin 2023.

D. Genetic Data

304. **Limited legal uses of genetic data**. The processing of genetic data in France is prohibited in principle and is subject to rare medical,[685] judicial,[686] or police[687] exceptions. Article 226-28-1 of the French CP states that '*any person requesting the examination of his or her genetic characteristics or those of a third party, or the identification of a person by his or her genetic fingerprints outside the conditions provided for by law, is punishable by a fine of €3,750*'. Even advertising the examination of a person's constitutional genetic characteristics is prohibited.[688]

305. **DNA recreational tests**. While the legal framework on genetics data is clear, the development of 'DNA' tests for recreational use in France has raised several concerns.[689] Beyond the illegality of such tests under French law, the issue is the risk of genetic data being captured by non-European private companies likely to use them for non-transparent purposes. In addition, the reliability of these tests is often called into question by geneticists themselves.

306. **Processing against gene doping**. The holding of the Olympic Games in Paris in 2024 has made it necessary to modernise France's anti-doping provisions, particularly to detect so-called gene doping. This term refers to the use of prohibited substances or techniques to manipulate cells or genes to improve sports performance. A new derogation has been introduced into the Civil Code[690] and the Sports Code[691] to allow the laboratory accredited by the World Anti-Doping Agency in France to carry out some genetic tests. These authorised treatments have been strictly defined. It involves examining the genetic characteristics of an athlete or comparing genetic fingerprints for the sole purpose of revealing the presence and use of a substance or method prohibited by the World Anti-Doping Code. In addition, athletes should be informed in advance, particularly when registering for a sporting competition, that these types of tests can be carried out. The athlete must also be informed *a posteriori* of '*the incidental discovery of genetic characteristics that may be responsible for a condition justifying preventive or therapeutic measures for himself or herself or for potentially affected family members …*'[692] The athlete may, however, object to the disclosure of such information. Additional guarantees have been added. Analyses must be carried out on pseudonymised samples and concern only the relevant parts of the genome. Under no circumstances may they be used for profiling or selecting athletes. The analyses are destroyed without delay if no trace of gene doping has been detected.

685. Article 16-10 Civil Code.
686. Article 16-111 Civil Code.
687. Article 16-12 Civil Code.
688. Article 16.10, IV Civil Code.
689. Galichet,charlotte, *stérin,anne-laure, abderrahim,myriam, bamba,sarata, bécam-touré,kadiatou, moukoko-priso,osiris: tests génétiques récréatifs: où est passé le RGPD?,* Expertises n° 465, pp. 63–69.
690. *See* Art. 16.10, III bis Civil Code.
691. *See* Art. L.232-12-2 Sport Code.
692. *See* Art. L.232-12-2, II, 2°) Sport Code.

E. Open Judicial Data and Processing of Sensitive Data

307. Article 44.5 LIL creates a legal ground for the processing relating to **the reuse of public information contained in the Open Data judicial decisions** which authorise the processing of sensitive data.[693] The only requirement is that '*the purpose or effect of these processing operations is not to allow the re-identification of data subjects*'.[694]

F. Sensitive Data Versus Highly Personal Nature Data

308. In France, as in other Member States, there is a third category of personal data between standard data and special categories of data (Article 9 GDPR including Article 10). This is data of a '**highly personal nature**', as the EDPB recalls.[695] The CNIL recalls that '*financial data, including payment card data, is classified as "highly personal data" because of the seriousness of the impact that its violation could have on the individuals concerned (use for fraudulent payments, for example*)'.[696] Both the CNIL and the *Conseil d'Etat* underlined that banking data are not sensitive data within the meaning of Article 9 GDPR[697] but require special attention. The CNIL has the same approach for the location data. In its case, *City scoot*, she mentions referring to EDPB positions[698] that location data are 'highly personal data' … because '*they have an impact on the exercise of a fundamental right: the collection of location data involves freedom of movement*'.[699]

693. This open judicial data is rules by Art. L.10 Code of Administrative Justice and Art. L.111-13 of the judicial organisation code.
694. *See* Art. 44.5 LIL.
695. Concept included for instance in the G29 Guidelines on Guidelines on DPIA and determining whether processing is 'likely to result in a high risk' for the purposes of Regulation 2016/679, adopted on 4 Apr. 2017, p. 9, point 4.
696. *See* Deliberation n° 2018-303 du 6 Sep. 2018 portant adoption d'une recommandation concernant le traitement des données relatives à la carte de paiement en matière de vente de biens ou de fourniture de services à distance et abrogeant la délibération n° 2017-222 du 20 juillet 2017.
697. CE, 10 Dec. 2020, n° 429571, point 6.
698. Beyond the above-mentioned position of the G29 of 2017, the CNIL refers to the EDBP, Guidelines 01/2020 on processing personal data in the context of connected vehicles and mobility related applications.
699. CNIL, SAN 2023-003, 16 Mar. 2023, point 27.

Part IV. Data Subject Rights

309. Chapiter II of the LIL is dedicated to data subject rights, with several cross-references to the dedicated articles of the GDPR. Most of these data subjects' rights are as many obligations as possible for data controller and processor who must ensure that the rights of data subjects are respected. Therefore, Article 12 GDPR introduces a new principle of transparency which applies to the information, communication, and modalities for the exercise of the rights of the data subject. Although the rights of data subjects have been harmonised across the Member States, their scope and certain modalities for exercises contain specific features in France.

310. The data subject rights can be exercised through an intermediary. 'The request may also be made by a person specially authorised for this purpose by the applicant, if that person can prove his identity and the identity of the principal, his mandate and the duration and precise purpose thereof. The mandate must also specify whether the authorised representative may receive the controller's or processor's response.'[700] In 2021, the CNIL adopted a recommendation which lists the different steps for a request to exercise rights through a representative and other practical modalities.

§1. Right to Be Informed

311. **Article 48 LIL specificities**. The right to be informed is the first data protection right which has been reinforced by Articles 13 and 14 GDPR. Those provisions list all the information to be provided to the data subject. In France, the right to be informed is provided by Article 48 LIL which refers to Articles 12 to 14 GDPR. The wording of Article 48 LIL provides two specificities regarding the right to be informed according to the GDPR. First, the second paragraph recalls the necessity of providing information to the child in clear and easily accessible language. Second, there is, in France, a right to be informed on the right to define directives concerning the fate of one's personal data after death.[701]

312. **Derogations to the right to be informed**. Article 48 LIL contains three derogations to the right to be informed. The right to be informed will not apply

700. Article 77 of the 2019 application decree of the LIL.
701. *See* Art. 48, para. 2 LIL. This right is detailed in Art. 85 LIL.

where personal data have not been obtained from the data subject and used '*in processing carried out on behalf of the State and in the interest of public security, to the extent that such restriction is necessary to comply with the purposes sought by the processing which are set forth in the act authorising the processing*'.[702] The second derogation applies to processing '*carried out by public authorities charged with official missions, such as tax and customs administration, or carrying out audits on the activity of natural or legal persons which may lead to the detection of an infringement or breach, and to administrative fines or penalties*'.[703] The third derogation concerns intelligence processing.[704]

313. **Illustrations**. The failure to comply with information and transparency obligations is at the heart of many French cases. These cases recalled the way in which the information is provided and the extent of the information that needs to be provided.

314. In the first post-GDPR *Google* case, the CNIL pointed out that the right to information is not respected when the information is scattered, so the essential elements are not accessible on the first few clicks and are not organised in an intelligible manner.[705] The *Conseil d'Etat* validated this approach, also stating that '*the requirements of conciseness, intelligibility, clarity and simplicity of the information laid down by the GDPR justify that it should not be excessively detailed so as not to discourage the user from becoming acquainted with it; all the relevant elements relating to the various purposes and the scope of the processing must be easily accessible to him*'.[706]

315. In its *Stop Covid application* opinion, the CNIL reaffirms the importance of the way in which information is provided to ensure that it is truly understandable to the data subject. The CNIL accepts that while all the information must be made available to the user within the application itself, it is possible to adopt a multi-level approach, with the main features of the processing being listed first. Above all, the CNIL stresses '*the need to provide information that can be understood by as many people as possible, given that a large proportion of the population is likely to be affected by the system*'. This means paying particular attention to people with disabilities and minors.[707] In deliberation concerning a major French retail group, the CNIL pointed out that in cases when the information concerns a wide audience, it is important '*to use simple vocabulary, short sentences and a direct style, but also*

702. Article 48, para. 4 LIL.
703. Article 48, para. 5 LIL.
704. Article 48, last paragraph. Such processing's are covered by Art. L.863-2 of the French Internal Security Code. *See* further para. 614.
705. *See* CNIL, SAN-2019-001, 21 Jan. 2019. *See also* SAN 2020-008, 18 Nov. 2020.
706. CE, 19 Jun. 2020, n° 430810, point 15.
707. CNIL, n° 2020-056, 25 May 2020 portant avis sur un projet de décret relatif à l'application mobile dénommée 'StopCovid'.

to avoid legal or technical terms, abstract or ambiguous terms and formulas such as "we could use your data", "a possible use of your data", "some data concerning you is used", etc'.[708]

316. The CNIL has also had occasion to point out the specific nature of the right to information for call recording devices. Each employee has the right to be informed individually of the installation of such devices for listening to and recording telephone calls. In France, this individual right is also covered by Article L.1222-4 of the Labour Code. The right to information implies that the information must be complete. The right to be informed is not respected when the data subject does not have 'granular information relating to the legal basis of each processing operation',[709] the DPO's contact details, and information on the third countries to which the data is transferred.

317. Recently, the *Conseil d'Etat* pointed out the limit of the right to information by recalling that this right applies only to information collected from him. In this case, the applicant wanted to know who had access to his file with the Caisse d'allocation familiale.[710]

§2. Right of Access

318. As the EDPB pointed out in its recently updated guidelines, the right of access '*includes three different components:*

- *Confirmation as to whether data about the person is processed or not,*
- *Access to this personal data and*
- *Access to information about the processing, such as purpose, categories of data and recipients, duration of the processing, data subjects' rights and appropriate safeguards in case of third country transfers*'.[711]

When the controller processes his or her data, the data subject has the right to obtain copies of it in a commonly used electronic form.

Article 49 LIL rules the right of access in France by recalling that it 'will be exercised by the data subject under the conditions laid down in Article 15 GDPR'. However, the right of access in France has its own specific features, both in terms of its scope and the way in which it is exercised.

708. CNIL, SAN 2020-008, 19 Nov. 2020, point 79.
709. CNIL, 14 juin 2021, San-2021-008, C.
710. CE, 24 Feb. 2022, n° 447495, point 5.
711. EDPB, Guidelines 01/2022 on data subject rights – Right of access, Version 2.0. adopted on 28 Mar. 2023.

I. French Scope of the Right of Access

319. **Territorial scope**. The territorial scope of the right of access is linked to the territorial scope of the LIL.[712] This means that requests for access must concern establishments located in France. This led the *Conseil d'Etat* to reject a request for access to data from financial institutions located in Switzerland, a subsidiary of a group whose parent company was established in France.[713]

320. **Right of access of Heirs**. French law contains specific provisions concerning the holders of the right of access. People other than those whose data is being processed can have a right of access. Article 85, II provides that, in principle, '*the heirs of the data subject may, after his death, exercise*' his data subject rights. This provision introduced in French law in 2016[714] is linked to the right to draw up instructions for the storage, erasure, and communication of personal data after his death. Heirs may be deprived of their right to access the deceased's data if the deceased left instructions to this effect. This right of access is nevertheless limited to certain purposes. The first one is the arrangement and settlement of the deceased's estate. To this end, the heirs may access the processing of personal data which concern them to identify and obtain information on the administration and division of the estate.[715] The second one is to enable heirs to obtain data from those responsible for processing the deceased's data that they take the death into account by closing or updating the deceased's account, for example.

321. Few cases illustrated the heirs' frustrations generated using their right to access by heirs. In a case where the heirs asked to access the deceased father's personal data held by financial institutions, the bank stated that it had no personal data concerning the deceased. The CNIL, therefore, closed the complaint, and the *Conseil d'Etat* upheld its decision.[716] Another case illustrated the impossibility of the heir obtaining the medical files of their late mother from her former GP. The request did not concern the organisation and settlement of the deceased's estate, and the mother had left no instructions as to what should happen to her personal data after her death.[717]

322. **Right of access and professional alert**. Processional alert systems also open up an extended right of access. The CNIL has specified that any person whose personal data is being or has been processed in the context of a professional alert

712. *See supra* para. 192.
713. CE, 5 Jul. 2021, n° 447088, point 5.
714. More details on the French inclusion of the data of deceased person in the concept of personal data. *See*, *supra* para. 203. The possibility of access to data of a deceased person by heirs has been accepted before 2016 in case where the deceased was the victim of an injury for which she had not had time to exercise her right to compensation. *See* CE, 7 Jun. 2017, n° 399446, M. B.
715. Article 85, II, 1° LIL.
716. CE, 5 Jul. 2021, n° 447088, point 7. The CNIL therefore closed the complaint and the *Conseil d'Etat* upheld its decision.
717. *See* CE, 18 Nov. 2021, n° 448729.

(whistleblower, presumed victims of the facts, persons targeted by the alert, witnesses and persons heard during the investigation, etc.), has the right to access it in accordance with the provisions of Article 15 of the GDPR.[718]

323. **Minors and right of access**. Since 2016, minors aged 15 or over in France have been able to decide that they alone should have access to their data for the purposes of research, studies or evaluation in the field of health. In other words, they may object to holders of parental authority also having access to their data.[719]

324. As far as the limitation of the right of access is concerned, the LIL refers to the limits introduced for specific processing situations of Article 85 and Article 89 GDPR.[720] The national limitations will be addressed in *infra* §8.

II. Direct Versus Indirect Right of Access

325. The right to access can be exercised directly or indirectly in France. In the first case, the data subject can directly contact the controller, whereas in the second case, access is granted via the CNIL.

326. **Indirect access to bank account files**. The indirect access concerns mostly[721] the bank and similar accounts file called in French FICOBA, Fichier des comptes bancaires. The FICOBA contains information on all types of accounts (current, savings, passbook, etc.) opened with a bank in France. The FICOBA is filled in and updated by the banks, and it is managed by the Directorate-General of Public Finances (DGFiP). Such indirect access is ruled by Article 52 LIL which refers to the procedure described in Article 118 LIL.

327. **Direct access to bank files of the *Banque de France***. Three other banks files deserve attention because they are often the subject of complaints to the CNIL in connection with the exercise of the right of access. This is the case for the Central Cheque Register (Fichier central des cheques, FCC in French)[722] which lists individuals banned from holding a cheque book or who have their card payment

718. CNIL, Deliberation n° 2023-064, 6 Jul. 2023 portant abrogation de la délibération n° 2019-139 du 18 juillet 2019 portant adoption d'un référentiel relatif aux traitements de données à caractère personnel destinés à la mise en œuvre d'un dispositif d'alertes professionnelles et adoption d'un référentiel relatif aux traitements de données à caractère personnel destinés à la mise en œuvre d'un dispositif d'alertes professionnelles, point 9.1.
719. Article 79 LIL.
720. *See* further para. 552.
721. *See* The indirect access concerns also files concern so-called regalian files that fall within either the purely national scope of the LIL or that of Directive 2016/80. *See* further paras 617 et seq.
722. For more details, *see* Banque de France, The Central Cheque Register (FCC), https://particuliers.banque-france.fr/sites/default/files/media/2021/12/22/654ta18_818236_depliant_fcc_web-en.pdf.

card confiscated. The second file is the national register of Household Credit Repayment incidents (FICP in French),[723] which lists individuals who have missed repayments on a loan or files an overindebtedness application. The National Register of Irregular Cheques (Fichier national des cheques irréguliers, FNCI) lists all cheque irregularities.[724] Those files are managed by the Banque de France; therefore, the right to access is exercised before the Banque de France.[725]

328. **Judicial guarantees**. Given the importance of the right of direct access, French law also provides for specific judicial guarantees for the right of access. The data subject can ask the competent court, 'including by way of summary proceedings', to order the necessary measures to prevent the 'concealment or disappearance' of data concerning them.[726]

III. Illustrations on the Implementation of the Right of Access in France

329. **Figures**. The CNIL's annual report attests to the importance of the right of access in France. In 2022, the CNIL received 1,512 complaints relating to difficulties in exercising the right of access, including 120 complaints concerning access to medical records under Article L.1111-7 Health Public Code.[727] The CNIL investigated 7,417 requests for indirect access, of which 5,803 were admissible. 93% of these requests concerned FICOB, the other files do not fall within the scope of the GDPR.

330. **Cases**. The Clearview case is a good example of violation of the right of access. The CNIL considered that 'Clearview AI did not facilitate the exercise of the complainant's rights by only agreeing to respond to the complainant's request for access after seven letters and more than four months after her initial request, and by demanding a copy of her identity document when the complainant had already provided information enabling her to be identified and a photograph of herself.'[728] In addition, the CNIL criticised Clearview for limiting the right of access to data collected in the twelve months preceding the request and restricted the right to two per year without this being specified in its confidentiality policy. In the Free case,

723. For more details *see* Banque de France, The national register Household Credit repament incidents, (FICP), https://particuliers.banque-france.fr/sites/default/files/media/2021/12/22/654ta18_818235_depliant_ficp_web-en.pdf.
724. More details, Banque de France, the National Register of Irregalur Cheques, https://particuliers.banque-france.fr/sites/default/files/media/2023/01/13/823017_depliant_fnci_en.pdf.
725. Article 15, arrêté du 26 octobre 2010 relatif au fichier national des incidents de remboursement des crédits aux particuliers, for the FICP.
726. *See* Art. 49 para. 2 LIL and Art. R.555-2 of the Code of Administrative Justice, for an illustration before the GDPR *see* CE, ord., 26 Nov. 2010, n° 342114, A.
727. This article provides that '*All persons have access to all information concerning their health held, ... by healthcare professionals, healthcare establishments, healthcare centres, birthing centres, the armed forces health service or the national invalids' institution, which is formalised or has been the subject of written exchanges between healthcare professionals ...*'.
728. CNIL, SAN 2022-019, 17 Oct. 2022, point 76.

the CNIL underlined that 'the data subject's right of access is a fundamental guarantee of the transparency of data processing methods'.[729] This company, known to the French for its inopportune telephone canvassing, was sanctioned for breach of the right of access because it refused to inform the data subject of the identity of the data broker who had provided the data. The need to provide precise and complete information is justified by the purpose of the right of access, which is to enable the data subject to verify the lawfulness of the processing and to exercise other rights, such as the right to rectification or erasure. Therefore, the CNIL recalls that the right of access may only be limited to indications of the 'nature of the sources, types of bodies, undertakings and sectors' when the data controller does not hold this information and it is impossible to identify the specific source of the data subject's personal data',[730] which was not the case here.[731]

331. The CNIL also ensures that information is provided within the time limits required by the GDPR. A company cannot justify the lack of a response on the grounds of internal difficulties. The CNIL rules that when a '*company relies on numerous commercial partners to supply data on prospective customers, ... it is therefore up to the company to organise itself in such a way as to be able to ensure that access requests are processed in a rigorously compliant manner and, in particular, to provide information on the origin of the data. In addition, the company was able to proceed in several stages to communicate the data it had immediately within the one-month period*'.[732]

332. In its *Criteo* case, the CNIL recalled that the information given to the data subject need to be complete but also intelligible. This was not the case because the company gave only a brief description of the purposes of each table without an explanation of each colon on these tables or its contents.[733]

333. Some French cases illustrate the need for the right of access to be exercised with due respect for the rights of others. In the *Free* case, the CNIL recalled that according to Article 15, §4 GDPR, it is when the data subject asks for a copy of its personal data that the rights and freedoms of others need to be respected.[734] Free may not use this as an excuse to give the name of the data broker from whom it has obtained the data of the data subject exercising his right of access.

334. By contrast, the *Conseil d'Etat* considered that Article 15 GDPR had 'neither the object nor the effect of authorising a person to know the identity of public

729. CNIL, SAN 2022-022 du, 30 Nov. 2022, point 37.
730. CNIL, SAN 2022-022, 30 Nov. 2022, point 37.
731. This CNIL Case echoes to the recent CJEU, 12 Jan. 2023, aff. C-154/21, RW c/ Österreischische Post AG.
732. CNIL, SAN 2022-011, 23 Jun. 2022 concernant la société Totalenergies Electricité Et Gaz France, point 42.
733. CNIL, SAN 2023-009, 15 Jun. 2023, point 111.
734. CNIL, SAN 2022-022, 30 Nov. 2022, point 36.

officials or employees who have consulted personal data concerning them in the performance of their duties within the recipient legal person or service'.[735]

335. The need to protect the rights of others is a current issue in the right to access of employees to their personal data and professional emails. The CNIL recalls that the right of access relates to personal data, not documents. However, if the employer transmits documents containing data rather than just the data itself, it must first take steps to ensure that the rights of third parties are respected. This may involve deleting or anonymising data that may infringe a third party's rights (business secrets, intellectual property, privacy, secrecy of correspondence, etc.).[736] When these measures do not allow the rights of third parties to be respected, the employer must refuse the right of access, giving reasons to the person concerned. Gregoire Loiseau[737] noted that the right of access is currently being used by employees to obtain documents to seek evidence in a possible dispute with their employer. It aims at circumventing the need to go before a judge[738] to obtain evidence in the employer's possession to prove the validity of the termination of a contract or the payment of overtime, for example.

§3. Right of Rectification

336. Article 50 LIL rules the right to rectification only by referring to Article 16 GDPR. It includes the right of individuals to have inaccurate or incomplete personal data corrected or completed. French cases illustrated that the rectification requested can be linked to the name of the data subject. The *Conseil d'Etat* recalled that right of rectification can be refused when the data subject requests a modification in the spelling in capital letters of the particle of its name. The judge considered that the requested correction was not intended to correct an inaccuracy and that no risk of confusion or error as to the data subject identity was at stake.[739]

337. Gender identity is also an area in which the right to rectification is claimed. The *Conseil d'Etat* has ruled that a person whose civil status has changed because of a court ruling can request the rectification of its data for the future by a company, but not for a previous order. The *Conseil d'Etat* considered that the old name did not constitute inaccurate data and that, moreover, the company was under a legal obligation to keep this order. The fact that the company offered to hide the details of this order on her home page account to please the data subject is also an element that the *Conseil d'Etat* considered.[740]

---

735. CE, 24 Feb. 2022, n° 447495, point 6.
736. CNIL Le droit d'accès des salariés à leurs données et aux courriels professionnels. https://www.cnil.fr/fr/le-droit-dacces-des-salaries-leurs-donnees-et-aux-courriels-professionnels.
737. *See* Gregoire Loiseau, *Les débordements du droit d'accès aux données à caractère personnel, La semaine juridiqe Social*, n° 41, 18 octobre 2022, 12.
738. Article 145 Civil Procedure Code.
739. CE, 3 Oct. 2018, n° 405939, point 7.
740. CE, 26 Jun. 2016, n° 477856, point 5.

338. The CNIL also fined a company that produced an online directory listing of French companies and that had not complied for more than three years with a request from a director to rectify his personal address on his profile and replace it with his business address.[741]

§4. Right to Erasure

339. Article 51 LIL rules the right to erasure by referring to Article 17 GDPR. The LIL completes this right by mentioning a right to erasure for the minor and by clarifying the practical modalities of the exercise of the right to erasure.

I. Right to Erasure for Minors

340. The right to erasure for the minor has been introduced in the LIL by the 2016 Digital Republic Law in anticipation of the GDPR. Article 51, II LIL provides that '*at the request of the data subject, the controller is obligated to erase personal data concerning the data subject without undue delay, which have been collected in relation to the offer of information society services if the data subject was a child at the time of collection. Where the controller has transmitted the data in question to a third-party controller, the controller, taking account of available technology and the cost of implementation, will take reasonable steps, including technical measures, to inform the third-party controller that the data subject has requested the erasure of any links to, or copy or replication of, those personal data*'.

341. The right of minors to erasure calls for three comments. On the one hand, this right might seem rather symbolic today, since it is now enshrined in the GDPR for all persons, including minors. Moreover, recital 65 of the GDPR is close to the wording of the right to erasure for minors of the LIL. On the other hand, the wording of Article 51, II LIL suggests that this right to erasure for minors would be more automatic than that governed by Article 17 GDPR. Finally, the exercise of the French right to erasure is explicitly submitted to an accelerated procedure. The controller has one month to erase and answer the data subject request. After that, the data subject 'may refer the matter to the CNIL, which will rule on the request within three weeks of receiving the complaint'.[742] Some French authors noticed this does not conform to the GDPR[743] which provides a possibility of extension '*by two further months where necessary, taking into account the complexity and number of the*

741. CNIL, SAN 2021-014, 15 Sep. 2021 concernant la Société nouvelle de l'annuaire français (SNAF), points 35–38.
742. *See* para. 2 of Art. 51 LIL.
743. Judith Rochfeld, Données à caractère personnel – Données des mineurs, Répertoire Dalloz IP/IT Communication, point 15.

requests'. One could consider that this accelerated procedure is covered by Article 23, §1, i) as a reinforcement of the processor's obligations for the protection of data subjects.[744]

II. French Disputes on Right to Erasure

342. In France, the implementation of the right to erasure has mainly given rise to disputes in three types of situations. First, as in other Member States, most disputes concern requests to the Google search engine to remove a link between a name and a page containing information relating to that person. This is the so-called right to de-listing or de-refencing, which was recognised by the CJEU in 2014.[745] The right to de-listing has been at the heart of a dialogue between the *Conseil d'Etat* and the CJEU to clarify its practical implementation. Second, the deletion of negative reviews, mainly from Google My Business, is the subject of intense litigation. Third, cases illustrate the use of the right to erasure before data controllers operate in a variety of fields where there is no legal basis for the processing.

A. *Right to De-listing*

343. **Scope of the de-listing's right**. The *Conseil d'Etat* asked the CJEU to rule on the dispute between Google and the CNIL over the geographical scope of this right. The CJEU rejected the CNIL's claim that dereferencing should be applied worldwide, essentially on the grounds that there was a unique worldwide processing made by Google. The CJEU ruled that de-listing should only apply to EU Member States search engine registries. The CJEU argued that the de-listing right is not an absolute right and needs to be balanced with other European fundamental rights. Such balance cannot be exercised outside of the EU, where the implementation of the fundamental rights may be different.[746]

344. **De-listing's right v. Information's Right**. The *Conseil d'Etat* asked the CJEU to clarify how to balance the right to de-listing with the right to information. Following the Court's response,[747] the *Conseil d'Etat* issued 13 rulings on the conditions under which the right to dereferencing must be respected.[748] In so doing, it has drawn up a set of instructions for Google and the CNIL on how to arbitrate between the right to de-listing and the right to information. Such arbitration is based on three main criteria. The characteristics of the personal data in question, such as their nature, their accuracy, how long they have been online, and the repercussions

744. In this sensé *see*, Thibault Douville, *Droit des données à caractère personnel*, Gualino 2021, p. 263.
745. CJEU, 13 May 2014, C-131/12.
746. CJEU, 24 Sep, 2019, C-507/17, points 60–65.
747. CJEU, 24 Sep. 2019, C-136/17.
748. For a synthesis of all these cases, *see* Conseil d'Etat, fiches juridiques, Droit à l'oubli, https://www.conseil-etat.fr/content/download/153672/file/Fiche%20juridique%20-%20Droit%20%C3%A0%20l%27oubli.pdf.

for the data subject, make it possible to assess the seriousness of the inference with data subject's fundamental right to privacy. The social role of the applicant, such as his or her reputation, role, and function in public life, makes it possible to assess the public's interest in accessing the information linked to their name. The conditions of access to the information question the fact that this information has been made public by the data subject or that it can be accessed by means other than googling his name; the fact that this information has been made public by the person concerned makes it possible to assess the proportionality of the invasion of privacy or right to information.

345. These criteria apply without further consideration in cases where the dereferencing concerns non-specific data (sensitive data within the meaning of Article 8 GDPR or data relating to criminal proceedings within the meaning of Article 9 GDPR). For example, the *Conseil d'Etat* ruled that an individual is entitled to request the dereferencing of links leading to web pages relating to a patent that he or she has registered and that mention his or her personal address. The judge considered that the public's interest in accessing this information was weak because the interested party had only filed one patent, which was old and had expired. Furthermore, researchers likely to be interested had other means of accessing this information.[749] By contrast, the *Conseil d'Etat* validated the decision of the CNIL to refuse the de-listing of information relating to the activity and professional details of a general practitioner, considering the overriding public interest in accessing this information.[750]

346. **De-listing's right of sensitive data**. When the de-listing right involves sensitive data, access to the personal data of the data subject must be strictly necessary for protecting the freedom of information of internet users. Consequently, the *Conseil d'Etat* acceded to the de-listing of a web page mentioning the data subject, a former member of the Church of Scientology, given that this information was old and that the data subject had since left his position in this organisation. In addition, the *Conseil d'Etat* underlined that the public could access this information by other means.[751]

347. When the de-listing right involves data relating to criminal proceedings, according to the CJEU position, the *Conseil d'Etat* applies the legal framework of the sensitive data with an additional obligation for the controller to update the information with the current judicial situation of the data subject. For example, the *Conseil d'Etat* considered public access to press articles relating to a mayor's conviction for condoning war crimes against humanity. The fact that this conviction had been quashed was not sufficient to remove the strict necessity of this information for the public, given the notoriety of the mayor. In addition, the website clearly indicated

749. CE, 6 Dec. 2019, n° 405910, point 11.
750. CE, 6 Dec. 2019, n° 4137/17, point 16.
751. CE, 6 Dec. 2019, n° 393769, point 13.

this more recent court decision, and Google had rearranged its list of results so that by typing the mayor's name, the reversal of his conviction appeared first.[752]

348. The *Cour de cassation* also overturned a decision of the Court of Appeal that did not assess the strict necessity of public information by applying the CJEU case law mentioned above. The dispute concerned the dereferencing of an Internet page reporting a conviction for tax fraud committed by the data subject in the context of his private life. The Court of Appeal had simply upheld the public's right to information, considering the interest of this information given that the person concerned was a chartered accountant.[753]

349. Recently, the *Conseil d'Etat* annulled a CNIL decision for failing to apply these criteria when it refused the de-listing to a press article that published the conviction of the data subject to various penalties for fraud, bankruptcy, forgery, breach of trust and concealed work. The *Conseil d'État* criticised the CNIL for failing to consider that the article in question no longer reflected the current legal situation of the person concerned, whose sentence had in the meantime been reduced. In addition, the applicant was not particularly well known, and the press article could be accessed using information other than the name of the person concerned.[754]

B. Deletion of Negative Comments on Google My Business

350. **A controversial issue**. Google My Business enables the creation of a professional identity card showing the name, address, telephone number, opening hours and website of professionals who appear in the list of search engine results or in a separate box. Internet users can then give their opinion on the professional concerned, which is expressed by means of stars and comments. Some of the medical professionals wanted to either delete this professional file to avoid having to manage reviews, particularly negative reviews or delete the negative reviews. To do this, some have tried to rely on data protection law. French judges agreed that both the professional identity card and the comments constitute processing of personal data. By contrast, French judges have conflicting views on the specific nature of the processing involved and its legal grounds which has led to contradictory solutions concerning the right of professionals to have their data deleted.

351. In 2021, the *Tribunal judiciaire of Paris* considered that the processing of patient reviews in Google My Business was necessary for the exercise of freedom of expression and opinion and could not therefore be deleted according to Article 17, §3 GDPR.[755] By contrast, in 2022, the *Tribunal judiciaire de Chambéry* judged that the processing of patient reviews in Google My Business was unlawful.

752. CE, 6 Dec. 2019, n° 405464, point 16.
753. Cass., 27 Nov. 2019, 18-14675, point 11.
754. CE, 23 Apr. 2023, n° 463487, point 4.
755. Tribunal judiciaire of Paris, 9 Mar. 2021, M. X./Google France, Google LLC et Google Ireland Ltd.

According to this second judge, the processing could not be based on the legitimate interest of the data controller because it has, in fact, a marketing purpose. As this processing was not necessary in the name of the right to information, the judge ordered the deletion of the data subject's file.[756]

C. Right to Erasure of Unlawfully Processed Data

352. The third area of application of disputes relating to the right to erasure concerns cases before the CNIL, where mostly French data controllers had no legal basis for their processing. The CNIL found that a French directory company had violated the right to erasure of a data subject by listing its personal address in the listing of its company. The CNIL pointed out that, according to the GDPR, '*where processing is lawfully based on the legitimate interest of the controller, the controller must comply with a request for erasure made by the data subject where the latter has objected to the processing of his or her personal data and the controller does not demonstrate compelling legitimate grounds for the processing*'.[757] In addition, the CNIL noticed after investigations that the French directory company did not comply with answering several requests for erasure in duly time.

353. Some cases illustrate the extent of the right to erasure. For example, in its *Criteo* case, the CNIL has noted that interrupting the display of personalised advertising does not mean that personal data involved has been erased.[758] In the same way, the CNIL ruled that the suspension of an email[759] or the deactivation of a client account[760] does not fully respond to a request for erasure.

354. In these cases, the CNIL is careful to specify the scope of what must be deleted. The CNIL recalls that data required under legal obligations or for evidential purposes may be stored in an intermediate archive.

§5. RIGHT TO RESTRICTION

355. Article 53 LIL enshrines the right to restrict processing solely by referring to Article 18 GDPR. This right does not call for any comment on its application in France. Suffice it to say that this right is closely linked to the exercise of other rights, such as the right of rectification and the right to object. Limitation allows data to be verified or retained to exercise a right.

756. Tribunal judiciaire of Chambéry, 15 Sep. 2022, Mme X./Google France, Google LLC & Google Ireland Ltd.
757. CNIL, SAN 2021-014, 15 Sep. 2021, Société nouvelle de l'annuaire français (SNAF), point 46. For another illustration *see* CNIL, SAN 2022-019, 17 Oct. 2022, Clearview AI, point 84, in which the CNIL recalls that it points out that when processing has no legal basis, erasure should be carried out as a matter of rights.
758. CNIL, SAN 2023-009, 15 Jun. 2023, Criteo, point 136.
759. CNIL, SAN 2022-022, 30 Nov. 2022, FREE, point 47.
760. CNIL, SAN 2021-008, 14 juin 2021, Brico privé, points 57–59.

§6. Right Not to Be Subjected to Automated Individual Decision-Making, Including Profiling

356. **Rationale of Article 47 LIL**. The chapter of the LIL devoted to the rights of data subjects does not include a specific article on the right not to be the subject of an exclusively automated individual decision within the meaning of Article 22 GDPR. This question is dealt with in Article 47 of the LIL in the form of a prohibition for the controller rather than data subject rights. The significance of this difference in approach is ambiguous, especially as Article 47 of the LIL refers to Article 22 GDPR only to specify the exceptions to the prohibition of these types of processing. In practice, although in some cases, the CNIL has qualified certain processing operations relating to targeted advertising[761] and facial recognition[762] as profiling, these decisions conclude that the data controller has failed to fulfil its obligations without relying on the data subject's right under Article 22 of the GDPR. In addition, the French law is more focused on the clarification of the legal regime of automated decision-making processing. For instance, the 2021 bioethics law is worth mentioning because it introduced a new right of explicability for automated decision-making processing (exclusively automated or not) for the benefit of the patient. Concretely, the law provides an obligation of explainability for the designers of certain algorithmic treatments for health professionals who use them for an act of prevention, diagnosis, or care. This article also provides for the obligation to inform the patient and to warn him or her, if necessary, of the interpretation that results from the processing of algorithmic data.[763] The LIL also contains two particularities regarding automated decision-making processing. The exception based on Article 22, §2 GDPR will be detailed below because it enters into the scope of the Article 23 GDPR limitations of rights.

357. **Application in the Justice Area**. Article 47 LIL starts by recalling a rule introduced by the 1978 LIL that 'No judicial decision involving an assessment of a person's conduct may be based on automated processing of personal data intended to evaluate certain personal aspects relating to that person.' Does this prohibition clearly rule out any fantasy of a robot judge in France? One might think so, even if the scope of this prohibition is ambivalent and could leave certain possibilities for algorithmic justice open. On the one hand, the prohibition of Article 47 LIL only applies to decisions involving a form of profiling within the meaning of the GDPR. In addition, the judicial decision itself needs to involve an assessment of the data subject's behaviour. This excludes any decision concerning the criminal or civil liability of the data subject. On the other hand, these conditions may not apply to other kinds of civil decisions, such as an order for payment.[764] Finally, the scope of this prohibition is broader than Article 22 GDPR, since it covers any form of decision and not just those taken exclusively on automated processing. This raises the

761. CNIL, MED 2018-022, 25 Jun. 2018.
762. CNIL, SAN 2022-019, 17 Oct. 2022, Clearview AI.
763. Article L.4001-3 of the Public Health Code.
764. *See* Thibault Douville, *Droit des données à caractère personnel*, p. 285.

question of whether French judges can use decision-making tools. In 2004, the Conseil d'Etat considered that 'while these provisions preclude a court from basing its decision solely on the results of automated data processing, they have neither the object nor the effect of prohibiting it from taking into account, among other assessment factors, the results of such processing'.[765] This includes the possibility for the judge to use automated statistical calculations made by health insurance to assess the professional conduct of an individual. Recently, the Conseil d'Etat has promoted the controlled development of legal assistance by the AI system for administrative justice.[766] As in other countries, the use of decision-support tools for judges and litigants is a subject of debate in France. The terms of this debate are linked to the development of judicial Open Data. The opening up of court rulings means that there is now enough judicial data to develop learning algorithms for analysing recurrences in past rulings. In France, this is referred to as 'quantitative justice', or even 'jurimetrics', rather than the more widely publicised term predictive justice. Experimentations of such tools by judges have started since 2017.[767] This raises concerns about the potential impact of these tools on the independence of judges, the risk of legal professionals being replaced by algorithms, and criticism of the relative performative effectiveness of such tools.[768] While the complete opening up of judicial decisions in France has been announced for 2025, the quality of judicial data is a recurring problem.[769] Beyond Article 22 GDPR and Article 47 LII, future European regulations on AI[770] should provide a response to some of the legal issues raised by using algorithmic tools in the judicial field.

358. Meanwhile, the opening of judicial decisions in France has led to a ban on the profiling of judges. 'The identity data of judges and members of the court registry may not be re-used for the purpose or effect of evaluating, analysing, comparing or predicting their actual or supposed professional practices.'[771]

765. *See* CE, 4 Feb. 2004, n° 240023.
766. *See* CE, Étude intelligence artificielle et action publique: construire la confiance, servir la performance, August 2022, La Documentation Française, p. 302.
767. *See* Christian Licoppe, *Laurence Dumoulin, Le travail des juges et les algorithmes de traitement de la jurisprudence. Premières analyses d'une expérimentation de 'justice prédictive' en France,* Revue Droit et Société, 2019/3, pp. 535–554.
768. *See* the abandonment by the French Justice Minister of the Datajust project, aimed to develope an algorithm to create an indicative benchmark for the compensation of victims of personal injury. Vincent Rivollier, Manon Viglino Christophe Quézel- Ambrunaz, Le retrait de Datajust, ou la fausse défaite des barèmes Dalloz 2022, p. 467.
769. In France, for example, there is no strict common framework for drafting judgments, especially for lower courts and usually first-instance cases mostly do not include metadata. *See* Bruno Mathis, Extracting Proceedings Data from Court Cases with Machine Learning, for more details on the technical challenges linked the valorisation of the judicial Open Data, article available at https://www.mdpi.com/2571-905X/5/4/79.
770. Regulation (EU) 2024/1689 of the European Parliament and of the Council of 13 Jun. 2024 laying down harmonised rules on artificial intelligence and amending Regulations (EC) No. 300/2008, (EU) No. 167/2013, (EU) No. 168/2013, (EU) 2018/858, (EU) 2018/1139 and (EU) 2019/2144 and Directives 2014/90/EU, (EU) 2016/797 and (EU) 2020/1828 (Artificial Intelligence Act), *OJ L, 2024/1689, 12.7.2024.*
771. *See* Art. L.111-13 of the Code of Judicial Organisation and Art. L.10 Code of Administrative Justice.

359. **French concretisation of Article 22 GDPR.** Article 47 LIL provides that 'No decision which produces legal effects concerning a person or significantly affects him or her may be taken solely on the basis of automated processing of personal data, including profiling.' By contrast to Article 22 GDPR, the French wording does not use the adverb 'similarly' in the situation of the decision which significantly affects the data subject without producing a legal effect. It is difficult to assess the significance of this difference, given that to our knowledge there has been no litigation in this area.

§7. RIGHT TO OBJECT

I. Common Right to Object

360. Article 56 LIL rules the right to object by referring to the Article 21 GDPR. Under this provision, the right to object allows data subjects to object to the processing of their personal data based on a legitimate interest of the controller or in the public interest. However, this right is not absolute. Its implementation requires a balancing of these interests against those of the data subject. Therefore, the *Conseil d'Etat* refused to grant parents the right to object to their children's data being stored on a Ministry of Education database because they have no legitimate interest in asking so. The parents '*confined themselves to invoking fears of a general nature concerning, in particular, the security of the database's operation, without mentioning any considerations specific to them or their children*'.[772] Recently, the *Conseil d'Etat* referred a question to the CJEU for a preliminary ruling, asking whether an SNCF traveller could object to the compulsory processing of his or her title.[773] The applicant argued that the collection of this information is not adequate, relevant and necessary for purchasing a ticket. In addition, the applicant considers that the mention 'Mr' or 'Mrs' could not apply to his or her situation. This case illustrates a new kind of balance of interest that could be extended to further application by gender rights activists in the future.

II. Right to Object to Processing for Direct Marketing Purposes

361. Beyond this common right to object, Article 21, paragraph 2 GDPR provides an automatic right to object to processing for direct marketing purposes. French cases involve mostly this second type of right to object. The *EDF* case illustrates that the right to object is a complementary right to the right to erasure. In this case, the data controller was convicted for failing to consider the data subject's opposition to the processing of his data for direct marketing purposes prior to a request for erasure.[774] This case also shows that often, the controller had not obtained reliable information about the data subject's consent to direct marketing

772. CE, 18 Mar. 2019, n° 406313, point 10.
773. CE, 21 Jun. 2023, n° 452850, point 8.
774. CNIL, SAN 2022-021, 24 Nov. 2022 EDF, points 56–58.

processing from the data brokers who had transferred the data to him.[775] Convictions are often linked to human and technical errors that did not allow the people concerned to validly object to receiving direct marketing emails or telephone calls.[776]

362. In addition, Article 56 LIL clarifies that 'This right will not apply where the processing meets a legal obligation or, under the conditions laid down in Article 23 of said Regulation, when the application of those provisions has been excluded by an express provision of the act authorising the processing.' These limitations will be seen in the next paragraph.

§8. Restrictions (National Implementation of Article 23 of the GDPR)

363. The LIL provides mainly to kind of restrictions on data subject's rights. On the one hand, Article 52, §3 LIL sets out a common limitation to the rights of access, rectification, and erasure of personal data. On the other hand, some provisions contain specific limitations on certain rights, which mainly are to the benefit of public authorities.

364. **Common limitation to the rights of access, rectification, and erasure of personal data**. Article 52, §3 LIL provides that 'for any processing carried out by the financial jurisdictions, when acting in their non-judicial capacity provided for in the Code of Financial Courts (code des juridictions financières), in particular where their functions are likely to reveal irregularities calling for the initiation of legal proceedings, the right of access may be restricted under the conditions laid down in points (e) and (h) of Article 23 (1) of Regulation (EU) 2016/679 of 27 April 2016'.

365. **Article 47 2°) LIL** authorises the exclusively automated individual administrative decision, including profiling with specific guarantees. First, such administrative individual decisions can neither be based on the processing of special categories of data nor be related to administrative complaints ('recours gracieux'). Second, these decisions need to make an explicit reference to the automated nature of the processing. The lack of this explicit reference is a cause for annulment of the administrative decision. Third, controllers have an obligation to control the algorithm and its development. This aims to impose the data controller on explaining in detail and in an intelligible manner the implementation of the processing of the data subject. This implies that the administration cannot use proprietary algorithms, whose *modus operandi* can hardly be disclosed to the data subject.[777] Thus, the will of the French legislator is to design a model of transparency of algorithmic decisions in coherence with its political commitment to an open government. Moreover, according to the *Conseil constitutionnel*, this obligation excludes pure machine

775. *See ibid.*, point 20.
776. CNIL, SAN 2022-011, 23 Jun. 2022, Totalenergies, points 51–52, SAN 2022-017, 3 Aug. 2022, ACCOR SA, point 70.
777. *Conseil Constititionnel* Decision No. 2018–765 DC du 12 juin 2018, point 70.

learning algorithms. It considered that '*the data processor must ensure managing the algorithmic processing and its changes to be able to explain, in detail and in an intelligible format, to the person in question how the data processing has been implemented to him/her. It results that, as an exclusive basis for an individual administrative decision, algorithms likely to revise by themselves the rules to which they apply cannot be used, without the oversight and validation of the data processor*'.[778] Therefore, there is, in France, a real right to 'explanability' for algorithmic decisions.[779] As the *Conseil d'Etat* mentioned, Article 47, §2 LIL is stricter than Article 22 GDPR as the European provision does not exclude 'the automated decision, which are not explicable'.[780] More globally, the *Conseil d'Etat* considered that the scope of the interdiction needs to be clarified.

366. **Exceptions to the right to information**. Article 48 LIL provides that the right to information will not apply to data collected indirectly and '*used in processing carried out on behalf of the State and in the interest of public security, to the extent that such restriction is necessary to comply with the purposes sought by the processing which are set forth in the act authorising the processing*'. The same exception applies '*when the processing is carried out by public authorities charged with official missions, such as tax and customs administration, or carrying out audits on the activity of natural or legal persons, which may lead to the detection of an infringement or breach, and to administrative fines or penalties*'.

367. **Exceptions to right of access**. According to Article 49, §2 LIL, the right of access does not apply to 'information to the effect that personal data has been transmitted pursuant to the first paragraph of Article L. 863-2 of the Internal Security Code'. This article rules the communication of information to the intelligence services by public administrative authorities.

368. **Exceptions to the right to object**. Article 56 LIL recalls that the right to object will not apply when the processing is based on legal obligations or by an express provision of the act authorising the processing. Therefore, beyond the LIL, national law contains numerous restrictions on data subject rights. For example, the *Conseil d'Etat* rejected the refusal of the right to object concerning the application for managing the files of foreign nationals in France (AGDREF2). The judge recalled that this processing was based on a legal obligation[781] and could not, therefore, be opposed.[782] This is the case of several files created for the interests of State

778. CC Decision No. 2018–765 DC, 12 Jun. 2018, point 71.
779. *See* Thierry Kirat, Olivia Tambou, Virginie Do, Alexis Tsoukias. Fairness and Explainability in Automatic Decision-Making Systems. A challenge for computer science and law. 2022, p. 33, available at https://hal.science/hal-03873607/document.
780. *See* Étude du Conseil d'Etat, Intelligence artificielle et action publique: construire la confiance, service la performance, La documentation Française, 2022, p. 349.
781. *See* Art. L. 142-1 et les Art. R.142-11 à R.142-25 of the code governing the entry and residence of foreign nationals and the right of asylum.
782. CE, 3 Jun. 2022. n° 452798, point 15.

security, defence, or public security.[783] This applies also to files with public interest purposes. As an illustration, Article 7 of the arrêté of 21 December 2021 implementing the processing of personal data relating to the traceability of waste, known as the 'National Waste Register', provided that no right to rectification and to object will apply to this processing which aims at the traceability of the waste.

369. **Exception to the right to communication in case of Data breach.** Article 85 of the Decree of application of the LIL provides an exception of the right to communicate with the data subject in case of a data breach. This exception applies when:

1 The processing of personal data likely to allow, directly or indirectly, the identification of persons whose anonymity is protected under Article 39 sexies of the law of 29 July 1881 on the freedom of the press;
2 The processing of administrative, financial and operational management data and the processing of health data for which notification of unauthorised disclosure or access is likely to represent a risk to national security, national defence or public safety with regard to the volume of data affected by the breach and the information relating to private life that it contains such as address or family composition.

783. *See*, for instance, the décret 2023-255 of 6 Apr. 2023 authorising the creation of an automated processing of personal data relating to the care of minors returning from areas of operation of terrorist groups (MRZOGT). The Art. 6 of this decree provides that there is no right to object, and an indirect right to access, rectification, limitation before the General Secretariat of the Interministerial Committee for the Prevention of Delinquency and Radicalisation. *See also* Art. 7 of the Decree No. 2023-64 of 3 Feb. 2023 creating a personal data processing system called 'NATALI', relating to the request of naturalisation. This provision specifies that the right of access may be subject to restrictions 'to ensure national security, protection against threats to public security and the prevention of such threats.'

Part V. Duties of Controllers and Processors

370. **Presentation of the duties of controllers and processors in the LIL.** The LIL includes an entire chapter on obligations incumbent on data controllers and data processors in the framework of the GDPR. The chapter contains five sections. The first section recalls some general obligations. Article 57 LIL begins with a reminder of the principle of responsibility as defined in Article 24 RGDP, the obligation of records of the processing activities of the controller[784] and the need in certain circumstances to design a DPO. The second section is dedicated to the obligation in case of processing with a high risk to the rights and freedoms of natural persons dealing with the need of DPIA. The third section deals with health data processing. The fourth and fifth sections clarify the obligations for the processing of archiving purposes in the public interest, scientific or historical research purposes or statistical purposes, and processing and freedom of expression and information.[785] Chapter III of LIL does not list all the obligations. In fact, some obligations are closely linked to the exercise of the rights of the data subjects or are concrete expressions of the key principles relating to processing and data.

§1. National Rules Regarding Duties of Controllers

371. Section I of Chapter III of the LIL refers only to two kinds of general obligations of the data controller.

I. Obligations Relating to Personal Data Breach

372. **Article 58 LIL** rules the notification of data breach to the CNIL and the communication to the data subject according to Articles 33 and 34 GDPR. In 2022,

784. For an illustration of a violation of this obligation by a company with one employee because the processing was 'its core business', *see* CNIL, SAN 2021-014, 15 Sep. 2021, SNAF, point 57. The CNIL edited models of register *see* https://www.cnil.fr/fr/RGDP-le-registre-des-activites-de-traitement and its own register is accessible at https://www.cnil.fr/sites/cnil/files/2023-07/registre_rgpd_de_la_cnil_juin_2023.pdf.

785. *See* further §§488 et seq.

4,088 data breaches were notified to the CNIL.[786] The CNIL considers that it is part of the obligation of accountability of the data controller to document the data breach in a register.[787]

373. **Data breach notification obligation.** The CNIL rules that the obligation to notify a data breach to its departments is an obligation of principle and that failure to notify is an exception which it interprets strictly. The CNIL condemned a controller for a violation of its data breach notification obligation because it had wrongly considered that the breach was not likely to give rise to risks to the rights and freedoms of individuals.[788] The data breach concerned the loyalty points card accounts of a French supermarket chain. The computer attack on its server had resulted in 4,000 successful authentications and 275 actual accesses to these customers' accounts. In its risk assessment, the CNIL rejected the controller's argument that its customers had not suffered any financial loss. The CNIL, on the other hand, ruled that '*the seriousness of the breach stems from the obviously malicious origin of this attack, the large number of people concerned, and the combination of several personal data items accessed as a result of the attack ...*'[789] It also rightly considered that there was a risk of 'credential stuffing' (the risk of attackers gaining access to the accounts of other web sites using these data, as many people use the same identifiers for many websites). Finally, this attack could also lead to risks of identity theft. The CNIL also recalls that the notification of a data breach is an obligation of the controller, even if the breach was caused by an error of the processor.[790]

374. Recently, the Conseil d'Etat clarified the extent of the obligation of the data controller. It considered that 'the obligation to notify the CNIL of a personal data breach likely to pose a risk to the rights and freedoms of individuals does not apply to the data controller in cases where the CNIL has itself informed it of the breach and has initiated its control on the basis of information brought to its attention elsewhere'.[791]

375. **Data Breach Obligation of Communication to the Data Subject.** In its *Slimpay* case, the CNIL condemned a payment institution for failing to communicate to the data subjects a data breach. The CNIL ruled that the data controller had wrongly considered that there was no high risk for the data subjects. The CNIL considered that the risk was high given that it involved banking data and that more than twelve million people were concerned. It also considered that the data subjects were easily identifiable without any disproportionate effort from the data controller. In addition, the CNIL stressed that the risk of phishing or identity theft for individuals

---

786. *See*, CNIL rapport annuel 2022, May 2023, p. 10. For monthly updated data *see* https://www.data.gouv.fr/fr/datasets/notifications-a-la-cnil-de-violations-de-donnees-a-caractere-personnel/.
787. *See* CNIL, SAN 2022-022, 30 Nov. 2022, FREE, point 76.
788. *See* CNIL, SAN 2020-008, 18 Nov, 2020, Carrefour.
789. CNIL, SAN 2020-008, 18 Nov. 2020, Carrefour, point 169.
790. CNIL, SAN 2023-008, 8 Jun. 2023. KG COM, point 172.
791. *See* CE. 22 Jul. 2022, n° 449694.

was high.[792] Finally, the CNIL rejected the argument of the controller based on Article 34, §3 GDPR of the non-necessity of the communication. The CNIL contested the conditions of application were not met. The controller had not taken appropriate protection measures for the security of the data affected by the breach, and the data remained accessible for five years.[793]

II. Obligation of Contract Between Controller and Processor

376. Article 69 LIL recalls the obligation for a controller to govern its relations with the processor by a contract or other legal act with reference to Article 28 GDPR. This can be illustrated by cases in which the CNIL has condemned a data controller for failing to fulfil this obligation. The CNIL carries out a formal check to ensure that such a contract exists, and the CNIL also checks that all the information required by the GDPR is written in the contract. The absence of signatures from certain processors and the lack of a clause specifying that the controller must process data only on documented instructions from the controller constitute an infringement of Article 28 GDPR.[794] Beyond these two provisions, the LIL contains several specifications of the obligations of the data controller, some of which have already been discussed.

III. Other National Obligations

377. First, the controller will have **specific obligations of information** beyond Article 12 GDPR in France. The controller has to inform the data subject on '*what will happen to the data concerning him on his death and will allow him to choose whether or not to share his data with a third party designated by him*'.[795] The controller implementing exclusively automated individual administration decisions must explain, if asked by the data subject '*in detail and in an intelligible manner, to the data subject how the processing concerning him has been carried out*'.[796]

378. Second, **the controller must be authorised for specific processing.**[797] This is the case for the processing 'in the interests of State safety, defence or public security and processing whose purpose is prevention, research, detection or prosecution of criminal offenses or the execution of criminal convictions or security measures'.[798] Prior authorisation is also required for processing carried out on behalf of the State, in the exercise of its public powers, in connection with genetic or biometric data necessary for the authentication or verification of individuals'

792. CNIL, SAN 2021-020, 28 Dec. 2021 point 85.
793. CNIL, SAN 2021-020, 28 Dec. 2021 point 86.
794. CNIL, SAN 2023-008, 8 Jun. 2023 KG COM, point 16. *See also* CNIL, n° SAN-2021-012, 26 Jul, 2021 Monsanto.
795. *See* Art. 85, III LIL. *See supra* para. 203 for the context of this right.
796. *See* Art. 47, III LIL. *See supra* para. 365.
797. *See* the Health processing *supra* para. 285 and States' processing *infra* para. 582
798. Article 31 LIL.

identities.[799] Finally, when the controller processes data in the health sector and researches health data, he will be submitted either to an authorisation or to a declaration of compliance with an existing CNIL referential.[800]

379. **French case law on the scope of the data controller's obligations**. Most of the cases are concentrated on the obligations of information of the data controller[801] and the obligation of security based on Article 32 GDPR.

380. **Violations of the security obligation** are mainly the result of human error, which attests to the lack of awareness and verification on the part of the data controller. The infringement of the obligation of security is often related to three types of negligence from the data controller: insufficient measures to restrict authorised access to its server, lack of measures to log server access, and insufficient data protection measures such as encryption. The CNIL recalls that '*the introduction of a robust authentication policy is a basic security measure which generally contributes to compliance with obligations*'.[802] This means having a robust password policy and secure password storage. These technical measures must consider the state of art. The CNIL considered that using a password consisting of six characters, including letters and numbers,[803] or a password of eight same type of characters,[804] is too weak a security measure. Similarly, the CNIL condemns the use of obsolete hash functions, such as MD5, to store passwords[805] globally, as well as the unencrypted storage and transmission of passwords to the company's subscribers.[806] The CNIL carefully ensures that banking data is kept secure, as it is highly personal data. For example, it found a breach of its security obligation by a company that used an obsolete mechanism for encrypting bank data[807] and, in addition, used a website using the unsecured HTTP protocol for the communication of banking data.[808]

381. In 2024, the CNIL edited an updated version of its guide, which consists of twenty-five practical sheets to help the controller comply with its GDPR security

799. Article 32 LIL.
800. *See supra* para. 285
801. *See* more illustration paras 313 et seq.
802. CNIL, SAN 2022-021, 24 Nov. 2022, Electricité de France, point 62.
803. CNIL, SAN 2022-020, November 2022, Discord Inc., point 71.
804. CNIL, SAN 2022-022, 30 Nov. 2022, FREE, points 56–57. *See also* SAN 2023-008, 8 Jun. 2023, KG COM in which the company used user's passeword with one character point 126.
805. CNIL, SAN 2022-021, 24 Nov. 2022, Electricité De France. For more details, *see also* the CNIL recommendation on password, Deliberation n° 2022-100, 21 Jul. 2022 portant adoption d'une recommandation relative aux mots de passe et autres secrets partagés, et abrogeant la delibération n° 2017-012 du 19 janvier 2017.
806. CNIL, SAN 2022-022, 30 Nov. 2022, FREE, point 62. The CNIL also condemned the inadequacy of the technical and organisational measures taken by Free to ensure the security of the personal data of the company's subscribers in the process of updating the Freebox boxes.
807. CNIL, SAN 2023-008, 8 Jun. 2023, KG COM, point 140.
808. CNIL, SAN 2023-008, 8 Jun. 2023, KG COM, point 148.

obligation.[809] In addition, the CNIL has adopted a recommendation to help data controllers secure data exchanges using the API[810] system, which recalls some good security practices for all stakeholders, including the controller. Although these CNIL documents are not legally binding, most sanctions decisions refer to them, pointing out once again that controllers were provided with information on how they were expected to fulfil their security obligations.

382. **General obligation of data protection by default**. In its *Discord* case, the CNIL invoked, for the first time to our knowledge, the general obligation of data protection by default.[811] The CNIL considered that Discord breached this obligation by setting by default that by clicking on the 'X' icon, its users only put the voice chat application in the background but did not close it. The CNIL considered that such a feature was not usual, and Discord should at least inform its users. Without this information, the users could have been unaware that they had not disconnected from the chat room and that their words were still being transmitted and heard by other members present in the chat room.

383. **Obligation of cooperation with the CNIL**. Several cases revealed an infringement of the obligation to cooperate with the CNIL. This obligation is based on Article 31 GDPR. Such infringement occurred when the data controller '*fails to respond satisfactorily to the CNIL's requests within the time limits set*'.[812]

§2. National Rules Regarding Duties of Joint Controllers

384. Article 59 LIL recalls that in case of joint controllers, additional obligations are provided by Article 26 GDPR. The CNIL pointed out that the mere existence of an agreement between joint data controllers is not sufficient to meet the requirements of Article 26 of the GDPR. '*The allocation of the obligations of the joint controllers must cover all the obligations laid down by the GDPR in order to determine, for each of these obligations, which of the joint controllers will be responsible for it.*'[813] Joint controllers breach their obligations under Article 26 GDPR when their agreement does not include their respective obligations in exercising the data subjects' rights and their duties in the event of a data breach and does not clarify which controller is in charge of carrying out the DPIA.

---

809. *See* CNIL pratique RGPD sécurité des données, available at https://www.cnil.fr/fr/guide-de-la-securite-des-donnees-personnelles. The most rect pratical sheets concern the cloud, mobile applications and artificial intelligence.
810. *See* CNIL Recommandation technique relative à l'utilisation des interfaces de programmation applicative (API) pour le partage sécurisé de données à caractère personnel, available at https://www.cnil.fr/sites/cnil/files/2023-07/recommandation_api.pdf.
811. *See* CNIL, SAN 2022-020, 10 Nov. 2022, Discord Inc.
812. CNIL, SAN-2022-019, 17 Oct. 2022, Clearview AI, points 88–93 and SAN 2021-014, 15 Sep. 2021, SNAF 2021, point 65 where there has been no satisfactory response to the five injunctions.
813. CNIL, SAN 2023-009, 15 Jun. 2023, Criteo, point 142.

§3. National Rules Regarding Duties of Processors

385. **Article 60 LIL**. Article 60 LIL recalls that since the GDPR processors have direct obligations and are submitted to the LIL. This provision focuses on the processor's obligation to follow the instructions of the controller included in their binding agreement. It refers to the obligation of the processor to maintain its record of processing under Article 30 GDPR. Finally, Article 60 LIL recalls the obligation of the processors to conclude a contract with further processors. In addition, Article 61 LIL refers to the Article 29 GDPR prohibition '*to process data except on instructions from the controller and unless otherwise provided for law or regulation*'.

386. **Illustrations**. In its *Dedalus* case, the CNIL found that a processor had failed in its obligation to provide a formal legal framework for the processing carried out on behalf of the controller. None of the documents relating to the contractual relations or maintenance contracts between the processor and the data controllers mentioned the information required by Article 28 GDPR. By sanctioning the processor for its obligation, the CNIL seems to have considered that this software company was the originator of these commercial documents transmitted to analysis laboratories, which were the data controllers.[814] This could be seen as an approach very similar to consumer law, where the professional party assumes greater responsibility. In this case, the CNIL also considered that by extracting more data than was requested by its controller, the processor failed in its obligation to follow the controller's instructions. In addition, the CNIL forcefully rejected the processor's argument that it was technically necessary to carry out an extraction on such a scale because of the tool it had at its disposal. The CNIL states that '*the processor cannot rely on an unsuitable tool to justify having exceeded the instructions of those responsible for processing. It could, for example, have opted for another tool enabling it to comply with the instructions given by its customers, as it says it is doing now, or at the very least deleted all the data that should not have been extracted*'.[815] Lastly, the CNIL noted several violations of the security obligation by this subcontractor, even though sensitive health data was at stake. '*The absence of encryption, the lack of automatic deletion of data after migration, the lack of authentication required from the Internet to access the public area of the server and the use of shared user accounts – all led to the data being made accessible to third parties, despite prior warnings of a personal data breach that led to the disclosure of a file containing the medical and administrative data of almost 500,000 people.*'[816]

387. In its *Slimpay* case, the CNIL recalls the scope of the obligation regarding the further processor. The CNIL considers that simply sending questionnaires to third-party processors does not enable the processor to comply with its obligation to ensure that subsequent subcontractors offer the sufficient guarantees required by the

814. CNIL, SAN 2022-009, 15 Apr. 2022, Dedalus Biologie, point 35.
815. CNIL, SAN 2022-009, 15 Apr. 2022, Dedalus Biologie, point 49.
816. CNIL, SAN 2022-009, 15 Apr. 2022, Dedalus Biologie, point 69. Therefore, the CNIL imposed a 1.5 million fines to the processor.

GDPR. The processor must be able to demonstrate that the sub-processors have completed and signed the questionnaire, at least. This does not validate the use of questionnaires, which are not binding. The processor also needs to check that the agreement with the further processors includes all the information required by Article 28 GDPR. The absence of details about the type of data concerned and the controller's obligations and rights constitute a breach of Article 28 GDPR.[817]

§4. DPIA and Prior Consultation

388. Article 62 LIL recalls the data controller's obligation to carry out a DPIA prior to processing when the processing is likely to result in a high risk to the rights and freedoms of individuals. Therefore, it refers to Article 35 GDPR. In addition, Article 63 LIL rules that the CNIL need to be consulted 'in the absence of measures taken by the controller to mitigate'[818] such high risk. Furthermore, the CNIL adopted several guidelines relating to DPIA. The first deliberation[819] includes a list of processing operations subject to DPIA and a list of processing not subject to DPIA, clarifying the conditions for the realisation of the DPIA and the cases where the controller must transmit the DPIA to the CNIL. This CNIL guidelines refers to the EDPB 2017 guidelines on DPIA.

I. List of Processing Subject to DPIA

389. The list of processing operations subject to DPIA includes for each case the EDPB criterion used for justifying the obligation of conducting a DPIA. Currently, the list contains the fourteen following processings:[820]

Types of Processing Operations	*Reference to the EDPB's Guidelines Criteria*
Processing of health data carried out by healthcare establishments or medico-social establishments for the care of individuals	– *sensitive data* – *vulnerable data subjects*
Processing of genetic data of vulnerable data subjects (patients, employees, children, etc.)	– *sensitive data* – *vulnerable data subjects*

817. CNIL, SAN 2021-020, 28 Dec. 2021, Slimpay, points 43 and 45.

818. *See* Art. 36 GDPR.

819. *See* Délibération n° 2018-326, 11 Oct. 2018 portant adoption de lignes directrices sur les analyses d'impact relatives à la protection des données (AIPD) prévues par le règlement général sur la protection des données (RGPD), point 3.

820. *See* Deliberation n° 2018-327 of 11 Oct. 2018 on the adoption of the list of processing operations for which a DPIA is required (Art. 35.4 GDPR), https://edpb.europa.eu/sites/default/files/decisions/list_of_processing_operations_for_which_dpia_is_required_fr.pdf.

Types of Processing Operations	*Reference to the EDPB's Guidelines Criteria*
Processing carried out for the profiling of data subjects for human resources purposes	– *profiling* – *vulnerable data subjects*
Processing carried out for the purpose of systematic monitoring of employees' activities	– *systematic monitoring* – *vulnerable data subjects*
Processing carried out for the management of alerts and reports (whistleblowing) in the field of social and health matters	– *vulnerable data subjects* – *evaluation/scoring* – *sensitive data*
Processing carried out for the management of alerts and reports (whistleblowing) in professional matters	– *vulnerable data subjects* – *evaluation/scoring* – *sensitive data*
Processing of health data that is necessary for establishing a data warehouse or a register	– *sensitive data* – *vulnerable data subjects*
Processing involving the profiling of persons that may lead to their exclusion from a contract or to its suspension or even termination	– *evaluation/scoring* – *combined data sets*
Mutualized processing of personal data related to verified contractual breaches, likely to result in a decision to exclude a data subject from the benefit of a contract, or to suspend or terminate it	– *combined data set* – *preventing data subjects from exercising a right*
Profiling processing using data coming from external sources	– *combined data set* – *evaluation/scoring*
Processing of biometric data of vulnerable data subjects (patients, employees, children, etc.) for the purpose of recognizing the data subject	– *sensitive data* – *vulnerable data subjects*
Processing aiming at evaluating applications for social housing and for their management	– *sensitive data* – *evaluation/scoring*
Processing carried out for the purpose of social or medico-social care	– *sensitive data* – *evaluation/scoring* – *vulnerable data subjects*

Types of Processing Operations	*Reference to the EDPB's Guidelines Criteria*
Processing of location data on a large scale	– *sensitive data* – *large scale*

II. List of Processing Not Subject to DPIA

390. Although this was optional, the CNIL published a list of the kind of processing operations for which a DPIA is, in principle, not required. This list needs to be strictly interpreted. It includes the following processings:[821]

Kind of Processing Operations
Processing operations, implemented under the conditions laid down by the applicable texts, solely for human resources purposes by employers with fewer than 250 people, except when profiling is used;
Processing carried out for the management of the relationship with suppliers;
Processing implemented under the conditions provided by the law relating to the management of the electoral register of municipalities;
Processing carried out for the management of working committees and councils;
Processing carried out by an association, foundation or any other non-profit institution for the management of its members and donors in the framework of its regular activities as long as the data is not sensitive;
Processing of health data necessary for the care of a patient by an individual healthcare professional in a medical practice, a pharmacy or a medical biology laboratory;
Processing carried out by lawyers in the individual practice of their profession;
Processing carried out by the clerks of commercial courts for the purpose of carrying out their activity;
Processing carried out by notaries for the purpose of carrying out their notarial activity and the drafting of notarial office documents;
Processing carried out by local authorities, as well as legal persons covered by public and private law, for the management of schools, as well as extracurricular and early childhood services;

821. *See* CNIL Deliberation No. 2019-118, 12 Sep. 2019 for adoption of the list of the kind of processing operations for which a DPIA is not required available in English at https://edpb.europa.eu/sites/default/files/decisions/fr_art35-5_gdpr_list_final.pdf.

Kind of Processing Operations
Processing carried out solely for the purpose of managing physical access controls and schedules for calculating of working times, excluding any biometric device. The processing does not reveal sensitive data or data of a highly personal nature;
Processing relating to breathalyser tests, implemented in the framework of transport activities, mandatory by law and restricted to the sole purpose of preventing drivers from operating vehicles while under the influence of alcohol or narcotics;

391. **Beyond the lists**. The CNIL admitted that some processings may not appear in either list. In such a situation, it is up to the controller and the processor to verify whether the processing involves a high risk to the rights and freedom of individuals.[822]

392. In its guidelines, the CNIL considered that the controller must ask for the authorisation of the CNIL for highly risked processing in the health area which does not conform to a referential of the CNIL.[823] In addition, some national acts which created processing include an obligation for the controller to conduct a prior DPIA.[824]

393. Furthermore, the CNIL adopted a specific declination of its general guidelines for connected objects[825] and guides relating to the method,[826] models,[827] and knowledge bases.[828] It also published an open software for conducting a DPIA.[829]

394. **Cases**. Despite all these documentation and tools, some cases illustrate that controller does not always comply with their obligation to carry out a DPIA. The CNIL considered that Discord '*should have carried out an impact analysis of the data processing implemented, given the volume of data processed by the company*

822. CNIL, SAN-2022-020, 10 Nov. 2022, Discord Inc, point 85.
823. *See* Délibération n° 2018-326 du 11 octobre 2018 portant adoption de lignes directrices sur les analyses d'impact relatives à la protection des données (AIPD) prévues par le règlement général sur la protection des données (RGPD), point 3.
824. *See,* for instance, Art. 154, 2019 Finance Law, for a three-year experimental processing authorising certain customs and tax officials to collect information on the Internet and social networks in order to detect certain types of fraud. *See also* for the implementation of devices for controlling access by biometric authentication to premises, equipment and IT applications in the workplace, Art. 11 of the CNIL Délibération n° 2019-001 du 10 janvier 2019 portant règlement type relatif à la mise en œuvre de dispositifs ayant pour finalité le contrôle d'accès par authentification biométrique aux locaux, aux appareils et aux applications informatiques sur les lieux de travail.
825. *See* https://www.cnil.fr/sites/cnil/files/atoms/files/cnil-pia-piaf-connectedobjects-fr.pdf.
826. https://www.cnil.fr/sites/cnil/files/atoms/files/cnil-pia-1-fr-methode.pdf.
827. https://www.cnil.fr/sites/cnil/files/atoms/files/cnil-pia-2-fr-modeles.pdf.
828. https://www.cnil.fr/sites/cnil/files/atoms/files/cnil-pia-3-fr-basesdeconnaissances.pdf.
829. https://www.cnil.fr/fr/outil-pia-telechargez-et-installez-le-logiciel-de-la-cnil.

and the use of its services by children'.[830] The CNIL rejected the argument of Discord which considered that its users were no longer children because they were more than fifteen years old. The CNIL rightly replied that '*while, pursuant to Article 8 of the GDPR and Article 45 of the Data Protection Act, a minor may consent alone to the processing of personal data relating to the direct provision of information society services from the age of fifteen, the fact remains that a minor between the ages of fifteen and eighteen is still a child, and therefore a vulnerable person*'.[831]

395. The purpose of the DPIA is not only to assess the risks but also to document how the controller or processor has complied with its obligations, particularly those relating to security. In addition, the *Conseil d'Etat* recalled that '*While this analysis is the responsibility of the data controller, it must in principle be carried out before the processing operation is implemented, and the analysis must be updated once the processing operation has actually begun in order to ensure that the risks to the rights and freedoms of natural persons associated with the processing of their personal data are taken into account on an ongoing basis.*'[832]

396. The question has arisen as to whether, when a regulatory act provides for the creation of a processing operation falling within the scope of the GDPR and whose implementation requires a DPIA, this DPIA must be carried out prior to the adoption of the act. The *Conseil d'Etat* replied in the negative, stating that the legality of an act instituting processing covered by the GDPR '*is not subject to the prior completion of the data protection impact assessment provided for in Article 35 §1 of this Regulation and its transmission to the Commission nationale de l'informatique et des libertés (CNIL)*'.[833]

§5. Data Protection Officer

397. **Figures**. In 2022, there were 31,757 DPOs in France for 89,841 bodies.[834] As far as the designation of the DPO is concerned, France did not use its margin of manoeuvre, which allowed it to add cases where a DPO would have to be appointed. Article 82 LIL application decree only provides that the DPO must be appointed by

830. CNIL, SAN 2022-020, 10 Nov. 2022, Discord Inc, point 84.
831. CNIL, SAN 2022-020, 10 Nov. 2022, Discord Inc, point 81.
832. CE, 6 Nov. 2019, n° 434376, point 13.
833. CE, 26 Jun. 2023, n° 465329, point 4, case relating to the Decree No. 2022-676 of 26 Apr. 2022 authorising the creation of an electronic means of identification known as the 'Service de garantie de l'identité numérique' (SGIN) (digital identity guarantee service). The purpose of the SGIN is to provide holders of a national identity card containing an electronic component with an electronic means of identification enabling them to identify and authenticate themselves to public or private organisations by means of an application that they install on their electronic communications terminal equipment enabling the contactless reading of this component. *See also* CE, 21 Oct. 2022, n° 459254; CE, 6 Nov. 2019, n° 434376.
834. *See* CNIL, annual Report 2022, p. 10. *See also* the Open Data list of the bodies with DPO at https://www.data.gouv.fr/fr/datasets/organismes-ayant-designe-un-e-delegue-e-a-la-protection-des-donnees-dpd-dpo/.

the controller or the processor in the cases provided for in Article 37 GDPR. In other words, a DPO will have to be appointed by three types of bodies:

- public authorities or bodies (except for courts in the exercise of their jurisdictional judicial functions);
- organisations whose basic activities require them to carry out regular and systematic monitoring of individuals on a large scale of individuals on a large scale;
- bodies whose basic activities lead them to process sensitive data on a large scale or relating to criminal convictions and offences.

398. **Definition of public authorities.** In its practical guide on DPO,[835] the CNIL recalls what is considered in France as 'public authorities or bodies'. It is the national, regional, local authorities, and public bodies such as public universities, schools, hospitals, independent administration authority, and independent administration authority. The CNIL opted for an organic approach to the concept of public authorities or bodies, which does not include legal entities under private law carrying out public service missions. Nethertheless, as the EDBP, the CNIL recommended for such private bodies to voluntarily designate a DPO.[836] A large proportion of these organisations should be obliged to appoint a DPO based on criteria 2 and 3 set out above.

399. **DPO and local authorities.** Some French public local authorities[837] still struggle with their obligation to designate a DPO. An investigation based on Open Data revealed that on 1 January 2022, only 47% of the French municipalities had designated a DPO.[838] In May 2022, the CNIL had to give formal notice to twenty-two local authorities to appoint a DPO.[839] In July 2024, the CNIL imposed for the first time a French municipality for failing to comply with its obligation to appoint a data protection officer despite the CNIL's injunction of December 2023.[840] However, Article 84 of the LIL application decree, like Article 37 of the GDPR, states that a DPO may be shared between different structures. The statistics currently

---

835. *See* CNIL, guide pratique RGPD, délégué à la protection des données, available at https://www.cnil.fr/sites/cnil/files/atoms/files/guide_pratique_rgpd_-_delegues_a_la_protection_des_donnees.pdf.
836. *See* above-mentionned guide pratique, p. 10.
837. 100% of cities, regions and municipalities with more than 100,000 inhabitants have appointed a DPO, as have 96% of départements *See* Data Publica, l'observatoire, Les collectivités territoriales et la donnée, p.17, available at https://uploads.strikinglycdn.com/files/fb1a0a45-317d-46f0-8246-ee980bea402b/DATA%20PUBLICA_resultats_enqu%C3%AAte%20VDEF.pdf.pdf?id=3943769.
838. Data Publica, l'observatoire, les délégués à la protection des données. Étude des nominations des communes de France, June 2022, p. 5 available at https://uploads.strikinglycdn.com/files/b0b5dfe8-1924-4034-8f0d-7c703b5cc94b/Enquete_DPO_20220601.pdf?id=3943340.
839. *See* CNIL Délibération MEDP-2022-001 du 5 May 2022.
840. *See* CNIL Délibération SAN-2023-018, 12 Dec. 2023 in which the CNIL noted the persistence of the breach even though the municipality of Kourou had been alerted by a letter from the CNIL in June 2021 of the need to appoint a DPO givent that it had more than 16,000 inhabitants. In May 2022, the CNIL issued a formal notice to the municipality which nevertheless failed to appoint a DPO. Then, the CNIL decided in December 2023 to impose a fine of Eur 5,000, together with a penalty of Eur 150 per day's delay to Kourou. Finally, in July 2024, the CNIL decided to pay the penalty of EUR 6,900; CNIL SAN-2024-009, 22 Jul. 2024, concernant la commune de Kourou.

available show that this possibility is exploited in the small local authorities or bodies with less than 250 employees. In 2021, nationally, around 86% of DPOs were in-house, including 54% mutualised, versus 14% of external DPOs.[841] Forty-seven per cent of the DPOs in France come from areas of expertise other than IT or legal.[842]

400. **French Certification of DPO**. Article 37, §5 GDPR merely states that 'the DPO shall be designate on the basis of professional qualities, and in particular, expert knowledge of data protection law and practices, and the ability to fulfil the tasks' harmonised in Article 39 GDPR. The LIL gave the CNIL the power to adopt certification standards and approve bodies responsible for issuing such certification.[843] The CNIL used it to identify the skills and expertise of the DPO.[844] In 2018, the CNIL adopted two referentiels, which have been recently updated.[845] The first one provides a list of seventeen skills that are required to be a certified DPO. The second one lists the criterion that need to be complied by organisms willing to be agreed by the CNIL for certifying the DPO skills based on the first above-mentioned referential. Currently, nine organisms have been agreed to deliver French DPO certification.[846] The DPO certification consists of an examination in the form of a multiple-choice questionnaire of at least one hundred questions on regulations, accountability and security. Only people with two years' professional experience in data protection or two years' experience in any other field, plus thirty-five hours' training on the subject, are allowed to pass this exam. Finally, this certification is only valid for three years. At the end of this period, DPOs wishing to continue to be certified must pass the examination again. While this certification is not compulsory to perform the duties of DPO, it does constitute for its holder, as the CNIL points out, 'proof of his or her adequacy with the level of knowledge requirements imposed by the GDPR'.[847]

401. **DPO's dismissal**. While the position of the DPO is harmonised by Article 38 GDPR, the *Conseil d'Etat* recently ruled on the condition of the DPO's dismissal. The *Conseil d'Etat* has upheld the CNIL's decision not to uphold the complaint of a DPO who had been dismissed by the company that employed him. First,

841. *See* Ministère du Travail, de l'Emploi, et de l'Insertion, Étude 2022, L'évolution de la fonction de délégués à la protection des données, p. 8.
842. *See ibid.*, 'These DPOs come in particular from other administrative and financial functions, quality and finance, quality, compliance and audit', p. 13.
843. For more details *see* further para. 423.
844. This is contradictory with the common position of DPAs that the certification should not be used for person. *See* EDPB, Guidelines 1/2018 on certification and identifying certification criteria in accordance with Arts 42 and 43 of the Regulation, point 55. the EDPB considers that the scope of certification under the GDPR is directed to processing operations or sets of operations.
845. *See,* CNIL Délibération n° 2023-062 du 13 avril 2023 modifiant la délibération n° 2018-317 du 20 septembre 2018 portant adoption des critères du référentiel d'agrément d'organismes de certification pour la certification des compétences du délégué à la protection des données (DPO) et la délibération n° 2018-318 du 20 septembre 2018 portant adoption des critères du référentiel de certification des compétences du délégué à la protection des données (DPO).
846. *See* https://www.cnil.fr/fr/organisme-agrees.
847. *See* CNIL, guide pratique du DPO, p. 15.

the *Conseil d'Etat* recalls the principles set out in Article 38 GDPR about the independence of the DPO. Second, the administrative judge refers to the CJEU Case law which clearly rules that Article 38 GDPR does not protect the DPO against any decision which terminates his or her duties and does not govern all labour relationship between the controller and its DPO employees.[848] Then, the *Conseil d'Etat* considered that this provision did not prohibit '*an employee performing the duties of DPO within the company from being dismissed within the company may be sanctioned or dismissed for breaches of the company's internal rules applicable to all its employees*'.[849] Finally, the *Conseil d'Etat* ruled that the CNIL, having listened to both parties, was able to accept the DPO dismissal in view of the company's alleged shortcomings, both in terms of its know-how and its failure to comply with the data protection instructions it had been given. In addition, the CNIL was able to validly reject the complainant's argument that she did not have the resources to carry out her duties, even though the company had granted her a team of three employees and a substantial budget. In other words, a bad DPO cannot use his independent status to prevent his dismissal from being organised in accordance with the rules of employment law. This echoes the former position of the French Labour Ministry, which considered that the position of the DPO is not one of the protected employees within the employment law code.[850]

848. *See* CJEU, 22 Jun. 2022, C-534/20, *Leistritz AG c/ LH*, point 28.
849. *See* Conseil d'Etat, 21 Oct, 2022, n° 459254, point 10.
850. *See* Rép. min. n° 2896: JO Sénat Q, 7 févr. 2019, p. 712.

Part VI. Code of Conduct and Certification

402. Article 72 of the LIL decree of application rules the procedure for the elaboration of the code of conduct in application of Article 40 GDPR.

403. **Approbation of the Cloud Infrastructure Service Providers Europe (CISPE) code of conduct**. In 2021, the CNIL approved the first European code of conduct dedicated to cloud infrastructure service providers (IaaS). This code, supported by CISPE, is aimed at cloud infrastructure service providers located in the European Union.[851] This certification is the result of a long process that began in 2019 when CISPE applied to the CNIL for approval of a draft transnational code of conduct in accordance with the provisions of Article 40.5 GDPR. As required by the GDPR, the CNIL's approval of this code was preceded by an opinion from the EDPB.[852] The purpose of this code is to enable its members to demonstrate to their customers that they meet the requirements of Article 28 of the GDPR, which requires data controllers to use only processors who provide sufficient guarantees that appropriate technical and organisational measures have been implemented. Adherence to this code of conduct can also be used to demonstrate the existence of these guarantees. This code should make it easier to comply in this sector of activity: it provides both a method of compliance and practical solutions to the problems identified by the professionals concerned.

The Code of Conduct is divided into five parts:

- a first part which specifies the geographical and material scope of the code of conduct (i.e. in which countries it applies and what it concerns);
- a second part which develops the data protection requirements;
- a third part, which deals with the requirements for transparency of security measures;
- a fourth part setting out the terms and conditions for subscribing to the code of conduct;
- a fifth part which sets out the proposed governance of the code of conduct.

851. CNIL, Délibération n° 2021-065 du 3 juin 2021 portant approbation du code de conduite européen porté par CISPE.

852. EDPB, Opinion 17/2021 on the draft decision of the French Supervisory Authority regarding the European code of conduct submitted by the CISPE, adopted on 19 May 2021.

Each part provides practical explanations of the problems encountered by professionals in the sector and gives concrete examples to help future members understand their obligations in terms of data protection.

The code of conduct also includes several appendices, including:

- an appendix listing technical and organisational best practices in terms of security;
- an appendix listing the points for checking compliance with the code of conduct, with numerous recommendations on the documentation to be put in place;
- a model declaration of adherence;
- a security breach notification template.

This code of conduct is not intended to govern data transfers outside the European Union. It does contain a reminder of the obligations of organisations in this respect. In addition, it stipulates that members of the code must offer their customers the option of storing and processing their data exclusively within the EEA.

404. **Accreditation of bodies responsible for monitoring certification.** Article 74 of the LIL decree of application clarifies the CNIL's powers to draw up or approve the criteria for certification reference systems and the accreditation of bodies responsible for monitoring certification. In 2020, the CNIL detailed a referential[853] procedure enabling it to approve the accreditation of organisations for monitoring the implementation of a code of conduct. On this basis, three organisations have been approved by the CNIL as supervisory bodies for the European code of conduct implemented by CISPE: Bureau Veritas Italia Spa, EY CERTIFY-POINT, and Laboratoire national de métrologie et d'essai (LNE).[854] The accreditation has been granted by the CNIL for a period of five years. However, it may be withdrawn at any time in the event of failure to comply and renewed following a new investigation.

853. *See* CNIL délibération n° 2020-050 du 30 avril 2020 portant adoption d'un référentiel relatif à l'agrément des organismes chargés de contrôler le respect des codes de conduite.

854. Délibération n° 2021-117 du 7 octobre 2021 portant agrément de Bureau Veritas Italia Spa en tant qu'organisme de contrôle du code de conduite européen porté par CISPE.

Part VII. International Transfers

§1. General Principles

I. Definition of the Concept of International Transfer

405. The GDPR harmonises the regime of international transfers without giving a legal definition of the 'notion of transfer of personal data to a third country or to an international organisation'. Before the GDPR, the CNIL specified that such '*transfer may be carried out by communicating, copying or moving data via a network (e.g. remote access to a database) or another medium, regardless of the type of medium (e.g. from a computer hard drive to a server)*'.[855] The EDPB has recently clarified this concept in order to assist stakeholders and ensure consistent interpretation between the DPAs of this concept. '*It has identified the following three cumulative criteria to qualify a processing operation as a transfer:*

1) A controller or a processor ('exporter') is subject to the GDPR for the given processing.
2) The exporter discloses by transmission or otherwise makes personal data, subject to this processing, available to another controller, joint controller or processor ('importer').
3) The importer is in a third country, irrespective of whether or not this importer is subject to the GDPR for the given processing in accordance with Article 3, or is an international organisation.'[856]

This definition integrated some of the remote access of personal data mentioned before by the former statement of the CNIL. In addition, the EDPB gives a broad definition of the notion of transfer. It includes further international transfer from controllers and processors, which are not established in the EU but submitted to the GDPR because they offer goods and services to the EU market or monitor behaviours of data subjects living in the EU, in the sense of Article 3, §2 GDPR.[857] By contrast, when the data is disclosed by the data subject or in case of internal processing without disclosure to another controller or processor, there is no international transfer. Therefore, when an employee of a controller in the EU travels on a

855. CNIL, Lignes directrices sur les transferts de données à caractère personnel hors UE, 2012.
856. *See* Guidelines 05/2021 on the Interplay between the application of Art. 3 and the provisions on international transfers as per Ch. V of the GDPR, adopted on 14 Feb. 2023, p. 7, point 9.
857. *See ibid.*, point 13 and the example 2, p. 9.

business trip to a third country and remotely accesses the personal data of its company, there is no international transfer.[858] When a data subject in the EU gives online her personal data to a company submitted to the GDPR for a purchase, it is not an international transfer.[859]

II. Legal Regime of International Transfers

406. **The GDPR Approach.** The legal regime of international transfers is based on three main principles. First, transfers to third countries or international organisations are, in principle, prohibited in order not to jeopardise the high level of personal data protection guaranteed in the EU. Second, the transfers may be authorised if they are covered by an adequacy decision attesting that the third country concerned, or certain types of data transfers to a third country or territory, protect the data in a way that is 'essentially equivalent'[860] to what the EU does. In this case, data falling within the scope of this adequacy decision may be transferred without any further authorisation. As the adequacy decision is a decision of the European Commission, its legality may be challenged before the CJEU if it turns out that the guarantees negotiated with the third country do not, in fact, ensure a level of protection that is 'substantially equivalent' to that of the EU. On two occasions, the adequacy decision allowing transfers to the USA has been invalidated by the CJEU.[861] This has placed transatlantic data transfers in a state of legal uncertainty despite attempts by the European DPAs[862] to help players find solutions to ensure their compliance. As many of the players in the digital world are Americans, these legal uncertainties have led to several disputes, including those in France, which will be discussed later. At this stage, it should be noted that on 10 July 2023, the European Commission adopted a new decision of adequacy with the USA.[863] As the CNIL mentioned on its website, controller and processor subject to the GDPR '*may now transfer personal data to certified organisations that have made an annual and public commitment to adhere to this legal framework. They are not obliged to implement a transfer tool under article 46 of the GDPR or to avail themselves of a derogation under article 49 of the GDPR*'.[864] In fact, the third principle of international transfers is to list other legal grounds on which international transfers can be founded in the absence of an adequacy decision. Among these tools, two are widely used: contractual clauses and Binding Corporate Rules (BCRs), which involve the national DPA. Since the GDPR, certification and code of conduct can also be tools

858. *See ibid.*, example 8, p. 11.
859. *See ibid.*, example 1, p. 9.
860. CJEU, 6 Oct. 2015, Schrems, C-362/14, point 73.
861. CJEU, 6 Oct. 2015, Schrems, C-362/14 on the decision of adequacy named Safe Harbor, and CJEU, 16 Jul. 2020, Schrems II, C-311/18, on the decision of adequacy named Privacy Schield.
862. *See* for instance EPDB, Frequently Asked Questions on the judgment of the Court of Justice of the European Union in Case C-311/18 – *Data Protection Commissioner v. Facebook Ireland Ltd and Maximillian Schrems* Adopted on 23 Jul. 2020; Recommendations 01/2020 on measures that supplement transfer tools to ensure compliance with the EU level of protection of personal data Version 2.0 Adopted on 18 Jun. 2021.
863. CJEU, 16 Jul. 2020, Schrems, C-311/18, on the decision of adequacy named Privacy Schield.
864. *See* https://www.cnil.fr/fr/adequation-des-etats-unis-les-premieres-questions-reponses.

for international transfers. These possibilities have yet to be fully exploited. Therefore, in 2022, the EDPS adopted two guidelines to promote the use of these tools.[865] Finally, Article 49 GDPR provides legal grounds for specific situations, which apply much more to one-off international transfers.

407. **French rules on international transfers.** In France, chapter VI of the LIL application decree rules the transfers of personal data outside of the EU, clarifying how the CNIL can authorised ad hoc contractual clauses and administrative agreements for international transfer. It also fixes some additional obligations for the controller and processor using a code of conduct or certification for international transfers. In complement, Article 73 of the same decree rules the procedure of approbation of the BCR in France.

408. **Approvement of BCRs by the CNIL**. According to Article 4, §20 GDPR, BCRs 'means personal data protection policies which are adhered to by a controller or processor established on the territory of a Member State for transfers or a set of transfers of personal data to a controller or processor in one or more third countries within a group of undertakings, or group of enterprises engaged in a joint economic activity;'. It is up to the CNIL to approve BCR of the controller or processor established in France. In case of the main establishment in France with secondary establishments in other EU Member States, the coherence system should apply. The CNIL must coordinate the approval of the BCR with other involved DPAs. Article 73 of the LIL application decree gives the CNIL six months, extendable to eight, to refer the matter to the EDPB for its opinion. The Commission must then approve the BCRs within one month of receiving the EPDB's opinion. Otherwise, the BCR request will be considered rejected. Since the GDPR,[866] the CNIL has approved five BCRs, which are related to employees and business contacts categories of data subjects.[867] All these CNIL deliberations are structured in the same way. The first part illustrates how the BCRs meet the requirements set out under Article 47, §1 GDPR. The CNIL verifies that the BCRs are legally binding, contain a clear duty for each participating member of the Group, and expressly confer enforceable third-party beneficiary rights to data subjects. More globally, the first part checks and lists that all the information required by Article 47 is part of the BCR. The second part of the deliberation recalls that the use of the BCR as a valid tool for international transfer needs further assessment by the controller and/or the processor. They need '*to determine if the guarantees provided for by the BCRs can be complied with in practice,*

865. *See* EDPB Guidelines 07/2022 on certification as a tool for transfers, Version 2.0, adopted on 14 Feb. 2023, Guidelines 04/2021 on Codes of Conduct as tools for transfers, Version 2.0, adopted on 22 Feb. 2023.
866. A list of pre-GDPR BCR approved before 25 May 2018 is accessible here.
867. *See* CNIL, Courtesy Non-Official Translation of National Decision Controller BCR Decision No. 2021-087 of 22 Jul. 2021 approving controller BCRs of CGI INC group; Decision No. 2022-016 of 17 Feb. 2022 approving controller BCRs of Webhelp. *See also* the three CNIL, Courtesy Non-Official Translation of National Decision processor, Decision No. 2021-088 of 22 Jul. 2021 approving processor BCRs of CGI INC GROUP; Decision No. 2022-017 of 17 Feb. 2022 approving processor BCRs of WEBHELP; Délibération n° 2022-113 du 17 novembre 2022 portant approbation des règles d'entreprises contraignantes (BCR) 'sous-traitant' du groupe LEYTON.

considering the circumstances of the possible impingement created by the third country legislation with the fundamental rights and the circumstances surrounding the transfer. If this is not the case, the data exporter in a Member State, if needed with the help of the data importer, should assess whether it can provide supplementary measures to ensure an essentially equivalent level of protection as provided in the EEA. Where the data exporter in a Member State is not able to take supplementary measures necessary to ensure an essentially equivalent level of protection as provided in the EU, personal data cannot be lawfully transferred to a third country under this BCR. Therefore, the data exporter is required to suspend or end the transfer of personal data'.[868]

It is also worth underlining that there is a European doctrine of the DPAs for the approval of BCR,[869] including a common application form and instructions for filling in.

409. **Ad hoc contractual clauses**. Beyond the standard contractual clauses adopted by the European Commission, national DPA can approve **'ad hoc' contractual clauses** as tools for international transfer. In France, this possibility is provided by Article 125 of the LIL application decree. To our knowledge, the CNIL has not adopted such clauses.

410. **French Issues related to the cancellation of the Privacy Shield.** The cancellation of the Privacy Shield, in France as in other European countries, raised legal issues regarding the use of Google Analytics, Microsoft 365, and American Cloud solutions. The CNIL has taken several positions for prohibiting the use of these common American tools. For example, in May 2021, it was recommended that higher education and research establishments should no longer use Microsoft's collaborative suite. It also gave a formal notice to a French website manager to stop using Google Analytics.[870] It is also the more political dimension of digital sovereignty that has been put forward by the French public authorities to no longer allow the deployment of Microsoft 365 in public administrations and to warn of the issues involved in the free subscription to Microsoft 365 to students and teachers. As a result, 'the inter-ministerial director of digital published a note on 15 September 2021 stating that the Microsoft 365 was not "*in line with the Cloud doctrine at the centre*" and *called for a halt to any deployment or extension of this solution as well as that of Google, which would be contrary to the GDPR*'.[871] The *Conseil d'Etat* has also been called upon to suspend the hosting of the Heath Data Hub by Microsoft. The applicants considered that this hosting did not conform to the international transfer rules of the GDPR. In the first case, the *Conseil d'Etat* underlined

868. *See* for instance points 7 and 8 of the Decision No. 2021-087 of 22 Jul. 2021 approving controller BCRs of CGI INC GROUP.
869. *See* Recommendations 1/2022 on the Application for Approval and on the elements and principles to be found in Controller BCRs (Art. 47 GDPR).
870. *See* CNIL, rapport annuel 2021, p. 47.
871. *See* the Education national Ministery answer to the deputy Philippe Lacombe Question n° 971, available at https://questions.assemblee-nationale.fr/q16/16-971QE.htm.

that the concerned health data was hosted in the Netherlands and that possible international transfers to the USA were covered by the Privacy Shield[872] or standard contractual clauses.[873] The second case was delivered after the annulment of the Privacy Shield by the CJEU. Therefore, the *Conseil d'Etat* considered that while the risk cannot be totally ruled out that the American intelligence services may request access to this data, this does not justify suspending the processing. The *Conseil d'Etat* considered that special precautions were only required under the supervision of the CNIL. Interestingly, the *Conseil d'Etat* argued that '*there is an important public interest in allowing the continued use of health data for the purposes of managing the health emergency and improving knowledge of SARS-CoV-2 …*'[874] Given the context of the pandemic, the *Conseil d'Etat* considered more prudent to validate Microsoft's hosting solution, and to encourage players to take precautions while awaiting a more permanent solution. Indeed, the political uproar surrounding this hosting had led the French public authorities to announce that they would eventually opt for purely European hosting rather than American hosting.

§2. Transfers in the Context of International Agreement

411. Article 125 of the LIL application decree also authorises the CNIL to approve administrative agreements as tools for international transfer. There is an administrative arrangement governing the transfer of personal data between the Autorité des Marché Financier (AMF) and its counterparts outside the EEA.[875] There is also an administrative arrangement governing the transfer of personal data between the Haut Conseil du Commissariat aux Comptes (H3C) and its American counterpart, the Public Company Accounting Oversight Board (PCAOB).[876] Each CNIL deliberation on the approval of the administrative agreement describes the context justifying the agreement and then the different points that the CNIL checks for its assessment of the agreement regarding the conditions required by the GDPR. It is worth underlining that while the CNIL is competent to approve such an administrative agreement, it decided to ask the opinion of the EDPB for the agreement with PCAOB. The CNIL considered that such European coordination was necessary because it was planned that this administrative arrangement would be used as a model for the supervision of transfers of personal data from other European homogeneous bodies with the PCAOB.

872. *See* CE Ord., 19 Jun. 2020, points 23–28.
873. *See* CE Ord., 24 Jul. 2020, point 5.
874. *See* CE Ord., 23 Oct. 2020, point 20.
875. *See* Délibération n° 2019-034 du 21 mars 2019 autorisant la mise en œuvre d'un arrangement administratif visant à encadrer les transferts des données à caractère personnel entre l'autorité des marchés financiers (AMF) et ses homologues en dehors de l'Espace Economique Européen (EEE).
876. Délibération n° 2021-032 du 18 mars 2021 autorisant la mise en œuvre d'un arrangement administratif visant à encadrer les transferts des données à caractère personnel entre le H3C et son homologue américain, le PCAOB.

Part VIII. Enforcement

§1. Supervisory Authorities

412. The CNIL is the French supervisory authority for the GDPR, the Police Justice directive and the e-privacy Directive. Since 2024, the CNIL is also the French competent authority for the DGA, and one of the French competent authorities for the DSA.[877] The CNIL is one of the oldest French AAIs, created in 1978. Since the GDPR, the status, competences, tasks and powers of the CNIL have been guaranteed at the EU level, as have the other DPAs. However, the GDPR leaves the Member States considerable room for manoeuvre when it comes to organising their DPA. From the outset, the CNIL has been a collegiate authority.[878] The CNIL is organised around a college, a restricted panel, an office and departments. Although its independence is guaranteed by both the GDPR and national law,[879] it does not have a legal personality.

I. CNIL's Composition

A. *Composition of the CNIL's College*

413. **A mixed composition**. The CNIL is composed of a college of eighteen members, twelve of whom are elected or appointed by the assemblies or courts to which they belong for a mandate of five years.[880] The CNIL has a half-political body with four parliamentarians (two MPs and two Senators). It is also a half-jurisdictional board with six representatives of high courts (two members of the *Conseil d'Etat*, two members of the *Cour de cassation*, two members of the French Court of Auditors, the *Cour des Comptes*, with counsellors status). The CNIL also includes five people qualified for their knowledge of digital technology and issues affecting individual freedoms. The final members are two representatives of the Economic, Social and Environmental Council and the President of the CADA

877. The other French competent authorities according to Art. 49 DSA, are the ARCOM (which is also the Digital Services Coordinator), and the DGCCRF.

878. *See* our Manuel de droit européen de la protection des données à caractère personnel Bruylant 2020, on the diversity of organisational models for national supervisory authorities, p. 354.

879. Loi n° 2017-55 du 20 janvier 2017 portant statut général des autorités administratives indépendantes et des autorités publiques indépendante.

880. *See* Art. 9 LIL, in the case of members of parliament, for a period equal to their elective term of office. For the majority of the members the mandate is renewable once.

(Commission for Access to Administrative Documents).[881] In addition, the president of the Defender of Rights (French Ombudsman) is part of the college of the CNIL but has a consultative vote. The presence of these last two ex officio members illustrates the growing need for interregulation.[882] In the future, it is likely that more institutional links will be created between the CNIL and other independent authorities working in related fields.[883]

414. **A composition often criticised**. The composition of the CNIL is regularly criticised for not having enough informatic profiles.[884] The future European regulation on AI[885] could lead to a far-reaching reform of the CNIL, with its college strengthened by more technical profiles and representatives of innovation players.[886] This could also reinforce the independence of the college of the CNIL from their technical services. The CNIL's relative independence from political powers has also been criticised.[887] Six members of the CNIL are appointed by Parliament and three by the Executive, including the President. This type of appointment procedure is perfectly acceptable under Article 53 GDPR, even though this provision also proposes an appointment procedure by an independent body. The CNIL president is designed by a decree of the President of the French Republic after a hearing of the Constitutional Law, legislation and General Administration standing committee of the *Assemblée nationale* and the *Sénat*. It is true that the CNIL's president can no longer be a member of parliament as he used to be. The presence of a government commissioner appointed by the Prime Minister, who attends all CNIL deliberations,[888] has also been the subject of reservations from scholars.[889] However, the government commissioner is not present at the deliberation. Furthermore, like many high positions in France, the president and secretariat of the CNIL are traditionally held by members of the *Conseil d'Etat*. The CNIL's president is currently required to hold office on a full-time basis, and '*his position is incompatible with any direct or indirect interest in a company in the electronic communications or IT sector*'.[890]

881. Article 14 LIL provides that the CNIL and the CADA can also have a common plenary if needed.
882. On interregulation activities of the CNIL *see* Rapport annuel 2022, pp. 28–29. *See also* our article L'émergence d'un modèle européen d'interrégulation en matière de protection des données personnelles, in Liber Amicorum – Hommage en l'honneur du professeur Joël Moneger, Lexis Nexis mai 2017, pp. 381–394.
883. This could apply to the competition authority and the ARCOM which is the competent authority for digital planforms and content regulation and ARCEP which is the authority for the telecom.
884. Currently, only two members of the CNIL college have an IT background, and only one member comes from the social sciences, as lawyers are the most represented in the CNIL.
885. Regulation (EU) 2024/1689 of the European parliament and of the council laying down harmonised rules on artificial intelligence (artificial intelligence act) and amending certain union legislative acts, OJL 12 July 2024.
886. *See* the statement of the *Conseil d'Etat* for such reform of the CNIL in Intelligence artificielle et action publique: construire la confiance, servir la performance, La documentation française 2022, p. 202.
887. *See* Suzanne Vergnolle, L'effectivité de la protection des personnes par le droit des données à caractère personnel, Thèse, 7 December, available at https://theses.fr/2020PA020042, https://hal.science/tel-03903958, p. 354.
888. *See* Art. 17 LIL.
889. *See* Suzanne Vergnolle, *supra* n. 892, p. 355.
890. *See* Art. 9 LIL.

In addition, the CNIL adopted in 2021 a deontology charter,[891] which applies to both the members of its college and its staff. This charter includes rules for the prevention and cessation of conflicts of interest, rules relating to the secrecy obligations, in particular, the confidentiality of the deliberation of the CNIL, and a more general duty of self-restrain. The charter clarifies how members and agents of the CNIL are required to exercise prudence and discernment about promises, proposals and offers of gifts, advantages, invitations, donations, favours, distinctions, and any other gifts made to them by third parties in the performance of their duties. It recalled different forms of incompatibilities with the mandate of members of the CNIL.[892] CNIL members must make a declaration of assets and interests to the High Authority for transparency in public life.[893] The Charter also includes rules concerning transfers to the private sector. Members and CNIL staff may not, for three years after leaving the CNIL, engage in activities within private structures that would not be compatible with their former position at the CNIL. Finally, the Charter provides the nomination of a compliance officer ('referent déontologue'), who should be appointed by the president of the CNIL for three years renewable. This compliance officer has a general mission to advise the members and the agents of the CNIL with their professional ethics obligations.

B. The Other Structures of the CNIL

415. **The restricted formation.** The restricted formation is a panel of five members of the college with its own chairman, who is not the president of the CNIL.[894] While the college elaborates on the doctrine of the CNIL, the restricted formation issues administration sanctions, as detailed below.[895]

416. **The board**. The board of the CNIL is made up of the President and the Vice-Presidents of the CNIL. It has several administrative tasks; among them, it may publish a formal notice issued against a data controller failing to comply with its obligations at the request of the President of the CNIL.

417. **The administration of the CNIL**. The CNIL consists of a team of mainly contractual State employees organised around five directorates under the coordination of the Secretary-General. In 2023, the CNIL had a 26.3 million budget and 288 employees.[896] Strengthening the CNIL's resources so that it can carry out its missions is a recurring concern.

891. Délibération n° 2021-095 du 17 juin 2021 portant modification du règlement intérieur de la Commission nationale de l'informatique et des libertés.
892. *See* Arts 12–13 of the Charter.
893. *See* Art. 15 of the Charter.
894. *See* Arts 9, 8 LIL.
895. *See infra* paras 474 et seq. More details on the CNIL composition and organisation *see* Thomas Dautieu, *La CNIL, évolution, indépendance et composition, Juriscl. Communication Fasc. 934.*
896. *See* CNIL, rapport annuel 2023, p. 11, more details on Human ressources at the CNIL, p. 23.

II. Competence, Tasks and Powers of the CNIL

A. *Geographical competence of the CNIL*

418. The CNIL's competence is linked to the territorial scope of the LIL.[897] The CNIL is the competent authority for all controllers and processors established in France. The CNIL will be the lead supervisory authority for the controllers and processors which have their main establishment in the EU in France.[898] As such, some of its draft decisions can be challenged before EDPB by another concerned DPA which expressed objections under Article 60, §4 GDPR.[899] The CNIL can also be a concerned supervisory authority in cases involving EU cross-border processing of personal data.[900] According to Article 4, §22 GDPR, this covers three main situations:

- when the controller or the processor has an establishment in France;
- when data subjects living in France are substantially affected or likely to be affected by the processing, and finally;
- when a complaint has been lodged with the CNIL.

419. **Illustrations of the competence of CNIL outside the one-stop-shop mechanism**. Involving the CNIL by lodging a complaint with it can be a strategy of associations such as None of Your Business (NOYB)[901] which was behind the first CNIL post-GDPR sanction concerning Google.[902] In this case, Google learned that it could not claim to have its main establishment in Ireland because, at this time, Google Ireland had no real decision-making power regarding the processing involved and the rules of confidentially of Google France. Therefore, the CNIL declared its competence in assessing the processing entering the scope of the activities of Google France.

420. It is also worth underlining that the one-stop-shop mechanism applies only to application of the GDPR and not to the application of Article 15 of the e-Privacy

897. *See* before para. 192.
898. *See* Art. 24 LIL. For an illustration *see* the Simpay Case in which the CNIL was the lead supervisory authority with other DPA from Germany, Spain, Italy and Netherland. CNIL, SAN 2021-020, 28 Dec. 2021, Slimpay, point 13, and CNIL, SAN 2022-017, 3 Aug. 2022, Accor SA. A list of eighty-one final One-Stop-Shop Decisions of the CNIL a Lead Supervisory authority is available at https://edpb.europa.eu/our-work-tools/consistency-findings/register-for-article-60-final-decisions_en?f%5B0%5D=article_60_lsa%3A685.
899. For an illustration *see*, Decision 01/2022 on the dispute arisen on the draft decision of the French Supervisory Authority regarding Accor SA under Art. 65(1)(a) GDPR which concerned one objection expressed by the Polish authority, regarding the amount of the fine set in the draft decision.
900. *See* a list of more than 339 cases in which the CNIL has been concerned supervisory authority https://edpb.europa.eu/our-work-tools/consistency-findings/register-for-article-60-final-decisions_en?f%5B0%5D=article_60_csa%3A685. The recent Vinted Case is an illustration of such a cooperation with the Lituanian DPA, *see* https://vdai.lrv.lt/en/news/a-company-operating-an-online-second-hand-clothing-trading-and-exchange-platform-is-fined-under-the-general-data-protection-regulation/.
901. *See* https://noyb.eu/en/project/dpa/cnil-france.
902. *See* CNIL, SAN 2019-001, 21Jan. 2019.

Directive.[903] Therefore, the CNIL is competent for controlling that access or recording to an electronic communication service may only be carried out provided that the subscriber or user has explicitly expressed, after receiving said information.[904] This explains why the CNIL regularly decides on the use of cookies or other tracking devices by French establishments for processing which takes place in the context of their activities, even if there are subsidiaries of American companies which have their main establishment in the EU in Ireland[905] or Luxembourg.[906] This competence of the CNIL has been validated by the *Conseil d'Etat*.[907]

421. The CNIL will also be competent for all controllers and processors that are not established in the EU but whose processing is entered into the scope of Article 3 GDPR. In other words, the CNIL will be competent for the processing activities related to offering of goods or services to data subjects living in France and for processing activities related to the monitoring of their behaviour in France.[908] Here, the one-stop-shop mechanism does not apply.[909]

B. Tasks of the CNIL

422. **Five main tasks of the CNIL**. Article 8 LIL lists the five main tasks of the CNIL. The first one is to inform the data subjects and the controllers of their rights and obligations. The second one is to ensure that personal data processing is carried out in accordance with the LIL, EU law and other French international commitments. The third one is to issue a seal for products and procedures attesting to their conformity. The fourth one is to analyse the new technologies and uses which could have an important impact on privacy or other fundamental rights or freedoms. The fifth one is to make observations before any court in connection with a dispute concerning the application of data protection law in France. Since 2024, the CNIL has two additional tasks related to the implementation and the control of obligations from the DGA and the DSA. Those new tasks will be mentioned separately.

423. **Overview of the documents that the CNIL can adopt**. The CNIL can adopt a wide range of documents to support compliance which have already been mentioned. It issues opinions on authorising State processing[910] and processing in

---

903. *See* EDPB Opinion 5/2019 on the interplay between the e-Privacy Directive and the GDPR, in particular regarding the competence, tasks and powers of DPAs, p. 80.
904. *See* Art. 16 LIL combined with Art. 82 LIL.
905. CNIL, SAN 2022-025, 29 Dec. 2022, Apple distribution international, points 61–62.
906. CNIL, SAN 2020-013, 7 Dec. 2020, Amazon Europe Core, point 41.
907. CE, 28 Jan. 2022, n° 449209, Google, point 12 and CE, 27 Jun. 2022, n° 451423, Amazon Europe Core, point 13.
908. For an illustration *see* CNIL, SAN 2022-019, 17 Oct. 2022, Clearview AI, point 37.
909. *See* for an illustration CNIL, SAN 2022-020, 10 Nov. 2022, Discord Inc, point 25. This American company does not have an establishment in the EU only a European representant in Ireland.
910. This cover all the processing in the scope of the Police Justice Directive, *See* for instance Délibération n° 2023-112 du 19 octobre 2023 portant avis sur un projet d'arrêté portant création par la

the health sector.[911] It adopts guidelines, referential[912] recommendations, methodology of research,[913] and standard regulations.[914] It may provide certification mechanisms for persons,[915] products, data systems or procedures, including processes of anonymization to promote Open Data policy. It adopts lists of processing with high risk for the rights and freedoms of the data subject and for which a DPIA is necessary.[916]

424. **Different types of CNIL consultation**. The CNIL is consulted 'on any draft bill or decree or any provision of a draft bill or decree relating to personal data protection or the processing of such data'.[917] As such, its opinions are made public and often invoked in the public debate. CNIL also does not hesitate to express its position and concerns on projects involving data protection by means of press releases.[918] In addition, the CNIL may be called upon by various parties, such as the courts, members of parliament and other national regulatory authorities, for their expertise in data protection. It should be noticed that all these doctrine activities of the CNIL are elaborated by the plenary session, which brings together all eighteen members every week based on agenda made public.

425. **Ethical and societal issues assessment.** The CNIL has an explicit task to conduct '*assessments on ethical and societal issues raised by developments in IT and digital technology*'.[919] In the exercise of this task, the CNIL has been organising an annual event since 2020 on ethical thinking called the 'air conferences'[920] (futures, innovations, revolutions). So far, the new relationship between work and technology, the ethics of Open Data, and digital education ethics have been discussed. The CNIL also published statements on specific technologies, such as its position on the deployment of so-called smart cameras in public spaces,[921] its overview of ethical challenges of AI,[922] and its paper on ethical,

direction générale des douanes et droits indirects d'un traitement automatisé dénommé 'Système d'Information du Renseignement des Navires et des Équipages' (SIRENE); More details *supra* para. 262.

911. *See* supra para. 285.

912. The referentiels are sometimes binding *see* para. 285, and others are only soft law *see* para. 287 or n. 640.

913. *See infra* n. 636.

914. *See* CNIL deliberation 2019-001, 10 Jan. 2019 portant règlement type relatif à la mise en œuvre de dispositifs ayant pour finalité le contrôle d'accès par authentification biométrique aux locaux, aux appareils et aux applications informatiques sur les lieux de travail.

915. *See supra* para. 400

916. *See supra* para. 389.

917. *See* Art. 8, 4), a) LIL. The list of these opinions can be find https://www.legifrance.gouv.fr/search/cnil?tab_selection=cnil&searchField=ALL&query=&page=1&init=true&facetteNatureDelib=Avis&timeInterval=.

918. *See* for instance CNIL 2023, the Merger of the Vitale card and the identity card: CNIL points out data protection concerns, https://www.cnil.fr/fr/fusion-de-la-carte-vitale-et-de-la-carte-didentite-les-points-dattention-de-la-cnil-concernant-la.

919. *See* Art. 8, 4, e) LIL.

920. *See* https://www.cnil.fr/fr/avenirs-innovations-revolutions-la-mission-ethique-de-la-cnil.

921. CNIL Caméras dites 'intelligentes' ou augmentées' dans les espaces publics, position sur les conditions de déploiement, July 2022.

technical, and legal issues of voice assistants.[923] Such documents are generally preceded by public consultation and debates. In addition, the CNIL is proud to have its proper digital innovation laboratory called the LINC. The LINC conducts experiments and publications such as studies, special reports,[924] innovation and prospective notebooks on a specific theme,[925] and blog posts. The LINC also creates tools such as the DPIA software[926] or the cookies Viz, a visualisation tool to measure the impact of cookies during your Internet browsing.[927] It should also be noted that in January 2023, the CNIL opened a new AI department (AID), which is part of the CNIL's Technology and Innovation Directorate. As explained on its website, '*the three main missions of the AID will be:*

- *improve the understanding of AI systems for the CNIL, professionals and individuals;*
- *strengthen CNIL's expertise for the identification and prevention of privacy risks related to the implementation of these systems;*
- *prepare for the implementation of the European regulation on AI (under discussion at the European level);*
- *develop relationships with the ecosystem (academia, start-ups, companies, etc.)*'.[928]

Since the creation of the AID the CNIL's Website has seriously expanded its content on AI (fact sheets, cal for consultation, FAQs, etc.).[929]

426. **The new tasks of the CNIL for the DGA and the DSA**. The CNIL is the French competent authority for the registration of data altruism organisations established in France.[930] As such, it examines applications for registration, according to a procedure that has yet to be specified by decree in *Conseil d'Etat*. The CNIL must then ensure that these data altruism organisations comply with all the requirements of Chapter IV of the DGA, such as transparency requirements, the requirement to operate on a non-profit basis, and the requirements to safeguard rights and interests of data subjects and data holders with regard to their data, (consent, purposes etc.). The CNIL is one the French competent authorities for the DSA. As such it has tasks linked to advertising on online platforms which have their main establishement in France or their legal representative. Firstly, the CNIL should control that such providers comply with their obligations of information on their advertising. This means

922. *See* Comment permettre l'homme de garder la main? Les enjeux éthiques des algorithmes et de l'intelligence artificielle, 2017.
923. *See* White paper 1 on the record Exploring the ethical, technical and legal issues of voice assistants, November 2020.
924. *See* the special report from April 2023 on Generative IA, https://linc.cnil.fr/dossier-ia-generative.
925. For an illustration the last issue of the Cahiers IP of the LINC is about data, footprints and freedoms, https://linc.cnil.fr/sites/linc/files/2023-07/cnil_cahier_ip9_0.pdf.
926. *See* https://www.cnil.fr/en/open-source-pia-software-helps-carry-out-data-protection-impact-assessment.
927. https://linc.cnil.fr/cookieviz-une-dataviz-en-temps-reel-du-tracking-de-votre-navigation.
928. *See* https://www.cnil.fr/fr/node/8698.
929. *See* https://www.cnil.fr/fr/tag/Intelligence%2Bartificielle%2B%28IA%29.
930. *See* Art. 124-1 to 124-3 LIL.

that '*the recipients of the service are able to identify, in a clear, consise and unambigious manner and in real time ... meaningful information directly and easily accessible from the advertisement about the main parameters used to determine the recipient to whom the advertisement is presented and, where applicable, about how to change those parameters.*'[931] Secondly, the CNIL must ensure that online platforms comply with the probition to present advertisements to recipients of the service based on profiling, which include the specific prohibition related to the case when they are aware that the recipient of the service is a minor.[932] France has decided to rely on the CNIL's expertise to entrust it with new tasks closely linked to the processing of personal data in the so-called targeted advertising ecocosystem.

C. Powers of the CNIL

427. **Overview**. The CNIL has basically four kinds of powers: investigation powers, corrective powers, and some limited powers to initiate or intervene in judicial processing. Authorisation powers and advisory powers have already been mentioned in relation to its tasks.[933]

1. Investigations Powers

428. **Overview**. The CNIL has extensive investigation powers which echoes Article 58, §1 GDPR. The CNIL investigation's powers are detailed in Article 19 LIL, section II of its application decree and chapter VII of its rules of procedure.[934] The CNIL also issued a control charter, which synthesises all these rules.[935] The CNIL has the possibility to investigate any controller or processor of personal data, including private companies, non-profit organisations, or public bodies. Four different types of investigations may be carried out by the CNIL: online investigations, on-site investigations, hearings at the CNIL premises, and document-based investigations. These investigation modalities can be combined and carried out only on behalf of the CNIL or in the framework of mutual assistance or joint investigations with other European DPAs. When a joint investigation takes place on French territory, the President of the CNIL could authorise agents of another DPA to be present alongside the agents of the CNIL and to be part of the audit and investigation with the same guarantee as the ones required for the staff of the CNIL.[936] The CNIL may also use these investigative powers as part of its new tasks relating to the DSA.

931. Article 26, I, d) DSA.
932. Article 28 DSA.
933. *See* paras 423–425.
934. A consolidated version of the rules of procedure of the Cnil is available at https://www.cnil.fr/fr/reglement-interieur-de-la-cnil#_Toc411938673.
935. *See* CNIL, Charte des contrôles de la CNIL, version 1 Jun. 2023, avalaible at https://www.cnil.fr/sites/cnil/files/2023-07/cnil-charte_des_controles.pdf.
936. *See* Art. 25, III LIL.

429. **Guarantees**. CNIL home visits need to respect certain guarantees. They may only be conducted by accredited agents of CNIL between 6 am and 9 pm and are limited to the places, premises, enclosures, facilities, or buildings used for the processing of personal data. When it is a private home, in case of emergency and when the controller objects to the visit, an authorisation is required from the judge in charge of sentencing (juge des libertés et de la détention des peines).

430. For their investigations, the CNIL members and accredited staff may ask for all documents required for the performance of their tasks, in whatever format, and take a copy of them. They may collect, on-site or upon summons, all useful and necessary information or proof for the fulfilment of their task. The need to respect medical confidentiality may require CNIL staff to be accompanied by a doctor.[937] The professional secrecy applicable to lawyer-client privilege and journalistic processing can be opposed to the CNIL agents.[938]

431. **Scope limitation**. Finally, it should be underlined that these powers of investigation do not apply in the context of processing relating to State security and to processing carried out by the courts in the exercise of judicial functions.

2. Corrective Powers

432. Article 20 LIL lists the corrective powers of the CNIL which echoes Article 58, §2 GDPR. The corrective powers are shared by the President of the CNIL and the restricted formation. The restrictive formation is a panel of five members with its own chairman who is not the president of the CNIL.[939] The CNIL may also use these corrective powers as part of its new tasks relating to the DSA. By contrast, a specific provision, Article 20-1 LIL, rules the corrective powers of the CNIL for its DGA's tasks.

433. **Police powers of the President of the CNIL**. The president of the CNIL can issue mainly three kinds of corrective measures as an alternative to sanctions for violations of data protection rules. On the one hand, the president can address **a warning** to a controller or his processor that the intended processing operations are likely to infringe the provisions. For instance, in 2021, the President of the CNIL issued a warning to a sports club planning to use a facial recognition system to automatically identify people subject to a stadium ban. The president of the CNIL recalled that such biometrics processing by a sports club for anti-terrorism purposes does not conform to the GDPR. It has no legal ground in France.[940] However, since January 2022, the President of the CNIL can issue a **reminder** to an organisation of

---

937. *See* below para. 558.
938. *See* below paras 559 and 560.
939. *See* Arts 9, 8 LIL.
940. *See* https://www.cnil.fr/fr/reconnaissance-faciale-et-interdiction-commerciale-de-stade-la-cnil-adresse-un-avertissement-un-club.

its legal obligations if it does not comply with the GDPR or the LIL.[941] For example, in March 2023, the CNIL reminded two organisations carrying out medical research of their obligations to carry out a DPIA and to provide individuals with adequate information.[942] The CNIL considered that the reminder '*make it possible, in the case of minor breaches that do not justify the imposition of public measures or financial penalties, to encourage compliance by data controllers and processors who have failed to comply with their legal obligations*'.[943] Finally, the president of the CNIL can issue **formal notices** to organisations that fail to comply with the provisions of the GDPR or the law, requiring them to do so within a specified period. The LIL provides four purposes for formal notices such as:

- complying with the data subject's requests to exercise his rights;
- bringing processing operations into compliance;
- communicating a data breach to the data subject;
- rectifying or erasing; or
- limiting a processing.

The formal notice sets out the facts and shortcomings identified by the CNIL and details what is expected of the data controllers or processors concerned in order to comply. The president of the CNIL can ask for a proof of compliance within a time limit set in the formal notice. This deadline may not be less than ten days, except in an emergency, when it may be twenty-four hours. In such case, the president, where appropriate, rules on the closure of the formal notice procedure. In 2022, the CNIL issued 147 formal notices, of which only 13 have been made public. It is up to the president to ask the Office of the CNIL[944] to make public the formal notice depending on the seriousness of the infringement observed or the number of people concerned. This publication has an educational purpose. It aims to alert other controllers likely to be confronted with the same violations, so that they can bring themselves into compliance.

434. **Corrective measures of the restricted formation**. Article 20 III LIL lists the corrective measures that can be issued by the restricted formation. It includes a reminder, an order to bring the processing into compliance, which may be accompanied by a coercive fine, a restriction on processing, a ban on processing, an order of the suspension of a processing operation or its decision of approval of a BCR, the withdrawal of certification or the approval of certification body and an administrative fine.[945]

941. This echoes Art. 58, §2, b) GDPR.
942. *See* https://www.cnil.fr/fr/donnees-de-sante-la-cnil-rappelle-deux-organismes-de-recherche-medicale-leurs-obligations-legales.
943. *See* Délibération n° 2021-035 du 25 mars 2021 portant avis sur les Arts 40, 41 et 42 du projet de loi relatif à la différenciation, la décentralisation, la déconcentration et portant diverses mesures de simplification de l'action publique locale (paragraphe on Art. 41 of the Bill).
944. The CNIL Office is made up the President and the two Vice-president of the CNIL. *See* Art. 9 LIL.
945. *See* below paras 471 et seq.

435. **Emergency powers of the restricted formation.** Article 21 LIL lists the emergency powers of the restricted formation of the CNIL.[946] In such cases, the restricted formation can adopt several kinds of temporary suspension, such as a temporary suspension of a certification, the accreditation of a certification body, the temporary suspension of a processing' authorisation, or a limitation of the processing. The restricted formation can also adopt an injunction to bring the processing into compliance or a reminder. In all these cases, emergency measures will be taken by the Restricted formation at the request of the CNIL president.

3. Powers to Initiate and Intervene in Judicial Proceedings

436. The CNIL has some limited powers to initiate and intervene in judicial proceedings which echoes Article 58, §5 GDPR.

437. First, the president of the CNIL has the power to request that the competent court, through summary proceedings and orders, under penalty as applicable, take any measures needed to safeguard human identity, human rights, privacy, and individual or public freedoms.[947] In 2021, the president of the CNIL used this power in a case where personal and medical data relating to almost 500,000 patients was illegally collected and compiled in a computer file that was made available online on a website hosted in Guernsey Island. Unable to act effectively and quickly against the host of the disputed site or the publisher or author of the disputed content, the CNIL obtained an injunction from the Tribunal to require French Internet providers to block the disputed site.[948]

438. Second, the CNIL should immediately inform the public prosecutor of the offence or crime of which it is aware.[949] In the same way, the public prosecutor must inform the CNIL of all proceedings relating to criminal offences in connection with data protection. This information includes the date and subject of the hearing and is intended to enable the CNIL to file its written observations and to develop them orally at the hearing.[950]

439. Finally, the LIL took into account the CJEU's *Schrems* ruling[951] and provided the CNIL the power to request to the *Conseil d'Etat* the suspension of a data transfer or an extension to the suspension of a transfer that it might have previously ordered after receiving a claim against such international transfer it considered

946. *See also* Art. 46-47-1 of the 2009 of the LIL application Decree.
947. *See* Art. 21, IV LIL.
948. *See* Tribunal Judiciaire de Paris, Ord. 4 March 2021, n° RG 21/51823.
949. *See* Art. 40 CPPP and Art. 8, I, 2°, f LIL.
950. *See* Art. 41 LIL.
951. CJEU, Case C-362/14, Judgment of 6 Oct. 2015, *Maximillian Schrems v. Data Protection Commissioner (Schrems 1)*, ECLI:EU: C:2015:650.

grounded. The aim here is to enable the *Conseil d'Etat* to ask if needed the CJEU for a preliminary ruling on whether the international transfer in question is contrary to the GDPR.[952]

§2. Remedies

440. GDPR Chapter VII on remedies provides that two kinds of remedies against the controller or the processor are at the disposal of the data subject: non-judicial and judicial. Article 77 rules the non-judicial remedy as the right to lodge a complaint with a supervisory authority. Article 79 deals with judicial remedies.

I. Preliminary Remarks

441. **The Data Subject's Choice between Non-judicial Remedies versus Judicial Remedies.** It is up to the data subject to choose between bringing its case before the judge or the supervisory authority. Generally, data subjects prefer to refer the matter to a supervisory authority when they want to have a violation of his or her rights or an infringement of the GDPR terminated. This is mainly due to the cost and the length of judicial proceedings. However, the data subjects must go before a court if they want to receive a compensation for such violation. Recently, the CJEU considered that the data subject could also exercise both remedies 'concurrently with and independently of each other' ... [953] 'It is for the Member States, in accordance with the principle of procedural autonomy, to lay down detailed rules as regards the relationship between those remedies in order to ensure the effective protection of the rights guaranteed by that regulation and the consistent and homogeneous application of its provisions, as well as the right to an effective remedy before a court or tribunal as referred to in Article 47 of the Charter'.[954] Currently, French law has no provision to link these two remedies. Common procedural law could nevertheless provide solutions to avoid possible contradictions between the CNIL's decision and those of the judges. If the judge rules before the CNIL, there are no difficulties. The CNIL is bound to respect the authority of judgments. If the CNIL has issued a ruling before the court, it is highly likely that the judge will be alerted to this by a party seeking to base its claims on the CNIL's position. The civil judge will have two possibilities. He could either refer the matter to the Tribunal des Conflits for a ruling on the validity of the CNIL decision, which is considered an administrative decision. He could also submit a preliminary question to the Conseil d'Etat on the validity of the CNIL. Only the Conseil d'Etat can overturn a CNIL decision.[955]

952. *See* Art. 39 LIL.
953. *See* CJEU, Case C-132/21 Judgment of 12 Jan. 2023, Budapesti, point 35.
954. *See* CJEU, 12 Jan. 2023, C-132/21, Budapesti, point 57.
955. On the impact of the Budapesti Case in France. *See*: Ludovic Pailler, *La Cour de justice de l'Union européenne, pompier pyromane malgré elle: l'articulation des voies de recours ouvertes à la personne concernée par un traitement de données à caractère personnel*, Légipresse 2023, p.161.

442. **Wide Margin of Manoeuvre of Member States in Remedies.** GDPR Chapter VII leaves Member States a wide margin of manoeuvre to implement remedies in their national law. This is an expression of the well-known principle of the institutional and procedural autonomy of the Member States, even more so as the procedure is not in itself a competence of the EU. In addition, the CNIL has a wide discretionary power in investigating controllers and processors and in investigating complaints from data subjects. So, it comes as no surprise that, five years after the GDPR came into force, the Commission has proposed a revision of the regulation aimed precisely at better harmonising procedural issues between DPA.[956] Pending the adoption of this first revision of the GDPR, this section will illustrate the French rules relating to data protection remedies.

II. Non-judicial Remedies

443. Article 8, §2, d) LIL provides that the CNIL 'processes claims, petitions and complaints lodged by a data subject or by a body, organisation or association, and examines or investigates the subject matter of the claim, to the extent necessary'.

A. *Need of a Complaint*

444. **Definition of a complaint**. Curiously, the LIL has maintained its original 1978 wording without clearly explaining the differences between a complaint, a petition, or a claim. This echoes the lack of definition in the GDPR of what a complaint in the sense of Article 77 GDPR exactly is.[957] In its rules of procedure, the CNIL clarifies that '*A complaint is considered to be any request made by an identified natural or legal person relating to facts likely to be contrary to the texts whose application is entrusted to the Commission.*'[958]

445. **Practical issues**. The definition of complaint given by the CNIL makes it clear that it reserves the right not to consider a request for information or interpretation as a 'complaint'. In its 2022 annual report, the CNIL notes that it declared 4,234 of the 12,193 complaints received inadmissible, while at the same time, the CNIL said that it received 19,610 requests.[959] These different figures demonstrate a lack of transparency regarding the nature of these requests, which are not complaints and the criterion used for the admissibility of a complaint. It is only clear that a complaint cannot be anonymous, must be in French and must contain precise

956. Proposal for a Regulation of the European Parliament and of the Council laying down additional procedural rules relating to the enforcement of Regulation (EU) 2016/679, 4 Jul. 2023.
957. *See* our commentary in General Data protection, Article by Article Commentary, *supra*, p. 1010.
958. *See* Art. 47 règlement intérieur de la CNIL. However, the CNIL website seems to widely use the terms claims and complaints as synonyms perhaps to be more in tune with the language of the public. https://www.cnil.fr/fr/cnil-direct/question/adresser-une-reclamation-plainte-la-cnil-quelles-conditions-et-comment.
959. *See* p. 37.

details, such as the name of the organisation concerned by the complaint, any relevant information about the situation and a copy of any documents that are essential to understanding the complaint. The complaints can be submitted either online or by post. In both cases, the CNIL points out that the person must first contact the organisation or the DPO concerned to report the infringements and wait for a month before lodging a complaint.

B. Individual Versus Collective Complaint

446. The complaint can be lodged by the data subject itself or an '*identified natural or legal person*'. Therefore, the intermediate should have a written mandate. This person could be the legal representative of the data subject or a body which according to Article 80 GDPR can be mandated by the data subject to exercise his right before the CNIL.

447. **French definition of the bodies for collective complaints**. In France, Article 37 LIL provides that four kinds of bodies enter this category. First, it can be an association that has complied with their disclosure requirements for at least five years and whose corporate purpose includes privacy protection or data protection. Second, it can be a consumer protection association representative at the national level and approved[960] when the processing of personal data affects consumers. Third, it can be a trade union organisation for employees or officials when the processing affects the interests of these concerned people. Fourth, it can be an association or an organisation whose corporate purpose is associated with the protection of rights and freedoms where such rights and freedoms are disregarded in personal data processing or an association of which that person is a member and whose statutory purpose involves the defence of interests in relation to the purposes of the contentious processing. These collective complaints have been used since 2018 in France by both the NOYB[961] association created by Max Schrems and the French association la Quadrature du Net.[962] These first collective complaints were about the GAFAM and were behind the CNIL's first post-GDPR sanction against Google.[963] It is true that this collective complaint can also be exercised by the above-mentioned body without a mandate of a data subject.

448. **Whistleblowers**. In 2022, the CNIL also announced[964] that it has set up a specific system for collecting and processing whistleblower reports as required by

960. There are around fifteen approved national associations in France, which come from either the trade union movement, the family movement or the consumer movement.
961. For a global overview of the complaints of NOYB before the CNIL. *See* https://noyb.eu/en/project/dpa/cnil-france.
962. *See* https://www.laquadrature.net/donnees_perso/.
963. *See* CNIL, SAN 2019-001, 21 Jan. 2019.
964. *See* https://www.cnil.fr/fr/lanceurs-dalerte-adresser-une-alerte-la-cnil.

French law.[965] This system '*is reserved for individuals who report or disclose information, without direct financial consideration and in good faith*' a violation of the GDPR or the LIL. This page provides an initial level of information so that people can assess whether they qualify for whistleblower status. Strangely enough, the CNIL's dedicated page refers to filing a standard complaint, inviting the individual to clearly indicate his status as a whistleblower. However, this CNIL page simply invites people to use the complaints teleservice, the CNIL mail or phone by identifying themselves as whistleblowers. This is particularly strange given that the CNIL itself has drawn up a set of guidelines relating to the processing of personal data for the purposes of personal data processing relating to the implementation of a professional alert system.[966]

C. The Limited Right of the Claimant

449. The right to lodge a complaint with the CNIL also implies an obligation for the CNIL to inform the initiator of the claim as to the progress and outcome of the investigation within a reasonable time, particularly if further investigation or coordination with another supervisory authority is required.'[967] Before the GDPR, the *Conseil d'Etat* had already ruled that '*the author of a complaint to the CNIL may, however in all cases, refer the failure of the CNIL to inform him of the action taken on his complaint to the juge …*'[968]

450. In practice, when the complaint is serious, the CNIL opens an investigation based on discussions between the data controller, or even the processors, and the CNIL's departments. In other words, once they have initiated the procedure, the people behind the complaint are not associated as a party to the case and cannot express their views. The *Conseil d'Etat* ruled that the CNIL's decision not to act on a complaint did not constitute an unfavourable individual decision, which, under French law,[969] would require a statement of reasons.[970]

D. The Limited Right of the Controller Involved

451. Furthermore, the CNIL remains in control of its relations with the data controller. As indicated in its internal rules, it is not obliged to reveal the identity of the person who lodged the complaint and may even decide to carry out an on-site

965. Loi n° 2022-401 du 21 mars 2022 visant à améliorer la protection des lanceurs d'alerte and the Décret n° 2022-1686 du 28 décembre 2022 relatif à l'abondement du compte personnel de formation d'un salarié lanceur d'alerte obliged 41 public bodies including the CNIL to have such a specific system for collecting and processing whistleblower reports.
966. CNIL Référentiel relatif aux traitements de données à caractère personnel destinés à la mise en œuvre d'un dispositif d'alertes professionnelles adopted in July 2019.
967. *See* Art. 8, 2, d) LIL.
968. *See* CE, 21 Jun 2018, n° 416505, point 2.
969. In particular Art. L.211-2 Code of the relationship between the public and the administration.
970. *See* CE, 21 Oct. 2022, n° 459 254, point 9.

inspection without telling the controller what the complaint is about. The CNIL often carries out a series of ongoing investigations, regularly asking the controller to provide clarification on a particular point, so that it is only at a late stage that the controller becomes aware of the concrete position of the CNIL whether a violation is committed or not. The CNIL is not subject to any specific deadline for closing the complaint or its investigations. Once the investigations have been carried out, the President of the CNIL can take two main decisions. He can close the procedure or refer the case to the restricted committee for corrective measures and sanctions. In a recent case, the *Conseil d'Etat* declared that the CNIL '*has wide discretionary powers*' as to the action to be taken on a complaint. The CNIL may '*take into account the seriousness of the alleged breaches with regard to the legislation or regulations it is responsible for enforcing it is responsible for enforcing, the seriousness of the evidence relating to these facts, the date on which they were committed, the context in which they were committed and, where appropriate, the nature of the complaint in which they were committed and, more generally, all the general interests for which it is responsible*'.[971] Although the CNIL's decision may be appealed to the *Conseil d'Etat*, the latter has admitted that it exercises only limited control. It simply checks that the CNIL has not committed a manifest error of assessment. It is only in the event of an appeal against a CNIL decision relating to the data controller's failure to comply with data subject rights that the *Conseil d'Etat* can exercise full control.

E. Solutions for Dealing with the Large Number of Complaints

452. Since the GDPR, the annual reports of the CNIL have noted the continued existence of a high level of complaints. Three solutions have been put in place to try and improve the handling of these complaints in 2022.[972] First, a simplified procedure has been in place to enable a single member of the restricted panel to deal quickly with a simple complaint.[973] The ordinary procedure and the simplified procedure are both based on a contradictory procedure. Those procedures implied the nomination of a rapporteur to further investigate the case and to give her or his opinion on the violations. Second, the CNIL creates a teleservice, which not only helps the person lodge their complaint but also allows them to have a kind of follow-up of their complaint. Third, the CNIL announced that an external service provider carries out certain administrative tasks as part of the investigation of complaints, even though it alone decides what action to take on complaints.

971. *See* CE, 21 Oct. 2022, n° 459 254, point 3.
972. *See* CNIL rapport annuel 2022, p. 37.
973. *See* Art. 22-1 LIL.

III. Judicial Remedies

453. The GDPR provides two kinds of judicial remedies. First, Article 78 GDPR rules the right of an effective judicial remedy against a supervisory authority. Second, Article 79 GDPR provides a right to an effective judicial remedy against a controller or a processor.

A. *Judicial Remedy Against a CNIL's Decision*

454. In France, the *Conseil d'Etat*[974] is competent in case of an appeal by a data subject or controller against a decision of the CNIL. Appeals against CNIL decisions regarding the global scope of the de-listing right/obligation,[975] against fines imposed by the CNIL,[976] or against guidelines of the CNIL[977] have been made before the *Conseil d'Etat*. However, the data subject right to a judicial remedy against a supervisory authority could be limited when he or she has no interest in acting against the CNIL's decision.[978] For instance, the data subject should not be able to contest the amount of the fine imposed on the controller. In such situation, only the controller concerned should be able to challenge such decision before the *Conseil d'Etat*. Interestingly, recently, the *Conseil d'Etat* declared that a controller could be considered a defender in a case where the data subject criticised the closure of its complaints against such controller by the CNIL.[979] This illustrates that it is not always clear who the parties are in the procedure before the CNIL and this could have some impact on the parties in future litigation before the judges.

455. The appeal must be lodged within two months of notification or publication of the CNIL's decision. An appeal may also be lodged by the data subject in the

974. *See* Art. R-311-1-4 Code of Administrative Justice.
975. *See* Droit à l'oubli, https://www.conseil-etat.fr/content/download/153672/file/Fiche%20juridique%20-%20Droit%20%C3%A0%20l%27oubli.pdf.
976. *See,* for instance, CE, 19 Jun. 2020, n° 430810 regarding the first post GDPR fines, in which the *Conseil d'Etat* considered that the 50 million fines imposed by the CNIL on Google was not disproportionate. The CNIL had rightly observed serious breaches of the obligation to provide information and transparency, as well as of the rules governing consent for processing for personalising advertising purposes. *See also* CE, 17 Apr. 2019, Optical Center, n° 422575 in which the CE reduced the EUR 250,000 fine imposed on Optical Center by the CNIL to EUR 200,000. The *Conseil d'Etat* considered that The CNIL did not take sufficient account of the promptness with which Optical Center took corrective measures to remedy the breaches of its security obligation. Point 7.
977. CE, 19 Jun. 2020, Association des agences conseils en communication n° 434684B regarding the CNIL guidelines on cookies in which the *Conseil d'Etat* considered that within the framework of non-binding guidelines, the CNIL could not deduce the general prohibition of wall cookies from the sole requirement of free consent.
978. *See* CE, 21 Jun. 2018, n° 416505, point 2. (Partially challenged the judgment of CE, 21 Oct. 2022, n° 459254, point 3).
979. Before the GDPR, the Conseil d'Etat, even considered that '*the author of the complaint has no interest in contesting either the decision taken at the end of this procedure, whatever its outcome, or the fate reserved for his complaint at the end of this procedure. In all cases, however, he is entitled to refer the CNIL's failure to inform him of the outcome of his complaint to the juge ...* .' *See* CE, 21 Jun. 2018, n° 416505, point 2.

event of an implied refusal by the CNIL. This is the case when the CNIL does not deal with a complaint within three months. It should be noted that in French law, the CNIL decision is enforceable as soon as it is notified, and an appeal to the *Conseil d'Etat* has no suspensive effect. The data controller must comply with the provisions of the decision or the imposed fine while awaiting the outcome of its administrative appeal. To remedy this, two so-called emergency procedures under French law can be used to ask the judge to suspend the implementation of the CNIL's decision.

456. On the one hand, **the summary proceedings procedure**[980] enables a request to be made to the interim relief judge to suspend the execution of the administrative decision or some of its effects pending a verdict on the merits. To do this, four conditions are required so that the interim injunctions are rarely granted. The decision must be the subject of an application for annulment or reversal, the procedure must be justified on the grounds of urgency (for example, because the CNIL has decided to make public the penalty imposed),[981] the decision must not already have been implemented in full and there must be serious doubt as to its legality. The suspension ordered by the interim relief judge is provisional and ceases to have effect as soon as the court hearing the case on the merits; in this case, the *Conseil d'Etat* has ruled on the application for annulment or reversal of the CNIL's decision. Depending on the degree of urgency, the decision to suspend implementation of the decision may be taken within a period ranging from forty-eight hours to one month. The interim relief judge's decision is subject to appeal or cassation.

457. On the other hand, **the interim relief procedure**[982] allows the interim relief judge to take any measures necessary to safeguard a fundamental freedom that the CNIL has infringed in a serious and manifestly unlawful manner. The judge will give a ruling within forty-eight hours. Three conditions are required. The case must be urgent, requiring the judge to intervene very quickly, and it must be shown that fundamental freedom is at stake and that the infringement is serious and manifestly unlawful.

458. Finally, it is worth mentioning that litigation on the visit by agents on the CNIL falls outside the jurisdiction of the *Conseil d'Etat* and, more globally, the administrative courts. The order issued by the liberty and custody judge authorising a visit to premises as part of a CNIL inspection after the person responsible has objected to the visit may be appealed to the First President of the Court of Appeal.[983] The First President of the Court of Appeal also has jurisdiction to hear appeals against the conduct of the visit.

---

980. *See* Art. L.521-1 of the Code of Administrative Justice on the 'référé suspension'.
981. By contrast, the *Conseil d'Etat* judges that the condition of urgency had not been met when a newspaper cited the serious consequences for its financial situation of the CNIL's refusal to authorise it to carry out the processing required to produce the hospital ranking in France. The newspaper argued that this issue was one of its best sellers. *See* CE Ord., 29 Dec. 2022, n° 469969.
982. *See* Art. L.521-2 du Code de la justice administrative on the 'référé-liberté'.
983. *See* Art. 19 LIL and Arts 28 and 29 of the 2009 Decree of application of the LIL.

B. Judicial Remedy Against a Controller or a Processor

1. Administrative Judges Versus Judicial Judges

459. **Competence of the administrative judges**. In France, administrative courts are competent in case of an action against a controller or a processor that is a public authority. It is only when the controller is a Ministry or an administrative independent authority that the *Conseil d'Etat* is competent. Thus, when the controller is a local authority, the *tribunal administratif* is first competent. The *Conseil d'Etat* can only rule on the case in cassation.

460. **Competence of the judicial judges.** In addition, judicial judges shall be competent to resolve conflicts between a data subject and a controller or a processor, which is not an administrative body. Therefore, most of the judgments on data protection by the civil courts are related to conflicts between employees and employers[984] or data subjects who have chosen to take judicial action against a private company. There is also the possibility of summary proceedings when the urgency justifies it.[985] Such summary proceedings have been used in cases related to the de-listing right against Google.[986]

2. French Group Action in Data Protection

461. **The various Group Actions in France**. Since 2016,[987] there has been in France a sectorial group action 'action de groupe' in data protection. This action is open to individuals who find themselves in similar situations and who are suffering from damages that resulted from a breach of statutory obligations by data controllers or processors. The purpose is to request the court to order the cessation of unlawful practices. A compensatory collective redress in data protection has been introduced within the adaptation of the GDPR.[988] The French group action in data protection can be filed before civil and administrative courts. Administrative courts are competent, if the group action is introduced against a controller or a processor that is a public authority. The agents may be: (i) associations that have been exercising their statutory activities in the field of privacy and data protection for at least five years; (ii) accredited consumer associations that are representative at the national level (if data processing affects consumers' interests); or (iii) trade unions (if data processing affects employees or civil servants' interests).[989] It is also worth

984. *See infra* paras 521 et seq. for some illustrations.
985. *See* Arts 834 and 835 CPPC.
986. *See* Olivia Tambou, Trois enseignement à tirer de la mise en œuvre juridictionnelle française de l'arrêt Google Spain in Tambou O., Bourton S. (dir.), *Le droit à l'oubli en Europe et au-delà/ The Right to be Forgotten in Europe and Beyond, Avril 2018, Luxembourg, Blogdroiteuropéen, Collection Open Access Book,* Available at: https://wp.me/p6OBGR-2QK.
987. The French data protection group action has been introduced in the LIL by the Digital Republic Law No. 2016-1547, 18 Nov. 2016.
988. *See* Art. 37 LIL.
989. *See* Art. 38 LIL.

underlining that France uses its margin of discretion by accepting that such bodies have the right to act independently of a mandate of the data subject.

462. **Limited application.** Group action in relation to personal data is still not widely used in France. This seems to be due to the limited number of structures that can bring a group action, the necessarily long duration of these procedures and the costs that this can entail. Only two group actions have been launched publicly in relation to personal data. The first one was launched in 2019 by the Internet Society against Facebook.[990] The NGO invoked seven infringements to the GDPR: the inadequate protection of user data against hacking, the inadequate information provided to users in the event of a data breach, the existence of 'tracking cookies' that collect information on non-members who consult Facebook, the limitation of Facebook's accountability for personal data in the general terms of use, the 'sensitive' nature of some of the data collected, in this case, data relating to sexual orientation, political opinions and religious beliefs, the absence of 'free and informed' consent from users of Facebook and its instant messaging subsidiary WhatsApp when data from the two platforms is cross-referenced, and the absence of any possibility for users to partially object to Facebook's data processing; The second one was also launched in 2019 by the consumer French association *UFC-Que Choisir?* against Google. The association considered that Google has illegally collected and exploited its users' data. It states on its website that 'users' consent to the collection and processing of personal data, for targeted advertising purposes, is not obtained in compliance with the regulations' and denounces a 'massive intrusion into users' private lives and the scale of the data processing'.[991] To date, there have been no judicial decisions on group actions for the protection of personal data. The ineffectiveness extends to all existing other sectorial group actions in France.[992] Therefore the legislator is currently considering a reform of group actions which aims to introduce a universal and more effective system.[993]

§3. Liabilities of the Controllers and Processors

463. **European specific regime for liability of the controller or processor.** Article 82 GDPR provides a specific European regime for the liability of the controller and processor when they cause damage to a person.[994] It also sets out rules for the conditions for joint liability, where more than one controller or processor is liable for the damage caused by the processing which infringes the GDPR rules. This covers the liability of joint controllers, the liability of both the controller and

990. https://www.isoc.fr/ebastille-mars-2019/.
991. https://www.quechoisir.org/decryptage-action-de-groupe-contre-google-vos-questions-nos-reponses-n68427.
992. Beyond the Data protection group action, there are currently a Consumer, Health, Discriminations, Environment group action, in France. There are seven different legal regimes of group action.
993. *See* Proposition de Loi n° 639 relative au régime juridique des actions de groupe, registred at the Assemblée Nationale on 15 December.
994. *See* our comment in General Data Protection Regulation, Article by Article Commentary, *supra,* p. 1041.

the processor and the plurality of liable processors. To simplify the action of the claimant, the GDPR provides that in case of joint liability, the person who suffered the damage has the choice of whether to sue the controller, the processor or both for full compensation. The controller or the processor, which paid the full compensation, is entitled to a recourse action against the co-liable processor or controller. In the end, everyone will share in the compensation to the extent of their involvement in the damage. Finally, Article 82, §3 GDPR establishes a tighter possibility of exemption of the controller and/or processor, where they can prove that they are not 'in any way responsible for the event giving the damage'.

464. Recently, the CJEU interpreted Article 82 GDPR by clarifying the three conditions necessary to give rise to the right to compensation, namely processing of personal data that infringes the provisions of the GDPR, damage suffered by a person,[995] and a causal link between that unlawful processing and that damage. These are cumulative conditions. The CJEU ruled that the concepts of 'the material or non-material damage' and of 'compensation for the damage suffered' are autonomous concepts of EU law which must be interpreted in a uniform manner in all the Member States.'[996] Then, the judge considers that Article 82 GDPR '*must be interpreted as meaning that the mere infringement of the provisions of that regulation is not sufficient to confer a right to compensation*'.[997] There is a right to compensation only when the damage suffered by a person is the result of the infringement of the controller or processor. The Court did not attempt to define the concept of damage further, merely pointing out that, according to the wording of Article 82, damage may be material or non-material. Material damage could be, for instance, damage to property or personal injury. Non-material damage could cover moral harm or non-pecuniary loss. The CJEU also clarified that the person concerned will have to demonstrate that he has suffered damage because of the breach of the GDPR.[998] In other words, the burden of proof rests on the plaintiff. However, this burden of proof can be eased because the plaintiff can rely on the existence of the many obligations set out in the GDPR for the controller and the processor and its accountability obligation. In addition, the CJEU denied the possibility for national law to require a certain threefold seriousness for the compensation for non-material damage.[999] It is also accepted that compensation must be paid in full. Finally, the CJEU considers that it is up to the national courts under domestic law to determine the amount of damages payable under the right to compensation granted by Article 82 GDPR.[1000] This first judgment as well as a series of other recent judgments[1001] have clarified

995. As Art. 82 GDPR refers to 'any person' it can be not only the data subject but also a legal person or a third party. *See* our comment on Art. 82 GDPR, *supra,* point 8.

996. *See* CJEU, 4 May 2023, *UI v. Österreichische Post AG*, C-300/21, point 30.

997. *See* CJEU, 4 May 2023, *UI v. Österreichische Post AG*, C-300/21, point 42.

998. *See* CJEU, 4 May 2023, *UI v. Österreichische Post AG*, C-300/21, point 50.

999. *See* CJEU, 4 May 2023, *UI v. Österreichische Post AG*, C-300/21, point 51.

1000. *See* CJEU, 4 May 2023, *UI v. Österreichische Post AG*, C-300/21, point 59.

1001. *See* CJEU, 14 Dec. 2024, *VX AT*, C-456/22 ECLI:EU:C:2023:988, in which, the Court ruled that the disclosure of personal data on their local authority's website without their consent could constitute non-material damage without having to exceed a de minimis threshold; CJEU, 21 Dec. 2023 Kanrakenversicherrung Nordhrein, c-667/21 EU:C:2023:1022, points 92 to 94, in which the

the interpretation of Article 82 GDPR in a way that makes it easier to identify the ad value of Article 82 GDPR in relation to traditional national liability regimes.

465. **French Liability related to Data Protection.** The LIL does not include clarification of the individual right to compensation and liability. However, several ways can be used to obtain compensation for damage relating to personal data.

I. Compensation Based on General French Civil Liability Rules

466. **Article 1240 Civil code**. General rule of French civil liability sets forth by Article 1240 Civil Code that '*any act of man, which causes damages to another, shall oblige the person by whose fault it occurred to repair it*'. As Article 82 GDPR, the wording of Article 1240 civil code shows clearly the three elements necessary to engage liability. Liability only arises from a fault if there is a direct causal relationship between the fault and the damage. As soon as these three criteria are fulfilled, a person is entitled to claim compensation for a broad scope of injuries: material and financial injuries, bodily injuries, and moral injuries (which include several aspects, notably pain, suffering and loss of enjoyment). French law is also governed by the principle of full compensation.

467. **Illustration**. Compensation may be claimed because of the non-material damage suffered by the data subject because of the infringement of their rights. In 2022, a civil judge ordered a bank to pay its customer EUR 15,000 in damages for non-material loss. The bank had improperly registered its customer in the Foreign Account Tax Compliance Act (FACTA) files, following its obligation to declare any customer considered to be a US taxpayer to the US tax authorities. The bank had not corrected its mistake even though its customer, a Frenchman born in Ottawa, had confirmed that he was not American and had asked several times for the erasure of the false information. The judge considered that the registration of the data subject in the FACTA file had caused him harm through the worry he could legitimately feel not only when crossing US borders but also about the possibility of prosecution by the US tax authorities. Interestingly, the judge rejected the possibility of compensation based on prejudice of anxiety. The judge considered that: '*The courts have already recognised that the anxiety caused to a victim by a liable third party may constitute compensable loss. This is the case for fear of imminent death,*

Court considered that Art. 82 GDPR 'provides for fault-based liability in which the burden of proof rests not on the person who has suffered damage, but on the controller'; CJEU, 25 Jan. 2024, BL, C-687/21 ECLI:EU:C:2024:72, in which the Court declared that Art. 82 GDPR 'fulfils a compensatory and not a punitive purpose'. §47, therefore this provision allows the damage acutually suffered as a result of the infringement of the GDPR 'to be compensated in full' §50. Finally, the Court recalls that 'the loss of control of the personal data for a short period of time may cause the data subject 'non-material damage', within the meaning of Art. 82(1) of the GDPR, giving rise to a right to compensation, subject to that person demonstrating having actually suffered such damage' … ; CJEU 11 Apr. 2024 *GP*, C-741/21, ECLI:EU:C:2024:288; CJEU 20 Jun. 2024 *AT*, C-590/22, ECLI:EU:C:2024:53§, in which the Court precises that the criteria for setting the amount of administrative fines laid down in Article 83 GDPR are not applicable to determine the amount of damages due as compensation for damage based on Art. 82 GDPR.

for the anxiety loss recognised for employees who have been victims of asbestos exposure, or for the loss of expectation and anxiety suffered by the relatives of victims of terrorist attacks or disasters. However, on the one hand, this anxiety must be sufficiently serious and linked to a particularly serious event to constitute an autonomous loss, and on the other hand, it must not overlap with a non-material loss that may encompass it.'[1002] This was here the case.

II. Compensation Based on Denigration and Parasitic Acts

468. More globally, compensation can also be sought in combination with other national grounds. In 2022, a civil court ordered Google to pay a dentist EUR 20,000 in compensation for non-material damage for failing to remove his Google My Business listing, despite his request to do so. The judge based his decision on multiple infringements of the GDPR[1003] and also found that Google had committed denigration and parasitic acts constituting misconduct. According to the case law, denigration consists of '*damaging the brand image of a company or a designated or identifiable product in order to divert customers by using reprehensible comments or arguments, whether or not they have an accurate basis; disseminated or issued in any case in such a way as to reach the customers of the company targeted, whether or not it is a competitor of the company that made them*'.[1004] In this case, the judge considered that the denigration was constituted because of the violence of the opinions left for this practitioner without Google being able to demonstrate that these opinions had a sufficient factual basis, as these opinions were not verified. In addition, the judge underlined that although Google was obviously not in competition with the dentist, it benefits directly from these reviews, which constitute an important element of its service values to Internet users and its commercial partners. Parasitism is the act of taking undue advantage of the know-how and human and financial efforts made by a company that is the victim of the actions of a person who usurps the reputation acquired by the competitor.[1005] The judge considered that '*By means of reviews and ratings, Google creates and organises, without having to say so and without having to spend the slightest penny, under the guise of the right to information, a competition between providers of the same service in a given region, enabling it to offer them, through its own free and paid services, the means to increase their visibility.*' To qualify as parasitic acts, the judge considered that the system allows Google to take advantage of the reputation of professionals. This is

1002. *See* Tribunal judiciaire de Grenoble, 7 Feb. 2022, Banque Rhône- Alpes, available at https://www.legalis.net/jurisprudences/tribunal-judiciaire-de-grenoble-4e-ch-civile-jugement-du-7-fevrier-2022/.

1003. The main issues were that the data was processed without the prior consent of the data subject, and that the doctor's right to object was not respected. There was also a failure to comply with the principle of fairness and transparency. More details on Google My Business in relation to the right to erasure *see* before paras 350–351.

1004. *See,* for instance, CA Versailles, 9 Sep. 1999. *See also* case law of the *Cour de Cassation* on the distinction between critique and denigration Cass., 16 Jun. 2005 or and freedom of expression and denigration Cass., 11 Jul. 2018.

1005. *See* Cass., 5 Jul. 2016, n° 14-10108.

reinforced by the fact that Google My Business is particularly locked, as it is currently very difficult for professionals to get out of it. As for the existence of moral prejudice, the judge based it on the unverifiable nature of the negative reviews. In addition, the judge also considered the fact that the dentist had always objected to her data being processed precisely to avoid having to deal with these reviews. Finally, it is worth underlining that the judge decided Google France, Google LLC and Google Ireland had jointly and severally to pay these damages. In this respect, the judge seems to consider that Google LLC, Google Ireland and Société Google France are, on the whole, joint controllers, although this point was not really discussed. The judge simply explicitly rejected Google France's request to be exonerated from liability. In so doing, the judge referred by analogy to the CJEU's *Google Spain* ruling. He deduced that Google France carries out its activities within the framework of the other Google companies and that it is also a data controller. While this judgment marks a step forward in the litigation surrounding the opinions of platforms,[1006] the economic stakes involved should lead to higher courts, and in particular, the *Cour de cassation,* clarifying this issue. The definitive recognition of the possibility of objecting to the processing of personal data within Google My Business on the grounds of the GDPR should also have an impact on the conditions under which such platforms can be held liable.

III. Compensation Based on Contractual Liability

469. Compensation can also be sought as part of contractual liability. For instance, recently, OVH, the French leader in cloud computing and a provider of website hosting services, has had to compensate its client for data loss resulting from a fire.[1007] OVH committed a breach of its contract by storing data and backups in the same building. As a consequence, the website of its client became totally unavailable to both end customers and partners. The data on these websites (pages, databases, customer data) was lost. Interestingly, the judge rightly refused to consider the fire as a case of force majeure and declared the contractual clause exempting OVH in the event of a fire null and void. The judge also declared null and void the limitation of liability clause drafted in advance by OVH. Such a clause in a contract of adhesion would transfer '*the risk onto the other party in an unjustified manner and without any consideration for the latter*'.[1008] Under this clause, OVH's liability was limited to the reimbursement of six months' subscription, in this case EUR 1,800. By contrast, the judge ordered OVH to pay around EUR 97,000 in damages for non-compliance with the general terms and conditions, including EUR 20,000 for image damage for its client.

1006. *See* for recent illustration on tribunal de Commerce de Paris, 25 May 2023, Socated et Cie, Galerie de l'Echaudé, Gowork.

1007. *See* Tribunal de Commerce de Lille Métropole, 26 Jan. 2023 SAS France Bati Courtage/SAS OVH. *See* for a similar case related to this fire and its consequences, Tribunal de Commerce de Lille 9 mars 2023, in which OVH was ordered to pay BluePad nearly EUR 144,839 for the various losses suffered.

1008. The prohibition of such clause is based on Art. 1171, §1 Civil Code.

470. It is worth underlining that in French law, limitation of liability clauses may be called into question in four cases. First, in the case of willful misconduct, where the debtor '*refuses to perform his contractual obligations*', even without '*intent to harm his co-contractor*'.[1009] Second, in the case of intentional fault, '*fault which presupposes the intention to cause the damage and not merely to create the risk of it*'.[1010] Third, the limitation of liability will be rejected when '*its scope of the essential obligation*'.[1011] It will be the case in the above-mentioned case where the limit on reparation is abnormally low. Fourth, there is no limitation in the case of gross negligence, which is '*characterised by behaviour of extreme seriousness, bordering on fraud and showing the inability of the debtor of the obligation to perform the contractual task which he had accepted*'.[1012]

IV. Group Action for Compensation

471. France used the opening clause provided by Article 80, §1 GDPR and introduced a group action for the exercise of the right to compensation. Article 37 LIL clarifies that such a group action applies to individuals '*in a similar situation … [who] suffer damage as a result of a similar type of failure of a personal data controller or processor to comply*' with the GDPR.

472. The group action is open to the same four kinds of bodies mentioned above for group action on the cessation of the infringement.[1013] Similarly, the controller or processor involved must be given prior notice. After four months, the body can go before the judge. It should be the civil judge if the processor or the controller is a private entity or the administrative judge if they are a public entity. In the group action for compensation, the judge will first adopt a judgment on the definition of the group and assess the liability of the controller and/or the processor. Then, each individual victim will have to apply to the controller or processor for compensation.[1014] In the event of disagreement, the matter may be referred to the court again. All types of damage are compensable (material, non-material and bodily injury). The complexity of this procedure rules out its use for small requests for compensation. This is one of the reasons why this system has not yet been applied.[1015]

1009. Cass., 1st civ., 4 Feb. 1969.
1010. Cass., 1st civ., 10 Apr. 1996.
1011. Cass., com., 29 Jun. 2010, Faurecia; Civil Code, Art. 1170.
1012. Cass., com., 3 Apr. 1990.
1013. *See infra* para. 447
1014. *See* Art. L.849-11 to L.849-20 of the Code of Civil Procedure, and the Art. L.77-10-7 to L.77-10-15 of the Code of Administrative Justice.
1015. *See* the intend of the trade union to invoke the collective action against which was rejected by the judge for procedural reasons Cour d'appel de Versailles, 6 Jul. 2023, n° 21/00233.

V. Compensation as a Complement to Penalty

473. In French law, the civil party may, in support of its claim, request compensation for the damages corresponding to the harm caused to it.[1016] This means that compensation can be sought as a complement to a penalty related to data protection.[1017]

§4. Administrative Fines

474. **Impact of the GDPR Harmonisation in France**. The CNIL has had the power to impose fines against controllers and processors since 2004.[1018] However, the amounts of such fines were lower than those introduced in Article 83 GDPR. The GDPR harmonisation of the administrative fines covers both the criteria for setting administrative fines and the graduation of the amount of the administrative fines.[1019] The GDPR defines two fine upper limits with an alternative between a lump sum or a percentage in case of an undertaking. The first limit is up to EUR 10 million or 2% of the total worldwide annual turnover of the undertaking. The second limit is up to EUR 20 million or 4% of the total worldwide annual turnover of the undertaking. The highest limit applies to infringements of the core provisions of the GDPR, such as the personal data principles of Article 5, the conditions of the consent, the data subject rights, the rule on international transfers, etc. Beyond the GDPR, the EDPB adopted guidelines on the calculation of administrative fines under GDPR to improve the coherency between the DPAs.[1020]

475. **Scope of the administrative fines**. Article 20 LIL recalls the GDPR's graduation of the administrative fines. It also clarifies that the CNIL cannot impose such administrative fines on the State. Therefore, France used its margin of manoeuvre given by the GDPR. According to Article 83, §7 GDPR, it was up to the Member States to decide on whether national public authorities or bodies acting as controllers or processors can be subjected to this regime of administrative fines as well. Thus, in France, only the State is excluded. By contrast, public local authorities can be imposed by the CNIL, despite the opposition of their representative during the negotiation on the GDPR adaptation of the LIL. The CNIL imposed its first administrative fine to a municipality for failure to comply with its obligation to appoint a DPO by December 2023.[1021]

1016. Article 418 CPPP.
1017. On the penalty, *see* below para. 483.
1018. *See* A. Debet (ed.), *Informatique et Libertés*, *supra* n. 430, p. 825.
1019. More details *see* my comment on Art. 83 GDPR in General Data Protection Regulation, Article by Article Commentary, *supra,* p. 1053.
1020. *See* EDPS, Guidelines 04/2022 on the calculation of administrative fines under the GDPR, Version 2.1 adopted on 24 May 2023.
1021. CNIL SAN-2023-018, Commune de Kourou, 12 December 2023 more details on this case *see* n. 847.

476. **French additional measures**. The LIL also provides for two types of injunctions that may be accompanied by a fine. First, the restricted formation can adopt an injunction to bring the processing into compliance with a 100,000-per-day delay fine due to the controller involved.[1022] Second, the restricted formation can adopt an injunction in the event of failure to respond to a previous formal notice of the CNIL, attached with a fine, the amount of which may not exceed EUR 100 per day's delay.[1023] Since 2022, fines under the simplified procedure[1024] have been capped at EUR 20,000, which can be attached to a fine, the amount of which may not exceed EUR 100 per day's delay.[1025] Here again, these fines do not apply in case of processing carried out on behalf of the State.

477. It should also be underlined that the restricted formation can publish the sanction, including the amount of the fine. The statistics given by the CNIL illustrate that more than half of its sanctions with fines are published.[1026]

478. Furthermore, the LIL provides clarification on the articulation between the administrative fine and a penalty in relation to the principle *non bis in idem*. '*When the restricted formation issues an administrative fine that is final before the criminal court has definitively ruled on the same o related facts, the criminal judge may order the penalty to be deducted from the administrative fine issued.*'[1027]

479. Administrative fines are not paid directly into the CNIL budget. CNIL fines are collected by the Treasury and included in France's general State budget.

480. **Illustrations**. In the context of administrative fines in France, the *Clearview* case is worth mentioning. In 2022, the CNIL imposed a EUR 20 million fine with an injunction not to collect and process without a legal basis personal data relating to data subjects on French territory in connection with the operation of the facial recognition software it markets and to delete all personal data relating to these data subjects. Clearview had two months to comply. A EUR 100,000 fine per day's delay was attached. Clearview did not comply. Thus, the CNIL made public in May 2023 the imposition of a penalty payment of EUR 5.2 million.[1028]

481. **Figures**. According to comparative statistics on GDPR fines,[1029] the CNIL used moderately its power to impose fines with sixty two fines,[1030] since the

1022. *See* Art. 20, III, 2) LIL, and Art. 21, I, 6 LIL.
1023. *See* Art. 20, IV LIL introduced in 2022.
1024. *See* §§452.
1025. *See* Art. 22-1 LIL.
1026. *See* Open Cnil sanctions given between 2019–2022, available at https://www.data.gouv.fr/fr/datasets/sanctions-prononcees-par-la-cnil/.
1027. *See* Art. 22 LIL.
1028. *See* CNIL, Délibération de la formation restreinte n° SAN-2023-005 du 17 avril 2023 concernant la société CLEARVIEW AI.
1029. *See* https://www.enforcementtracker.com/?insights.
1030. By contrast in the same period, the Spanish DPA issued 888 fines, but with an total of EUR 82,150 millions

application of the GDPR until July 2024. However, the CNIL ranks third[1031] among the DPAs that have imposed the highest fines since the GDPR, with total fines of around EUR 371 million in July 2024. Until that date, the highest fine awarded by the CNIL was its first post-GDPR EUR 100 million fine against Google, which dates to January 2019. The CNIL's constant approach is, therefore, to give priority to supporting controllers and processors in their compliance. The CNIL only fines particularly serious breaches for data subjects and when it faces a persistent lack of cooperation by the controller or processor to achieve compliance.

§5. PENALTIES

482. **Overview of the French penalties**. Article 84 GDPR provides that '*the Member States shall lay down the rules on other penalties applicable to infringements*' of the GDPR. Most of these penalties are grouped together in the CP in a section dealing with violations of privacy. This section carries penalties of up to five years' imprisonment and EUR 300,000 in fines.

483. First, certain penalties apply to failure to comply with the rules governing the principles applicable to processing. This will be the case for processing carried out without prior formalities,[1032] fraudulent, unfair, or unlawful data collection,[1033] retention of data for longer than the period stipulated by law,[1034] and misuse for other purposes.[1035] Second, failure to meet certain obligations of data controllers is subject to penalties. For example, there may be non-compliance with the accountability principle[1036] or failure by a controller, or processor to notify of a data breach.[1037] Third, unlawful processing of specific data is also a criminal offence. This applies equally to sensitive data within the meaning of Article 9 GDPR, to data relating to criminal offences and convictions within the meaning of Article 10 GDPR,[1038] and to the French national identification number.[1039] Article L.226-21 CP provides an offence for the illicit international transfer to a third country or an international organisation. Fourth, the CP specifies offences for disregarding the rights of the persons concerned, such as the right to information,[1040] the right to access[1041] and the right to object,[1042] the right to erasure and to limitation.[1043] Fifth, the CP foresees some criminal offence in the event of obstruction of CNIL's action, such as opposing the performance of the tasks entrusted to its members or authorised agents,

1031. Behind Luxembourg and Ireland.
1032. Article L.226-16 CP.
1033. Article L.226-18 CP.
1034. Article L.226-10 CP.
1035. Article L.226-21 CP.
1036. Article L.226-17 CP.
1037. Article L.226-17-1 CP.
1038. Article L.226-19 CP.
1039. Article L.226-16-1 CP. On this number called NIR *see infra* paras 511–512.
1040. Article R.625-10 CP.
1041. Article R.625-11 CP.
1042. Article 220-18-1 CP.
1043. Article R.625-12 CP.

refusing to communicate to them by concealing or by information and documents that are useful for their mission, communicating information that does not comply with the content of the recordings as they were at the time of the request or which does not present this content in a directly accessible form.[1044] In this case, the penalty is one year's imprisonment and a EUR 15,000 fine.

484. **Focus on recent French penalties**. Two types of penalty that deserve attention because they are often mentioned by the media: the revenge porn and the doxing. Since 2016, revenge porn has been covered by Article L.226-2-1 CP which provides a penalty of one year's imprisonment and a fine of EUR 45,00. This is considered a special case of capturing and broadcasting images or words in a private place without the person's consent. In the case of revenge porn, the courts must assess the sexual nature of the images and the intent to harm the person disseminating them. The absence of the person's consent may relate to the dissemination of these images to third parties and not necessarily to the taking of them. The penalty is up to two years imprisonment and a fine of EUR 60,000. Since 2021, a doxing penalty has been introduced in the CP. It is related to the tragic death of a professor of geography who was beheaded in 2020 for showing caricatures of the Prophet Mohammed in a lecture on freedom of expression. This crime was made possible by the dissemination of these coordinates on social networks. Article 223-1-1 CP provides that '*The act of disclosing, disseminating or transmitting, by any means whatsoever, information relating to the private, family or professional life of a person enabling that person to be identified or located for the purpose of exposing that person or exposing members of that person's family to a direct risk of harm to the person or property of which the perpetrator could not have been unaware is punishable by three years' imprisonment and a fine of 45,000 euros*.' The penalty is increased to five years imprisonment and a fine of EUR 75,000 when the person concerned by the doxing is a public authority, an elected representative, a journalist or a minor.

485. Although the press has occasionally reported situations involving doxing,[1045] to our knowledge, this penalty has not been applied.

486. In 2024, two new penalties have been introduced in French law which can be related to personal data processing. First, Art.226-8 CP establishes an offence against the dissemination of deepfake. It punishes 'the act of making known to the public or to a third party... visual or audio content generated by algorithmic processing and representing the image or words of a person, … '. This text tackles AI-generated content constituting personal data processing. However, it lays down three conditions that in practice should not facilitate its implementation. On the one hand, the offence will only be constituted in the absence of consent from the data subject. It is not specified whether this consent must be in line with the conditions laid down in Article 7 GDPR. On the other hand, this does not apply to cases where

1044. Article L.226-22-2 CP.

1045. *See,* Un site d'ultradroite appelle à 'éliminer' des avocats signataires d'une tribune contre le RN, le parquet saisi, *Le Monde* 4 juillet 2024.

it is obvious that the content is algorithmically generated. Finally, this does not apply to content that expressly mentions the use of such algorithmic processing. The penalty is two years' imprisonment and a fine of €45,000. Second, Art. L.131-35-1 CP an additional penalty of suspension of accounts for access to online services, otherwise known as banning from social networks, for people convicted of certain online offences. This could apply to the failure to comply with a request from an administrative authority to remove child pornography content, the disseminating images of violence or video or photo montages, particularly of a sexual nature, using the words or image of a person without their consent. The suspension is for a maximum of six months, or even one year if the person is a repeat offender. If the supplier fails to comply with the judge's request for suspension, it may itself be liable to a fine of €75,000.

487. To sump up, France has been steadily stepping up its penalties in relation to personal data protection, even if for the time being these penalties are rarely applied.

Part IX. Specific Processing Situations

§1. Processing for Journalistic Purposes and Academic, Artistic or Literary Expression

488. Article 80 LIL establishes a specific regime for the processing of journalistic purposes and academic, artistic, or literary expression. This provision aims to reconcile the right to the protection of personal data with the right to freedom of expression as required by Article 85 GDPR. This appeals to three kinds of comments.

I. French Exclusion of the Non-professional Journalist

489. The specific regime proposed by Article 80 LIL refers to processing with the purposes of the professional exercise of the activity of a journalist in compliance with the ethical rules of this profession. France clearly excludes its application to the processing of bloggers who are mainly not journalists by profession. France considered it could be stricter than the wording of Article 85, §1 and §2 GDPR. This interpretation is not consistent with the CJEU case law. The CJEU opts for a broader interpretation of the concept of processing of personal data solely for journalistic purposes. According to the CJEU, *'journalistic activities' are those which have as their purpose the disclosure to the public of information, opinions, or ideas, irrespective of the medium which is used to transmit them'*.[1046] The CJEU has, therefore, a functional and not an organic definition of journalistic activities. The CJEU even admitted that the fact that a person is not a professional journalist does not exclude the fact that the recording of the video and its publication on YouTube cannot be seen as processing for journalism purposes.[1047] France's restrictive interpretation illustrates its ancient reluctance to non-professional forms of journalism.[1048] At the same time, in France, since the yellow jacket movement, there has been a recurring debate about the lack of legitimacy of the traditional media. More globally, the recognition of a right to information through whistleblowers questions this restrictive French approach. French fears should be more focused on the guarantees

1046. *See* CJEU, 6 Dec. 2008, *Satakunnan Markkinapörssi and Satamedia*, C-73/07, -point-- 61.
1047. *See* CJEU, 14 Feb. 2019, *Sergejs Buivids*, C-345/17, point 55.
1048. The reference of professional journalist has been existing in the LIL since 1978 and has not been updated for the French adaptation of the LIL to the GDPR.

of the necessity of the use of the exemption than the scope of it. The fight against online fake news and disinformation must be fought by other means.[1049]

II. Authorised Derogations

490. Article 80, §1 LIL provides several derogations for the processing implemented for journalistic purposes and academic, artistic, or literary expression. It will be up to the controller or processor to justify that these derogations are necessary and respect the proportionality principle. Article 80 LIL authorises derogations to the principle of storage limitation to the prohibition of the processing of sensitive data and data relating to criminal convictions and offences. Article 80 LIL also establishes derogations to data subject rights, such as the right to information, the right of access, the right of rectification, and the right to restriction. Finally, processings with the above-mentioned purposes are not submitted to the chapter on international transfer of the GDPR. This list is a limitative list. Therefore, a newspaper cannot invoke Article 85 GDPR and Article 80 to derogate from its obligation of prior formalities for Health data processing.[1050]

491. In addition, Article 80, §2 LIL provides that these derogations 'shall not prevent the application of the provisions of the Civil Code, the laws relating to the media and the CP that provide for the conditions of the exercise of the right of reply ('droit de réponse') and that prevent, limits, compensate and, if necessary, sanction violations of privacy and attacks on the reputation of individuals'.

III. Other French Specificities

492. Beyond Article 80 LIL, Article 4, §2 LIL mentions that French law is applicable to the processing of journalistic purposes and the purposes of academic, artistic, or literary expression when the controller is established in France. In addition, Article 19 LIL protects journalistic sources in case of a visit by the agents of the CNIL to the premises of the controller.[1051]

493. Finally, it is worth mentioning that the LIL do not contain provisions for balancing the freedom of expression with the right to erasure or the de-listing right. Before the GDPR, the *Cour de cassation* judged that there is no obligation for a press institution to delete the name of the person in its archive or to limit access to this information.[1052] Since the GDPR, this position has been maintained by civil

1049. *See* for instance in France, Loi organique et loi ordinaire du 22 décembre 2018 relatives à la manipulation de l'information.

1050. *See* CE, 30 Jun. 2023, n° 469964, point 16. In this case, the CE considered that the balance between the freedom of expression and data protection has been made by the CNIL in assessing the request of authorisation of of Health data processing.

1051. *See* below para. 560.

1052. *See* Cass., 12 May 2016, 15–17.729.

courts. For instance, the *Tribunal judiciaire* of Paris rejected a request for the deletion and anonymisation of a conviction of a former sports club manager published by a newspaper.[1053] In this case, the judge recalled that both the right to object and the right to erasure must be reconciled with the right to freedom of expression. In addition, it refers to Articles 80 LIL and 85 GDPR, for underlining that '*when the data controller is a press organisation, requiring it … to remove personal data from an article, such as the first and last names of a person covered by a court decision which is the subject of the article, thereby depriving the article of any interest, would be likely to exceed the restrictions that can be placed on the freedom of the press*'.[1054]

§2. Processing of Personal Information Versus Public Access to Official Documents

494. Article 7, §1 LIL provides that the LIL 'not preclude the application, for third parties of provisions concerning access to administrative documents and to public archives'. The holder of a right of access to administrative documents is, therefore, authorised to access a third party's personal data.[1055]

I. French Right to Access Administrative Documents

495. **A right recognised since 1978.** In French law, the right to access administrative documents was established in 1978[1056] at the same time as the right to protection of personal data. A specific authority, the Commission d'accès aux documents administratifs (CADA), has been created to assist citizens in exercising their rights and the administration in fulfilling its obligations. Therefore, since 1978, '*any person has had the right to access information contained in an administrative document whose conclusions have been challenged*'.[1057]

496. **Broad concept of administrative document**. The concept of administrative documents is broadly interpreted. It means completed documents[1058] produced or received by the State, local authorities,[1059] and persons governed by public or private law as part of their public service tasks.[1060] These cover reports, minutes,

1053. *See* Tribunal judiciaire de Paris, 17e chambre presse civile, 30 Jun. 2021, n° 20/05100.
1054. *Ibid.*
1055. *See* Art. 7, §2 LIL.
1056. *See* Loi n° 78-753 du 17 Jul.1978, portant diverses mesures d'amélioration des relations entre l'administration et le public et diverses dispositions d'ordre administratif, social et fiscal, which is codified in Book III of the Code of Relations between the Public and the Administration (CRPA).
1057. *See* Art. L.311-3 of the CRPA.
1058. Article L.311-2 CPRA excludes preparatory documents.
1059. *See* Art. L.2126 General Local Authorities Code (CGCT in French) which establishes that any natural or legal person has the right to request communication of the deliberations and minutes of the municipal council, the budgets and accounts of the municipality and municipal by-laws.
1060. *See* Art. L.300-2 CRPA.

statistics, and information contained in digital files, which could include personal data, algorithms, and source code.[1061] This also covers a register in sense of Article 30 GDPR or a DPIA in sense of Article 35 GDPR.[1062]

497. **A relative right to receive communication**. This right to receive communication of administrative documents is subject to a request from the interested party and was intended to be a one-off measure. This communication can take several forms, such as on-site consultation, reproduction or sending by email, including a publication online when it is possible. There are, however, two types of limitations to communication of administrative documents. Some administrative documents may not be disclosed because they are covered by secrecy[1063] or other public interests. Other administrative documents may only be disclosed to the interested party to protect private interests, in particular privacy, medical and business secrecy. This also covers cases where the administrative document contains '*an assessment or value judgement on a natural person, named or easily identifiable*'.[1064] As an illustration, the CADA considered that the CNIL did not have to communicate the letter sent to a controller for the closure of the procedure because it '*reveals behaviour likely to be prejudicial to the company being audited, just like the reminder of its obligations which is motivated by the infringements observed*'.[1065] In addition, the CADA underlined that the letter mentioned the content of a file, which could identify other employees. Thus, the rule is that documents may only be disclosed to the applicant after occultation of the non-disclosable information.[1066] When this is not possible, there is no communication with the applicant.[1067]

II. Open Data Versus Data Protection

498. Beyond the communication of administrative documents, the 2016 Digital Law Republic enshrines the principle that information held by public authorities should be open by default. Open Data is becoming public policy at both national

1061. *See* Art. L.300-2 CRPA.
1062. *See* CADA, opinion 20225787, adopted on 15 Dec. 2022, on the register of the Caisse Nationale des Allocations Familiales (CNAF) (French national family allowance fund), and the DPIA for the implementation relating to processing of the CNAF as part of its policy to combat fraud, which has been transmitted to the CNIL. Interestingly, the CADA considered that such document should be freely disclosed to anyone who so requests with occultation on protected data on such as personal data where appropriate.
1063. *See* Art. L.311-5 CRPA.
1064. Article L.311-6 CRPA.
1065. *See* CADA opinion n° 20213252, adopted on 8 Jul. 2021.
1066. Article L.311-7 CRPA.
1067. For an illustration CE, 17 Mar. 2022 n° 449620, points 5 to 7. The *Conseil d'Etat* rejected the request for 8,957 documents because it required extensive work to remove information relating to private life and industrial and commercial secrecy. On the one hand, such blanking out would have made the documents unreadable. On the other hand, this would have placed a disproportionate workload on the administration, given the resources at its disposal.

and European levels, thanks to the adoption of directives.[1068] At the European level, France is considered a pioneer and trendsetter.[1069]

A. *French Open Data Regime Rules on Personal Data*

499. The French Open Data regime is based on two components. First, the publication of administrative documents, which may be voluntary or mandatory for public authorities. Thus, this publication is made without the consent of the data subject either on the grounds of a legal obligation or the necessity for the public service task of the administration. Second, the possibility of re-using these administrative documents by any person for commercial or no commercial purposes. Personal data issues could be at stake at both stages.

500. **Exceptions of the publication without anonymisation**. As far as the publication of administrative documents is concerned, Article L.312-1-2 CRPA establishes that the data needs to be anonymised except if the data subject has given its consent to the publication or if the publication is provided by law.[1070] In addition, a decree lists nine categories of administrative documents that can be published without having been anonymised.[1071] These are documents required for public information relating to:

- the organisation of the administration, in particular, organisational charts, directories of administrations and the list of persons entered on a promotion table or a list of suitable candidates for access to a step, grade, body or employment category in the civil service;
- the organisation of economic, associative and cultural life, in particular, the national register of associations and the register of companies and their establishments;
- the conditions under which regulated professions and regulated professional activities are organised and practised, in particular, those relating to the practice of the professions of notary, lawyer, bailiff and architect;
- teaching and research, and in particular, the results obtained by candidates in administrative examinations and competitions or those leading to the award of national diplomas;
- the organisation and practice of sporting activities;

1068. *See* the later one the Directive (EU) 2019/1024 of the European Parliament and of the Council of 20 Jun. 2019 on Open Data and the re-use of public sector information (recast).

1069. *See* the European Commission, Open Data Maturity report 2023, Publications of the European Union, p. 142.

1070. For instance, Art. L.127-10 Environnemental Code related to the plot division and representation of buildings; or Art. L.112-A of the Book of Tax Procedures, which states that 'In order to contribute to the transparency and real estate markets, the tax authorities shall make freely available to the public, in electronic form electronic form, the information it holds about the property values declared in connection with transfers that have taken place over the last five years'.

1071. Décret n° 2018-1117 du 10 décembre 2018 relatif aux catégories de documents administratifs pouvant être rendus publics sans faire l'objet d'un processus d'anonymisation.

- the conditions for organising and exercising political life, such as the national directory of elected representatives ('Répertoire national des élus');
- the conditions under which tourist activities are organised and carried out;
- activities subject to formalities laid down by legislative or regulatory provisions, in particular in relation to town planning, occupation of the public domain and protection of personal data; and
- certain administrative documents held by public archive services and other bodies responsible for providing a public archiving service.

501. The absence of anonymisation is justified by the need to inform the public. This means that when the processing of personal data does not fall within the scope of this information, it should be anonymised.

502. **Role of Data controller of the administration**. The communication and the publication of personal data included in an administrative document is personal data processing. Thus, the public administration concerned is a data controller.[1072] Therefore, data protection provision should apply and the data subject right of information, the right to access, and the right of rectification should be respected. When the processing is not based on a legal obligation but the execution of a public service task, data subject should be able to exercise its right to object for reasons relating to their situation. This is the case for the publication of individual planning decisions.

503. **Reuse of administrative documents**. One of the purposes of the communication and the publication of administrative documents is to authorise their reuse for purposes other than those of the public service mission for which the documents were produced or received. When these documents contain personal data, re-users must comply with the GDPR and the LIL.[1073] The CNIL and the CADA have established a guide for the re-users, which details their obligations regarding the GDPR.[1074] The re-user of public data is a data controller. As such he must ensure that its processing complies with the following key principles of Article 5 GDPR such as lawfulness, fairness, transparency, purpose limitation, storage limitation, accuracy, integrity, accountability. The recent implementation of the platform *Ma data* can be mentioned here as an illustration. *Ma Data* is a private platform which aims to facilitate access to administrative documents. It enables users to send requests for access to administrative documents to over 50,000 listed authorities, and to obtain any responses and associated documents. All requests, responses and documents produced are automatically published. Therefore, the platform engaged itself to systematically delete the email addresses and business telephone numbers of agents involved in providing answers before publication. Following the opinion

1072. The CADA systematically recalls this in its opinion post-GDPR by mentioning GDPR relevant provisions including Art. 82, for instance CADA opinion 20180650, Adopted in 13 Sep. 2018.
1073. *See* Art. L322-2 CRPA.
1074. *See* CNIL, CADA, Guide pratique de la publication en ligne et de la reutilisation des données publiqus Open Data.

of the CADA,[1075] the platform informs its users on the need to have some of their personal data for the necessity of its services of sending their request to public authority concerned. As far of the publication on the platform is concerned, the data subject has a right to object to it, or to use a pseudonym. Finally, according to the minimisation principle, the email address of the user will not be published, and it will not be transmitted to the administration.

504. It is also worth mentioning that the need for coherent articulation between data protection and right to access administrative documents has led to the integration of the president of the CADA in the CNIL college.

505. There are some specific regimes for publication of administrative documents which are related to the digital transformation of the French administration. This is the case for the local authorities' administrative documents and the Open Data of the judicial decisions.

B. *Publication of the Local Authorities' Administrative Documents and Personal Data*

506. From 1 July 2022, the General Local Authorities Code (CGCT) requires the electronic publication of regulatory acts and decisions of a non-regulatory or individual nature taken by local authorities.[1076] As far as the municipalities are concerned, Article R.2131-1 of the same code sets out the details of this publication. Under the terms of these provisions, the documents concerned are '*made available to the public on the municipality's website in their entirety, in a format that cannot be modified and under conditions that ensure their preservation, guarantee their integrity and enable them to be downloaded. The electronic version of these documents must include a mention, in legible characters, of the first name, surname and position of the author, as well as the date on which the document was posted on the municipality's website. The period of publication of the document may not be less than two months*'.

507. The CADA[1077] and the *Conseil d'Etat*[1078] consider that personal data which are not justified and useful for informing the public about local management must, therefore, be removed before the document is disclosed or published unless such removal would render the document irrelevant (in which case it cannot be disclosed or published).

1075. For an illustration, *see* CADA opinion 20213227, adopted on 8 Jul. 2021.
1076. This publication obligation applies to communes, groups of communes, departments and regions. *See* Art. L.2121-15, Art. L.3121-13, Art. L.4132-12, Art. L.5211-1 et Art. L.5711-1 du CGCT.
1077. *See* CADA, Conseil 20221096 – Séance du 21/07/2022, and its sheet on 'La publication des documents des collectivités territoriales liés à l'exercice de leur pouvoir discretionnaire.'
1078. CE, 17 Mar. 2022, n° 449620, point 5.

508. For documents published without prior anonymisation, the CADA recommends[1079] preventing the indexing of identifying data by external search engines, such as the use of a 'robots.txt' file or a captcha system.

C. Open Data of Judgments

509. The Open Data of Judgments is another example of a specific regime aiming to secure data protection rules. Article 44.5 LIL creates a legal ground for the processing relating to the reuse of public information contained in the Open Data of Judgments which authorises the processing of sensitive data.[1080] The only requirement is that '*the purpose or effect of these processing operations is not to allow the re-identification of data subjects*'.[1081] Therefore, the first and second names of the parties or third parties, judges and registrars are systematically occulted. Additional identification details may be withheld at the request of the judge or presiding judge if there is a risk to the privacy or security of individuals. In practical terms, these blackouts are carried out by the *Cour de cassation* and the *Conseil d'État*. Automated processing is supplemented by manual checks of varying degrees of detail, depending on the sensitivity of the case. Thus, the *Conseil d'Etat* and the *Cour de cassation* are controllers of such processing of pseudonymisation. Consequently, any interested party may apply to the *Cour de cassation* or the *Conseil d'Etat* to have additional identifying details removed where there is a risk to security or privacy. The right to access and rectification also needs to be invoked before these Courts.

510. As far as the reuse of French judgments is concerned, there is a legal prohibition of reuses for the profiling purposes of judges and registrars.[1082] Furthermore, the *Conseil d'Etat*[1083] and the *Cour de cassation*[1084] have each published general conditions for the use of their data. These general conditions recall that the reuser must respect data protection rules and that it needs to notify the court '*the persistence, in a court decision, of elements of obvious re-identification of the natural persons mentioned therein*'.

1079. *See* CADA, sheet on 'La publication des documents des collectivités territoriales liés à l'exercice de leur pouvoir discretionnaire.'

1080. This open judicial data is rules by Art. L.10 Code of Administrative Justice and Art. L.111-13 of the Judicial Organisation Code.

1081. *See* Art. 44.5 LIL.

1082. *See* Art. L.111-13 Code of the Judicial Organisation which provides that '*The identity data of judges and members of the court registry may not be re-used for the purpose or effect of evaluating, analysing, comparing or predicting their actual or presumed professional practices. Violation of this prohibition is punishable by the penalties.*'

1083. *See* https://www.courdecassation.fr/conditions-generales-dutilisation-pour-la-reutilisation-des-donnees-issues-des-decisions-de-justice.

1084. *See* https://opendata.justice-administrative.fr/cgu.html.

§3. Processing of the National Identification Number

511. **The French Numéro d'Inscription au Répertoire (NIR).** In France, the national identification number is called NIR. This is a thirteen-digit number[1085] completed by a two-digit control key, assigned to each person at birth in France, and to the French nationals born abroad. This national number is a personal data and a unique identifier. The NIR is recorded on the Vitale card and enables each insured person to obtain the benefits to which they are entitled.

512. **Listed categories of controllers of the NIR.** Article 30, §1 LIL established the NIR could be only processed by categories of controllers and purposes of processing determined by a decree. The 2019-341 decree[1086] lists such categories in the following areas: social protection, health, the work, employment and public sector, finance, tax and customs, justice, public statistics, census, education, and housing. Article 30, §2 provides some exceptions, such as the use of the NIR by the official public statistics which do not involve sensitive data, and criminal convictions and offences data, processing for scientific, historical research purposes. This is also the case for processing carried out to provide online e-government services and some health processing.[1087] In all these exceptions, the NIR must be encrypted and replaced with an unintelligible statistical code.

§4. Processing in the Context of Employment

513. **No specific provision in the LIL.** There are no express provisions in the LIL relating to the processing in the context of employment, which concretises Article 88 GDPR. At this stage, it is worth recalling that Article 88, §1 GDPR empowers the Member States to adopt more specific rules for the employment context in a broad field of application. It covers all national provisions regarding the processing of employees' personal data, from recruitment and working conditions to termination of employment relationships. Then, Article 88, §2 GDPR frames the wide margin of manoeuvre of the Member States. It recalls that these national rules must include safeguard measures relating to transparency, personal data transfer of employees in the groups of undertakings, and monitoring systems at the workplace. French-specific rules to ensure the protection of employees' rights and freedoms regarding the processing of their personal data in the context of employment relationships are scattered mainly in the French Labour Code.

1085. The 1st digit corresponds to the individual's sex (one for men and two for women); the 2nd sequence, consisting of two digits, corresponds to the individual's year of birth; the 3rd sequence, consisting of two digits, corresponds to the insured person's month of birth; the 4th sequence, also consisting of two digits, corresponds to the department of birth; the 5th sequence, consisting of three digits, corresponds to the INSEE code of the commune of birth; the 6th sequence, consisting of two digits, corresponds to the serial number of the civil register in the month of birth.

1086. Décret n° 2019-341, 19 Apr. 2019 relatif à la mise en œuvre de traitements comportant l'usage du numéro d'inscription au répertoire national d'identification des personnes physiques ou nécessitant la consultation de ce répertoire.

1087. *See* Art. 30, §6, 2 LIL.

I. Main Provisions on the Labour Code for Personal Data Protection Interest

514. **Article L.1121-1 Labour** is a generic provision on workers' rights and freedoms that can be invoked in many contexts, including in relation to personal data. According to this provision, '*No one may impose restrictions on the rights of individuals or on individual and collective freedoms that are not justified by the nature of the task to be performed or that are not proportionate to the aim pursued.*' This provision protects employees' private, personal and family lives, freedom of expression, religious freedom and professional freedoms, in particular, union freedom.

515. **Specific obligations of information.** In employment relations, the principle of transparency is essential, both in cases where the processing has a legal basis and for processing that may rely on the employee's consent. The Labour Code sets out several obligations information for employment processing of personal data. Some provisions impose an obligation to provide information about the employees.

516. **Individual information of the job applicant or employee.** First, the job applicant[1088] and the employee[1089] must be expressly informed, prior to their implementation, of the professional assessment methods and techniques used in relation to him/her.[1090] This prior information is crucial, as employees cannot refuse to be assessed by their employer if they have been informed in advance of the professional assessment methods and techniques used in the company. This information will enable the employee to ensure that the assessment methods are objective and transparent (no discriminatory assessment criteria nor criteria likely to generate stress).

517. Second, no personal information concerning a job applicant[1091] or an employee[1092] may be collected by a system that has not been brought to the employee's attention beforehand. As the *Cour de cassation* often points out, the employee's right to information is the counterpart to the employer's right to control and monitor the activity of his staff.[1093] As the GDPR requires, this information should enable the employees to know the purposes of the processing and to understand the processing that will be carried out on their data. This information is crucial because it is the first necessary step in exercising subject rights.[1094]

1088. *See* Art. L.1221-8 Labour Code.
1089. *See* Art. L.1222-3 Labour Code.
1090. *See* more details on the CNIL Website on evaluation annuelle des salariés: droits et obligations des employeurs, https://www.cnil.fr/fr/levaluation-annuelle-des-salaries-droits-et-obligations-des-employeurs.
1091. *See* Art. L.1221-9 Labour Code.
1092. *See* Art. 1222-4 Labour Code.
1093. *See* Cass. soc., 22 Sep. 2021, 20-10.843, point 6.
1094. *See* Cour d'Appel d'Amiens Chambre prud'homale 4 mai 2023.

518. Third, employees may be informed in various ways, such as in their contract of employment, the internal regulations, or even in a charter on IT or digital usage annexed to the contract of employment, and in case of video surveillance by means of posters.

519. **Obligations of information of the employee representative bodies**. In France, a 'Comité social et économique' (CSE) has to be implemented in any enterprise employing more than eleven employees.[1095] For companies with more than fifty employees, the employer is obliged to consult the CSE beforehand on working conditions and any plans to 'introduce new technologies'.[1096] The *Cour de cassation* has even ruled that this obligation to inform and consult the CSE extends to employee monitoring systems, even though monitoring is not the primary and exclusive purpose.[1097] This case concerned a traceability tool used by a banking institution to control internal operations and procedures, as well as to monitor and control risks. This processing was based on a legal obligation. However, the tool had also been used by the employer to check whether the employee was carrying out consultations other than those with customers in his portfolio. The judge considered that the employer should have informed and consulted the CSE on the use of this system for this last purpose.

520. **Importance of the transparency principle in work environment**. Compliance with the principle of transparency is very important for the employer. On the one hand, collection of employees' personal data without their knowledge is likely to infringe on their privacy. This will be the case for surveillance devices, which collect data without the knowledge of workers, such as a hidden camera and hidden microphone.[1098] Such surveillance tools allow the employer to have access to both professional and private discussions. This will also be the case when the employer is not sufficiently transparent about the purposes of the surveillance processing. For example, the geolocation of an employee is used to prevent theft and check the mileage of the vehicle but cannot be used to monitor the use of the vehicle by the employee outside working hours.[1099] The use of a geolocation system outside working hours is considered to violate the employee's privacy.[1100] On the other hand, failure to inform employees and staff representatives not only invalidates the arrangements for monitoring employees but also prevents the employer from using the information collected as evidence.[1101]

1095. *See* Art. L.2311-2 Labour Code.
1096. *See* Art. L.2312-8 Labour Code.
1097. Cass. soc., 11 Decembre 2019, n° 18-11792 FSPB.
1098. *See* for instance Tribunal correctionnel de Paris, 19 Mar. 2022, RG n° 00/02830, Carsy c/ Couturier.
1099. *See* Cass. soc., 22 Mar. 2023, n° 21-24.729, point 4.
1100. *See also* Cass. soc., 22 Mar. 2023, n° 21-22.852, In this case, the Cour of Cassation judged that 'the implementation of the company's vehicle geolocation system had enabled permanent monitoring of the employee, by collecting data relating to the location of his vehicle outside his working hours and days, so that this significant infringement of his right to a personal life was disproportionate to the aim pursued'. Point 9.
1101. Cass. soc., 11 Decemb. 2019, n° 18-11792 FSPB.

II. Collection of Personal Data and Evidence in Labour Relations

521. **Right of the employers**. An employer in dismissal proceedings cannot use the geolocation data collected outside the employee's working hours to prove the employee's misconduct.[1102] However, the *Cour de cassation* has accepted that, under certain conditions, unlawful evidence based on the collection of data without the prior knowledge of the employee or the information/consultation of the CSE may be admissible. The *Court de cassation*, therefore, considers that judges must check whether the disputed evidence was essential to the exercise of the employer's right and whether the infringement of the employee's right to respect for her personal life was not strictly proportionate to the aim pursued. In other words, there is a need for a fair balance between the right of evidence, the protection of personal data and the protection of privacy. The use of unlawful evidence relating to the non-informed collection of personal data in the context of the employment will only be accepted on condition that the employer has no other means of proof at his disposal.[1103] For example, an employer cannot use video surveillance recordings illegally installed on its premises to prove thefts committed by an employee when it has an audit report enabling it to prove the employee's misconduct.[1104]

522. **Right of the employees**. Personal data processing as a means of evidence in the employment context can also be used to the benefit of the employee. The *Cour de cassation* ruled that employees could ask their employer for the records of other employees to prove cases of discrimination, either men or women[1105] or because of union membership.[1106] The judge applied the same rationale on the need for a fair balance between privacy and data protection on the other employees' side and ruled on proof for the applicant. In both cases, the judge admitted that the use of unlawful evidence based on personal data processing will only be accepted because '*it was essential to the exercise of the right to evidence of the employee and proportionate to the aim pursued i.e. the defence of the employee's legitimate interest in equal treatment*'.[1107] The Court admitted that '*in order to present evidence suggesting the existence of the alleged pay inequality between her and some of her male colleagues, the employee was entitled to obtain the pay slips of eight other employees occupying positions of comparable level to hers in management, sales or*

1102. *See* Cass. soc., 22 Mar. 2023, n° 21-24.729, point 9 or Cass. soc., 22 Mar. 2023, n° 21-22.852, point 10.
1103. *See* Cass. soc, 25 Nov. 2020, 17-19.523 as a first application before the GDPR where the Cour admitted that 'the unlawfulness of a piece of evidence under the provisions of Law no. 78-17 of 6 January 1978, as amended by Law no. 2004-801 of 6 August 2004 (...) does not necessarily mean that it should be dismissed from the proceedings', point 16. This statement is based on an interpretation of the Arts 6 and 8 of the EHRC and Art. 9 Civil Code, and Art. 9 of code of civil procedure. In a former case, the *Cour de Cassation* admitted the use of SMS sent by the employer to the employee as evidence of harassment against an employer without referring to data protection but by rejecting the unfair nature of the use of this method of proof the Cass. soc., 23 May 2007, 06-43.209, point 3.
1104. *See* Cass. soc., 22 Mar. 2023, n° 21-17-802, point 9.
1105. *See* Cass. soc., 8 Mar. 2023, n° 21-12.492.
1106. Cass. soc., 1 Jun. 2023, n° 22-13.238 F-B, Sté Renault Trucks c/ U.
1107. *See* Cass. soc., 8 Mar. 2023, 21-12.492 point 10.

market functions'.[1108] The Court also took into account that the processing for evidentiary purposes had been minimised. Personal data was withheld, except for surnames and forenames, contractual classification, detailed monthly remuneration and total gross remuneration per calendar year.[1109]

III. Employees' Monitoring

523. Employees' monitoring is an area in which national law must provide guarantees for employees. These guarantees are mainly based on Article 9 Civil Code relating to privacy or on the above-mentioned provisions of the Labour Code, in particular, Article L.1121-1 and the GDPR. Case law and CNIL deliberations illustrate the variety of areas in which the employees' rights and the employers' obligations have been clarified.

A. *Usual Prohibitions of Permanent Surveillance*

524. The use of permanent employees' surveillance tools is prohibited. The constant video surveillance of an employee working alone in the kitchen constitutes a disproportionate interference with his personal life.[1110] The recording of all of the employees' telephone conversations with the customer service department of a distance-selling company has been considered an infringement of the minimisation principle.[1111] The CNIL considered that the use of keyloggers, insidious spyware which enables to remotely record all actions performed on a computer made by an employee, is, in principle, an illegal type of surveillance.[1112] The CNIL also considers that surveillance cameras must not allow employees' workstations to be viewed continuously. It encourages employers to redirect or move cameras.[1113] During the COVID-19 pandemic, the CNIL recalls that the employer cannot require its employees to videoconference throughout their working hours to ensure that they are present behind its screen. Permanent screen sharing or any '*obligation for employees to perform actions on a regular basis to demonstrate their presence behind the screen, such as clicking on an application every X minutes or taking photos at regular intervals, are also prohibited*'.[1114]

525. The CNIL recently condemned Amazon France for setting up continuous surveillance of its employees using two tools to measure their performance. One

1108. *See* Cass. soc., 8 Mar. 2023, 21-12.492, point 9.
1109. This minimisation safeguard echoes to the CJEU, 2 Mar. 2023, C-268/*21 Norra Stockholm Bygg AB see* in particular, point 18.
1110. *See* Cass. soc., 23 Jun. 2021, n° 19-13.856.
1111. CNIL, SAN 2020-003, 28 Jul. 2020. The CNIL considered here that it was an infringement of the minimisation principle.
1112. *See* CNIL, les outils informatiques au travail, 2018.
1113. *See* CNIL, SAN 2019-006, 13 Jun. 2019, point 9.
1114. CNIL Question réponse sur le télétravail, https://www.cnil.fr/fr/les-questions-reponses-de-la-cnil-sur-le-teletravail.

was a system for measuring the speed in real time of whether an item had been scanned in less than 1.25 seconds after the previous one. The second was a system for measuring work interruptions with such accuracy, potentially requiring employees to justify every break or interruption. The CNIL ruled that this processing had an excessive impact on the interests and fundamental rights of employees, in particular 'their right to the protection of their private and personal life as well as their right to working conditions that respect their health and safety'. Such processing could not therefore be based on the company's legitimate interests within the meaning of Article 6 GDPR.[1115]

B. Control to Access the Internet or Emails of Employees

526. There is a certain tolerance for the private use of work tools in France, provided this is not abusive.[1116] Employers, therefore, have the possibility of controlling their employees' access to the Internet, fixing conditions for email, prohibiting the downloading of software, connecting to chat rooms or blocking access to certain illegal sites. The CNIL recommended the implementation of the digital charter uses or the inclusion of this issue in internal regulations. By doing so, the employer must be careful not to lay down rules '*provisions restricting the rights of individuals or individual and collective freedoms in a way that is neither justified by the nature of the task to be performed nor proportionate to the aim pursued*'.[1117] The connections made by the employee using the IT equipment provided by the employer for work purposes are presumed to be of a professional nature. Thus, the employer may consult them even in the absence of the employee.[1118] This solution has been extended to the consultation SMS on business smartphones[1119] and to a USB key[1120] made available by the employer.

527. **Blurred boundary between private and professional email**. There is abundant case law relating to the access of the employer to the email and files of its employees when dealing with legal issues of their private or professional nature. The principle of the inviolability of correspondence applies to the employer. The employer cannot access emails sent and received from the employee's personal email account.[1121] The tools provided by the employer are subject to a presumption of professionalism. Initially, the *Cour de cassation* ruled that the employer could

1115. *See* CNIL SAN-2023-021, 27 Dec. 2023, https://www.cnil.fr/en/employee-monitoring-cnil-fined-amazon-france-logistique-eu32-million; Braun, S. France and Germany. Amazon Fined by CNIL for Excessive Monitoring of Employees in France – Is the Situation in Germany Contrary to This? European Data Protection Law Review Volume 10, Issue 1 (2024), pp. 83–88.

1116. *See* Cass. soc., 29 Oct. 2014, n° 13-18.173; CA Paris, 12 Sep. 2019, n° 17/09980.

1117. Article 1321-3 Labour Code.

1118. Cass. soc., 9 Jul. 2008, n° 06-45.800. For an illustration of abusive use justifying a dismissal *See* Cass. soc., 9 Feb. 2010, n° 08-44.632. (the employee spent an hour a day, during the shift, on online shopping sites).

1119. Cass. com., 10 Feb, 2014, n° 13-14.779.

1120. Cass. soc., 12 February 2013, n° 11-28.649.

1121. *Cour de cassation*, 26 Jan. 2016, n° 14-15.360.

have access to these files or emails unless they were specifically identified as personal.[1122] Subsequent case law is more nuanced in favour of the employer. In 2005, the *Cour de cassation* considered that '*the employer may only open files identified by the employee as personal contained on the hard disk of the computer made available to him in the presence of the employee or the latter duly summoned* '.[1123] In 2019, the *Cour de cassation* considered that even when a professional email of an employee is involved, the Court of Appeal has to check '*whether this email concerned the private life of the latter, so that it was covered by the secrecy of correspondence and could not be produced in support of legal proceedings*'.[1124] By not doing so, the Court of Appeal deprived its decision of a legal basis in the light of Article 8 EHRC and Article 9 of the Civil code. This case law illustrates the practical difficulties of clearly demarcating the boundary between private and professional life. The development of teleworking and the use of BYOD are accentuating the porosity of the boundary between private and professional life. The employer's need to maintain a degree of control over the digital activities of its employees may also be justified for reasons of security, including the security of personal data. During the COVID-19 epidemic, the CNIL urged both employers[1125] and employees[1126] to use digital tools to secure their exchanges.

C. Video Surveillance of the Employees

528. The video surveillance of the employees in France calls for a few comments. Employers may use video surveillance to ensure the safety of people and property in the workplace. By contrast, video surveillance cannot be used to locate employees. The CNIL has pointed out that 'continuous filming of an employee's workstation is therefore disproportionate, unless there are special circumstances relating, for example, to the nature of the task in hand. This is the case when an employee is handling objects of great value or when the data controller is able to justify theft or damage to these areas'.[1127] This was not the case in this small enterprise. Therefore, the CNIL considered that this video surveillance system constituted an interference in the private lives of employees in their workplace and infringed on their individual freedom. It declared that the system did not comply with the GDPR's principle of minimisation and Article L.1121-1 of the Labour Code. The CNIL recalls on its website that cameras cannot be installed in certain locations, such as toilets, employees' rest areas, and the union premises and corridors leading to them.[1128]

1122. Cass. soc., 2 Oct. 2001, n° 99-42.942, Société Nikon France.
1123. Cass. soc., 17 May 2005, n° 03-40.017.
1124. Cass. soc.. 25 Sep. 2019, 18-11.009, point 2.
1125. *See* https://www.cnil.fr/fr/les-conseils-de-la-cnil-pour-mettre-en-place-du-teletravail.
1126. https://www.cnil.fr/fr/salaries-en-teletravail-quelles-sont-les-bonnes-pratiques-suivre.
1127. CNIL, n° MED 2019-025, 5 Nov. 2019. *See also* MED 2018-024 du 2 Jul. 2018, in which the CNIL considered that neither could it justify the constant supervision of an employee in a public school who is responsible for registration.
1128. https://www.cnil.fr/fr/la-videosurveillance-videoprotection-au-travail.

529. Employers must comply with certain conditions when installing a video surveillance system. As mentioned before, prior information about the employees and a consultation with the CSE is required. The CNIL considers that this information must be provided '*by signs permanently and visibly displayed in the premises concerned, which must include at least the pictogram of a camera indicating that the premises are under video protection*'.[1129] The information must be complete and match with what Article 13 GDPR requires. It would be up to the employer and, if applicable, his DPO to assess whether a DPIA is needed. The processing of the video surveillance[1130] should also be included in the register of processing, and the duration of the processing should be indicated.

530. **A dual Regime in France**. The regime of video surveillance depends on the locations filmed. The surveillance of workplaces open to the public (such as restaurants, cinemas, supermarkets, sales areas, counters, etc.) or filming even partially in public spaces (public entrances, exits, garages, etc.) is governed by the French CSI. The installation of this type of device is limited '*to ensuring the protection of the immediate surroundings of their buildings and installations, in places particularly exposed to the risk of assault or theft*'.[1131] The device must be authorised by the Prefet. Video surveillance systems filming areas not open to the public, such as shop storerooms, warehouses, or closed condominiums, including if the employees have access to these places, are simply subject to LIL. When access to these premises is forbidden to employees, the employer does not have to inform employees of the presence of the cameras, and these video recordings constitute a lawful means of proof.[1132]

531. It is worth underlining that the CNIL is competent to receive complaints on video surveillance, including the application of the CSI. It is an annual report, and the CNIL constantly notes that video surveillance of employers is one of the important subjects in employee complaints.[1133]

D. *Geolocation of Employees*

532. **Limited legal uses**. As geolocation is a particularly intrusive technique that is the subject of much litigation, the CNIL has reiterated that it can only be used for the following purposes:

- Tracking, justifying, and invoicing the transport of people, goods or services directly linked to the use of the vehicle. For example: ambulances as part of the dematerialisation of health insurance invoicing.

1129. https://www.cnil.fr/fr/la-videosurveillance-videoprotection-au-travail.
1130. This period should not exceed one month, in principle.
1131. *See* Art. L251-2 CSI.
1132. *See* Cass. soc., 19 Apr. 2005, 02-46.295, point 3.
1133. *See,* for instance CNIL rapport annuel 2022, p. 39.

- Ensure the safety of employees, goods, or vehicles in their charge, and in particular recover the vehicle in the event of theft (for example, with an inert device that can be activated remotely as soon as the theft is reported).
- Better allocation of resources for services to be carried out in dispersed locations, particularly for emergency interventions. For example, identify the nearest employee to a lift breakdown or the nearest ambulance to an accident.
- Tracking working hours when this cannot be done by any other means.[1134]
- Comply with a legal or regulatory obligation requiring the implementation of a geolocation system due to the type of transport or the nature of the goods being transported.
- Check compliance with the rules governing the use of the vehicle.[1135]

By contrast, geolocation cannot be used to permanently track an employee. The Cour de cassation recently recalled that geolocalisation cannot be registered outside the employee's working hours.[1136] Thus, employees must be able to deactivate the collection or transmission of their geographical location outside working hours. Geolocation cannot be used to check compliance with speed limits.

533. The use of such geolocation devices must respect employees' rights. This implies not only full prior information but also a right of access to their geolocation data. The employer will be subject to obligations concerning the security of the data processed, the inclusion of such processing in its register, and the carrying out of a DPIA if necessary. Lastly, the CNIL specifies that employers are required to keep geolocation data for a period of two months. This period may be extended to one year when the data is used to optimise rounds or to provide proof of work carried out where it is not possible to provide such proof by any other means. Finally, they may be kept for five years if they are used to monitor working hours.[1137]

E. Access Control to Business Premises by Biometrics Authentication

534. **Binding standard regulation of the CNIL.** Access control to business premises by biometrics authentication has also received particular attention from the CNIL which has adopted 'règlement type' (standard regulation) on this subject.[1138] This standard regulation supplements or clarifies certain obligations of the GDPR and the LIL regarding this processing of sensitive data. Unlike recommendations, the standard regulation is binding for the controller and processor. It must be applied to any public or private employer imposing a device using biometric data on its

1134. *See* for instance Cass. soc., 3 Nov. 2011, 10-18.036.
1135. *See* https://www.cnil.fr/fr/la-geolocalisation-des-vehicules-des-salaries.
1136. *See* Cass. soc., 22 Mar. 2023, 21–22.852, point 9.
1137. *See* https://www.cnil.fr/fr/la-geolocalisation-des-vehicules-des-salaries.
1138. CNIL Deliberation n° 2019-001, 10 Jan. 2019 portant règlement type relatif à la mise en oeuvre de dispositifs ayant pour finalité le contrôle d'accès par authentification biométrique aux locaux, aux appareils et aux applications informatiques sur les lieux de travail.

employees (employees, trainees, temporary employees, volunteers, people in civic service, civil servants, etc.) to control access to premises, applications, and professional tools. This standard regulation stipulates that employers must justify the need to use a biometric process to control their professional access. The employer must document precisely why he needs to use this type of system and the choice made between different kinds of biometrics processes at his disposal. Only authentication based on a person's morphological characteristics (iris, fingerprint, hand vein network, etc.) is authorised. Authentication using biological samples (blood, saliva) is prohibited. It also classifies the biometric processes that can be used into three categories depending on the degree of control of the persons concerned over their template. The concept of template refers to measurements that are stored when the morphological (fingerprint, hand shape, iris, etc.) of the data subject is processed. The CNIL encourages employers to favour type 1 templates, which are under the control of the data subjects.[1139] This means that the only durable storage medium is held by the person themselves, for example, in the form of a badge or smart card. Then, the standard regulation fixes rigorous specifications for organisational and technical security measures. It also recalled that such device implementation needs a DPIA.

IV. Processing of Health Data of the Employees

535. Processing of health data of employees has been an important topic during the COVID-19 pandemic. It should be remembered that in France, during this period, a state of health emergency was declared and lasted from March 2020[1140] until 1 August 2022.[1141] In this changing legal context, the CNIL has helped employers clarify their various obligations about the processing of their employees' health data. The CNIL has clarified that employers may only collect their employees' health data in three circumstances.[1142] First, employers were required to process reports of contamination with COVID-19 made by their employees. These processing operations should only be made for the purposes of protecting employees and the public in compliance with Article L.1121-1 of the French Labour Code. Employers are prohibited from requiring their employees to report temperature readings to their superiors every day and from collecting medical questionnaires from all employees. The employer was also not authorised to require the presentation of screening tests or a sworn statement that a test has been carried out, including in cases where an employee/agent has reported being positive for COVID-19. Second, laws governing the state of health emergency have made it compulsory for

1139. Type 2 templates are those whose the durable storage medium is shared between the employer and employees. Type 3 templates are those whose permanent storage medium is controlled by the employer.

1140. *See* Loi n° 2020-290, 23 Mar. 2020 d'urgence pour faire face à l'épidémie de COVID-19 which has been extended several times.

1141. *See* Loi n° 2022-1089, 30 Jul. 2022 mettant fin aux régimes d'exception créés pour lutter contre l'épidémie liée à la COVID-19.

1142. *See* https://www.cnil.fr/fr/covid-19-questions-reponses-sur-la-collecte-de-donnees-personnelles-sur-le-lieu-de-travail.

establishments to be open to public (restaurants, bars, trains, etc.) to present the vaccination pass. In such cases, employees of such establishments were required to present proof of their vaccination status to their employer, who was authorised to retain proof of this verification until such time as the system is no longer in force. Third, French law imposes a vaccination obligation on nursing staff, mainly employees of health establishments, retirement homes, and establishments catering to the disabled.[1143] Furthermore, the CNIL has carried out ongoing checks on the tools used to manage the epidemic, which were mainly proposed by the government. In particular, the CNIL has issued a series of public reports to Parliament on the implementation of large-scale and unprecedented health data processing tools.[1144]

536. Behind the COVID-19 rules, there are several legal obligations for employers to collect health data of their employees, such as the management of accidents at work.[1145] By contrast, in the event of sick leave, the employer does not need to be informed of the nature of the employee's illness.

V. Documents of Interest from the CNIL on Common Processing Related to Work

537. The CNIL has adopted several documents about GDPR compliance obligations in the workplace. All these documents are non-legally binding. However, the CNIL often refers to it in its deliberations, particularly those involving sanctions. Two documents cover routine processing in the work environment.

538. **The referential on the processing of personal data for the purposes of personnel management.**[1146] This first document sets out the main purposes for which the data may be processed and the legal bases for doing so. It also lists the categories of personal data concerned, the potential recipients and the retention periods. In addition, it specifies the rights of the individuals concerned and the security measures to be taken. Finally, it sums up the cases where a DPIA must be done and where no DPIA are required.

1143. *See* the list in Art. 12 de la loi relative à la gestion de la crise sanitaire du 5 août 2021. This obligation did not apply in case of medical contraindication or presentation of a certificate of recovery. This legal obligation has been the subject of public debate due to the opposition of certain health professionals to vaccination. This led to the suspension of 4,000 out of 1.2 million healthcare professionals. *See* Press Release of the French Hospital Federation. https://www.fhf.fr/sites/default/files/2022-11/20221108_FHF_R%C3%A9actionVaccination.pdf.

1144. CNIL, Deliberation n° 2022-061, 19 May 2022 portant avis public sur les conditions de mise en œuvre des systèmes d'information développés aux fins de lutter contre la propagation de l'épidémie de COVID-19 (octobre 2021 à avril 2022).

1145. *See* Art. L.441-3 Social Security Code.

1146. Deliberation No. 2022-126, 23 May 2022 portant modification de la délibération No. 2019-160 du 21 novembre 2019 portant adoption d'un référentiel relatif aux traitements de données à caractère personnel mis en œuvre aux fins de gestion du personnel.

539. **The guide on recruitment.**[1147] This second document proposes an FAQ on the topic through nineteen practical sheets.

540. **The referential on the processing of personal data for implementing a professional alert system.**[1148] The CNIL opts for a large definition of this concept. A professional alert system covers a tool that enables a person (employee, co-contractor, third party, etc.) to bring to the attention of an organisation a situation, behaviour or risk that may constitute a breach of the law or ethical rules adopted by the organisation in question, such as a breach of a charter or code of conduct. In other words, the referential deals with internal whistleblowing systems that are compulsory in France and ethical alerts set up voluntarily by private or public bodies. The first category includes the whistleblowing systems introduced by the so-called Sapin II law.[1149]

541. According to French law, 'A whistleblower is a natural person who reports or discloses, without any direct financial consideration and in good faith, information relating to a crime, an offence, a threat or harm to the general interest, a violation or an attempt to conceal a violation of an international commitment duly ratified or approved by France, of a unilateral act of an international organisation taken on the basis of such a commitment, of European Union law, or of a law or regulation.'[1150]

542. Article 8 of the Sapin II law obliges public authorities and companies with fifty or more employees/agents to set up a secure system for collecting and processing reports that guarantees the confidentiality of the identity of the person reporting the problem. Reports can be made either internally or externally to trusted third parties listed by the decree implementing the law.[1151] Such an external alert can be made before the CNIL. As usual, the referential covers a common topic (purposes, legal grounds, categories of personal data involved, security, and data subject's rights). It focuses on the minimisation principle at different stages (alert investigation of the alert and once the decision has been taken on the action to be taken in response to the alert) and how to proceed to enable an anonymous whistleblower when this is legally possible. It also sets out the implications of outsourcing the processing of alerts. The CNIL also underlines that the referential aims to help the controller with their DPIA, which is compulsory for the implementation of a professional alert system.

1147. CNIL, guide du recrutement, les fondamentaux en matière de protection des données personnelles et questions réponses, adopted on 23 Jan. 2023.
1148. CNIL, Référentiel relatif aux traitements de données à caractère personnel destinés à la mise en oeuvre d'un dispositive d'alerte, adopted on 6 Jul. 2023.
1149. Loi n° 2016-1691 du 9 décembre 2016 relative à la transparence, à la lutte contre la corruption et à la modernisation de la vie économique modified by Loi n° 2022-401 du 21 Mar. 2022, which transposed the Directive (EU) 2019/1937 of the European Parliament and of the Council of 23 Oct. 2019 on the protection of persons who report breaches of Union law.
1150. Article 6, Loi n° 2016-1691, 9 Dec. 2016.
1151. Décret n° 2022-1284 du 3 octobre 2022 relatif aux procédures de recueil et de traitement des signalements émis par les lanceurs d'alerte et fixant la liste des autorités externes instituées par la loi n° 2022-401 du 21 mars 2022 visant à améliorer la protection des lanceurs d'alerte.

543. **A guide for trade unions.**[1152] This guide is intended to cover processing operations specific to trade union organisations (membership management, management of organised activities, transmission of membership files, etc.), management of organised activities, transmission of membership files, etc.).

§5. Processing for Scientific Research, Public Archiving and Statistical Purposes

544. The regime of these three kinds of specific processing is very similar which allows for a common analysis.

I. Scope of These Derogations

545. **Processing carried out by public archive services concerned.** Article 78 LIL provides derogations for personal data processing carried out by public archive services for archival purposes in the public interest by referring to Article 89 GDPR. The scope of this derogation is threefold restrictive.

546. First, this concerns only public archives, while the wording of Article 89 GDPR and Recital 158 authorises the State to include private '*records for general public interest*'. The French Heritage Code defines the archives as *'all documents, including data, whatever their date, place of storage, form or medium, produced or received by any natural or legal person and by any public or private service or body in the course of their activity*'.[1153] The Heritage Code also gives a broad and functional legal definition of the concept of conservation of archives for public interest. The aim is to meet the needs '*of the management and justification of the rights of natural or legal persons, public or private, as well as for the historical documentation of research*'.[1154] In this context, public archives comprise three types of documents.[1155] On the one hand, this covers documents resulting from the activity of the State, local authorities, public establishments and other legal entities governed by public law, as well as the acts and documents of parliamentary assemblies. On the other hand, this includes documents resulting from the management of a public service or the performance of a public service mission by private law entities. Finally, this concerns the minutes and registers of public or ministerial officers and the registers of notarised civil solidarity pact agreements. The rest of the documents are private archives.

547. Second, the derogation applies only to definitive public archive services for archival purposes in the public interest. This concerns documents that are no longer

1152. CNIL, Guide de sensibilisation au RGPD, Organisations syndicales de salariés, Februay 2023, It contains twelve practical information sheets.
1153. Article L.211-1 Heritage Code.
1154. Article L.211-2 Heritage Code.
1155. Article L.211-4 Heritage Code.

of interest to the departments but are of historical, heritage or scientific interest. These are documents from so-called intermediary archives that have been sorted for their interest by the authority that held them.

548. Third, the derogation applies only to the document of the definitive public archive services for archival purposes in the public interest, which contains personal data.

549. **Processing for scientific or historical research purposes.** There is no real precise definition in French law of processing for scientific or historical research purposes. GDPR 159 Recital considers that '*the processing of personal data for scientific research purposes should be interpreted in a broad manner including for example technological development and demonstration, fundamental research, applied research and privately funded research. In addition, ... it should also include studies conducted in the public interest in public health*'. As mentioned before,[1156] the LIL has introduced a specific regime for processing health research. Article 72 clarifies that this regime is applicable to '*Automated processing of personal data whose purpose is or will be research or studies in the field of health and the assessment or analysis of treatment or prevention practices or activities.*'

550. **Processing for statistical purposes**. The term 'statistical purposes' is defined by Recital 162 sentence 3 GDPR as 'any operation of collection and the processing of personal data necessary for statistical surveys or for the production of statistical results'. In France, a specific law only rules public statistics.[1157]

II. Derogations for the Benefits of Such Processing

551. The rules governing such processing are based on two types of possible derogation: derogations from the rights of data subjects and derogations from some key principles.

552. **Derogations to Data Subjects Rights.** Article 78 LIL recalls, in the same terms as Article 89 GDPR, that these three kinds of processing may derogate some data protection rights. This does not apply to the right to erasure. Personal data processing carried out by public archive services for archival purposes in the public interest may derogate from the right of access, rectification, limitation, portability, and to object. Personal data processing for scientific or historical research purposes or statistical purposes may derogate from the right of access,[1158] rectification, limitation, and to object. However, these derogations only apply if these rights make it impossible or seriously hamper the achievement of these purposes. It is also worth

1156. *See supra* para. 286.

1157. Loi n° 51-711 du 7 juin 1951 sur l'obligation, la coordination et le secret en matière de statistiques.

1158. *See also* Art. 49,§1 LIL.

recalling that the information obligation of the controller does not apply when such information is impossible or would involve a disproportionate effort.[1159]

553. Appropriate conditions and safeguards provided for in Article 89 have been introduced in French law.[1160] Data resulting from these three kinds of processing may only be accessed or modified by authorised persons. These persons shall comply with the ethical rules applicable to their sectors of activity. Such data may not be disseminated without first being anonymised. This anonymisation obligation can only be lifted under strict conditions. The interests of third parties in such dissemination outweigh the interests or the fundamental rights and freedoms of the data subject. In the case of research results, dissemination must be absolutely necessary for their presentation. The data disseminated must be adequate, relevant, and limited to what is necessary regarding the purposes for which they are processed. Dissemination of data contained in public archives is subject to authorisation.

554. The digitalisation of the public archive combined with some Open Data obligations has resulted in special conditions for the publication of archive documents containing personal data on the Internet. Documents containing sensitive data or data relating to criminal convictions or offences may only be published on the Internet after a period of a hundred years unless authorised by the CNIL.[1161] Other documents may be freely published without anonymisation.

555. **Derogations to Data Principles.** The LIL provides that such processing may derogate from the principle of purpose limitation. Article 4, §2 LIL provides data processing for archiving purposes in the public interest, scientific and historical research purposes, and statistical purposes that may be considered compatible with the purposes for which the data were initially collected. These processings should not be used to take decisions with respect to data subjects. The LIL also foresaw a derogation to the storage limitation for these three kinds of processing. '*Personal data may be kept beyond that period if they are processed exclusively for archiving purposes in the public interest, for scientific or historical research purposes, or statistical purposes.*'[1162]

1159. *See* Art. 79 LIL.
1160. *See* Art. 116 of the 2019 Decree of application of the LIL.
1161. *See* Art. D.312-1-3 CRPA.
1162. *See* Art. 4, §5 LIL.

Part X. Specific Data Protection Regimes

§1. Obligations of Professional Secrecy

I. Respect of Professional Secrecy During the Visit of the CNIL Agents

556. **Two-Faceted Nature of Professional Secrecy. Article 19, III LIL** sets out the powers of the CNIL in relation to controllers and processors that are subject under law to an obligation of processional secrecy as required by Article 90 GDPR. It is part of a provision which deals with the CNIL powers to monitor processing operations.[1163] While the CNIL's agents should have access in principle to all the information and documents required for the performance of their task,[1164] professional secrecy can limit their investigation powers. Article 19, III LIL illustrates the two-faceted nature of professional secrecy. On the one hand, it constitutes an obligation both for CNIL staff and for the organisations inspected, which must protect certain data.[1165] Beyond data protection law, there is in French law a criminal offence for the disclosure of such data protected by professional secrecy.[1166] On the other hand, it constitutes a right for the inspected organisations not to disclose this protected data, including to CNIL agents.

557. Professional secrecy can be opposed to CNIL's agents in respect of requests for information, justifications, copies, proof, access to IT programmes and data and their transcriptions for the purpose of their investigation. It should be considered that according to the GDPR, this applies only '*to personal data which the controller or processor has received as a result of or has obtained in an activity covered by that obligation of secrecy*'.[1167]

558. **Three kinds of Protected Professional Secrecy by Article 19, III LIL.** Article 19, III only mentioned three kinds of professional secrecy that can be

1163. More details on the powers of the CNIL. *see* before paras 428–431.
1164. Article 18 LIL even recalled that such principle apply to 'Government ministers, public authorities, executives of state-owned or private companies, heads of various associations and more generally owners and users of data processing and personal data filing systems' except when they are bound by professional secrecy.
1165. For the controller and the processor, this implies reinforced technical and organisational security measures, *See* §560.
1166. *See* Art. 226-13 of the CP which provides that 'The revelation of secret information by a person who is in possession of it either by virtue of his status or profession, or by virtue of an office or temporary assignment, is punishable by one year's imprisonment and a fine of 15,000 euros.'
1167. *See* Art. 90 GDPR.

opposed to the CNIL agents: professional secrecy in relations between a lawyer and his client, secrecy of the journalistic sources, and medical secrecy. Article 19, III LIL does not refer to business secrets or bank secrecy which are linked to the privacy of legal persons.

559. **Medical secrecy**. Article 19, III only provides clarification on medical secrecy. It clarifies the scope of medical secrecy, which applies to information necessary *'for the purposes of preventive medicine, medical research, medical diagnosis, administration of care or processing, or health service management'*.[1168] In other words, there is a large variety of health professionals who are submitted to secrecy, not only doctors.[1169] Finally, this article details the regime of such medical secrecy by stating that '*Communication of personal data concerning health contained in this category of processing may only be requested under the authority and in the presence of a physician.*'[1170] This means that the CNIL's staff will not have access to these data but to the report of the physician on their processing.[1171] This specific guarantee was introduced into French law in order to reconcile the right to personal data with the obligation of medical secrecy. This echoes the emergence in France of a collective dimension to professional secrecy. This essentially involves securing exchanges between two professionals bound by secrecy.[1172] Finally, this specific rule also illustrates that it is only in very limited cases that professional secrecy may prevent CNIL staff from accessing certain data. Professional secrecy is, therefore, not an absolute right and cannot be invoked to conceal a breach of the GDPR from CNIL staff. The CNIL has already condemned doctors for a lack of security for their medical data following online investigations which reveal the disclosure of health data.[1173] Like medical secrecy, the other two types of secrecy listed in Article 19, III of the LIL are based solely on legal sources[1174] and have a limited scope of application.

1168. *See* Art. 79, III.
1169. This includes not only various medical professions, such as physiotherapists, nurses etc., but also a group of professionals in the so-called social and medico-social sector, including, for example, social workers, but also laboratories.
1170. *See* Art. 79, III last paragraph. More details on the selection of this physician *see* Art. 36 of the 2019 decree of application of the LIL.
1171. *See* Art. 36 of the 2019 decree of application of the CNIL.
1172. As an illustration, the concept of share secrecy has been introduced in 2002 in France between the members of a medical team. *See* Art. L.1110-4, II of the Public Health Code which rules that: 'II – A professional may exchange information relating to the same person under his care with one or more identified professionals, provided that they are all involved in his care and that this information is strictly necessary for the coordination or continuity of care, prevention or his medico-social and social follow-up.' The concept of share medical secrecy was also at the core of the collect of Health Data relating to COVID-19 in France based on the State of health emergency law.
1173. CNIL, SAN 2020-015, 7 Dec. 2020, (EUR 6,000 fines); CNIL SAN 2020-014 du 7 Dec. 2020 (fine of EUR 3,000 which was reduced to EUR 2,000 by the *Conseil d'Etat*); *the Conseil d'Etat* ruled that since the CNIL was aware of the data breach because of an inspection, there was no infringement to the obligation to notify the CNIL of such a data breach. *See* CE, 7 Jul. 2022, n° 449694.
1174. The *Conseil constitutionnel* has stated on several occasions that 'no constitutional provision specifically enshrines ... a right to secrecy of journalists' sources.' *See,* for instance, CC, 24 Jul. 2015,

560. **Professional secrecy of the lawyer**. The professional secrecy in relations between a lawyer and his client is enshrined in a 1971 law that has been amended on several occasions. In its current version, the law provides that '*In all matters, whether advising or defending, consultations sent by a lawyer to his client or intended for his client, correspondence exchanged between the client and his lawyer, between the lawyer and his colleagues, with the exception of correspondence marked "official", interview notes and, more generally, all documents in the file are covered by professional secrecy.*'[1175] This covers not only the information received from the client but also the information received about them and/or about a third party in the context of the client file.[1176] This includes, in particular, the names of the clients, the lawyer's agenda, and the pecuniary settlements.[1177] This secrecy does not match the legal privilege in common law which, in general, is extended to in-house lawyers.[1178] This means that the CNIL agents will have full access to data related to communications between in-house lawyers and officers, directors or employees of their employer, or information obtained from them. In addition, many common processings in law firms are not covered by professional secrecy. This will be the case for human resources processing, the management of suppliers and IT service providers, some of the processing linked to the website, and some linked to the management of physical access to the firm's premises. Furthermore, lawyers can be expected to meet their accountability obligation to the CNIL by taking special measures to protect their data covered by professional secrecy. Therefore, French bar associations published a practical guide for the lawyer which recalls all their obligation regarding the GDPR.[1179] In most cases, CNIL's agents will not need to have access to data covered by professional secrecy to check that the lawyer has fulfilled his obligations. This is undoubtedly one of the reasons why no specific guarantee has been included in the LIL to allow such access. Under French law, the presence of the President of the Bar is only required for criminal searches and seizures or administrative home visits.[1180] A prior authorisation of a judge is not

n° 2015-478 QPC, point 15, and CC, 10 Nov. 2016, n° 2016-738 DC, point 17. It extended this statement to lawyers' professional secrecy in 2022. *See* CC 2022-1030 QPC du 19 Jan. 2023, in which the *Conseil constitutionnel* stated that 'although these provisions [Article 16 of the Declaration of human and civic rights of 1789] guarantee the rights of the defence, no constitutional provision specifically enshrines a right to secrecy of lawyers' exchanges and correspondence'. Point 9.

1175. Article 66-5 Loi n° 71-1130 du 31 décembre 1971 portant réforme de certaines professions judiciaires et juridiques. *See also* the introductory article to the CPP.

1176. CA Paris, Ch. 1, s. A, 30 Nov. 1994.

1177. *See* Art. 2 of the internal rules of the French Bar Association which is dedicated to the professional secrecy of the lawyer.

1178. For more details about the difference between legal privilege and professional secrecy of the lawyer in France *see* Nicolas Michon, *Legal privilege et secret professionnel: elements de comparaison*, AJ penal 2019, p. 588.

1179. Conseil National des Barreaux, Barreaux de Paris, Conférence des Bâtonniers, Guide pratique: les avocats et le RGPD, 2ème édition 2023, Here again, the guide focused on the security obligation, p. 43. The National Bar Association has also created an IT tool called e-barreau which enable the lawyers to have a secure access to their files, email, and agenda.

1180. *See* Art. 56-1 Criminal Procedure Code which provides that searches of a lawyer's office or home may only be carried out by a magistrate in the presence of the President of the Bar or his delegate, following a written, reasoned decision by the liberty and custody judge to whom the matter has

required for general inspection of the CNIL[1181] because the controller can always object to it. Thus, a lawyer controller has the possibility of objecting to impose to the CNIL to obtain a judge's authorisation to carry out its inspection.[1182]

561. **Secrecy of journalists' sources.** The right to secrecy of journalists' sources has been included in Article 2 of the law of 29 July 1881 on freedom of the press since 2010.[1183] The scope of this secrecy is doubly limited. On the one hand, it only concerns professional journalists. This means a person who '*work in a professional capacity in one or more press, online or audiovisual communication companies or one or more press agencies, where they regularly gather information and disseminate it to the public for remuneration*'.[1184] On the other hand, the law considers that 'an overriding public interest' may allow measures to be taken that infringe this secrecy. The measures must be strictly necessary and proportionate to the legitimate aim pursued. It is difficult to imagine why CNIL's staff might need access to such sources to carry out their monitoring duties of a journalist. The law specifies that an attack on journalistic sources requires a specific investigation into a journalist's entourage and habits to find his or her sources. Here again, such secrecy is protected above all in the context of criminal proceedings.

562. To conclude, the main purpose of Article 19, III LIL is to remind CNIL officers that they do not have access to data protected by medical secrecy, lawyer-client secrecy and the secrecy of journalistic sources. It recalls that the controller submitted to this secrecy obligation must take additional measures to protect these data. This should include anticipating the possibility of a CNIL inspection which would enable the authority to control it without having access to this protected data. This could be, for instance, done by using special organisational and technical measures relating to these categories of data which need to be in their register. Finally, during an inspection, controllers and processors will have to object to CNIL's access to data covered by their secrecy obligations. These objections need to be justified and reasoned because they must be recorded in the minutes drawn up during the CNIL inspection.[1185] To our knowledge, there have been no disputes concerning the CNIL's access to the data protected by professional secrecy mentioned in Article 19, III of the LIL.

---

been referred by that magistrate, indicating the nature of the offence or offences being investigated, the reasons justifying the search, the purpose of the search and its proportionality in relation to the nature and seriousness of the facts.

1181. A prior authorisation of the judge will be required for inspection of private home including of a lawyer and when for emergencies reasons there is no prior information about the control of the CNIL *See* Art. 19, I, §3 LIL & Art. 19, II.

1182. *See* Art. 19, II LIL.

1183. *See* Loi n° 2010-1 du 4 janvier 2010 relative à la protection du secret des sources des journalistes.

1184. *See* Art. 2, §2 of the 1881 Act.

1185. Article 37 of the Décret n° 2019-536 du 29 mai 2019, Pris pour l'application de la loi n° 78-17 du 6 janvier 1978 relative à l'informatique, aux fichiers et aux libertés. This article provides that the written report of the inspection should refer 'to the legislative or regulatory provisions to which, where applicable, the person questioned refers, as well as the nature of the data he or she considers to be covered by these provisions'.

563. **Other LIL Provisions on Secrecy**. Beyond Article 19, III LIL, several provisions recall the general obligations of secrecy of the members and staff of the CNIL. First, the CNIL members,[1186] civil servants[1187] of the CNIL, are bound per status by professional secrecy. '*CNIL staff members are bound by a duty of confidentiality with regard to any facts, acts or information which has come to their knowledge in the course of the performance of their tasks.*'[1188] The CNIL's internal regulations also allow its chairman to limit the presence of outsiders at plenary and bureau meetings '*for reasons relating to the protection of professional secrecy and the secrecy of government deliberations*'.[1189] The President of the restricted formation of the CNIL '*may, at the request of the data controller in question or on its own initiative, restrict the public nature of the hearing in the interests of public order, or when the protection of secrets protected by law so requires*'.[1190] This possibility goes beyond the three kinds of professional secrecy mentioned in Article 19, III LIL. It includes, for instance, the protection of business secrecy.[1191] In addition, the request may be rejected by the President of the restricted formation if he considers it unjustified.[1192]

II. Emblematic Cases of Professional Secrecy Related to Personal Data

564. There are some emblematic cases concerning the protection of professional secrecy in relation to personal data. In 2020, the *Conseil d'Etat* annulled a decree on the certification of hospital accounts for breach of medical secrecy. The decree provided for auditors to have access to all patients' medical data for their certification mission. According to the Public Health Code, such auditors are subject to professional secrecy. However, they may only access the necessary medical personal data within the strict limits of what is necessary for their missions. Allowing auditors access to all patients' medical data without any technical or organisational measures went beyond what was strictly necessary for the performance of their certification mission. The illegality of the decree is linked to the lack of pseudonymisation of the medical data 'to guarantee the protection of the data subject's right to

1186. *See* article 9 de la loi du 20 janvier 2017 portant statut général des autorités administratives indépendantes et des autorités publiques indépendantes.
1187. *See* l'article 26 de la Loi n° 83-634 du 13 juillet 1983 portant droits et obligations des fonctionnaires.
1188. *See* Art. 11 LIL.
1189. *See* Art. 9 of the internal rules of the CNIL.
1190. *See* Art. 65 of the internal rules of the CNIL. In such cases, the decision of the restricted formation should include the reasons why the proceedings were held in camera. *See* for an illustration SAN 2020-015, 7 Dec. 2020 CNIL, in which the session was held in camera because the personal data submitted for discussion was protected by medical confidentiality.
1191. CNIL, SAN 2020-009, 18 Nov. 2020 in which the hearing was held on camera because the information presented was protected by business secrecy, as provided for in Art. L 151-1 of the French Commercial Code.
1192. *See,* for instance, CNIL, SAN 2022-018, 8 Sep. 2022 concernant le GIE INFOGREFFE. In such cases, the CNIL's decision does not specify the secrecy invoked by the controller.

respect for medical confidentiality, as set out in the aforementioned provisions of Article L. 1110-4 of the Public Health Code'.[1193]

565. While this case explicitly mentioned the GDPR, most of cases are not based on the LIL but on Article 226-23 CP. Some criminal convictions concern the consultation of data covered by professional secrecy by a professional for private purposes. For example, a hospital nurse was fined for breach of professional secrecy for repeatedly consulting the digital medical file of a patient who was not on her ward but was her extra-professional tenant with whom she was in conflict.[1194] Some case laws also illustrate that medical secrecy is a right in favour of the patient, whose consent will be necessary for the disclosure of his medical data to third parties.[1195] There is currently a debate on the application of this rule when an insurance company's medical advisor calls in an expert to assess an insured person's medical file as part of a bodily injury compensation procedure.[1196]

§2. Churches and Religious Associations

566. **France is a secular republic**. This principle of secularism has been enshrined in the Constitution since 1956.[1197] The 1905 law separating Church and State is the cornerstone of secularism in France. This law abolished the Concordat of 1802, under which the State recognised four religions (Catholic, Reformed Protestant, Lutheran, and Jewish) organised and funded under public law. Worships thus ceased to be public institutions, and their activities are now organised within an associative framework. This historical and cultural background explains why, in France, there are no autonomous data protection rules for churches and religious associations before and even more after the GDPR.[1198] Similarly, there is only one independent supervisory authority, the CNIL. Article 91 GDPR is meaningless in France, where only the GDPR and the LIL are to be considered.

567. The only mention of religions is in Article 6 LIL, which prohibits, in principle, the processing of sensitive data, in particular, data relating to religious beliefs. This provision merely refers to Article 8 GDPR for the list of exceptions to this prohibition.

1193. *See* CE, 25 Nov. 2020, n° 428451, point 10.
1194. https://www.estrepublicain.fr/faits-divers-justice/2020/11/20/condamnee-pour-violation-du-secret-professionnel.
1195. *See* for instance Cass. Crim., 16 Mar. 2021, n° 20-80.125.
1196. *See* Patrick Mistretta, *Secret professionnel médical ou secret de polichinelle ? A propos des avis médicaux sur pièces*, AJ Pénal 2022, p. 467.
1197. *See* Art. 1 of the 1946 Constitution and currently Art. 1 of the 1958 Constitution which provides that: 'France shall be an indivisible, secular, democratic and social Republic. It shall ensure the equality of all citizens before the law, without distinction of origin, race or religion. It shall respect all beliefs. … '
1198. This also applies to those parts of France where, for historical or political reasons, the 1905 Law does not apply (Alsace Moselle and certain overseas territories such as French Guiana, Mayotte, New Caledonia, Polynesia, Wallis and Futuna and Saint-Pierre and Miquelon).

§3. French Transposition of the Police Justice Directive

568. **Title III of the LIL.** Title III of the LIL transposes the specific provisions for the Police Justice Directive. This title comprises twenty-seven articles divided into four chapters. Chapter 1, although entitled General Provisions, deals with a heterogeneous set of rules. It covers the scope of the processing operations submitted to this title, the processing of sensitive data, and the procedures for authorising certain processing. It details the cases in which a DPIA is required, the rules governing further processing operations, the procedures for subcontracting, the conditions for implementing special categories processing (archiving, scientific research, historical data and processing for statistical purposes), and the legal framework of the automated decision. Chapter 2 is devoted to the obligations of the controller and processor, while Chapter 3 deals with the rights of data subjects, and Chapter IV is focused on international transfers. Title III LIL contains numerous references to the GDPR or to the common provisions of Title I of the LIL.

569. **Issue**. The structure chosen to transpose the Police Justice Directive into the LIL raised issues about the scope of the processing covered by the Directive and, consequently, the title III of the LIL. The stakes are high because the legal regime of processing under the scope of the directive differs significantly from the legal regime of the GDPR and other purely national processing relating to state security and intelligence. In France, the transposition of the Police Justice Directive led to reform in the legal regime for video protection, which until then had only been partially subjected to the LIL.[1199]

I. The French Scope of the Police Justice Directive

570. **Purpose criteria**. Article 87 LIL points out the two cumulative criteria that determine the scope of the Police Justice Directive processing which are related to the purposes and the status of the controller or a processor. Thus, title III of the LIL applies to processing for '*the purposes of the prevention, investigation, detection or prosecution of criminal offenses or the execution of criminal penalties, including the safeguarding against and the prevention of threats to public security*'. In France, this covers both administrative police activities focused on prevention and judicial police activities focused on the punishment of offences.

571. **French public competent authority**. Article 87 LIL clarified that the controller or the processor must be a '*public competent authority or any other body or entity entrusted to exercise public authority and public powers*'. This covers in France, the police, judicial authorities, the Ministry of Interior and all kinds of

1199. Before May 2023, the LIL applies only when videoprotection recording were used 'in automated processing automated processing or contained in files structured according to criteria that enable identify, directly or indirectly, individuals'. Other processing fell within the scope of the law No. 95-73 of 21 Jan. 1995. This was revised by the Loi n° 2023-380 du 19 mai 2023 relative aux jeux Olympiques et Paralympiques de 2024 et portant diverses autres dispositions. Video protection is codified in Arts L.251-1 to L.255-1 of Internal Security Code.

administrative directorates with criminal investigations powers such as the customs and direct tax directorate (Direction Générale des Douanes et Droits Indirects, DGDDI),[1200] the DGCCRF from the Ministry of the Economy, Finance and Industrial and Digital Sovereignty. The concept of competent public authority within the meaning of the Police Justice Directive thus covers a very large number of entities, although no list has been drawn up under French domestic law. Recently, the *Conseil d'Etat* itself acknowledged the current complexity of the administration's investigative powers and, in the absence of an exhaustive inventory, attempted to draw up a first categorisation.[1201]

572. **Main Police Files concerned**. Many so-called police files[1202] fall within the scope of Title III of the LIL. The four best-known can be mentioned here. First, criminal records (Traitement d'Antécédents Judiciaires, TAJ) are used as part of criminal investigations (to find the perpetrators of offences) and administrative investigations (such as investigations prior to certain public or sensitive jobs).[1203] Second, the National DNA database (Fichier National des Empreintes Génétiques, FNAEG) is used to facilitate the identification and search for offenders using their genetic profile and for missing persons using the genetic profile of their descendants or ascendants.[1204] Third, the wanted persons file (Fichier des Personnes Recherchées, FPR)[1205] is used to facilitate searches carried out by the police and gendarmerie at the request of the judicial, military, or administrative authorities. It lists all persons who are the subject of a search or verification of their legal situation. Fourth, the Automated Fingerprint File (Fichier automatisé des Empreintes Digitales, FAED) stores fingerprints (fingers) and palm prints (palms) to facilitate the search for and identify the perpetrators of crimes.[1206]

573. **Requirement of a case-by-case Analysis**. In practice, the scope of application of Title III LIL needs to be determinate case-by-case for each category of processing. Such an analysis is necessary to verify whether the processing operations

1200. For an illustration regarding a processing called SIRENE implemented by the DGDDI and used by the National Customs Coast Guard, to record all persons checked at sea or alongside the quayside and to combat fraud. *See* CNIL MED-2023-018 du 3 avril 2023 mettant en demeure le ministère de l'économie, des finances et de la souveraineté industrielle et numérique.

1201. *Conseil d'Etat*, étude réalisée à la demande du Premier Ministre, Les pouvoirs d'enquêtes de l'administration, Avril 2021, La documentation française.

1202. A distinction is often made between police files used for judicial police missions and those used primarily for administrative police missions. The latter are used for public security, State security and defence purposes. *See*, for example, V. Gautron, *Fichiers de police, Répertoire de droit pénal et de procédure pénale*, Dalloz. There is no real up-to-date mapping of all the files concerned, nor any clear categorisation of these files. In 2018, a report by the Assemblée Nationale nevertheless drew up a table of 106 files available to security forces. *See* Rapport d'information n° 1335, D. Paris P. Morel-à L'Huissier, *Les fichiers mis à disposition des forces de sécurité*, annexe 4.

1203. *See* Art. 230-6 to 230-11of the Criminal Procedural Code.

1204. *See* Art. 706-54 of the Criminal Procedural Code. There is also a file on perpetrators of sexual or violent offences (FIJAIS), *see* Art. 706-53-1 of the Criminal Procedural Code.

1205. Décret n° 2010-569 du 28 mai 2010 relatif au fichier des personnes recherchées.

1206. Décret n° 87-249 du 8 avril 1987 relatif au fichier automatisé des empreintes digitales géré par le ministère de l'intérieur.

do indeed relate to criminal offences within the meaning of the Police Justice Directive. The notion of criminal offence is an autonomous concept under EU law, as the CJEU has repeatedly pointed out.[1207] Thus, the *Conseil d'Etat* examined whether a processing enabling tax and customs officials to collect personal data freely accessible on social networks was related to criminal offences. To this end, the *Conseil d'Etat* examined in detail each of the purposes of the processing. It noted that the processing aimed to investigate customs offences punishable by prison sentences or severe fines imposed by the criminal courts. In view of the nature of these various offences and the nature and severity of the penalties incurred, these constitute criminal offences within the meaning of the Police Justice Directive. There were no difficulties in linking the part of the processing aiming exclusively at the investigation of offences classified as criminal under French law to the scope of title III of the LIL.[1208]

574. **Mixed file issues**. The detailed analysis of each category of processing is also necessary in case of mixed files, i.e., those with purposes that fall within the scope of the GDPR and the Police Justice Directive. The same applies to several mixed files, with both public security purposes falling within the scope of the Police Justice Directive and national security purposes. For example, the above-mentioned wanted persons file (FPR) is divided into 21 sub-files, grouping together the persons concerned according to the legal basis of the search. Beyond categories of processing which fall within the scope of the Directive Police Justice (for example, the 'E' for general Foreigner Police, 'IT' for inadmissibility to the territory, 'M' for runaway minor, 'AL' for insane persons, 'PJ' for judicial police search, etc., there is also a famous 'S' category which is dedicated to person search for State Security.) Furthermore, each category includes several search patterns associated with a course of action. In 2019, there were some 120 search patterns.[1209] Thus, within the same file, the applicable regime may differ according to the purpose of the processing in question.

575. In certain cases, the *Conseil d'Etat* has ruled that mixed purposes of the processing nevertheless make it possible to apply a single regime to all processing. To do this, it tried to determine whether there is a primary purpose for the processing. In this case, the *Conseil d'Etat* considers that the overall purpose of the processing must fall within the scope of the directive for the latter's rules to apply. In other words, in the event of a secondary purpose falling within the scope of the Directive Police Justice, the regime applicable will be that of the GDPR. The *Conseil d'Etat's* ruling on 'accidental Americans' illustrates such kind of situation. The term accidental Americans covers people who are considered US taxpayers, even though they have an individual's extremely weak links to the United States, for example, people who have acquired American nationality only because they were born on US soil. The US FACTA requires banks in foreign countries to transmit to the US tax authorities all accounts held by US citizens. This includes the accidental

1207. *See*, for instance, CJEU, 26 Feb. 2013, *Aklagaren c/ Hans Akerberg Fransson* C-617/10.
1208. *See* CE, 22 Jul. 2023, Nos 451, 653, points 6–7.
1209. *See*, CNIL, FPR, available at https://www.cnil.fr/fr/fpr-fichier-des-personnes-recherchees.

Americans. Alongside FACTA, France signed an agreement with the United States, enabling the exchange of tax information. The *Conseil d'Etat* was asked to determine whether the processing carried out under this international agreement fell within the scope of the Police Justice Directive or the GDPR. The *Conseil d'Etat* considered that while the processing at issue has several purposes, including the prevention, detection and prosecution of criminal offences, the main purpose is to improve compliance with their tax obligations by French and American taxpayers by combating tax fraud and evasion. Therefore, it falls within the scope of the GDPR and not that of the Directive Police Justice.[1210] The *Conseil d'Etat* has also clarified the legal framework for linking files for different purposes. The *Conseil d'Etat* has reiterated that the combination of two file systems constitute a new processing. It refers to the European harmonised definition of processing enshrined in Article 2 LIL. Thus, in case of combination of a file system with a GDPR purpose with a file system with Directive Justice Police purposes, the new processing should fall within the scope of the Police Justice Directive and the title III of the LIL.[1211]

576. **Restrictive interpretation of the competent authority**. Whenever an authority processes criminal data falling within the scope of the Police Justice Directive, it is necessary to check whether the type of function it performs about this data makes it a competent authority within the meaning of Title III of the LIL. For example, a lawyer may process data relating to offences contained in his clients' files, but he is not a 'competent authority'. Thus, this situation is not covered by the Police Justice Directive. Verification that a controller is a competent authority is also required for public authorities. As an illustration, the government considered that the National Gaming Authority (ANJ), when it acts as the manager of the file of those banned from gambling, is not a competent authority within the meaning of Title III, so this processing falls within the scope of the GDPR. In its analysis, the government seems to have considered that the ANJ has circumscribed powers in this area. The ANJ is required to issue bans on gambling at the request of the court without ruling on the legality or appropriateness of these bans. As such, it does not exercise any prerogative of public competent authority regarding the management of this file, although the purpose of this file falls within the scope of the Police Justice Directive.[1212]

1210. *See* CE, Ass., 19 Jul. 2019, 424216, point 18.

1211. Application by analogy of the rule laid down by the *Conseil d'Etat* in the context of the combination of a GDPR purpose file system with Interests of State Security processing. CE, 27 Mar. 2020, n° 431350, points 9–10.

1212. *See* CNIL Délibération n° 2020-133 du 17 décembre 2020 portant avis sur un projet d'arrêté portant autorisation d'un traitement de données à caractère personnel dénommé 'Fichier des personnes interdites de jeux', in which the CNIL takes up the government's arguments and suggests that the choice was not so obvious. *See also* CE opinion n° 396212 – 27 Nov. 2018 on the Application for managing the files of foreign nationals in France (AGDREF 2). The *Conseil d'Etat* considered that 'The primary purpose of this data processing, which is to record data relating to the right of residence of foreign nationals holding a long-stay visa valid as a residence permit, is not the prevention and detection of criminal offences, the conduct of investigations and prosecutions in this area or the execution of criminal penalties, and is not covered by Directive (EU) 2016/680 of the European Parliament and of the Council of 27 Apr. 2016 but by Regulation 2016/679 of the European Parliament and of the Council (General Data Protection Regulation).'

All these situations illustrate that both the CNIL and the *Conseil d'Etat* ensure that the scope of application is strictly defined.

577. **Reuse of Personal Data collected for Police Justice Purposes**. Article 91 LIL provides that personal data collected by the competent authorities for Directive Police Justice purposes may not be processed for other purposes. By exception, the reuse is only possible if authorised by national or EU law. This includes, for example, the situation of the reuse for the processing carried out for such purposes, including for archiving purposes in the public interest, scientific or historical research purposes or statistical purposes.[1213] Article 92 LIL deals with the reuse for a Directive Police Justice purpose other than those for which data were collected. It recalls that such reuse needs to be necessary and proportionate for that purpose. Article 91, §2 LIL recalls in other cases; the GDPR will apply unless the processing is carried out for an activity for purely national purposes such as State security and defence.

II. Specificities of the Processing of Sensitive Data

578. Article 88 LIL transposes in the Police Justice Directive legal framework for processing of sensitive data. In contrast to the GDPR, the ban on such processing can only be lifted on three grounds. Such processing must be laid down by a legislative or regulatory provision, or it must be necessary to protect the vital interests of a natural persona, or it relates to data which are manifestly made public by the data subject. But above all, the processing of sensitive data within the scope of the Police Justice Directive is only authorised where absolutely necessary.

579. **Absolute necessity of the processing**. Despite resistance from rights and freedoms associations, the *Conseil d'Etat* has systematically validated the absolute necessity of processing under the scope of the Police Justice Directive.[1214] For example, the *Conseil d'Etat* ruled that this was the case for the decree creating the weapons information system, which ensures the traceability of firearms on French territory.[1215] The *Conseil d'Etat* considered that this decree only allows the collection of data relating to a person's political opinions, religious beliefs, trade union membership or health in cases of absolute necessity. It emphasised the decree provides '*that the data must be strictly necessary, adequate, and not excessive, and*

1213. *See* Arts 91, §3 and 92, §2 LIL for such categories of processing.

1214. For an illustration the assessment of the absolute necessity of processing a person's genetic data in the FAED and FNAEG files, by the *Cour de cassation see* Cass. Crim 4 Apr. 2024 No. 23-84-520, §§13-20.

1215. This system enables the collection of sensitive data resulting from administrative investigations, the purpose of which is to ensure that the person applying for authorisation to manufacture, sell, acquire, hold, carry or transport firearms does not behave in a manner incompatible with the issue of such authorisation. This processing is compulsory under directive (EU) 2017/853 du 17 May 2017 and falls within the scope of the Police Justice Directive.

solely for the purposes assigned to the processing, in compliance with the conditions applicable to it. It prohibits any selection of a particular category of persons on the basis of this data alone'.[1216]

580. The *Conseil d'Etat* also validated the processing of sensitive data by the Gendnotes application, a note-taking application that enables military personnel to collect sensitive data during preventive actions, investigations or interventions required to carry out their judicial and administrative policing missions. The *Conseil d'Etat* based its assessment of absolute necessity on three factors. First, the decree clearly specified that such processing could only be carried out in cases of absolute necessity. Second, this condition was assessed solely on the needs of the operation in progress. Third, while this sensitive data may only be entered in the free comment zones, it was forbidden to select a particular category of person based on this information alone.[1217]

581. Last example, the *Conseil d'Etat* validated Article R.40-26 of the CPP, which allows photographs of suspects to be entered into the Criminal Records Processing System (TAJ), containing the biometric data needed to implement a facial recognition system. The purpose of this processing is to enable authorised agents to identify people using facial recognition software. To justify this absolute necessity, the *Conseil d'Etat* emphasised that the number of people registered in the TAJ was so large that officers could not carry out this identification work manually. '*However, such identification based on a person's face and reconciliation with the data recorded in the TAJ may prove to be absolutely necessary in the search for the perpetrators of offences and the prevention of breaches of public order, both of which are necessary to safeguard rights and principles of constitutional value.*'[1218] The Conseil d'Etat then goes on to give a detailed list of all the safeguards adopted by the government to limit these processing possibilities to what is absolutely strictly necessary. Biometric data may only be collected because of the nature or circumstances of the offence or when the description of the person is based on specific, objective, and permanent physical characteristics. Processing should only be carried out if there is any doubt as to the identity of the person. Finally, the identification is the responsibility of the officers and not exclusively of the facial recognition software.[1219]

This guarantee echoes the one introduced in Article 95 of the LIL, which concerns exclusively automated decisions.

III. Automated Decisions Processing

582. Article 95 LIL is the counterpart to Article 47 of the LIL, which applies to the GDPR processing.[1220] Article 95 LIL reaffirms the ban on automated court

1216. CE, 27 May 2021, n° 441977, point 8.
1217. CE, 13 Apr. 2021, n° 439360, point13.
1218. CE, 26 Apr. 2022, n° 442364, point 5.
1219. *See* CE, 26 Apr. 2022, n° 442364, points 6–7.
1220. *See* paras 356–359.

decisions involving an assessment of a person's behaviour in the scope of the Police Justice Directive. This concerns both exclusively automated decisions and decision-support systems. French judges are, therefore, prohibited from using any profiling tool to make their decisions in the scope of the Police Justice Directive. In addition, Article 95 LIL prohibits other exclusively automated decisions, including profiling, which produce legal effects about an individual or significantly affect him or her. Contrary to, within the scope of the Police Justice Directive, the legislator has not used its room for manoeuvre to authorise certain exclusively automated decisions. Finally, Article 95 LIL also enshrines the ban on profiling, which will lead to discrimination based on sensitive data.

IV. Prior Formalities

583. **Compulsory Authorisation.** Article 89 LIL provides that all processing operations falling within the scope of the Police Justice Directive require authorisation.[1221] This authorisation procedure is described in Articles 31–36 LIL. Depending on the case, this will involve a law or an order ('arrêté') of the competent minister(s), passed following the reasoned and published opinion of the CNIL or a decree of the *Conseil d'Etat*. A law[1222] or a decree of the *Conseil d'Etat*[1223] is necessary for processing of sensitive data and when the processing is carried out on behalf of the State. Processing that is particularly likely to affect the rights and freedoms of data subjects may, in practice, require both legal authorisation and an implementing decree for their implementation. For example, the 2020 Finance Act authorised the tax and customs authorities to collect and automatically process content freely accessible on websites and social networks in order to investigate criminal offences.[1224] The law specifies that the terms and conditions for the application of this processing will be set by a decree in the *Conseil d'Etat* issued after consultation with the CNIL.[1225] This prior formality system concerns both certain GDPR processing operations[1226] and those covered by the Police Justice Directive.[1227]

1221. Examples of infringement of this obligation of prior authorisation will be given later one *see* paras 586–587.
1222. For instance, mobile cameras for municipal police officers were authorised by Law No. 2018-697 of 3 Aug. 2018 *see* Art. L.241-2 CSI.
1223. *See,* for instance, the décret n° 2020-151 du 20 février 2020 portant autorisation d'un traitement automatisé de données à caractère personnel dénommé 'Application mobile de prise de notes' (GendNotes).
1224. Article 154 of the 28 Dec. 2019, Finance Act for 2020.
1225. *See* décret n° 2021-148 du 11 février 2021 portant modalités de mise en œuvre par la direction générale des finances publiques et la direction générale des douanes et droits indirects de traitements informatisés et automatisés permettant la collecte et l'exploitation de données rendues publiques sur les sites internet des opérateurs de plateforme en ligne.
1226. *See* above para. 582.
1227. In its 2022 activity report, the *Conseil d'Etat* highlights the inconsistency of this system, which does not take sufficient account of the rational of the 2018 European personal data package. It suggests that the government should limit the number of cases in which processing operations can be authorised by a *Conseil d'Etat* decree and should make greater use of authorisation by decree of

584. **DPIA**. Article 90 LIL deals with the necessity of DPIA where processing operations are likely to result in a high risk to the rights and freedoms of natural persons.[1228] The CNIL considered that the processing operations linked to the use of drones with onboard cameras are likely to give rise to a high risk for the rights and freedoms of data subjects. '*This high risk arises, on the one hand, from the characteristics of drones, which are flying objects carrying a camera capable of filming at high resolutions, anywhere and at any time. They are therefore capable of filming anyone walking in public spaces, tracking them, and processing intangible personal data such as facial features. The risk also arises from the use of drones by […], particularly during demonstrations, when people's political opinions, religious or philosophical beliefs, or trade union membership, are likely to be revealed. Finally, the risk is aggravated by the fact that the processing is potentially carried out without the knowledge of individuals, who are often unaware of the presence of drones, the activation of the camera and the capture of their image. This risk is exacerbated in this case by the fact that people are not informed of the flights being made.*'[1229] Similarly, the CNIL considered that the SIRENE processing, which enables customs to record all persons inspected at sea or at dockside for combating fraud purposes, should have been subject to a DPIA. The file included the processing of geolocation data for ships, leading to almost systematic surveillance of their crews and many people concerned.[1230] Unlike GDPR processing operations, there is no list of processing operations for which a DPIA is systematically required. However, these examples show that the CNIL uses the same criteria as for GDPR processing operations to determine whether there is a high risk to the rights and freedoms of individuals. It should also be mentioned that where processing is carried out on behalf of the State, this DPIA must be sent to the CNIL with the request for its prior opinion.[1231]

V. Controller and Processor Obligations

585. **Obligations inspired by the GDPR**. Under the scope of the Directive Police Justice, controllers and processors are subject to obligations largely inspired by the GDPR. In fact, Title III of LIL contains numerous references to the GDPR. This is particularly true of Article 96 LIL, which states that controllers must be bound by a contract with their processor. This is also the case of Article 102 LIL, which transfers to this title the controller's general accountability the obligation of data protection by design and data protection by default from the GDPR. Article 99 LIL refers to the GDPR for the security obligations of controllers and processors,

the public authority controller of the processing operation under the Police Justice Directive. *See Conseil d'Etat*, activité juridictionnelle et consultative des juridictions administratives en 2022, p. 373.

1228. *See* for example, CNIL, SAN 2021-003, 12 Jan. 2021.

1229. CNIL SAN 2021-003 du 12 Jan. 2021, point 40.

1230. *See* CNIL, MED-2023-018, 3 Apr. 2023 mettant en demeure le ministère de l'économie, des finances et de la souveraineté industrielle et numérique, IV, A.

1231. *See* Art. 90, §2 LIL. In practice, this clarification is welcome because the public authorities tend to send their DPIA to the CNIL late.

and Article 100 LIL for the obligation of register. Article 102 refers to the GDPR for the obligation of notification of data breaches. It only complements the GDPR by a specific obligation of notification of data breach to controller of other Member States in cases where the data breach has been transmitted by or to a controller established in the other Member States. Article 103 refers to the GDPR in relation to the obligation of the designation of the DPO. It clarifies that this obligation does not apply to the courts acting in their judicial capacity. Otherwise, the status, position, and tasks of the DPO are similar to the GDPR. It should be recalled here that the competent public authorities under the Police Justice Directive must have a DPO.

586. Furthermore, the controllers are submitted to the same key principles on processing as from the GDPR. Therefore, the CNIL has decided to publicly call the Ministry of the Interior to order five infringements relating to the FAED, the judicial police identification database containing the fingerprints of persons implicated in criminal proceedings. The CNIL considered retention in the file of data that was not provided for by law. The CNIL discovered that the retention of data for a period exceeded that provided for by law. The FAED contained retention of data relating to people who have been acquitted, discharged, had the case dismissed or had the case dropped. Such information should have been deleted. There was inadequate data security due to a weak password. Finally, the data subjects were not individually informed when their prints were taken and transferred to the FAED.[1232] As a reminder, the CNIL cannot impose fines on the State,[1233] which explains why, despite the scale of the violations, it has only issued a call to order with an injunction to comply.

587. The use of drones with onboard cameras by the Paris police *Préfecture* to ensure compliance with lockdown during the COVID-19 pandemic has also been sanctioned by the CNIL. This processing, which came under the Police Justice Directive, was unlawful because it was not based on an authorisation under national law.[1234]

588. A recent case shows that police authorities are not the only ones who failed to comply with this prior authorisation requirement. The *Tribunal administratif* of Lille ordered the deletion of a police custody local file, including personal data of people relating to the demonstrations against pension reform. The file called 'monitoring criminal proceedings: movement on pension reform' has been created by the judicial judges without any legal basis.[1235]

1232. *See* CNIL n° SAN-2021-016 du 24 Sep. 2021 concernant le ministère de l'intérieur.
1233. *See* before para. 475.
1234. *See* CNIL n° SAN-2021-003 du 12 Jan. 2021, point 43.
1235. *See* TA de Lille, Ordonnance du 19 May 2023, Nos 2304177, 2304186. Interestingly, the administrative judge rejected the Ministry of Justice's argument that this processing was a part of the CASSIOPEE file. This file records information relating to complaints and denunciations received by magistrates during legal proceedings, in order to improve the time taken to process proceedings and to ensure that victims are kept informed. The administrative judge ruled that this was a

589. Beyond these similar obligations to the GDPR, the Police Justice provides two new and specific obligations. These obligations aim to give additional guarantees for criminal processing by clarifying the categories of data processed and making the processing traceable.

590. **Specific Obligations for the Police Justice Processing.** Article 98 LIL transposes into the LIL the obligation to make a clear distinction between personal data of different categories of data subjects. This involves distinguishing between people suspected of an offence, guilty parties, victims or third parties. This obligation echoes the principle that personal data relating to facts must be distinguished from data based on personal assessments.[1236] These obligations complement the general principle that data processed must be accurate and kept up to date. In practice, the absence of prior authorisation and DPIA for processing often conceals a failure to comply with this obligation to distinguish between the categories of individuals whose personal data has been included in the unlawful file. This was the case for the above-mentioned SIRENE file.[1237]

591. Article 101 introduces into the LIL the new logging obligation laid down in Article 25, §1 Police Justice Directive. The purpose is to enable the justification of the date and time of collection, alteration, and consultation, as well as disclosure, including transfers, combination, and erasure of such data. It also aims to identify the person who consulted or disclosed personal data and the identity of the recipients of such personal data. The *Conseil d'Etat*'s opinions show that this logging obligation has not always been put in place for processing operations that took place before the Directive came into force.[1238]

592. Case law illustrates the importance of these specific obligations for the rights and freedoms of data subjects. The decisions based on unlawful access to certain data contained in a file generally have no legal basis. For example, a person who is not authorised to consult the TAJ cannot validly refuse individual authorisation to carry out port security inspections based on this consultation.[1239] Similarly, an application for naturalisation cannot be refused based on a consultation in the TAJ of personal data showing a decision to dismiss or close a case.[1240] The CPP explicitly states that this type of data may not be used in the context of administrative investigations carried out to examine an application to acquire French nationality.[1241] For its part, the Cour de cassation has intervened on a number of occasions

---

different processing because the data collected in an Excel file was not included in the Cassiopée file. The absence of common purposes was also invoked.

1236. *See* Art. 94 LIL.

1237. *See* CNIL n° MED-2023-018 du 3 avril 2023 mettant en demeure le ministère de l'économie, des finances et de la souveraineté industrielle et numérique.

1238. *See* for instance CE, 22 Mar. 2022, n° 404773 mentioned in *See* Conseil d'Etat, activité juridictionnelle et consultative des juridictions administratives en 2022, p. 309 related to provisions the prison Code.

1239. CE, 22 Jun. 2022, n° 452969.

1240. CE, 17 Apr. 2023, n° 468859.

1241. *See* Arts 230-6, 230-8, R.40-23 et R.40-29 CPP.

to point out that it is up to the investigating judge to verify whether the judicial police officer, customs officer or agent under their control is actually authorised to consult a police file.[1242] In order to reduce the number of cases in which police files are quashed for lack of formal authorisation to consult them, the legislature has introduced a presumption of authorisation for officers accessing these files in the course of investigations and enquiries.[1243] This means that investigative acts carried out without authorisation being mentioned in the minutes of the proceedings do not automatically render the proceedings null and void.[1244] However, it must be possible for a magistrate to check at any time, either on his own initiative or at the request of the person concerned, whether special and individual authorisation to consult the file has been granted. Lastly, at this stage of the procedure, the aim is only to verify that the authorisation has been granted and not to examine the legality of the authorisation on its merits. The investigating judge does not have to check the content of the authorisation. He does not have to examine the precise nature of the data to which the official may have access.[1245]

VI. Data Subject Rights

593. **Similar GDPR rights**. Under the Police Justice Directive, the data subject has several rights which are similar to the GDPR: the right to information,[1246] the right of access,[1247] the right of rectification or erasure[1248] and the right to restrict processing. The data subject also has a right to object. For the latter, there are two exceptions. There is no right to object when the processing is founded on a legal obligation or when it has been excluded by an express provision of the document establishing the processing.[1249]

1242. Cass. Crim. 26 Jun. 2018, No. 18-80.596 in which the *Cour de cassation* penalised the investigating chamber because it had been content with the report of the judicial police officer gathering information relating to a customs inspection and on which appeared the result of the consultation of the file in order to deduce the existence of clearance, the cassation intervened on hypothetical grounds. Cass. Crim. 19 Feb. 2019, No. 18-84.67, in which the *Cour de cassation* considers that there is no irregularity even if access was only possible with a personalised access code issued only to authorised persons.
1243. Cf. Art. 15-5 CPP issued of the Loi No. 2023-22, 24 Jan. 2023. This provision has been declared conform to the French Constitution by the *Conseil constitutionnel* 19 Jan. 2023, No. 2022-846 DC, *Loi d'orientation et de programmation du ministère de l'intérieur*, §101.
1244. Cass. Crim 3 Apr. 2024, No. 23-85- 513, *See also* Cass. Crim. 5 Mar. 2024, No. 23-84.626; Cass Crim. 5 Mar. 2024, No. 23-84.864; Cass. Crim. 19 Mar. 2024, No. 23-85.539; Cass. Crim 30 Apr. No. 23-85.910.
1245. Cass. Crim 3 Apr. 2024 No. 23-8-513, §19 in which the *Cour de Cassation* recalls that the mere mention, in the proceedings, of the existence of such authorisation is sufficient to establish proof thereof.
1246. Article 104 LIL.
1247. Article 105 LIL.
1248. Article 106 LIL.
1249. This is the case, for instance, for the TAJ processing. *See* Art. R-40-33, I Code of Criminal Procedure. There is also no right to object to the Gendnotes application *See* Art. 5 decret décret n°2020-151 du 20 février 2020 portant autorisation d'un traitement automatisé de données à caractère personnel dénommé 'Application mobile de prise de notes' (GendNotes); and to the abovementioned Weapons Information System.

594. **Data subject rights restrictions**. Article 107 LIL provides that data subject's rights may be restricted for five reasons. This could be for:

- avoiding obstructing official or legal inquiries, investigations or procedures;
- avoiding prejudicing the prevention, detection, investigation or prosecution of criminal offences or the execution of criminal penalties;
- protecting public security;
- for protecting national security;
- for protecting the rights and freedoms of others.

595. These restrictions are provided for in the document establishing the processing. This is, for example, the case of the aforementioned Gendnotes application, in which decree provides that restrictions may be placed on rights to information, access and rectification of data. These restrictions are intended to avoid hindering investigations, enquiries or administrative or judicial proceedings or to avoid hindering the prevention or detection of criminal offences, investigating or prosecuting criminal offences, executing criminal penalties, or jeopardising public security or national security.[1250] These restrictions may nevertheless be subject to control by the CNIL. In other words, the data subject can exercise his rights through the CNIL. The instruction will be made by one of the members of the CNIL who belongs to or has belonged to the *Conseil d'Etat*, the *Cour de cassation* or the *Cour des comptes* (Court of Auditors).[1251] The rights of data subjects under the scope of the Police Justice Directive may be exercised either directly before the controller or indirectly before the CNIL, as with the GDPR.[1252]

VII. International Transfers

596. The last chapter of Title III of the LIL dedicated to the transposition of the Police Justice Directive deals with international transfers to third countries or recipients established outside the EU.

597. Article 112 LIL submits international transfers to four cumulative conditions. The first conditions are the same as those relating to the scope of the directive. The transfer must be necessary for one of the purposes of the Police Justice Directive. It must be an international transfer to the foreign competent authorities within the meaning of the Police Justice Directive. In case of transferred data from another foreign state, such state must have authorised this further transfer '*except when the new transfer is necessary for the prevention of an immediate and serious threat to public security of another State or to safeguard the essential interests of France*'.[1253] Finally, like the GDPR, international transfer needs to be grounded on

1250. For another application of restrictions of rights based on Art. 107 LIL, *see* the R.312-90 Internal Security Code regarding the before mentioned weapons information system.
1251. *See* Art. 108 LIL.
1252. *See* before paras 325–328.
1253. *See* Art. 112, §3 LIL.

an adequacy decision of the European Commission. In the absence of such an adequacy decision, international transfer must be based on a legally binding instrument which provides appropriate safeguards, or the controller must assess that appropriate safeguards exist. In the latter situation, some additional obligations are imposed on the controller. The controller must notify the CNIL of the categories of transfer. It must also document the date and time of the transfer, information about the receiving competent authority, the justification for the transfer and the personal data transfer. The CNIL may request access to this information.

598. Apart from these cases, a controller may nevertheless transfer data or authorise the transfer of data already transferred to a third country only if the transfer is necessary for certain purposes. Article 113 LIL sets out an exhaustive list of five specific reasons. The transfer must be necessary to:

- the protection of the vital interest of the data subject or of another person;
- safeguard legitimate interests of the data subject where French law so provides;
- to prevent an immediate and serious threat to public security of another State;
- for one of the Police Justice Directive purposes;
- for the establishment, exercise or defence of legal claims relating to these purposes.

In the latter two situations, the controller must balance the fundamental rights and freedoms of the data subject against the public interest of the proposed transfer. In case of transfer to protect the legitimate interest of the data subject, the controller must again document the date and time of the transfer, information about the receiving competent authority, the justification for the transfer, and the personal data transfer. The CNIL may request access to this information.

599. Finally, Article 114 LIL refers to specific cases of international transfer. Those one-off transfers are possible when five cumulative conditions are met:

- The international transfer must be necessary for the performance of the task of the competent authority for one of the purposes of the Police Justice Directive.
- The public interest necessitating the transfer must override the fundamental rights and freedoms of the data subject.
- The transferring controller considers that the classical transfer to the other authority will not be effective. This covers the situation of a late transfer.
- The transferring controller must inform the competent authority of the other State as soon as possible.
- The transferring controller must inform the recipient of the exclusive purpose of the transfer.

It should also inform the CNIL. Here again, the controller has obligations to document the date, the time of the transfer, information about the recipient, the justification for the transfer, and the data transferred.

§4. National Security Services

I. Scope of the Title IV LIL

A. *State Safety and Defense as Part of National Security Strategy*

600. **State Safety versus National Security**. Title IV of the LIL deals with the processing in the interests of State safety and defence carried out on behalf of the State. The LIL and, more globally, French law does not give an exhaustive definition of such processing, which is outside of the scope of the EU law. While the LIL was rewritten when it was adapted to the European personal data package, the outdated term State Safety (*sûreté nationale*) has been retained. However, since 1992, this term has been replaced in the CP by that of 'the fundamental interests of the Nation'.[1254] Moreover, since the end of the Cold War, France has associated its defence policy with the term national security.[1255] This semantic shift reflects a paradigm shift. The distinction previously made between internal and external security no longer seems relevant in the face of geopolitical developments and new threats such as terrorism and the fight against organised crime. This has led to the gradual development of a body of laws and regulations governing defence and national security. In addition to the adoption of national defence and security strategies,[1256] France adopted a defence code in 2004,[1257] a CSI in 2012,[1258] and an intelligence law in 2015.[1259] The scope of the processing covered by Title IV LIL should be analysed in light of this body of law.

601. **Definition of the National Security Strategy**. There is not a clear legal definition of the concept of national security. The Defence Code simply defines the components of the national security strategy. The Defense Code clarified that '*the purpose of the national security strategy is to identify all the threats and risks likely to affect the life of the Nation, particularly as regards the protection of the population, the integrity of the territory and the permanence of the institutions of the Republic, and to determine the responses that the public authorities must provide*'.[1260] While the '*aim of defence policy is to ensure territorial integrity and the*

1254. *See* Loi n° 92-686 du 22 juillet 1992.
1255. *See* the 2008 White Paper on Defence and National Security introduced the concept of national security, which aims to 'counter the risks and threats likely to affect the life of the Nation'.
1256. Theses defence and national security strategies are included in White Paper. The 2018 White paper mentioned above and the 2013 White Paper on Defence and National Security. The Military programming laws give concrete form to these strategies in terms of purposes and means. *See* the last one Loi n° 2023-703 du 1er août 2023 relative à la programmation militaire pour les années 2024 à 2030 et portant diverses dispositions intéressant la défense.
1257. Ordonnance n° 2004-1374 du 20 décembre 2004 relative à la partie législative du code de la défense, which has been ratified by the Loi n° 2005-1550 du 12 décembre 2005 modifiant diverses dispositions relatives à la défense.
1258. Ordonnance n° 2012-351 du 12 mars 2012 relative à la partie législative du code de la sécurité intérieure.
1259. Loi n° 2015-912 du 24 juillet 2015 relative au renseignement. Currently Book VIII Internal Security Code provide the legal framework for French intelligence, (Arts L.801-1 to L.898-1).
1260. Article L.1111-1, §1 Defence Code.

protection of the population against armed aggression. It contributes to the fight against other threats likely to jeopardise national security. It ensures compliance with alliances, treaties and international agreements and participates, within the framework of the European treaties in force, in the common European security and defence policy'.[1261] The Defense Code focuses on the concentric articulation of France's national defence and security strategy. Therefore, national security is an all-encompassing concept that aims to protect against both risks and threats, whereas national defence focuses solely on threats. Military defence involves the use of armed force. This all-encompassing function of national security, conceived as an interministerial policy, is clearly set out in the Defence Code, which states that '*All public policies contribute to national security.*'[1262]

602. **Impact on data protection**. This cross-cutting approach to national security has resulted in two types of constant demands involving the processing of personal data. On the one hand, it legitimises the ongoing improvement of the technological surveillance tools made available to the security forces. On the other hand, it fuels the need for exchanges of information between security forces to provide reliable and up-to-date information for protecting the nation. Since 2015, there has been a succession of laws[1263] attempting to provide legal certainty for these claims while guaranteeing the rights and freedoms of individuals. The legitimacy of this constant deployment of new forms of surveillance of the French population is the subject of a public debate, leading to repeated legal and constitutional disputes[1264] that go beyond the framework of data protection.

In this context, the determination of which processing operations fall within the scope of Title IV must be made by a detailed analysis of the purpose of the processing operation concerned.

B. Processing in the Interest of the Defence

603. The *Conseil d'Etat* clarified the notion of 'processing in the interest of the defence'. To do this, it used an analysis grid based on a body of consistent evidence. First, it is necessary to consider not only the purpose of the tool, its intended and potential uses, but more generally, the framework and context in which the processing is carried out (its place in the exercise of the responsibilities of the Ministry's authorities). Second, the number and quality of recipients and accessors should be considered. Finally, the nature of the data of the processing is also important evidence. In other words, 'processing in the interest of the defence' cannot be all the

1261. Article L.1111-1, §3 Defence Code.
1262. *See* Art. L.1111-1, §2 Defence Code.
1263. *See* for the last years, lois n° 2021-646 du 25 mai 2021 pour une sécurité globale préservant les libertés; Loi n° 2021-998 du 30 juillet 2021 relative à la prévention d'actes de terrorisme et au renseignement; Loi n° 2022-52 du 24 janvier 2022 relative à la responsabilité pénale et à la sécurité intérieure; Loi n° 2023-380 du 19 mai 2023 relative aux jeux Olympiques et Paralympiques de 2024 et portant diverses autres dispositions; Loi n° 2023-610 du 18 juillet 2023 visant à donner à la douane les moyens de faire face aux nouvelles menaces.
1264. *See* for instance CC 2015-713 DC, 23 Jul. 2015; 2021-822 DC, 30 Jul. 2021.

processing of the Ministry of Defence, nor be limited to the processing related to the preparation or the implementation of operational activities of armed forces, nuclear activities or intelligence activities. The *Conseil d'Etat* concluded that the Flash Event was processing in the interest of the defence because:

- Its purpose was to put in place an immediate procedure for reporting serious events relating to the Ministry's activities, and the exclusively informative purpose of the processing itself cannot be dissociated from the process decisions are taken by the Ministry's authorities;
- the recipients of the information collected are the Minister of Defence himself and his cabinet, as well as the Chief of Staff of the Armed Forces and as well as, where applicable, the hierarchical or management authorities and the directorates, departments, organisations and public under the supervision of the Ministry;
- the information that may be collected concerns information relating to related to the Ministry's specific missions and activities, such as information relating to members of foreign armed forces stationed or in transit, intrusions by land, sea or air, overflights of the Ministry's premises
  over the Ministry's premises by drones, malicious damage to sensitive equipment or shooting and sensitive equipment or fire and ammunition accidents.[1265]

C. State Safety Processing

604. The above-mentioned methodology could be used to determine on a case-by-case basis whether a processing operation is of interest to 'State Safety' within the meaning of Title IV of the LIL. This approach will be necessary for all so-called mixed processing, i.e., those which have a cross-cutting State safety and public security purpose. As all such processing is subject to authorisation,[1266] the starting point for the analysis will be to verify all the above-mentioned evidence in the act of establishing the processing. This concerns the three so-called public security files for which the controller is the Minister of the Interior.

605. **Main public security Files.** First, the file administrative enquiries related to public security (EASP in French)[1267] aims to carry out administrative investigations for recruitment, assignment, tenure, authorisation, approval or accreditation of a range of jobs, in particular, those involved in the exercise of the state's sovereignty in the field of security and defence. The administrative investigation aims to verify that the conduct of the persons concerned is not inconsistent with the performance of the functions or duties envisaged. Second, the file for preventing breaches of public security (PASP in French) which purpose is '*to collect, store and analyse information concerning natural or legal persons and groups whose individual or collective activity indicates that they may be a threat to public security or State*

1265. *See* Conseil, 10 Jan. 2021, Opinion No. 401686 on the project of decree on Flashevent.
1266. The authorisation regime is fixed in Arts 31 to 36 LIL. *see* before para. 582.
1267. *See* Art. R-236-1 to R-236-10 Internal Security Code.

safety'.[1268] Third, the Information Management and Prevention of Threats to Public Security (GIPASP in French)[1269] collects, stores and analyses information concerning natural or legal persons and groups whose individual or collective activity indicates that they may pose a threat to public security or State security. This concerns people likely to take part in terrorist activities, to undermine the integrity of the territory or institutions of the Republic or to be involved in collective acts of violence, particularly in urban areas or at sporting events.

606. For all these processings, the CSI clarified that data concerning 'State safety' is 'data which reveals activities likely to harm the fundamental interests of the Nation or to constitute a terrorist threat to these same interests. Such data, individually or in groups, is identified in the processing'.[1270]

607. **The sovereignty files**. A decree[1271] sets out the list of processing operations relating to State defence or public safety for which the regulatory acts authorising them do not have to be published. Those seven teen militaries and/or intelligence files are presumed to be in the scope of Title IV of the LIL. These include the CRISTINA file of the DGSI, the file for processing alerts for the prevention of radicalisation for terrorist purposes (FSPRT), the DGSE (TREX), the Defence Intelligence and Security Directorate file (SIRCID), the Military Intelligence Directorate (DOREMI) and the Intelligence Directorate of the Paris Police Prefecture: GESTEREXT.

608. Those processing are not submitted to the supervision of the CNIL[1272] nor to the Commission Nationale des Contrôle des Techniques de Renseignements (CNCTR). However, since 2015, control of the intelligence processing has been entrusted to this AAI, but this does not include in practice these so-called sovereignty files.[1273]

II. Regime of the Processing Related to Intelligence Techniques

609. **The tasks of the CNCTR**. The CNCTR exercises *a priori* and *a posteriori* control over all intelligence techniques used in France, which can include processing in the interest of State safety.

610. **Ex ante control of the CNCTR.** The CSI stipulates that the use of intelligence techniques by the French intelligence services must be authorised by the

1268. *See* Art. R-236-11 CSI.
1269. *See* Art. R-236-20 CSI.
1270. *See,* for instance, Art. R236-1, §2 CSI.
1271. *See* Décret n° 2007-914 du 15 mai 2007 pris pour l'application du I de l'article 33 de la loi n° 78-17 du 6 janvier 1978 relative à l'informatique, aux fichiers et aux libertés.
1272. *See* Art. 3 of the above-mentioned Décret n° 2007-914 du 15 mai 2007.
1273. According to the CNCTR the argument of the intelligence services is based on Art. L.883-2 CSI which provides that the CNCTR cannot have access to 'information communicated by foreign services or international bodies, or which could inform the commission, directly or indirectly, of the identity of sources specialised intelligence services'. *See* 2022 CNCTR, 7ème rapport d'activité 2022, p. 71.

Prime Minister[1274] after consultation with the CNCTR.[1275] The intelligence techniques[1276] that may be used and the services[1277] concerned are listed exhaustively. The CNCTR must check that all these elements have been respected when it delivers its opinion. The CNCTR also checks that the public authority implementing these intelligence techniques respects privacy and data protection law.[1278] In the event of a negative opinion of the CNCTR, the processing operation cannot be implemented, and the matter is referred to the *Conseil d'Etat* for a ruling.[1279] In 2022, while only 1.6% of CNCTR opinions were negative, most of the negative opinions concerned the prevention of collective violence.[1280] In those cases, the use of intelligence techniques requested included surveillance of political activism mostly on an abstract motivation evoking a risk of serious disturbance of the public peace.

611. **Ex post control of the CNCTR.** The CNCTR can also carry out *ex post* checks on the implementation of intelligence techniques. In most cases, this

1274. The Groupement interministériel de contrôle (GIC) is a service with national competence attached to the Prime Minister and responsible for centralising requests for authorisation to use intelligence techniques issued by the following services, and a part of the intelligence collected. *See* Art. R-823-1 CSI.

1275. In 2022, the CNCTR received 89,502 prior requests for the use of intelligence techniques by the services. *See* CNCTR, 7ème rapport d'activité 2022, p. 19. The CNCTR notes a steady increase in requests, but also a rise in more intrusive techniques.

1276. The title V of the Book VIII CSI listed the authorised intelligences techniques, such as Access of the administrative authorities to connection data which can be in real time or in differed time; real-time geolocation; security interception which include the controversial Interception of communications by IMSI catcher, (*see* Art. L.852-1), the interception of international communications i.e., emitted or received from abroad (Arts L.854-1 et seq. CSI) the capture of images in a private place or of words spoken in a private capacity, or collection and capture of computer data. *See* Part I, Privacy Surveillance by State Intelligence Services.

1277. Article R.811-1 CSI provides the list of the six French services of intelligence: three are from the Ministry of Defense: The DGSE, the Defence Intelligence and Security Directorate (DSRD), the DRM. Two are from the Economy Ministry: The National Directorate for Customs Intelligence and Investigations (DNRED), the Intelligence Processing and Action against Illicit Financial Circuits (TRACFIN), and one are from the Ministry of interior), the DGSI. Except for DRM and TRACFIN, thoses services called the first circle able to use all intelligence techniques abovementioned. The national coordinator for intelligence and the fight against terrorism and, within it, the national counter-terrorism centre, placed under the authority of the national coordinator for intelligence and the fight against terrorism, the specialised intelligence services, the intelligence academy and the intelligence services inspectorate form the French intelligence community. Furthermore, there is a so-called second circle of intelligence services which can occasionally carry out intelligence missions using more limited techniques and for more limited purposes. *See* Art. L.811-4 CSI. This applies, for example, to the national prison intelligence service, whose scope of action is limited to prison premises (*See* Art. R.811-2 CSI).

1278. *See* Art. L.801-1CSI which provides that 'Respect for privacy, in all its aspects, in particular the confidentiality of correspondence, the protection of personal data and the inviolability of the home, is guaranteed by law. The public authorities may only interfere with privacy where this is necessary in the public interest, as provided for by law, within the limits set by the law and in accordance with the principle of proportionality … The National Commission for the Monitoring of Intelligence Techniques shall ensure compliance with these principles under the conditions laid down in this Book.'

1279. *See* Art. 821-1 CSI.

1280. *See* CNCTR, 7ème rapport d'activité 2022, p. 25.

involves documentary and on-site inspections at the premises of the intelligence services and, more rarely, remote controls. The results of inspections carried out by the CNCTR show the limits of this system. On the one hand, on-site inspections are necessarily quantitatively limited[1281] due to a lack of human resources and time. Second, the results of these checks consistently reveal irregularities. These irregularities seem minor during the implementation phase of intelligence techniques. The CNCTR emphasises the existence of techniques implemented without authorisation or beyond the authorisation period, for example. On the other hand, most irregularities are concentrated in the phase of exploitation of the data collected, so it is conceivable that many of them concern processing of personal data. The CNCTR seems to be faced with two majors and recurring difficulties in its controls.[1282] First, the difficulty of tracing the use of the data collected. Second, the lack of centralisation of the computer data collected and the monitoring of international electronic communications. While the CNCTR cannot access them remotely, it does not really have the technical means to analyse the exploitation of such massive data. These two constraints mean that the CNCTR can only carry out spot checks. Nevertheless, it has observed some worrying irregularities, such as data being used in breach of the law, for example, for purposes other than those provided for by law, or for the authorisation requested, or exploitation of data on a different person than the one initially targeted or targeting a person who had been excluded in the authorisation.[1283] It is interesting to note that these two constraints identified by the CNCTR run counter to the law. The CSI states that the CNCTR must have '*permanent, full and direct access to the statements, registers, information collected, transcriptions, extractions and transmissions mentioned in this book, to the systems for tracing the information collected and to the premises where this information is centralised* …'.[1284]

612. Finally, it should also be underlined that, in addition to the checks, CNCTR may carry out the work on its own initiative. It may be contacted by any person to find out whether no intelligence technique has been unlawfully used against him. In this case, the CNCTR checks the techniques invoked to verify that they have been or are being used in compliance with the CSI. It shall notify the complainant that the necessary checks have been carried out without confirming or denying that they have been implemented.[1285]

1281. In 2022, the CNCTR did 121 on-site inspections including 30 on the surveillance international of communication. While most of these inspections are made in the region of Paris, the CNCTR carried out around fifteen visits throughout France, including overseas territories.
1282. *See* CNCTR, 7ème rapport d'activité 2022, p.51.
1283. *See* CNCTR, 7ème rapport d'activité 2022, p.47.
1284. Article L.833-2 CSI.
1285. *See* Art. 833-4 CSI for national surveillance and Art. L.854-9 CSI for the surveillance of the international electronic communications. Each year, the CNCTR receives around fifty requests. Following its inspections, the CNCTR may make recommendations to the Prime Minister, and if these are not followed, it may refer the matter to the *Conseil d'Etat. See* Art. L.833-6 CSI and L-833-8 CSI. These possibilities have yet to be exploited in practice.

613. By contrast, the CNIL remains the competent authority for the exercise of the data subjects for the processing of interesting State safety and defence provided by Title IV LIL.[1286]

III. Data Subject Rights

A. *Limited Similar GDPR Rights*

614. For the processing in interests of State safety and defence, the LIL provides right to information, right to object, and a right to erasure and provides some prohibitions relating to the automated decision. These rights are more limited than those under the European data protection package.

615. Article 116 LIL lists the information that should be transmitted to the data subject[1287] in case of direct or indirect collection of his data. In the latter situation, the right to information can be limited when necessary for the purpose of the processing or when the information will be impossible or involve a disproportionate effort.

616. Article 117 LIL provides a right to object which will not apply when the processing is grounded on a legal obligation or when it is excluded by the act which authorises the processing. In this area, the right to object will be often excluded.

617. Article 118 LIL provides that the right to access, the request to object, to erasure, and to rectification should be exercised through the CNIL in principle (so-called above already mentioned for other parts of the LIL indirect access).[1288] It is only when the purpose of the processing does not run counter to the direct exercise of the data subject rights that this can be envisaged in the act authorising the processing.[1289] Article 119 lists all the information that should be given by the controller or take action in case of direct exercise of the data subject rights.[1290]

1286. *See* further para. 616.
1287. The identity of the controller, the purpose of the processing, whether or not it is compulsory to provide such data, the possible consequences of a failure to provide data, the recipients or categories of recipients of the personal data, his rights, and where applicable the international transfers, the retention period or at list the criteria used to determine that period.
1288. According to the CNIL reports, the indirect rights requests in the area of the processing in the interest of State safety and defence seems kind low in comparison of the other sectors of the indirect access. They represent less than 7% of the indirect access requests. Sovereignty files such as CRISTINA or DFSE files each account for 0.8% of indirect accesses. The file that is the subject of the most indirect requests is the TAJ file, but the CNIL report does not differentiate between Police Justice processing and those with a State safety and defence purpose. *See* annual report of the CNIL 2022, p. 41.
1289. *See* Art. 119 LIL.
1290. This includes the confirmation as to whether or not personal data concerning him are being processed, information about the purposes of the processing the categories of data processed, the recipients to whom the personal data have been disclosed, the existence of international transfers,

B. Focus on the Right of Access

618. Some cases concerning the exercise of access rights illustrate the practical application of this procedure. It should be noted that since 2015, the *Conseil d'Etat* has been competent to exercise a degree of control over the exercise of indirect duties in this area.[1291]

619. First, the *Conseil d'Etat* often recalls that in the absence of a prior application to the CNIL for access to information likely to concern him in a processing in interest of State safety, the data subject cannot challenge the refusal made against him by the controller of the processing.[1292] Second, the *Conseil d'Etat* is also competent to rule directly on appeals concerning the use of intelligence techniques relating to the sovereignty files mentioned before. Third, in the event of an indirect exercise before the CNIL, in the absence of the agreement of the data controller, the CNIL can often only inform the complainant that it has carried out the necessary checks and that the procedure is closed. In other words, the complainant does not obtain the information he or she is primarily interested in, i.e., whether he or she is mentioned in the file. This elliptical response could just as easily mean that he or she is in the file and that his or her data has been legally collected after checking or that he or she is not in the file. The only option for the complainant is then to refer the matter to the specialised section of the *Conseil d'Etat* for it to verify the legality of the CNIL's decision. The same applies if the complainant does not refer to the CNIL but to the CNCTR to find out whether he or she has been the subject of an intelligence technique.[1293]

620. These cases are dealt with by a dedicated configuration of the *Conseil d'Etat* called 'formation spécialisée' (specialised panel), whose members and public rapporteur are authorised ex officio to protect national defence secrets. The agents assisting them must have national defence secrecy clearance to have access to the information and documents required to perform their duties. The procedure before the specialised panel includes an adjustment to the procedural rules of ordinary law, in particular, the adversarial rule. Thus, the parties are heard separately when national defence secrecy is at stake. The indirect exercise of rights leads to an asymmetrical application of the adversarial principle before the CNIL, the CNCTR and the specialised panel of the *Conseil d'Etat*. While these authorities and the administrative judge receive all the claimant's written submissions, the claimant does not receive the documents covered by national defence secrecy. Before the *Conseil d'Etat*, the hearing is held on camera. The public rapporteur's conclusions are delivered in the absence of the parties. The reasoning is not necessarily detailed

---

the communication of the personal data undergoing processing and of any available information as to their origin, the information about the logic involved in the automatic processing and how to challenge such the decision based on it.

1291. Article L. 841-2 CSI and Ch. III bis of the Administrative Justice Code.

1292. *See* for an example, CE, 21 Oct. 2022, n° 459497, point 5.

1293. *See* before para. 610.

in terms of the merits. The *Conseil constitutionnel*[1294] and the *Conseil d'Etat*[1295] itself judged that this procedure complies with the requirements of Articles 6 and 8 of the European Convention for the Protection of Human Rights and Fundamental Freedoms. This seems to be in line with European case law.[1296]

621. In practice, the specialised panel conducts an in-depth review of the controller's decision to refuse access to the processing concerned, the CNIL's decision, or the CNCTR's decision. There are different possible scenarios. First, it appears that the claimant is not mentioned in the disputed file or that the personal data concerning him or her are not illegal. The *Conseil d'Etat* rejects the claimant's arguments without further clarification.[1297] Second, the processing or part of the processing that is the subject of the dispute contains personal data concerning the individual that is inaccurate, incomplete, equivocal, or out of date, or the collection, use, communication or storage is prohibited. Then, the specialised panel informed the data subject without reference to any element protected by the secrecy of national defence. The specialised panel '*may order that such data be corrected, updated, or deleted, as appropriate. If it is asked to do so, it may compensate the applicant*'.[1298] The specialised panel found that 'ambiguous data likely to have consequences for the applicant's personal situation'[1299] appeared in a DGSE file and considered that this constituted a fault likely to engage the responsibility of the State and having caused direct and certain damage to the person concerned. It then assessed this non-material damage and damage to the professional reputation of the person concerned at EUR 10,000. However, it did not order the deletion and rectification of the data,[1300] which had already been done. This case demonstrates the importance of appealing to the specialised panel following the CNIL's response, as only the specialised panel can rule on compensation for damages. It is highly likely that the CNIL was behind the deletion of the ambiguous data from the disputed file, even though nothing has been revealed on this subject.

IV. Automated Decision Processing Regime

622. Article 120 LIL copies/pastes the ban on court decisions involving an assessment of a person's behaviour based on automated processing of personal data intended to evaluate certain personal aspects relating to a data subject. In addition, Article 120 LIL bans the other exclusively automated decision which produces legal

1294. CC, 23 Jul. 2015, n° 2015-713 DC, point 86.
1295. CE, formation spécialisée, 19 Oct. 2016, No. 400688.
1296. *See* ECHR, 10 juill. 1998, 20390/92 et 21322/92, *Tinnelly & Sons Ltd et a. et Mc Elduff et a. v. UK*, §78, and CJEU, 18 Jul. 2013, C-584/10 P, C-593-10 P et C-595/10, ECLI:EU:C:2013:518.
1297. *See* for example, CE, 24 Mar, 2022, n° 452803, point 8.
1298. *See* Art. L.773-8 Administrative Justice Code.
1299. *See* CE, 21 Dec. 2020, n° 427059, point 7.
1300. The first case in which the *Conseil d'Etat* order the erasure of the data of a plaintiff in a Safety State processing dates back to 2017. *See* CE, 5 May 2017 n° 396669. Interestingly, the prior investigations of the CNIL revealed that the disputed file did not contain personal data of the claimant while the specialised panel considered that the DRSD's file contained applicant's unlawful personal data before ordering its deletion. *See* respectively point 4 and point 9.

effects concerning a data subject or significantly affects him by using or evaluating certain personal aspects related to him. The difference with the Police Justice Directive processing is that Article 120 LIL does not contain an explicit reference to profiling which could lead to discrimination based on sensitive data.

V. Controller and Processor Obligations

623. The controllers and the processors of processing on State safety and defence are submitted to the same common obligations mentioned before in Title 1 of the LIL. Title IV of the LIL contains only two additional provisions on this subject. Article 121 LIL recalls the obligation of security of the data controller, focusing on the need to consider the risk of the processing. It is asked that the controller take '*all necessary precautions to maintain the security of the data and to prevent it from being distorted, damaged or being accessed by unauthorized third parties*'.

624. The *Conseil d'Etat* recalled that Article 121 LIL requires 'the controller of a processing operation to guarantee the security of the data and to ensure that the processing is used in accordance with the rules laid down by the act authorising its creation, do not affect the lawfulness of the act authorising the processing'.[1301] In other words, the security principle relies on the accountability principle of the data controller. The plaintiff cannot invoke that the data controller has not taken sufficient security measures for its processing (here, the above-mentioned Gendnotes application) to ask for the annulment of the regulation on which it is based such processing. The law does not oblige the security measures that the controller must take, which should be described in the instrument establishing the processing. It is much more important for the CNIL in *a posteriori* control to assess whether the security measures taken comply with the principles of privacy by design and by default and guarantee a level of security appropriate to the risk.

625. Article 122 LIL recalls the obligation of the processor. In particular, the processor must provide sufficient guarantees to ensure the implementation of security and confidentiality. The obligations of the processor regarding these two topics should be clarified in the contract between the processor and the controller.

VI. International Transfer

626. The last of the Title IV LIL deals with international transfer. Article 123 LIL reiterates the principle that international transfers are prohibited unless the third country provides a sufficient level of protection, both in terms of the rules in force in that third country and the practical way in which those rules are applied. Article 124 LIL lists the three kinds of situations in which this prohibition may be lifted because a third country does not provide sufficient protection. First, an international transfer can be based on the explicit consent of the concerned person. This may

1301. CE, 13 Apr. 2021, n° 439360, point 19.

seem to be a curious hypothesis in terms of processing for State safety and defence. On the one hand, the data subject is not always informed that his or her data is being processed in this area. On the other hand, consent can only be valid if it is freely given, a condition that will not always be met in the case of processing carried out by a public authority based on a legal obligation, for example.

627. Second, six grounds for international transfers relate to the purpose of the processing, which must be one of the following:

1. To protect the life of that person.
2. To protect public interest.
3. To comply with obligations necessary for the establishment, exercise, or defence of legal claims.
4. To consult, under regular conditions, a public register established by legislative or regulatory provisions that is intended for consultation by the public or persons having a legitimate interest.
5. For the performance of a contract between the controller and the data subject or to take steps at the request of the data subject prior to entering a contract.
6. At the conclusion or execution of a contract concluded or to be concluded, in the interest of the data subject, between the controller and a third party.

628. Third, an international transfer may also be based on a decree adopted after a reasoned opinion from the CNIL. In this case, processing must guarantee a sufficient level of protection for the privacy and fundamental rights and freedoms of natural persons by virtue of the contractual clauses or internal rules to which it is subject. In event of sovereignty files, which are based on a regulatory act exempt from publication, the decree authorising the transfer is also exempt from publication.

Selected Bibliography

Braun, S. *France and Germany Amazon Fined by CNIL for Excessive Monitoring of Employees in France – Is the Situation in Germany Contrary to This?,* 10(1) European Data Protection Law Review, 2024, pp. 83–88.

Code de la protection des données personnelles, annoté et commenté, Dalloz, 6ème édition 2024.

Code du numérique, Lexis Nexis 2024.

Debet, A., Massot J. & Metallinos, N. *Information et Libertés. La protection des données à caractère personnel en droit français et européen*, Paris, Lextenso Éditions, 2015.

Douville, T., *Droit des données à caractère personnel*, LGDJ 2023.

Dumortier, J. et al., *Europe, Privacy and Data Protection Law, Privacy and Technology Law*, Kluwer 2022.

Féral Schuhl Chr., *Le Cyberdroit, le droit à l'épreuve d'internet*, Dalloz, 8 ed., 2020.

Lami, H., *France CNIL Confirms Google's Compliance with Earlier Injunctions on Cookie Banners*, 9(3) European Data Protection Law Review, 2023, pp. 350–352.

Lami, H., *France the Constitutional Council Validates the Use of Augmented Video Recognition Technology for the Olympics,* 9(2) European Data Protection Law Review, 2023, pp. 214–218.

Malgieri, G., *R.I.P.: Rest in Privacy or Rest in (Quasi-)Property? Personal Data Protection of Deceased Data Subjects Between Theoretical Scenarios and National Solutions* (30 March 2018). *Data Protection and Privacy: The Internet of Bodies*, edited by Ronald Leenes, Rosamunde van Brackel, Serge Gutwirth & Paul De Hert (Brussels, Hart, 2018), Available at SSRN: https://ssrn.com/abstract=3185249.

Perray R., *Jusriclasseur Fasc. 274-23: Données à caractère personnel.* Principes fondamentaux relatifs aux traitements de données à caractère personnel. Minimisation.

Perray R., *Juriscl. Fasc. 274-24 Données à caractère personnel.* Principes fondamentaux relatifs aux traitements des données à caractère personnel. Exactitude.

Perray R., *Juriscl. 274-28 Données à caractère personnel.* Principes fondamentaux relatifs aux traitements de données à caractère personnel. Intégrité et confidentialité.

Spiecker I. Papakonstantitnou V. & Hornung G. De Hert P., *General Data Protection Regulation, Article by Article Commentary*, Nomos 2023.

Tambou, O., *France Lessons from the First Post-GDPR Fines of the CNIL Against Google LLC*, 5(1) European Data Protection Law Review 2019, pp. 80–84.

Selected Bibliography

Tambou, O., *Manuel de droit européen de la protection des données à caractère personnel*, Bruylant 2020.

Tambou, O., *GDPR Implementation Series France: The French Approach to the GDPR Implementation,* 4(1) European Data Protection Law Review 2018.

Tambou, O., *France the New French Antiterrorism Law: Towards a Balance Between Security and Liberty after the State of Emergency*?, 3(4) European Data Protection Law Review, 2017, pp. 518–523.

Tambou O. & Bourton B. (ed.), Le droit à l'oubli en Europe et au-delà. The Right to be Forgotten in Europe and Beyond, Avril 2018, Luxembourg, Blogdroiteuropéen, Collection Open Access Book, Disponible sur Internet: https://wp.me/p6OBGR-2QK.

Vergnolle S., *L'effectivité de la protection des personnes par le droit des données à caractère personnel*, Bruylant 2022

www.ingramcontent.com/pod-product-compliance
Lightning Source LLC
Chambersburg PA
CBHW071433230926
51846CB00001B/208
9789403512693